The Handbook of Women, Psychology, and the Law

Andrea Barnes

Editor

The Handbook of Women, Psychology, and the Law

Alliant International University

CALIFORNIA SCHOOL OF PROFESSIONAL PSYCHOLOGY

EDUCATION · TRAINING · SERVICE · RESEARCH

CSPP

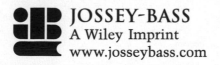
JOSSEY-BASS
A Wiley Imprint
www.josseybass.com

Published by Jossey-Bass
A Wiley Imprint
989 Market Street, San Francisco, CA 94103-1741   www.josseybass.com

Jossey-Bass books and products are available through most bookstores. To contact Jossey-Bass directly, call our Customer Care Department within the U.S. at 800-956-7739 or outside the U.S. at 317-572-3986, or fax to 317-572-4002.

Jossey-Bass also publishes its books in a variety of electronic formats. Some content that appears in print may not be available in electronic books.

Library of Congress Cataloging-in-Publication Data

The handbook of women, psychology, and the law / Andrea Barnes, editor.—1st ed.
    p. cm.
    Includes bibliographical references and index.
    ISBN 0-7879-7060-3 (alk. paper)
    1. Women—Social conditions. 2. Women—United States—Social conditions.
3. Women—Psychology. 4. Women—Legal status, laws, etc.—United States.
5. Sex discrimination against women. I. Barnes, Andrea, date
HQ1154.H2298 2005
305.42—dc22   2004020313

Printed in the United States of America
FIRST EDITION
HB Printing   10 9 8 7 6 5 4 3 2 1

—⁓— Contents

To those teachers who, through their kindness and their example, showed me the importance of understanding women's lives. Thanks to Steve Schiavo, Laurel Furumoto, Elizabeth Douvan, Leslie Espinoza, and Martha Minow.

—ᴟ— Introduction

When a baby is born, there is one thing we want to know: Girl or boy? It is good manners to ask about the health of the baby first, and of course we want to know how mother and child fared during the birth. But once we are assured of their health and safety, we want to know: Girl or boy? We have to know, because without that piece of information, our imaginations are stuck. We want to be able to think about how this new member will fit into the rest of the family. We want to think about how we will interact with the new child. Will she follow in the footsteps of the family business tycoons, or artists, or teachers? Will we identify with him? Will we make a point of giving him career advice so that he can avoid the mistakes we made? Will we want to give her beauty advice? Will he be the shortstop or quarterback we can brag about? Will she be the devoted child who makes up for those times when we did not feel loved? Will he carry on the family name? How will she fit in our models for how families work? Is this a child who will help cook the Thanksgiving turkey? Is this the child who will clean up afterward—or the child who will sit and watch football while others clean? Will we encourage this child to be nice? Ambitious? Accommodating? Proud?

Our imaginations require that we know the gender of the new person. Only with that information can we begin to organize our expectations and our perceptions. The classic study of infants by Rubin, Provenzano, and Luria (1974) first documented this process, and the results have been replicated since (Karraker, Lake, & Vogel, 1995). Adults looking at the very same babies will describe them differently depending on their belief about the baby's gender. If the adults thought they were looking at a female infant, she was described as sweet, fragile, and fine-featured. If the adults thought they was looking at a male infant, he was described as strong, vigorous, and energetic.

Research on attachment relationships (Main, 1996) has demonstrated that the quality of the relationship between a mother and a child when the child is one year old can be predicted from the mother's responses to an interview about her own relationships with her parents. The mother's interview took place during the pregnancy, before the baby was even born and available to influence the relationship. This speaks to the power of our expectations to influence our behavior and, even more subtle, the power of our expectations to influence what we see. The research subjects saw a more vigorous baby when they thought he was male. The interviewed mothers saw their new babies through the lens of their own personal relationship histories.

Gender is a core attribute that organizes our thinking consciously and unconsciously. We know this based on psychological research. We know this based on the history of sex discrimination law. We know this when we see Julia Sweeney's *Saturday Night Live* ambiguously sexed character, Pat. At the heart of every Pat sketch is the determination of the other characters to figure out if Pat is male or female. We relate to their frustration because we also want to know. We laugh with the same frustration at the way Pat's partner, "Chris," is equally ambiguous. We are uncomfortable not knowing.

This book offers a sampling of the many ways that gender affects experience. Whether the context is domestic or international, a courtroom or a business or a clinic, gender matters. It influences ideas and expectations, and they shape behavior and laws. Across settings, the experiences of women are shaped by patterns of power and dominance, cultural expectations, economic disparities, and internalized models of social relationships that are defined by gender.

The experiences of women are also shaped by absence and invisibility: what does not get noticed, discussed, valued, or included. This includes invisibility in the workplace. As Fletcher (1999) demonstrates, the relational work that women are expected to do does not quite make it into the job evaluation. It includes the "second shift" of the average working mother, which occurs after she comes home from her paid employment, when she has the primary responsibility for the care of the emotional and physical needs of family members (children, husband, elderly parents, or parents-in-law). She has this responsibility because she is female. She may ask for "help" in these duties, but that they are her responsibility is not likely to be questioned (Hochschild & Machung, 2003). It includes the routine exclusion of women as subjects in health care and drug research, because their inclusion makes the subject pool less "homogeneous" and more complicated statistically (Epstein, 1996), even when women will be the consumers of the drugs.

In every context, we see the power of language to define experience. When it is men defining the experience of women, the results can be surprising. In the law pregnancy is not seen as a gender-related issue because health benefits divide employees into "pregnant people" and "nonpregnant people" (*Geduldig* v. *Aiello,* 1974). Using this logic, a company can choose not to pay for the health care costs of pregnancy, even if it does cover illnesses related to the prostate. Under similar logic, erectile dysfunction is viewed as a health disorder for which insurance should cover the cost of treatments such as Viagra, while pregnancy is not a health problem and insurers should not be required to cover the cost of birth control pills. Those psychological and legal scholars who use a power and dominance model to explain gender relations will readily note the irony: that we are enabling men to have more sex and simultaneously making it more difficult for women to protect themselves from the consequences of that sex.

Jean Baker Miller (2003), a psychiatrist who has written about the psychological effects of gender, notes the following:

> Power is very real and is operating in front of us all the time. Quite amazingly, those who have the most power in our society almost never talk about it, and even more amazingly, they induce many of the rest of us not to recognize it, either. [Through distorted representations of groups in film] we absorbed . . . untruths routinely every week. . . . This is one example of how the "cultural materials" of a dominant group mystify its operation of power.
>
> For various historical reasons, a dominant segment in any society tends to divide people with less power into groups by race, class, gender, sexual preference, and the like. The dominant group often gains tremendous power over the less powerful groups in economic, social, political, and cultural realms. But dominant groups do not usually say, "I have great power over your life; I want to keep it and, if possible, increase it because I'm afraid of losing any of it to you."
>
> It is important to recognize that there are different kinds of power. We use the term "power-to" to mean the ability to make a change in any situation, large or small, without restricting or forcing others. The term "power-over" we apply to situations or structures in which one group or person has more resources and privileges and more capacity to force or control others. Structural power reinforced by power-over practices obstructs growth and constructive change.

Dominant groups usually manufacture false belief systems that act to perpetuate their power-over position and sustain their separation from subordinate groups. Patricia Hill Collins (1990), an African-American sociologist, discusses the impact of controlling images. She notes that dominant groups tend to create sets of images about themselves and about each of the "subordinate" groups. These controlling images are always false, yet they exert a powerful influence, holding each group in its place and maintaining the status quo. We absorb these images about others and ourselves, usually without fully realizing it. . . . This is part of the way dominant groups mystify their power-over practices and entice many of us into cooperation [p. 5].

MYSTIFICATION AND BIOLOGY

The concept of mystification helps us understand how gender stereotypes can be perpetrated, maintained, and internalized, until we are almost convinced they are true. We live in a culture that provides contradictory messages about almost everything, and gender is no exception. Any challenge to the status quo is met with opposition. Frequently, that opposition takes the form of biological mandates, or "natural law," which suggest that women are limited by the immutable characteristic of sex and it is the result of biology, nature, genetics, or, more recently, evolutionary forces that require women to be in a culturally inferior position.

When women began to assert their rights to education, property, and the vote, the science of the times warned of the health dangers of a higher education. The data were clear: women with college educations tended to have fewer children. In the late 1800s, the explanation was biological: education was literally impairing women's fertility, primarily by exhausting them with all that thinking (Barnes, 1985).

If the health dangers were not enough to keep women from seeking an education, then the genetic explanation was available. The variability hypothesis argued that only males could be expected to achieve great things. This "scientific" hypothesis pointed to the data: the historical records demonstrated that only men had made great intellectual and societal achievements. It also demonstrated that there were more men than women institutionalized for "mental defects." The conclusion was clear: men were genetically endowed with more potential to reach extremes in both directions, while women were resigned to mediocrity. The subtext was, Why bother educating women, who could achieve only modest goals (Barnes, 1985)?

As late at the 1960s, women at Harvard Law School were formally required to justify their presence. Alumnae have described an annual ritual, a dinner hosted by the school's dean, Erwin Griswold, where the guest list included all of the women in each class (and none of the men), along with selected faculty and their wives. After dinner the students were called upon, one by one, to answer Griswold's horrifying question, "Why are you at Harvard Law School, taking the place of a man?" (Hope, 2003). While the history of legal education in the United States was primarily that of exclusion of women, professional psychology was not dramatically more liberal. Women began earning Ph.D.s in psychology in the late 1800s, but they did it at the cost of a personal life. One could choose to be a professional or have a family, but not both. Institutions of higher education, even those most accepting of women as professors, required that they leave teaching once they married (Barnes, 1985).

MYSTIFICATION AND THE PSYCHE

By the early 1900s, psychology was beginning to explain gender inequalities as the result of intrapsychic conflicts. It was not that there was inherently a problem with women's legal, cultural, or economic status. The problem was that women did not willingly accept their inferiority. Freud himself had warned his colleagues, "We must not allow ourselves to be deflected . . . by . . . the feminists, who are anxious to force us to regard the two sexes as completely equal in position and worth" (quoted in Steinem, 1994, p. 20). Modern psychoanalysis continues to struggle with Freud's concept of penis envy. One strategy is to dismiss it as children's fantasy or magical thinking based on a child's naive understanding of anatomy. This leaves open the opportunity to outgrow the "natural inferiority" that little girls experience at the discovery that they are without a penis or to compensate by acquiring a man—and therefore vicarious ownership of a penis.

One strategy is to "equalize" the child's dilemma: girls wish they had a penis, and boys wish they could have babies, because children (and perhaps adults) do not want to acknowledge any limitations. All difference is loss at the preoperational level of cognitive development (Fast, 1990). In classical psychoanalytic theory, the core issue is power:

who has the advantage between the sexes and who is lacking and therefore inferior. Girls make the heartbreaking discovery that they are not "as good as boys," and they spend their lives trying to make up for it. The question of sexual identity is thus complicated by the value judgment that says girls are lesser.

Chodorow (1978) redefined the early childhood struggle as one of connection and separation. In this scenario, it is the boys who have the more difficult challenge of separating from the nurturing mother in order to identify with the same-sex parent. Boys have to give up the regressive pull toward mother in order to be "masculine." Those who do not will face the ultimate criticism from peers: that they are weak, sissies—in other words, like girls. This model offers an explanation for the intensity of feeling around masculinity, and the ever-present fear of being emasculated, as if masculinity were a fragile and precarious state of being, subject at any time to being lost or stolen. Women do not worry about "losing" their femininity any more than they worry about misplacing an arm or a leg.

What these theories have in common is the locus of control. Feelings about gender identity come from within and are an inherent part of the developmental process of all humans. They are ultimately biologically based, the result of millions of years of evolution, and they are unlikely to be changed.

MYSTIFICATION THROUGH THE LANGUAGE OF PROTECTION AND PHYSICAL STRENGTH

While psychologists theorized about the nature of gender identity for the individual, the law was required to make concrete decisions about the importance of gender in employment and other social relationships. Early legal decisions purported to want to protect women from the strains of the industrialized workplace by limiting hours (*Muller v. Oregon,* 1908). Making assumptions about the physical characteristics of women, these early decisions also helped promote stereotypes. It was now a legal fact that women were not as strong as men, and it was a legal value to protect women. More specifically, this was a value to protect women's bodies.

Consider the comments of Gloria Steinem (1994) about the history of the treatment of women's bodies:

Though cultural differences were many, there were political similarities in the way women's bodies were treated that went as deep as patriarchy itself. Whether achieved through law and social policy, as in this and other industrialized countries, or by way of tribal practice and religious ritual, as in older cultures, an individual woman's body was far more subject to other people's rules than was that of her male counterpart. Women always seemed to be owned to some degree as the means of reproduction. And as possessions, women's bodies then became symbols of men's status, with a value that was often determined by what was rare. Thus, rich cultures valued thin women, and poor cultures valued fat women. Yet all patriarchal cultures valued weakness in women. How else could male dominance survive? In my own country, for example, women who "belong" to rich white men are often thinner (as in "You can never be too rich or too thin") than those who "belong" to poor men of color; yet those very different groups of males tend to come together in their belief that women are supposed to be weaker than men; that muscles and strength aren't "feminine." . . .

If I had any doubts about the psychological importance of cultural emphasis on male/female strength difference, listening to arguments about equality put them to rest. Sooner or later, even the most intellectual discussion came down to men's supposed superior strength as a justification for inequality, whether the person arguing regretted or celebrated it. What no one seemed to explore, however, was the inadequacy of physical strength as a way of explaining oppression in other cases. Men of European origin hadn't ruled in South Africa because they were stronger than African men, and blacks hadn't been kept in slavery or bad jobs in the United States because whites had more muscles. On the contrary, males of the "wrong" class or color were often confined to laboring positions precisely because of their supposedly greater strength, just as the lower pay females received was often rationalized by their supposedly lesser strength. Oppression has no logic—just a self-fulfilling prophecy, justified by a self-perpetuating system. . . .

The more I learned, the more I realized that belief in great strength differences between women and men was itself part of the gender mindgame. In fact, we can't really know what those differences might be, because they are so enshrined, perpetuated, and exaggerated by culture. They seem to be greatest during the childbearing years (when men as a group have more speed and upper-body strength, and women have better balance, endurance, and flexibility) but only marginal during early childhood and old age (when females and males seem to have about the same degree of physical strength). Even during those middle years, the range of difference among men and among women is far greater than the generalized difference between males and females as groups. In multiracial societies like ours, where males of some races are smaller than females of others, judgments based on sex make even less sense. Yet we go right on assuming and praising female weakness and male strength. . . .

But there is a problem about keeping women weak, even in a patriarchy. Women are workers, as well as the means of reproduction. Lower-class women are especially likely to do hard physical labor. So the problem becomes: How to make sure female strength is used for work but not for rebellion. The answer is: make women ashamed of it. Tough hard work requires lower-class women to be stronger than their upper-class sisters, for example, those strong women are made to envy and imitate the weakness of women who "belong" to, and are the means of reproduction for, upper-class men—and so must be kept even more physically restricted if the lines of race and inheritance are to be kept "pure." That's why restrictive dress, from the chadors, or full-body veils, of the Middle East to metal ankle and neck rings in Africa, from nineteenth-century hoop skirts in Europe to corsets and high heels here, started among upper-class women and then sifted downward as poor women were encouraged to envy or imitate them. So did such bodily restrictions as bound feet in China, or clitoridectomies and infibulations in much of the Middle East and Africa, both of which practices began with women whose bodies were the means of reproduction for the powerful and gradually became generalized symbols of femininity. In this country, the self-starvation known as anorexia nervosa is mostly a white, upper-middle-class, young-female phenomenon, but all women are encouraged to envy a white and impossibly thin ideal [Steinem, 1994, pp. 94–96].

MYSTIFICATION OF POWER AND DOMINANCE

Jean Baker Miller (2003) reminds us that gender definitions have served as a means of domination and control, with this control often achieved through violence. To change the definitions of gender "appropriateness" is revolutionary and dangerous. Women have been killed for their difference (the witchcraft trials in Salem, Massachusetts, in the late seventeenth century). Women have been killed for their conformity (funeral pyres for the wives of deceased men). Women are killed for the behavior of others (honor killings of rape victims). Women are still routinely mutilated in Africa, and they are routinely beaten in America (domestic violence).

Gender equality is not an academic or philosophical issue. It has life-and-death implications for women, whether it involves access to safe abortions in Western culture, access to medications needed to treat HIV in Africa, or protection from murder (as an adult female in rural India or as a newborn female infant in China). In recent news stories, we have seen rape trials treated as "he said–she said" relational disputes. We have discovered numerous police departments that have hundreds of "rape kits" in storage that were never sent off for DNA analysis. The explanations were consistent: it was too expensive to analyze this evidence of a crime. The results were also consistent: alleged rapists went free or never went to trial in the first place. This is violence by omission.

MYSTIFICATION THROUGH INVISIBILITY

Law professor Leslie Espinoza (1997) describes the way in which even informed and well-intentioned professionals can disregard the perspectives and feelings of women:

> After a while, try as we might, domestic attorneys, whether we are clinical law professors or representing for-pay clients, become inured to the most shocking of social taboos. Abuse becomes normalized for us. Rape of a child is awful, but it happens. Family law attorneys have routine ways of redressing the situation. This is the standard response: temporary protective orders in district court, divorce action filed in the probate court, and temporary orders during the pendency of the divorce providing for support, custody, and protection. The temporary probate court orders become permanent upon the final adjudication of the case.
>
> The standard response is comforting to the attorney—you get to feel like the knight in white armor. It allows you not to think of the reality of what this family is going through. . . . A contextual understanding of what happened does not really matter. Only enough of the background to support the outcome is relevant.
>
> . . . We do not wrestle with the impact of gender-related trauma. Likewise we do not recognize that race matters. . . . Our legal distance

validates the dysfunctional normalization of abuse that usually occurs in abusive families.

. . .The stories of women who are traumatized by abuse are suppressed by the normalization of violence toward women and children. Subordination of women—treating them like objects of property—is our cultural legacy. Historically, this violence has been acknowledged as the private right of men ruling families. Violence and rape of women are now tacitly allowed by the suppression of knowledge about abuse and the failure of the society to redress abuse. When women and children do speak, their stories are distorted to make them willing victims, liars, provocateurs, and crazies.

. . . Who is listening and how they listen affect the ability of the speaker to talk. There is an interaction between speaker and listener. In a symbiotic way they can work together for deeper levels of understanding [pp. 904, 905, 908, 915, and 923].

PSYCHOLOGY AND THE LAW

The courts must make decisions about cases before them in a timely manner. The U.S. Constitution guarantees a "fair and speedy trial" to criminal defendants. The courts do not have to rely on the most current research on gender, but they do have to provide decisions that are consistent with past legal decisions (that is, precedent). Court decisions tend to reflect well-established social norms and conservative interpretations of the law, because the obligation to follow precedent tends to prevent dramatic changes in legal decision making. In examining legal cases related to women, we can see how the judges are viewing women and their role in society, and we can see how that role is then expanded or constricted as a result of their decisions. The courts give power to enforce gender roles when they define what is acceptable and not acceptable (not constitutional) treatment of women by employers, insurers, or the government itself. Scholars analyzing legal cases must spend as much time reading between the lines as they do reading the words of Supreme Court justices, since much of what affects women is in the unspoken assumptions made by those in power.

ABOUT THIS BOOK

This book brings together the perspectives of legal scholars, practicing attorneys, academic psychologists, and clinicians. Our hope is that this juxtaposition of ideas and perspectives will provoke valuable discussion. How does the law view women, and is it consistent with what academic researchers are presenting from their empirical research? In what ways have both fields fallen under the power of stereotyping and the mystification that seems to justify inequality? What should each field do when they become aware of both the overt violence related to gender (wartime rape, honor killings, infanticide) and the quiet "disappearing" of women, that is, the invisibility of the contributions of women to every aspect of life?

The differences between membership in a dominant social group and membership in a subordinate social group are profound and pervasive, influencing every aspect of life: money, health, education, family relationships, employment, even the cost of living. While this book can only hope to begin to describe one aspect of the dominant-subordinate experience—that of sexism—there are very few individuals who have the luxury of fighting on only one battleground. The function of prejudice is to simplify and objectify. The status quo of the dominant culture is maintained to the extent that groups are described in stereotypes and pitted against each other. These are the oldest tricks in the book: divide and conquer; create an us and a them; set a standard that few can reach, so that individuals feel different from each other and lesser than one another. Although gender is the focus of this book, it is presented with the understanding that women come to every encounter with many characteristics: racial identity, socioeconomic status, mental and physical health, sexual identity, educational achievement, occupation, family structure, and individual personality and history.

The book begins with history. Natalie Porter gives an overview of psychological research and theory related to gender, and Andrea Barnes describes the evolution of gender-related legal decisions.

The workplace is the next focus. Nancy Lynn Baker and Jay M. Finkelman look at sexual harassment in the workplace, first from the individual's perspective and then from the viewpoint of the organization. Joyce K. Fletcher describes the way that women's contributions to the workplace, particularly the interpersonal management and team-building behaviors that are essential to the effective functioning of a company, can become invisible when they do not fit a model of productivity and documentation. Lisa Wilson then describes the ambivalence of the courts in cases involving pregnant employees.

The next group of chapters examines issues related to women's health and sexuality. Andrea Barnes presents an update of both the psychological and legal sides of abortion. Judith C. Appelbaum and

Virginia S. Davis report on the gender gap in health insurance coverage. Jennifer R. R. Hightower presents a cross-cultural overview of women and depression.

The criminal justice system is then examined. Phyllis Goldfarb reviews the way courts have dealt with battered women, and she describes recent legal interventions for women who were incarcerated after killing their batterers. Patricia Rozee describes efforts to "undo" the effects of media messages and gender stereotypes in her chapter on rape resistance. Gretchen Borchelt discusses rape from an international perspective, particularly its use as a weapon of war.

The book ends with a global perspective on gender, addressing both cross-national issues and specific gender issues that have affected particular countries. Shannon M. Roesler addresses the use of religion as justification for human rights abuses against women. Catherine Toth describes the challenges of women in the U.S. armed forces, who face bias at home and end up in legal limbo when serving abroad. Teresa Mugadza describes the legal discrimination against women in southern Africa, and Valata Jenkins-Monroe relates the personal experiences of Ugandan women in the context of an AIDS epidemic. Renee Huebner describes the dilemma of being female, and giving birth to female children, in China, where the one-child policy and the devaluing of women have put women in the position of having to make impossible choices between their daughters and their own survival.

ACKNOWLEDGMENTS

This book could not have been completed without the tireless dedication of Jennifer Hightower, the generosity of the authors who contributed chapters, the patience of Seth Schwartz at Jossey-Bass, and the resources of Alliant International University.

January 2005   ANDREA BARNES, J.D., Ph.D.
Alhambra, California

References

Barnes, A. (1985). *Traditional attitudes and nontraditional life choices: The early women psychologists.* Paper presented at the annual convention of the American Psychological Association, Los Angeles.

Chodorow, N. J. (1978). *The reproduction of mothering.* Berkeley: University of California Press.

Collins, P. H. (1990). *Black feminist thought.* New York: Routledge.

Epstein, S. (1996). Tort reform to ensure the inclusion of fertile women in early phases of commercial drug research. *University of Chicago Law School Roundtable, 3,* 355–390.

Espinoza, L. G. (1997). Legal narratives, therapeutic narratives: The invisibility and omnipresence of race and gender. *Michigan Law Review, 95*(4), 901–937.

Fast, I. (1990). Aspects of early gender development: Toward a reformulation. *Psychoanalytic Psychology, 7*(Suppl.), 105–117.

Fletcher, J. K. (1999). *Disappearing acts: Gender, power and relational practice at work.* Cambridge, MA: MIT Press.

Geduldig v. Aiello, 417 U.S. 484 (1974).

Hochschild, A. R. (1983). *The managed heart: Commercialization of human feeling.* Berkeley: University of California Press.

Hochschild, A. R., & Machung, A. (2003). *The second shift* (2nd ed.). Berkeley: University of California Press.

Hope, J. R. (2003). *Pinstripes and pearls: The women of the Harvard law class of '64 who forged an old girl network and paved the way for future generations.* New York: Simon & Schuster.

Karraker, K. H., Lake, M. A., & Vogel, D. A. (1995). Parents' gender-stereotyped perceptions of newborns: The eye of the beholder revisited. *Sex Roles: A Journal of Research, 33,* 687–701.

Main, M. (1996). Introduction to the special section on attachment and psychopathology: 2. Overview of the field of attachment. *Journal of Consulting and Clinical Psychology, 64*(2), 237–243.

Miller, J. B. (2003). Telling the truth about power. *Research and Action Report, Center for Research on Women, 25*(1), 4–5.

Muller v. Oregon, 208 U.S. 412, 421 (1908).

Rubin, J. Z., Provenzano, F. J., & Luria, Z. (1974). The eye of the beholder: Parents' views on sex of newborns. *American Journal of Orthopsychiatry, 43,* 720–731.

Steinem, G. (1994). *Moving beyond words.* New York: Simon & Schuster.

The Handbook of Women, Psychology, and the Law

CHAPTER ONE

Psychological Gender Differences

Contemporary Theories and Controversies

Natalie Porter, Ph.D.

P sychology has played a key role in the policy and legal arenas pertaining to the rights and protections of women. Sweeping changes have occurred for women in society since the mid-1990s. Women's rights, protections, and roles have been transformed in virtually all aspects of American society, most notably in the family, higher education, and the workplace. Psychology has both contributed to and benefited from these changes. The field itself has undergone major shifts during the past few decades that have involved both the inclusion of women in the profession and the inclusion of research and theory in areas that pertain to the lives of women.

Although gender has been a topic of research, theory, and speculation throughout the history of the field of psychology, the psychology of women developed as a formal field only in the 1970s. The focus on women in psychology came about with the rise of the feminist movement in the broader society, paralleling the relationship between cultural and social movements and psychology that has existed throughout the history of psychology (Furumoto, 1998; Minton, 2000). Research in gender, sex differences and stereotypes, the workplace and workplace discrimination, sexual harassment, reproductive rights, family violence, sexual assault, and childhood sexual abuse has burgeoned over the past few decades as women have become researchers and clinicians and as the experiences of women have become legitimate topics of inquiry.

Questions about sex differences in attitudes, traits, behaviors, and abilities are central to both psychological inquiry and mainstream culture. It would be difficult to find another area of psychology that has received an equivalent amount of attention yet where the results and interpretations are as hotly contested and as murky. Controversy exists about whether the research on sex differences substantiates the existence of differences, whether the magnitude of the differences is sufficient to be regarded as important or relevant, whether the intragroup differences so outweigh the intergroup differences as to render the topic unimportant, and whether the differences are so context dependent that they reflect little about men's and women's actual behaviors in society. The etiology of sex differences, whether artifact, social construction, social status, social structure and role, or evolution, is also an area of disagreement, with research providing support for multiple perspectives. This chapter lays out the current research and perspectives about sex differences, beginning with quantitative research methods and conclusions and progressing to qualitative, discursive, and epistemological positions and methodologies.

HISTORICAL CONTEXT OF CURRENT RESEARCH

The Psychology of Sex Differences by Maccoby and Jacklin (1974) is generally viewed as the first major contemporary review of the topic, but the study of sex differences in American psychology is as old as the discipline itself. Much of the early research was based on evolutionary theory interpreted to support a social structure that equated women's roles with procreation and child rearing and men's roles with work and authority over the family. Jeanne Marecek (2002) quotes a tract written in the late 1800s that embodies this perspective: "All that is distinctly human is man; all that is truly woman is reproductive" (p. 255). The writings on sex differences by the renowned early psychologist G. Stanley Hall used evolutionary theory to promote sex segregation in education because of the presumed necessity to maintain the sex differences inherent in the nature of boys and girls (Minton, 2000). Although Hall supported the education of several early women psychologists when he was president of Clark University (1888–1920), he also served as a leader in an anticoeducation movement, because he believed that girls and boys required segregated socialization in order to fulfill their distinct social roles. Girls were to be prepared for motherhood and the perpetuation of society through child rearing. Boys were to be prepared for the roles that created, led, improved, or otherwise contributed to civilization. Their socialization required that they not be unduly influenced and feminized by their teachers and mothers during adolescence (Diehl, 1986).

Helen Thompson Woolley was one of the first psychologists to systematically investigate sex differences, to some extent in reaction to the types of assertions and conclusions about sex differences that her colleagues had drawn. She published a body of empirical work pertaining to sex differences in cognitive, motor, and sensory abilities as well as a critique of the work of her colleagues (Thompson, 1903; Woolley, 1910, 1914). She argued that differences in abilities between males and females were relatively small and did not justify the interpretations of her male colleagues. She was one of the first to counter the prevailing biological explanations for sex differences with social and structural theories.

Sex comparisons in research continued mostly in a piecemeal fashion over the next sixty years, culminating with *The Psychology of Sex Differences* (1974), in which Maccoby and Jacklin reviewed nearly fifteen hundred empirical studies that had reported sex differences in some form, evaluating their methods, instruments, results, and conclusions. Like Woolley (1910, 1914), they concluded that the literature documented relatively few or relatively small sex differences, given the level of professional and popular attention devoted to the topic. Their conclusion was that the research supported that differences existed in four areas—verbal, quantitative, and spatial cognitive abilities and the trait of aggression—with women scoring higher on verbal abilities and men higher on the other variables.

CONTEMPORARY RESEARCH FINDINGS

Research on sex differences has only increased since Maccoby and Jacklin's book. Marecek (2002) estimated that by 1985, over sixteen thousand studies of sex differences were reported in the literature. A major change that has occurred since the publication of *The Psychology of Sex Differences* in 1974 is the shift in the method of reviewing results across studies from cataloging those with significant results (p value) in order to locate trends or themes to using quantitative methods of meta-analysis. In the latter process, effect sizes (d value), derived from the standard deviation of the sex comparison for each study, are averaged (Cooper, 1979). This method is considered an improvement over earlier, more informal techniques of analysis because it evaluates effect size rather than statistical significance, which is tied to sample size, and because it involves establishing and complying with criteria-based rules for inclusion and aggregation that are uniformly applied throughout an analysis (Eagly, 1995a). This technique of aggregating and evaluating the effect sizes of studies in a particular research literature along a continuum has been applied to many areas of psychology, including sex differences, where meta-analyses of comparisons of men's and women's emotions, attitudes, traits, and behaviors across research studies have been conducted over the past two decades.

These meta-analytic techniques have not quelled the controversy about the existence or importance of sex differences. There is still little agreement on or clear direction about what traits, abilities, and attributes differ between men and women and about the size of these differences, their relevance to functioning in contemporary society, or their etiology. Critics of this approach counter that it does not solve the "file drawer phenomenon," meaning that only studies with some positive findings are published and available for another researcher's meta-analysis, while the studies with no results are filed in researchers' drawers. Meta-analysis attends only to those that have seen the light of day. A second critique is that studies may employ very different measures to evaluate the same disposition, and these measures may be lumped together in meta-analysis without truly knowing whether they are measuring similar or different qualities (Marecek, 2002).

Cognitive Abilities

Meta-analytic techniques have been used to evaluate hundreds of studies measuring cognitive and intellectual sex differences and have resulted in a range of interpretations of the results. Hyde (1981, 1994) has argued that sex differences in verbal, quantitative, and spatial cognitive abilities are small and diminish in late adolescence and adulthood. Halpern (1992) has interpreted the data as demonstrating that stable and significant sex differences exist for particular cognitive abilities even when the overall levels of quantitative and verbal sex differences appear to diminish over time (for example, in adolescence and adulthood). She and others cite research that has been focused on the specific dimensions of verbal, spatial, and quantitative abilities that seem to account for stable sex differences, such as visuospatial ability involving the mental rotation of three-dimensional objects, where males score higher than females (Masters & Sanders, 1993), verbal fluency (Halpern, 1992), and quantitative problem solving (Halpern, 1992).

Personality and Social Attitudes, Traits, and Behaviors

Social and personality researchers have analyzed sex differences using quantitative techniques on synthesized databases from a vast array of databases in social, personality, clinical, organizational, and sports psychology. Eagly (1995a) has made the case for their analyses confirming sex differences: "The psychologists who have conducted most of these syntheses of sex-related differences in social behavior and personality are in general agreement that their meta-analytic findings yield evidence of differences. A major theme of much of the interpretive writing based on these new syntheses is that empirical research has provided evidence for numerous nontrivial differences in many aspects of behavior" (p. 148). Eagly asserts that these researchers have provided evidence of sex differences in many more areas than claimed by Maccoby and Jacklin in 1974.

Costa, Terracciano, and McCrae (2001) analyzed synthesized databases of the Revised NEO Personality Inventory (Costa and McCrae, 1992) from twenty-six cultures made up of 23,031 adults and college-age participants. The authors concluded that modest-sized but cross-culturally consistent gender differences were found that were similar to stereotypes held about gender differences. Women tended to score higher on agreeableness, warmth, openness to feelings, and neuroticism, whereas men scored higher on openness to ideas and assertiveness. This review supports earlier work by Fiengold (1994) and Nolen-Hoeksema (1987). Fiengold (1994) had previously used meta-analysis to review sex differences on nine of the thirty personality traits of the Revised NEO Personality Inventory (Costa & McCrae, 1992). He found that men scored higher in assertiveness, whereas women scored higher on gregariousness, trust, and tender-mindedness. Nolen-Hoeksema (1987) found that women score higher in symptoms of depression cross-culturally. Nevertheless, Costa et al. (2001) interpreted their findings as showing that individual variation within sexes is greater than the differences between the sexes on these personality traits.

Eagly (1995a) summarizes the vast array of sex difference research in the areas of social and personality psychology: "Thematic analysis of demonstrated sex differences in social behavior suggests that they conform to stereotypic expectations that women are communal and men are agentic. In general, women tend to manifest behaviors that can be described as socially sensitive, friendly, and concerned with others' welfare, whereas men tend to manifest behaviors that can be described as dominant, controlling, and independent" (p. 154). For example, quantitative syntheses of nonverbal and vocal behaviors by Hall and her colleagues have concluded that women are better at decoding nonverbal expressions and smile more, whereas men touch women more than women touch men, use more dominant eye gaze patterns, and interrupt and hold the floor in conversation more than women (Hall, 1978; Hall & Halberstadt, 1986; McClure, 2000; Stier & Hall, 1984).

In a vein similar to Eagly's statement already quoted, Cross and Madson (1997) consider the majority of social and personality sex differences to reflect differences in traits of independence and interdependence. They use the definitions proposed by Markus and Kitayama (1991) based on whether one views oneself as separated from (independence) or connected to others (interdependence). A person who values independence focuses on self-fulfillment, whereas one with an interdependent perspective emphasizes the fulfillment of one's place in the broader social context. Cross and Madson (1997) provide examples from the existing literature in social sex differences as support for their position. They note research findings showing that women cite interpersonal problems as sources of distress more than men do (Pratt, Golding, Hunter, & Sampson, 1988; Walker, de Vries, & Trevethan, 1987); that women are more likely to talk about interpersonal subjects, whereas men talk about sports and politics (Heatherington et al., 1993; McFarland & Miller, 1990); that women pay more attention to information related to relationships than men do (Josephs, Markus, & Tafarodi, 1992; Ross & Holmberg, 1992); and that men attend to information pertaining to themes of social dominance (Maccoby, 1990).

Gabriel and Gardner (1999) suggest that both men and women are interdependent, but that their type of interdependence differs. They define *interdependence* as relational or collective and hypothesize that men demonstrate more collective (group-oriented and agentic) interdependence and women more relational (dyadic and intimate) interdependence. Their results across five studies investigating cognitive, emotional, and behavioral differences did not find sex differences in participants' tendencies toward independence versus interdependence. However, they did demonstrate sex differences in whether the type of interdependence manifested was relational or collective. Women described themselves in more relational terms, scored higher on a measure of relational "self-construal," reported more emotional experiences linked to relationships, appeared more attuned to information pertaining to the relationships of others, and were motivated to behave in ways that maintained close relationships. The male participants described themselves in more collective terms, scored higher on a measure of collective self-construal, reported more emotional experiences linked to groups, appeared attuned to information pertaining to group memberships of others, and were motivated to behave in ways that supported their groups (Gabriel & Gardner, 1999).

ARE SEX DIFFERENCES OF SUFFICIENT MAGNITUDE TO MATTER?

Not surprising, central to the controversy about the existence of sex differences is the disagreement among researchers about the consistency across studies and the magnitude of the differences that have been reported. Eagly (1995a) contends that many feminist researchers want to ignore or minimize sex differences for fear that they perpetuate social inequities. She summarizes the arguments put forth by the critics of the sex differences research: that differences are small and often inconsistent, results frequently are artifacts due to improper methods, and findings often conflict with stereotypes about sex differences, creating a second source of inconsistency (Eagly, 1995a, 1995b). Eagly (1995a) counters each of these arguments; she asserts that the meta-analyses of traits, abilities, and behaviors have demonstrated a range of consistent findings with effect sizes comparable to those in most accepted areas of psychology. She estimates that most effects in psychology for well-known research are in the moderate range of around "one half of a standard deviation or less; considerably larger effect sizes are relatively unusual" (p. 151). Compared to this standard, she points out that several aggregated findings of particular sex differences show large effect sizes (examples include a test of visuospatial abilities, nurturance, and facial expressiveness), with most differences falling in the small-to-moderate range of effect sizes. Eagly points out that even small effect sizes can have significant cumulative real-world consequences and impact. To provide a context for the relevance of these effect sizes, Eagly (1995a) cites Cohen's explanation (1977) of the benchmarks pertaining to each effect size category: small effect sizes represent group distributions that are 85 percent overlapping and are more common in studies lacking good experimental or measurement control, such as new areas of research; moderate effects are 33 percent nonoverlapping and 67 percent overlapping and represent group differences that are noticeable in daily life; and large differences are highly visible (47 percent nonoverlapping and 53 percent overlapping). Thus, Eagly's assertion is that most of the sex difference literature has findings that at least are noticeable in ordinary life. With regard to the other critiques of sex difference research, Eagly (1995a) asserts that researchers have increasingly taken into account and controlled for experimental artifacts.

Hyde and Plant (1995) take issue with Eagly's assertions, first, that feminist researchers have one perspective about the value of identifying or minimizing the existence of sex differences, and second, that the effect sizes of aggregated research in sex difference research are equivalent to those in other major areas of psychology. Hyde and Plant (1995) maintain that feminist empiricists have existed along a continuum; in addition to those who argue that sex differences do not exist or that this research promotes inequity for women, there have been many feminist empiricists who have taken the position that clear differences between men and women exist, and still others who have taken a more mixed position—that some sex differences are in fact large, while others are quite insignificant. The authors use Gilligan's work on moral reasoning (1982) as one example of a feminist researcher concluding that men and women fundamentally differ in moral reasoning, with men assuming a justice (agentic) perspective and women a care (communal) perspective. Hyde and Plant (1995) also cite the research in sex differences in nonverbal behavior as another widely accepted area of research by feminist scholars in spite of large sex differences. Examples include sex differences in touching behavior (Hall, 1978), smiling, verbal interruptions (McMillan, Clifton, McGrath, & Gale, 1977; Porter, Geis, Cooper, & Newman, 1985), and other differences in conversational style and meaning (Tannen, 1990). In addition, feminist psychologists disagree about whether differences in some abilities, such as cognitive abilities, represent substantial (Halpern, 1992) or insignificant differences (Hyde et al., 1990; Hyde & Linn, 1988).

Hyde and Plant (1995) reviewed the aggregated sex differences studies that had been conducted previously. They concluded that the effect sizes for the many sex differences reviewed in these meta-analyses were smaller than the figures given by Eagly (1995a) and smaller than the findings of meta-analyses of other psychological phenomena. They found that the magnitude of gender differences varied substantially from one variable to another, with one-fourth of the sex differences studies revealing effect sizes close to zero, 35 percent showing small effects, 27 percent moderate effects, and 13 percent large and very large effects. They compared these results with the aggregated analyses of other established areas of psychology, where only 6 percent of the research fell into the close-to-zero category, 29 percent in the small effects category, 38 percent in the moderate category, and 27 percent in the large and very large group. They argue that these comparisons support their contentions that sex differences are generally not of the same magnitude as other psychological findings and the impact of these differences needs to be questioned. However, these researchers still advocate for the understanding of the differences that fall into large effect sizes. "An important direction for research will be to sort out the larger from the smaller gender differences to give special attention to understanding the processes that create the larger differences" (Hyde & Plant, 1995, p. 161).

It is important to note that even in areas of sex difference research showing robust effect sizes, men and women overlap in abilities, traits, attitudes, and behaviors more than they fall into two separate groups. It is this overlap that is the source of controversy. In some ways, the controversy about effect size boils down to the question of whether the glass is half empty or half full. On the one hand are researchers making the case that research on sex differences is an area worthy of study, with findings that will lead to our understanding of important phenomena. For example, is it not important to know that men are responsible for most of the violent crime in the United States if one is developing interventions or policies? Doesn't knowing that most sex offenders are male lead not only to better-targeted intervention and research efforts but to more informed legal and social policies as well? Wouldn't recognizing that women suffer more from depression aid in prevention and treatment efforts? Wouldn't awareness of sex differences in quantitative problem solving and visuospatial abilities lead to more effective teaching techniques for women? Aren't sex differences in cognitive abilities as important to understand as social class differences? Researchers who see the glass as half full line up on the side of these arguments, asserting that the differences found in research cumulatively "make a difference" in society (Martell, Lane, & Emrich, 1995).

Other researchers question why psychologists would attend to sex differences rather than individual differences given that men and women overlap so substantially on every trait studied. They remind us that for 60 percent of the psychological variables that show significant sex differences, the group distributions for men and women overlap between 85 percent and almost completely. For the large effect sizes found only for 13 percent of the attributes studied, a 50 percent overlap between men and women still exists. Thus, these researchers argue that knowing that a person is male or female provides very little predictive value on where he or she would fall on any particular trait. The "half-empty group" argues that the continued focus on sex differences in the light of their insignificance contributes to the unequal status of women because the justification of sex discrimination and even unequal treatment under the law has been based primarily on sex differences. Hyde and Plant (1995) make this point: "Any possible bias that may have been introduced by minimalist psychologists [that is, those who minimize differences] is more than balanced by the effects of the popular media, which glamorize and magnify findings of gender differences and are bored to tears with findings of no difference" (p. 161).

THE ORIGINS OF SEX DIFFERENCES

Psychological theories pertaining to the causes of sex differences primarily fall into the biological (essentialist) and social psychological (constructionist) domains. Wood and Eagly (2002) broadly summarize these positions: "Essentialist perspectives emphasize the basic, stable sex differences that arise from causes that are inherent in the human species such as biologically-based evolved psychological dispositions. . . . Social constructionist perspectives emphasize the variation in sex differences across social contexts that emerges from the means of male and female within particular contexts" (p. 700). Although essentialist theories have been proposed from other perspectives, pertaining to parenting (Chodorow, 1978), moral development (Gilligan, 1982), and "ways of knowing" (Belenky, Clinchy, Goldberger, & Tarule, 1986), biological and evolutionary theories are the predominant ones.

Evolutionary theories postulate that basic sex differences are the result of the adaptations of ancient men and women to distinct survival problems. In brief, sex differences in psychological attributes stem from different reproductive pressures and levels of parental investment, and mate selection (Buss, 1995; Buss & Kenrick, 1998; Geary, 2000). Nurturance and relational qualities were adaptive for women as they experienced pregnancy, childbirth, and child rearing. Women needed to be more selective about mates because they invested more in the offspring and preferred males who could provide and protect successfully. Long-term mates were in their best interest and that of their offspring; thus, women historically have competed for more socially dominant, competitive, and aggressive men (Kenrick & Li, 2000). As men competed for sexual access to women, aggressiveness, competitiveness, and risk taking evolved because these traits increased their chances of being selected. Men's control over women's sexual behavior and their sexual jealousy came about to ensure their paternity. Evolutionary psychologists recognize that environmental conditions can influence the pattern of evolved traits but continue to attend more to demonstrating the universality of sex differences (Eagly & Wood, 1999). Wood and Eagly (2000) dispute that cross-cultural data support the evolutionary perspective, showing instead greater flexibility in mate selection and social organizations than that argued by the evolutionary perspective. They contend that the conclusions of evolutionary psychologists far outstrip their findings. Others maintain that the evolutionary perspective becomes a way to rationalize male domination and aggression toward women (see Marecek, 2002).

Social structural and constructivist theories emphasize contextual and social psychological principles over biological determinism. Social role theorists posit that sex differences emerge from men and women assuming different family and occupational roles (Eagly, 1987). The sex differences found in these family and occupational roles may occur for a number of reasons: from the greater status and power associated with men's roles (Geis, 1993), from sex-specific divisions of labor based on differing physical abilities (Eagly, 1987), and from different economic and ecological contexts (Wood & Eagly, 2000). Because these factors will vary across cultures and periods, the organization of the social structure and, thus, sex roles will differ as well. Structural theories argue that sex differences and roles are not universal but related to these contextual conditions.

Wood and Eagly (2000) have developed a biosocial model that integrates the essentialist perspective with a social psychological perspective. Their theory focuses on the "interactive elements between the physical attributes of men and women and the social contexts in which they live" (p. 701). This interactionist perspective is one in "which psychological and physical sex-linked attributes are repeatedly constructed or emergent in response to the evolved attributes of the species, the developmental experiences of each sex, and the situated activity of men and women in society" (Wood & Eagly, 2000, p. 1062).

The theory has the following elements:

1. Men and women are distributed differentially into societal roles, resulting in differences in social behavior.

2. These differences in social behavior occur through many processes, such as the formation of gender roles, where each sex is expected to have psychological dispositions congruent with the tasks usually performed by that sex.

3. These gender roles become stereotypical of women and men and guide social behavior, shaped by various processes of socialization, expectancy confirmation, and self-regulation.

4. Biological processes such as hormonal regulation and changes work in unison with psychological processes to direct the sexes toward specific social roles and to improve their functioning in these roles.

5. These causes of psychological sex differences arise from other determinants that have defined the positions of men and women in the social structure: sex differences in physical attributes and the behaviors associated with these differences (such as women's child rearing and men's greater size and upper-body strength) and the contextual factors within a society. These determinants have influenced social roles because of the ability of one sex or the other to perform particular tasks more efficiently in a society that is based on complementary relationships.

Although the biosocial model includes biological components, it differs significantly from the evolutionary theories. Wood and Eagly

(2000) dispute that the types of sexual selection pressures that contributed to physical sex differences are related to sex differences in dispositions. In their review of a considerable literature, they show that psychological sex differences in humans have not consistently covaried with physical ones or shared antecedents.

EPISTEMOLOGICAL, SOCIAL CONSTRUCTIVIST, AND POSTMODERN PERSPECTIVES

This chapter so far has focused on the quantitative research pertaining to psychological sex differences. Many contemporary theorists question whether quantitative research is the only way, or even a valid way, to approach these issues. They argue that women can be understood only in a context that includes the intersection of structural variables such as social, economic, cultural, and ecological contexts. Any human can be understood only as a function of the interaction of race, ethnicity, gender, class, sexual orientation, disability, and age.

Many psychologists also dispute the objectivity theoretically inherent in quantitative research methodologies, arguing that one's social identity, values, and own social "location" shape all aspects of one's research and conclusions (Harding, 1986). For example, Minton (2000) has made the compelling argument that as North American psychology was emerging and searching for an identity, it adopted the androcentric biases emerging in early twentieth-century American culture. Leading psychologists of the time such as G. Stanley Hall and James McKeen Cattell were proponents of a cultural shift in the view of masculinity from the turn-of-the-century ideal of gentle introspection to a rawer, instinctually based ideal characterized by independence, aggressiveness, and competitiveness (epitomized by Teddy Roosevelt and the Rough Riders). One manifestation of this shift in psychology was its move away from its roots in philosophy to an empirical science where control and "objectivity" replaced introspection and qualitative methods. However, the shift itself occurred in the context of particular social identities and values and the power and status of individual men to define the field of psychology.

Marecek (2002) compares the efficacy of qualitative with quantitative research methods in truly understanding women. She describes qualitative inquiry as embedding "psychology in rich contexts of history, society, and culture. It not only re-situates people in their life worlds, but also regards them as reflexive, meaning-making, and intentional actors" (p. 259). She contends that qualitative research frequently provides more accurate and meaningful information about people's lives because it captures psychological reality through the use of more natural language, allows more depth and input by participants, resulting in a more active collaboration, and dispels false notions of objectivity that often pervade one's methods, findings, and interpretations.

Kaschak (1992) has concentrated on feminist epistemology and the deconstruction of patriarchal social structures. She uses an epistemological approach, or making known the rules or meaning of "meaning," to illuminate the rules behind the relationships between the sexes. She questions whether sex differences can even be discovered, because in a patriarchal society, "the masculine always defines the feminine by naming it, containing it, engulfing, invading, and evaluating it. The feminine is never permitted to stand alone or to subsume the masculine" (p. 5).

By taking the noun *gender* and transforming it into a verb form, Kaschak reveals the epistemology of gender. In a gendered, or "engendered," world, gender is not static. Gendering is an active, interactive, and continuous process that is embedded in all aspects of our existence, our relationships, and our meanings. To truly understand the embeddedness of gender throughout our social structures means to recognize that changes in these relationships and structures cannot occur within the context of the same rules. Regarding sex differences, Kaschak (1992) points out that women are penalized for being too feminine as well as too masculine. They are presented with the paradox that to follow the rules is to be confronted with negative consequences for being female, and not to follow the rules is to be confronted with negative consequences for not being female enough. As women walk this tightrope between expressing too little or too much femininity, there are few payoffs for doing what is expected.

Kaschak (1992) offers the Antigone myth as the embodiment of women's roles and sex differences within patriarchal family and cultural structures. It is emblematic of the realization that men exist always with the expectation that they are entitled to the love and caretaking of women, just as Oedipus expected his daughter Antigone to sacrifice her life to care for him. In a patriarchal, gendered society, women's development is tantamount to preparation to serve men. Attachment to one's mother or other women or even conscious attempts to raise children in nonsexist ways cannot change these relationships or alter the course of gender in the broader context. In fact, in an Oedipal/ Antigone world, women are separated from each other, as the role of mothers is to prepare their daughters for the same servitude.

Kaschak (1992) provides examples of the pervasiveness of the embeddedness of gender. Self-concept is "embodied" for women, meaning that it exists only within the context of the female body. For women, esteem is the result of the internalization of a social, rather than an individual, construct that revolves around the attributions given to women by men about women's bodies. *Relational,* according to Kaschak, is defined as being responsible for the success of relationships with others or for being sensitive to the needs of others, even when these needs go unexpressed or even unrecognized by men who assert their independence and separateness while expecting nurturance and support.

Other feminist psychologists have considered language, or discourse, as the primary source of shaping gender relations (and sex differences) and subsequently of understanding them (Hare-Mustin & Marecek, 1990). From this theoretical perspective, language creates reality. Through language, men and women negotiate their relationships and are either enabled or restricted in what they perceive about themselves and their social relationships. In a patriarchal society, men define the roles of both men and women through discourse, determining when women will manifest feminine behavior and when they are "permitted" to venture from strictly sex-typed roles.

Brown and Ballou have provided a feminist critique of sex differences in both personality theories and psychopathological constructs. In *Personality and Psychopathology: Feminist Reappraisals* (1992) and *Rethinking Mental Health and Disorder* (2002), they have exposed the inadequacy of traditional quantitative approaches for understanding women's distress, their psychological development, or the static construct called "personality" as it pertains to women. They have pointed out that no psychological theories or constructs that fail to account for oppression in the lives of women can ever effectively be used to understand or treat women.

Worell and Remer (1992) elaborated on the ways in which assumed sex differences in psychopathology have resulted in bias in the psychological assessment and diagnosis of women. They have described the process as similar to a self-fulfilling prophecy where the outcomes are determined by initial assumptions. Assumptions of sex differences have had an impact on our understanding of psychopathology because of researchers' "(a) disregarding or minimizing the effect of the environmental context on individual's behaviors; (b) giving different diagnoses to women and men displaying similar symptoms; (c) misjudgments in selection of diagnostic labels due to sex-role stereotyped beliefs; and (d) using a sex-biased theoretical orientation" (p. 151).

Although the themes of these contemporary feminist theorists are wide ranging, there are common themes in the topics they have pursued. Attention to context, the diversity of women's lives, and the impact of multiple oppressions, such as race, ethnicity, class, or sexual orientation, on women are central to the work of these theorists. These authors have struggled to move beyond sex or gender as a dichotomous category to describe women's development, growth, and dilemmas in all of their complexity and depth.

References

Belenky, M. F., Clinchy, B. M., Goldberger, N. R., & Tarule, J. M. (1986). *Women's ways of knowing: Development of self, voice, and mind.* New York: Basic Books.

Brown, L. S., & Ballou, M. (Eds.). (1992). *Personality and psychopathology: Feminist reappraisals.* New York: Guilford Press.

Brown, L. S., & Ballou, M. (Eds.). (2003). *Rethinking mental health and disorder: Feminist perspectives.* New York: Guilford Press.

Buss, D. M. (1995). Evolutionary psychology: A new paradigm for psychological science. *Psychological Inquiry, 6,* 1–30.

Buss, D. M., & Kenrick, D. T. (1998). Evolutionary social psychology. In D. T. Gilbert, S. T. Fiske, & G. Lindzley (Eds.), *The handbook of social psychology* (4th ed., Vol. 2, pp. 982–1026). New York: McGraw-Hill.

Chodorow, N. J. (1978). *The reproduction of mothering: Psychoanalysis and the sociology of gender.* Berkeley: University of California Press.

Cohen, J. (1977). *Statistical power analysis for the behavioral sciences* (Rev. ed.). Orlando, FL: Academic Press.

Cooper, H. (1979). Statistically combining independent studies: A meta-analysis of sex differences in conformity research. *Journal of Personality and Social Psychology, 37,* 131–146.

Costa, P. T., Jr., & McCrae, R. R. (1992). *Revised NEO Personality Inventory (NEO-PI-R) and NEO Five-Factor Inventory (NEO-FFI) professional manual.* Odessa, FL: Psychological Assessment Resources.

Costa, P. T., Jr., Terracciano, A., & McCrae, R. R. (2001). Gender differences in personality traits across cultures: Robust and surprising findings. *Journal of Personality and Social Psychology, 81,* 322–331.

Cross, S. E., & Madson, L. (1997). Models of the self: Self-construals and gender. *Psychological Bulletin, 122,* 5–37.

Diehl, L. A. (1986). The paradox of G. Stanley Hall: Foe of coeducation and educator of women, *American Psychologist, 41,* 868–878.

Eagly, A. H. (1987). *Sex differences in social behavior: A social role interpretation.* Mahwah, NJ: Erlbaum.

Eagly, A. H. (1995a). The science and politics of comparing women and men. *American Psychologist, 50,* 145–158.

Eagly, A. H. (1995b). Differences between women and men: Their magnitude, practical importance, and political meaning. *American Psychologist, 51,* 158–159.

Eagly, A. H., & Wood, W. (1999). The origins of sex differences in human behavior: Evolved dispositions versus social roles. *American Psychologist, 54,* 408–423.

Fiengold, A. (1994). Gender differences in personality: A meta-analysis. *Psychological Bulletin, 116,* 429–456.

Furumoto, L. (1998). Gender and the history of psychology. In B. M. Clinchy & J. K. Norem (Eds.), *The gender and psychology reader* (pp. 69–77). New York: Appleton.

Gabriel, S., & Gardner, W. L. (1999). Are there "his" and "hers" types of interdependence? The implications of gender differences in collective versus relational interdependence of affect, behavior, and cognition. *Journal of Personality and Social Psychology, 77,* 642–655.

Geary, D. C. (2000). Evolution and proximate expression of human paternal investment. *Psychological Bulletin, 126,* 55–77.

Geis, F. L. (1993). Self-fulfilling prophecies: A social psychological view of gender. In A. E. Beall & R. J. Sternberg (Eds.), *The psychology of gender* (pp. 9–54). New York: Guilford Press.

Gilligan, C. (1982). *In a different voice: Psychological theory and women's development.* Cambridge, MA: Harvard University Press.

Hall, J. A. (1978). Gender effects in decoding nonverbal cues. *Psychological Bulletin, 85,* 845–857.

Hall, J. A., & Halberstadt, A. G. (1986). Smiling and gazing. In J. S. Hyde & M. C. Linn (Eds.), *The psychology of gender: Advances through meta-analysis* (pp. 136–158). Baltimore, MD: Johns Hopkins University Press.

Halpern, D. (1992). *Sex differences in cognitive abilities* (2nd ed.). Mahwah, NJ: Erlbaum.

Harding, S. (1986). *The science question in feminism.* Ithaca, NY: Cornell University Press.

Hare-Mustin, R. T., & Marecek, J. (1990). *Making a difference: Psychology and the construction of gender.* New Haven, CT: Yale University Press.

Heatherington, L., Daubman, K. A., Bates, C. Ahn, A., Brown, H., & Preston, C. (1993). Two investigations of "female modesty" in achievement situations. *Sex Roles, 29,* 739–754.

Hyde, J. S. (1981). How large are cognitive gender differences? A meta-analysis using *w* and *d. American Psychologist, 36,* 892–901.

Hyde, J. S. (1994). Can meta-analysis make feminist transformations in psychology? *Psychology of Women Quarterly, 18,* 451–462.

Hyde, J. S., Fennema, E., & Lamon, S. J. (1990). Gender differences in mathematics performance: A meta-analysis. *Psychological Bulletin, 107,* 139–155.

Hyde, J. S., & Linn, M. C. (1988). Gender differences in verbal ability: A meta-analysis. *Psychological Bulletin, 104, 53–69.*

Hyde, J. S., & Plant, E. A. (1995). Magnitude of psychological gender differences: Another side to the story. *American Psychologist, 50,* 159–161

Josephs, R. A., Markus, H. R., & Tafarodi, R. W. (1992). Gender and self-esteem. *Journal of Social and Personality Psychology, 63,* 391–402.

Kaschak, E. (1992). *Engendered lives: A new psychology of women's experience.* New York: Basic Books.

Kenrick, D. T., & Li, N. (2000). The Darwin is in the details. *American Psychologist, 55,* 1061–1062.

Kimmel, M. S. (1996). *Manhood in America: A cultural history.* New York: Free Press.

Maccoby, E. E. (1990). Gender and relationships. *American Psychologist, 45,* 513–520.

Maccoby, E., & Jacklin, C. (1974). *The psychology of sex differences.* Palo Alto, CA: Stanford University Press.

Marecek, J. (2002). After the facts: Psychology and the study of gender. *Canadian Psychology, 42,* 254–267.

Markus, H., & Kitayama, S. (1991). Culture and the self: Implications for cognition, emotion, and motivation. *Psychological Review, 98,* 224–252.

Martell, R. F., Lane, D. M., & Emrich, C. E. (1995). Male-female differences: A computer simulation. *American Psychologist, 51,* 157–158.

Masters, M. S., & Sanders, B. (1993). Is the gender difference in mental rotation disappearing? *Behavior Genetics, 23,* 337–341.

McClure, E. B. (2000). A meta-analytic review of sex differences in facial expression processing and their development in infants, children, and adolescents. *Psychological Bulletin, 126,* 424–453.

McFarland, C., & Miller, D. T. (1990). Judgments of self-other similarity: Just like other people, only more so. *Journal of Social and Personality Psychology, 16,* 475–484.

McMillan, J. R., Clifton, A. K., McGrath, D., & Gale, W. S. (1977). Women's language: Uncertainty or interpersonal sensitivity and emotionality? *Sex Roles, 3,* 545–560.

Minton, H. L. (2000). Psychology and gender at the turn of the century. *American Psychologist, 55,* 613–615.

Nolen-Hoeksema, S. (1987). Sex differences in unipolar depression: Evidence and theory. *Psychological Bulletin, 101,* 259–282.

Porter, N., Geis, F. L., Cooper, E., & Newman, E. (1985). Androgyny and leadership in mixed-sex groups. *Journal of Personality and Social Psychology, 49,* 808–823.

Pratt, M. W., Golding, G., Hunter, W., & Sampson, R. (1988). Sex differences in adult moral orientation. *Journal of Personality and Social Psychology, 56,* 373–391.

Ross, M., & Holmberg, D. (1992). Are wives' memories for events in relationships more vivid than their husbands' memories? *Journal of Social and Personal Relationships, 9,* 585–604.

Stier, D. S., & Hall, J. A. (1984). Gender difference in touch: An empirical and theoretical review. *Journal of Personality and Social Psychology, 47,* 440–459.

Tannen, D. (1990). *You just don't understand: Women and men in conversation.* New York: Morrow.

Thompson, H. B. (1903). *The mental traits of sex.* Chicago: University of Chicago Press.

Walker, L. J., de Vries, B., & Trevethan, S. D. (1987). Moral stages and moral orientation in real-life and hypothetical dilemmas. *Child Development, 58,* 842–858.

Wood, W., & Eagly, A. H. (2000). Once again, the origins of sex differences. *American Psychologist, 55,* 1062–1063.

Wood, W., & Eagly, A. H. (2002). A cross-cultural analysis of behavior of women and men: Implications for the origins of sex differences. *Psychological Bulletin, 128,* 699–727.

Woolley, H. T. (1910). Psychological literature: A review of the recent literature on the psychology of sex. *Psychological Bulletin, 7,* 335–342.

Woolley, H. T. (1914). The psychology of sex. *Psychological Bulletin, 11,* 353–379.

Worell, J., & Remer, P. (1992). *Feminist perspectives in therapy: An empowerment model for women.* New York: Wiley.

CHAPTER TWO

Women and the Law

A Brief History

Andrea Barnes, J.D., Ph.D.

U ntil relatively recently, women were legally invisible. Inheritance laws passed property from fathers to sons, and marriage laws passed women from fathers to husbands as if they were property. Children were the property of their father and belonged to their father in the case of divorce. Even the money or property that women owned independently before marriage became the property of the husband on marriage. These legal patterns have existed in both Western and Eastern cultures. While it is beyond the scope of this chapter to examine the anthropological aspects of why this pattern emerged, it is not difficult to see how it was maintained: by preventing women access to a legal voice, through either standing in court or the vote, and by preventing women from accumulating their own wealth, there have been few means of enforcing a more equitable status for women. Ultimately, change began through the efforts of women to organize themselves—to gain power in numbers where it was not available any other way.

In the United States, the first Women's Rights Convention in Seneca Falls, New York, on July 19 and 20, 1848, represents a starting point for organized action to change the legal status of women. The convention produced the Declaration of Sentiments and Resolutions, modeled after the Declaration of Independence. The list of grievances in the declaration, which follows, not only contained an attack on specific discriminatory statutes but also provided a statement of fundamental feminist principles, attacking the "supremacy of man," the unequal allocation of power in family, state, and church, and the different moral codes applied to men and women (Becker, Bowman, & Torrey, 1994):

THE DECLARATION OF SENTIMENTS
SENECA FALLS, JULY 19–20, 1848

When, in the course of human events, it becomes necessary for one portion of the family of man to assume among the people of the earth a position different from that which they have hitherto occupied, but one to which the laws of nature and of nature's God entitle them, a decent respect to the opinions of mankind requires that they should declare the causes that impel them to such a course.

We hold these truths to be self-evident: that all men and women are created equal; they are endowed by their Creator with certain inalienable rights; that among these are life, liberty, and the pursuit of happiness; that to secure these rights governments are instituted, deriving their just powers from the consent of the governed. Whenever any form of government becomes destructive of these ends, it is the right of those who suffer from it to refuse allegiance to it, and to insist upon the institution of a new government, laying its foundation on such principles, and organizing its powers in such form, as to them shall seem most likely to effect their safety and happiness. Prudence, indeed, will dictate that governments long established should not be changed for light and transient causes; and accordingly all experience hath shown that mankind are more disposed to suffer, while evils are sufferable, than to right themselves by abolishing the forms to which they were accustomed. But when a long train of abuses and usurpations, pursuing invariably the same object, evinces a design to reduce them under absolute despotism, it is their duty to throw off such government, and to provide new guards for their future security. Such has been the patient sufferance of the women under this government, and such is now the necessity which constrains them to demand the equal station to which they are entitled.

The history of mankind is a history of repeated injuries and usurpations on the part of man toward women, having in direct object the establishment of an absolute tyranny over her. To prove this, let facts be submitted to a candid world.

He had never permitted her to exercise her inalienable right to the elective franchise.

He has compelled her to submit to laws, in the formation of which she had no voice.

He has withheld from her rights which are given to the most ignorant and degraded men—both natives and foreigners.

Having deprived her of this first right of a citizen, the elective franchise, thereby leaving her without representation in the halls of legislation, he has oppressed her on all sides.

He has made her, if married, in the eye of the law, civilly dead.

He has taken from her all right in property, even to the wages she earns.

He has made her, morally, an irresponsible being, as she can commit many crimes with impunity, provided they be done in the presence of her husband. In the covenant of marriage, she is compelled to promise obedience to her husband, he becoming, to all intents and purposes, her master—the law giving him power to deprive her of her liberty, and to administer chastisement.

He has so framed the laws of divorce, as to what shall be the proper causes, and in case of separation, to whom the guardianship of the children shall be given, as to be wholly regardless of the happiness of women—the law, in all cases, going upon a false supposition of the supremacy of man, and giving all power into his hands.

After depriving her of all rights as a married woman, if single, and the owner of property, he has taxed her to support a government which recognizes her only when her property can be made profitable to it.

He has monopolized nearly all the profitable employments, and from those she is permitted to follow, she receives but a scanty remuneration.

He closes against her all the avenues to wealth and distinction, which he considers most honorable to himself. As a teacher of theology, medicine, or law, she is not known.

He has denied her the facilities for obtaining a thorough education—all colleges being closed against her.

He allows her in church, as well as State, but a subordinate position, claiming Apostolic authority for her exclusion from the ministry, and with some exceptions, from any public participation in the affairs of the Church.

He has created a false public sentiment by giving to the world a different code of morals for men and women, by which moral delinquencies which exclude women from society, are not only tolerated but deemed of little account in man.

He has usurped the prerogative of Jehovah himself, claiming it his right to assign for her a sphere of action, when that belongs to her conscience and her God.

He has endeavored, in every way that he could to destroy her confidence in her own powers, to lessen her self-respect, and to make her willing to lead a dependent and abject life.

Now, in view of this entire disfranchisement of one-half the people of this country, their social and religious degradation—in view of the unjust laws above mentioned, and because women do feel themselves aggrieved, oppressed, and fraudulently deprived of their most sacred rights, we insist that they have immediate admission to all the rights and privileges which belong to them as citizens of the United States.

In entering upon the great work before us, we anticipate no small amount of misconception, misrepresentation, and ridicule; but we shall use every instrumentality within our power to effect our object. We shall employ agents, circulate tracts, petition the State and national Legislatures, and endeavor to enlist the pulpit and the press in our behalf. We hope this Convention will be followed by a series of Conventions, embracing every part of the country.

Firmly relying upon the final triumph of the Right and the True, we do this day affix our signatures to this declaration.

During the convention, the participants also adopted the following resolutions:

Whereas, The great precept of nature is conceded to be, "that man shall pursue his own true and substantial happiness." Blackstone, in his Commentaries, remarks that this law of Nature being coeval with mankind, and dictated by God himself, is of course superior in obligation to any other. It is binding over all the globe, in all countries and at all times; no human laws are of any validity if contrary to this, and such of them as are valid, derive all their force, and all their validity, and all their authority, mediately and immediately, from this original; therefore,

Resolved, That such laws as conflict, in any way, with the true and substantial happiness of woman, are contrary to the great precept of nature and of no validity, for this is "superior in obligation to any other."

Resolved, That all laws which prevent women from occupying such a station in society as her conscience shall dictate, or which place her in a position inferior to that of man, are contrary to the great precept of nature, and therefore of no force or authority.

Resolved, That woman is man's equal—was intended to be so by the Creator, and the highest good of the race demands that she should be recognized as such.

Resolved, That the women of this country ought to be enlightened in regard to the laws under which they live, that they may no longer publish their degradation, by declaring themselves satisfied with their present position, nor their ignorance, by asserting they have all the rights they want.

Resolved, That inasmuch as man, while claiming for himself intellectual superiority, does accord to woman moral superiority, it is pre-eminently his duty to encourage her to speak, and teach as she has an opportunity, in all religious assemblies.

Resolved, That the same amount of virtue, delicacy, and refinement of behavior that is required of woman in the social state, should also be required of man, and the same transgressions should be visited with equal severity on both man and woman.

Resolved, That the objection of indelicacy and impropriety, which is so often brought against woman when she addresses a public audience, comes with a very ill grace from those who encourage, by their attendance, her appearance on the stage, the concert, or in feats of the circus.

Resolved, That woman has too long rested satisfied in the circumscribed limits which corrupt customs and a perverted application of the Scriptures have marked out for her, and that it is time she should move in the enlarged sphere which her great Creator has assigned her.

Resolved, That it is the duty of the women of this country to secure to themselves their sacred right to the elective franchise.

Resolved, That the equality of human rights results necessarily from the fact of the identity of the race in capabilities and responsibilities.

Resolved, therefor, That, being invested by the Creator with the same capabilities, and the same consciousness of responsibility for their exercise, it is demonstrably the right and duty of woman, equally with man, to promote every righteous cause by every righteous means; and especially in regard to the great subjects of morals and religion, it is self-evidently her right to participate with her brother in teaching them, both in private and in public, by writing and by speaking, by any instrumentalities proper to be used, and in any assemblies proper to be held; and this being a self-evident truth, growing out of the divinely implanted principles of human nature, any custom or authority adverse to it, whether modern or wearing the hoary sanction of antiquity, is to be regarded as a self-evident falsehood, and at war with mankind.

Resolved, That the speedy success of our cause depends upon the zealous and untiring efforts of both men and women, for the overthrow of the monopoly of the pulpit, and for the securing to woman an equal participation with men in the various trades, professions, and commerce [Bartlett and Harris, 1998].

The Declaration of Sentiments shows that, from the start, a belief in sex equality drove the feminist campaign to win the vote. To feminist minds, women's inability to vote was a central feature of their oppression by men: "Having deprived her of this first right of a citizen, the elective franchise, thereby leaving her without representation in the halls of legislation, he has oppressed her on all sides" (Brown, 1993, pp. 2178–2179).

Women's advocates pressed for the vote not only as a means to improve women's lives, but also because it would symbolize recognition of women's "equal personal rights and equal political privileges with all other citizens" (Brown, 1993, p. 2178). As the first right of a citizen, suffrage means citizenship; it is the very substance of self-government.

On November 1, 1872, while "reading her morning paper," the *Rochester Democrat and Chronicle*, Susan B. Anthony noticed an editorial urging readers to register to vote (Winkler, 2001, p. 1506). She and her sister immediately marched down to the Board of Registry, housed in a local barbershop, and demanded that the inspectors permit them to register. Anthony responded to the inspectors' initial refusal with an aggressive verbal assault, launching into a thorough argument as to why the U.S. Constitution guaranteed women suffrage. Unable to defend their position against Anthony and under the strong advice of the U.S. supervisor present that day, the young inspectors allowed Anthony to register. The evening newspapers covered the story extensively, and within days, fifty Rochester women had registered, fourteen in Anthony's ward alone (Winkler, 2001).

The Grant administration, having won reelection, informed Anthony three weeks later, on Thanksgiving Day, that it was bringing criminal charges against her. She was charged with fraudulent voting in violation of the Civil Rights Act of 1870, a federal law passed to prevent the Ku Klux Klan and other southern whites from casting multiple ballots to dilute the effect of freedmen's votes (Winkler, 2001).

The logic was based on the view that women were not individual citizens but extensions of their husbands and fathers. Thus, a vote by a woman was viewed by the legal system as a second vote by the man she was most closely related to (Becker et al., 1994). Ironically, Anthony herself was not allowed to speak during her trial. As a woman, she was declared by Judge Hunt to be incompetent to testify on her own behalf (Winkler, 2001; *United States* v. *Anthony,* 1873).

Unlike *United States* v. *Anthony* (1873), the case of *Minor* v. *Happersett* (1874) was at least allowed to reach the U.S. Supreme Court. The Supreme Court rejected Virginia Minor's assertion that the right to vote was one of the privileges and immunities of citizenship under the Fourteenth Amendment to the Constitution. The Court unanimously held that although women were citizens, the framers had never intended to enfranchise them (Becker et al., 1994). After these failures, the suffrage movement essentially gave up on the courts and turned to the political arena, pursuing constitutional change.

THE EQUAL RIGHTS AMENDMENT

The first version of an equal rights amendment (ERA) to the Constitution was introduced in 1923 and simply stated, "Men and women shall have equal rights throughout the United States and in every place subject to its jurisdiction. Congress shall have power to enforce this article by appropriate legislation."

Between 1923 and 1969, the ERA was proposed yearly in Congress but was defeated by a coalition of conservatives opposed to change in the status of women and by such progressive women reformers as Eleanor Roosevelt, who feared that an ERA would invalidate sex-specific protective legislation (Becker et al., 1994). It is important to note that this was an active process, an annual review of the status of women and an annual decision to keep women in their current, subordinate position.

PROTECTIVE LEGISLATION

In the nineteenth and early twentieth centuries, gender-specific legislation tended to have as its stated goal the protection of women from the harsh demands of the industrial workplace. Prior to labor union victories related to the length of the workday or workweek, the Supreme Court, in *Lochner* v. *New York* (1905), held that a state statute limiting the number of hours employees could work was unconstitutional as a violation of the contract clause. Three years later, in *Muller v. Oregon* (1908), the Supreme Court upheld similar legislation limiting the hours women could work in laundries. Becker et al. (1994) note that during this period, some state statutes limited the number of hours women could work in a day or week, mandated lunch and rest periods, or limited the number of pounds women could be required to lift. While such legislation, at least when applicable only to jobs held primarily by women, helped women combine wage work and domestic obligations in the short term, it inevitably reinforced harmful stereotypes as well. This protective legislation also legally excluded women from full participation in the economy (Taub & Schneider, 1993).

CONSTITUTIONAL STANDARDS FOR EQUALITY

In 1948, the U.S. Supreme Court started its gender-based equal protection analysis process in *Goesaert* v. *Cleary.* The Michigan law at issue in *Goesaert* forbade women from working in a bar unless they were the wife or daughter of a bar owner. The Court, which found that Michigan had a right to forbid women from working in a bar, held that the state's interest in protecting women was not unreasonable; moreover, the state's action forbidding women from working in a bar, it held, was not unconstitutional merely because the interest could have been achieved in a different manner (Riedel, 2003). Applying a "rational basis" standard, the Court found a rational relationship between the goal to be achieved (the protection of women in a bar) and the means of obtaining that goal (forbidding women to work in a bar, implicitly requiring that they be under the protection of a male relative).

Reed v. *Reed* (1971) is frequently cited as the first case to support the legal equality of women. At issue was an Idaho probate law requiring that where a man and a woman were equally entitled to act as administrator of an estate, "males must be preferred to females." The rationale was based on stereotyped views of men and women and the assumption that men were likely to be better qualified for the position because they tended to have more business experience than women. This added expertise would reduce the workload and be administratively more convenient for the state. But the U.S. Supreme Court unanimously held that this type of preference was not constitutional: the statutory provision giving a mandatory preference for appointment as administrator to a male applicant over a female applicant otherwise equally qualified and within the same entitlement class under the Probate Code violated the equal protection clause of the Fourteenth Amendment. Chief Justice Warren Burger, in writing the opinion for the Court, noted that "a classification must be reasonable, not arbitrary, and must rest upon some ground of difference having a fair and substantial relation to the object of the legislation, so that all persons similarly circumstanced shall be treated alike" (p. 76).

This case marked a fundamental change in the gender-based equal protection analysis. In *Reed*, although the Court applied the rational basis test, the Court recognized that the reduction of workload was a legitimate goal but held that the denial of equal protection was not justified for the purpose of administrative convenience (Riedel, 2003).

In the following years, the Supreme Court refined its analysis of gender-based cases. The Court seemed to be slow to settle on a standard by which to evaluate these cases. The apparent inconsistencies across these early cases likely reflected the broader society's uncertainty as to how seriously to take sex discrimination.

In *Frontiero* v. *Richardson* (1973), the Court struck down a military regulation that created a presumption of dependency for the wives of military men while requiring proof of dependency for the husbands of military women. The plaintiff, a married woman who was an officer in the U.S. Air Force, argued that she was denied equal protection by laws automatically giving spousal benefits to married men but denying them to married women absent a showing that the wife provided more than half of the husband's support (Becker et al., 1994). The Court noted that gender classifications were "inherently suspect" and stated that courts should apply higher scrutiny if the classification promulgates a belief of inferiority based on immutable characteristics. Under this standard, it was easy to strike down the statute in *Frontiero* since administrative convenience was the sole justification for differential treatment of women and men in the air force (Becker et al., 1994).

A year later, in *Schlesinger* v. *Ballard* (1975), the Court upheld a different military regulation, this one giving preferential promotional treatment to women but not to men. The Court noted that men and women were "not similarly situated with respect to opportunities for professional service" and recognized that the regulation was in place to help the women (Riedel, 2003, p. 141).

Siegel (2002) notes that "the modern law of sex discrimination is built on the understanding that there is no constitutional history of relevance to the question of women's citizenship" (p. 953). In *Frontiero,* Supreme Court Justice William Brennan argued that sex discrimination was like race discrimination and therefore fell under the equal protection clause of the Fourteenth Amendment. Comparing the history of women and blacks throughout the nineteenth century, Brennan noted that "neither slaves nor women could hold office, serve on juries, or bring suit in their own names, and married women traditionally were denied the legal capacity to hold or convey property or to serve as legal guardians of their own children.... And although blacks were guaranteed the right to vote in 1870, women were denied even that right ... until the adoption of the Nineteenth Amendment half a century later" (*Frontiero* v. *Richardson,* 1973, p. 1769). Brennan persuaded the Court to apply "heightened scrutiny" in analyzing sex-based cases, although not the "strict scrutiny" required in race-based cases.

In *Craig* v. *Boren* (1976), the Court struck down a law that distinguished according to gender when it prohibited the sale of alcohol to men under age twenty-one and to women under age eighteen. The Court adopted and applied a standard of "intermediate scrutiny," requiring a sex-based law to be "substantially related" to the achievement of "important governmental objectives." This was a more difficult standard to meet than a "rational relationship" between the law and the stated goal, but was not as difficult to meet as the strict scrutiny test applied to race-based cases. The strict scrutiny standard required that the law be necessary to achieve a "compelling" state interest. Siegel (2002) notes that the Court never explained why it had chosen to apply a different standard to sex and race discrimination cases. Possible explanations are suggested:

> First, the framers of the Fourteenth Amendment were thinking about questions of race discrimination, not sex discrimination. Thus, it is appropriate for courts to apply a less rigorous standard of review to questions concerning equal citizenship for women; bluntly put, the nation never made a collective constitutional commitment to respect women as equals of men. Second, and very much related to this lack of constitutional history, the difference in standards reflects a pervasive intuition that the problem of sex discrimination is not as grave, harmful, or significant in American history as the problem of race discrimination.... Third, underneath it all, there is a sense that sex discrimination is at root different from race discrimination. Sex distinctions are not always harmful (or based on animus) the way race distinctions are; it is not clear that we are prepared to embrace a

model of sex-blindness, in matters of love or war [Siegel, 2002, pp. 954–956].

Before the Supreme Court could apply an intermediate level of scrutiny, it needed to define a case as sex-based discrimination. In *Personnel Administrator of Massachusetts* v. *Feeney* (1979), the Court ruled that a policy giving civil service hiring preference to veterans did not employ a sex-based classification within the meaning of the equal protection clause, despite the fact that the law clearly benefited men (because only men were classified as veterans). Similarly, in *Geduldig* v. *Aiello* (1974), the Court ruled that a policy denying employment benefits to pregnant women did not employ a sex-based classification within the meaning of the equal protection clause. Remarkably, the Court held that discrimination on the basis of pregnancy is not discrimination against women, but distinguishes between pregnant people and nonpregnant people (who may be male or female). This was not a unanimous decision by the Court, and Justice Brennan noted the strained reasoning in his dissent (with Justices William Douglas and Thurgood Marshall concurring):

> In my view, by singling out for less favorable treatment a gender-linked disability peculiar to women, the State has created a double standard for disability compensation: a limitation is imposed upon disabilities for which women workers may recover, while men receive full compensation for all disabilities suffered, including those that affect only or primarily their sex, such as prostatectomies, circumcision, hemophilia, and gout. In effect, one set of rules is applied to females and another to males. Such dissimilar treatment of men and women, on the basis of physical characteristics inextricably linked to one sex, inevitably constitutes sex discrimination [*Geduldig* v. *Aiello*, 1974, p. 501].

LEGAL THEORY

Legal decisions tend to be multilayered statements that reflect both articulated legal reasoning (reliance on precedent, deference to legislative intent) and unspoken, perhaps even unconscious, assumptions about culture and social roles. Supreme Court decisions have particular power because they can dictate the decision-making rules for all lower courts. Supreme Court decisions also address the most basic legal values of our culture in interpreting the scope of constitutional rights. Legal scholars studying gender-related Court decisions have described recurring themes: Should women be treated the same as men, or differently? If they are to be treated differently, under what conditions? When is differential treatment discrimination, and when is it a means of leveling the playing field so that the result is greater fairness? Where did the standards for treatment develop in the first place, and is there a bias in what is considered "neutral" treatment?

Sameness and Difference

There is a legal assumption that fair, or equal, treatment means treating people the same way. In legal language, the courts refer to "similarly situated" people deserving the same treatment. Many legal scholars argue, however, that men and women are never similarly situated because the social and cultural forces that make meaningful distinctions in the experiences of men and women begin at birth. The courts have traditionally determined "sameness" based on an unspoken male model of "normal" or "neutral," so that sameness for women has meant how much women are the same as men. The question of how the law should treat pregnancy has challenged legal scholars and courts to review notions of equality. Minow (1988) notes:

> The Supreme Court's treatment of issues concerning pregnancy and the workplace highlights the power of the unstated male norm in analysis of problems of difference. The court considered, both as a statutory and a constitutional question, whether discrimination in health insurance plans on the basis of pregnancy amounted to discrimination on the basis of sex. In both instances, the Court answered negatively because pregnancy marks a division between the groups of pregnant and nonpregnant persons, and women fall into both categories. Only from a point of view that treats pregnancy as a strange occasion, rather than a present, bodily potential, would its relationship to female experience be made so tenuous; and only from a vantage point that treats men as the norm would the exclusion of pregnancy from health insurance coverage seem unproblematic and free from forbidden gender discrimination [p. 342].

Espinoza (1997) compares this "sameness equality" in gender-based cases with the idea of color blindness in race-based cases. In gender-based cases, sameness equality often perpetuates discrimination because the standard by which men and women are to be measured is one defined by men and established with men in mind. Espinoza notes that "sameness" equality fails to recognize the lived reality of the disparity of power between men and women and denies the valuable differences women have and wish to retain.

Similarly, "the power of colorblindness is that it makes us feel that we are being fair. It becomes the standard for behavior. We focus on the process of justice—Blacks and whites took the same test, the voting districts were historically and geographically drawn, and so on. Colorblindness hides the actual exclusion and suppression of outsiders" (Espinoza, 1997, p. 932).

Krieger and Cooney (1983) note that this model of formal equality rests on assumptions that promote the formal appearance of equality over the equality of effect. Problems with the doctrine of formal equality, or treating like cases alike, include its subjectivity, the false promise of neutrality, and the assumption that it is possible to ignore a person's sex (Weisberg, 1993). It fails to acknowledge the interdependence of men and women and the responsibility for the care of others that tends to fall more heavily on the shoulders of women.

Finley (1986) argues that the special treatment–equal treatment debate is fundamentally flawed. It accepts the culture's ideal of homogeneity—that men and women are alike—and it relies on a Western male ideal of isolated autonomy, self-sufficiency, and individual rights based on noninterference. Finley notes that "the defenders of the American ideal of homogeneous equality wrote in sweeping terms about the commonalities among American citizens, yet their descriptions bore a striking resemblance to the world of the white, Anglo-Saxon Protestant male. The American melting pot has been a cauldron into which we have put black, brown, red, yellow, and white men and women, in the hope that we will come up with white men" (p. 197).

The analysis of equality (equal treatment for similarly situated people) requires some measure of similarity and difference. These categories can only be measured against some standard: Similar to what? Different from what? The role of men in defining that standard and in assigning significance to ways in which women are different means that the whole premise of equality jurisprudence rests on the idea that whatever is male is the norm (Finley, 1986). Women are equal to the extent that they can act like men.

Finley notes that an equality analysis model that focuses on making comparisons with the male norm makes it well suited for perpetuating existing disparities in power. Because those in power are the ones who make the attribution of difference, they see themselves as normal and everyone else as other. Equality analysis has been used to legitimize discrimination rather than eradicate it. For example, in the guise of equality, it may seem fair to deprive women of health care coverage or employment protections for pregnancy. Withholding benefits from all can be justified in the name of equal treatment, although the impact on male and female employees is far from equal. Federal legislation requiring employers to allow unpaid medical leaves (the Family Medical Leave Act), for example, sounds fair and equal, but it disadvantages women. Few employees, male or female, can afford to stop working for pay, but women are the ones more likely to be in the position of having to take this time off, without pay. Women are the ones who have the physical recovery after childbirth, and women typically have the responsibility for the care of children and elders. Even in families where labor is divided equally, women are likely to be the ones to take unpaid leave because their traditionally lower incomes make it a sensible financial decision (thereby perpetuating their lower income as a result of their absence from work).

Dominance and Subordination

Catherine MacKinnon argues for an alternative to the formal equality theory and its emphasis on sameness and difference. She notes that the sameness standard's definition of equality as gender neutrality "results in equality only when women are not distinguishable from men. In in stances when there is no male standard (i.e., pregnancy), it becomes sex discrimination to give women what only women need; and it is not discrimination to treat women differently by denying to women what only women need. In contrast, men's differences from women are already affirmatively compensated before men even enter the courtroom. Thus . . . the sameness standard misses the fact of social inequality (e.g., women's poverty, financial dependence, motherhood, and sexual accessibility) imposed by male supremacy" (Weissberg, 1993, p. 214).

When courts use a sameness analysis, they are accepting the status quo as the standard against which to judge discriminatory treatment: whether women are being treated differently in comparison to the male norm. MacKinnon argues that no amount of group difference justifies treating women as subordinate. Dominance analysis demands equal power for women in society (Weissberg, 1993, p. 215).

Colker (1987) also argues that the special treatment–equal treatment debate focuses on the wrong question. She argues for an "antisubordination principle" that is similar to the "disparate impact" model of discrimination analysis. The antisubordination perspective views discrimination as the method that results in blacks and women having less power. The analysis focuses on the results, not the intent of the one doing the discriminating. If the result of legislation is to disempower women, then the intent (even if it is well intentioned and "protective") does not matter.

Essentialism

Sameness-difference approaches focus on whether men and women are treated similarly in similar situations and challenge the courts to define the standards of comparison (Same as what?). Dominance approaches argue that any differential treatment is suspect because the dominant groups (white Anglo-Saxon males) have historically used the law to maintain their social dominance over women. Both approaches suggest that unequal treatment and the legal decisions that support it must be carefully scrutinized for bias.

Essentialism shifts the debate to women's self-definition (Weisberg, 1993). Essentialism suggests that in certain basic, essential ways, women are alike in their experience of the world. It is characterized by two "central assumptions: first, the meaning of gender identity and the experience of sexism are similar for all women; and, second, any differences between women are less significant than the traits they have in common" (Weisberg, 1993, p. 335). According to the work of social science researchers, women are viewed as being essentially different from men in their reasoning about moral and ethical issues, in their relationships, and in their motivations. The essentialist perspective does not attribute these characteristics to biology, as was done a century earlier, but to the effects of growing up female in a sexist Western culture.

Antiessentialists argue that essentialism ignores women's diversity and has "taken the experiences of white middle-class women to be representative of all women" (Weisberg, 1993, p. 336). Weisberg notes, "In so doing, [essentialists] obscure women's diversity; reinforce the privilege of white middle-class women; result in other women being labeled as 'different,' deviant, and lacking; distort feminism in the same way as masculine privilege has done; contribute to feminism being exclusionary in its concerns; and, ultimately, forestall the possibility of social change" (p. 336).

Minow (1988) argues that there is a need for a new language in the discussion of feminism and law: "In critiques of the 'male' point of view and in celebrations of the 'female,' feminists run the risk of treating particular experiences as universal and ignoring differences of racial, class, religious, ethnic, national, and other situated experiences" (p. 47).

CONCLUSION

This debate among legal scholars, male and female, touches on the most basic questions about humanity and social relationships. Given the unique history of every individual, at what point does difference matter? The debate is about where to draw meaningful lines between people, dividing groups up for differential treatment. We have rejected the legitimacy of racial segregation and have made religious freedom a core value in the Constitution. When "immutable" traits are used to disadvantage one group and preferentially advantage another, we (through our courts and legislatures and our daily social behavior) usually declare that unfair and illegal. Yet gender remains a fuzzy category, and we as a society have not been able to draw clear lines around when there should be equal treatment and when there should be special treatment.

The debate is also about whether we should draw distinctions among groups, and to what extent we can allow distinctions that directly affect an individual's ability to work, earn an adequate living, or be free from sexual harassment. The challenge of respecting individuals also includes seeing them rather than letting them become invisible and voiceless. This chapter is about that debate as it applies to men and women, but Miller (2003) reminds us that dominant groups behave in consistent ways toward socially subordinate groups, so the basic questions of fairness go beyond male-female distinctions.

References

Bartlett, K. T., & Harris, A. P. (1998). *Gender and the law: Theory, doctrine, commentary.* Frederick, MD: Aspen.

Becker, M., Bowman, C. G., & Torrey, M. (1994). *Cases and materials on feminist jurisprudence: Taking women seriously.* St. Paul: West.

Brown, J. K. (1993). Note: The Nineteenth Amendment and women's equality. *Yale Law Journal, 102,* 2175–2204.

Colker, R. (1987). The anti-subordination principle: Applications. *Wisconsin Women's Law Journal, 3,* 59–80.

Craig v. Boren, 429 U.S. 190, 197 (1976).

Espinoza, L. G. (1997). Legal narratives, therapeutic narratives: The invisibility and omnipresence of race and gender. *Michigan Law Review, 95*(4), 901–937.

Finley, L. M. (1986). Transcending equality theory: A way out of the maternity and workplace debate. *Columbia Law Review, 86,* 1118–1181.

Frontiero v. Richardson, 411 U.S. 677, 93 S. Ct. 1764, 36 L. Ed.2d 583 (1973).

Geduldig v. Aiello, 417 U.S. 484, 94 S. Ct. 2485, 41 L. Ed.2D 256 (1974).

Goesaert v. Cleary, 335 U.S. 464 (1948).

Krieger, L. J., & Cooney, P. N. (1983). The Miller-Wohl controversy: Equal treatment, positive action and the meaning of women's equality. *Golden Gate University Law Review, 13,* 513–572.

Lochner v. New York, 198 U.S. 45, 25 S. Ct. 539, 49 L. Ed. 937 (1905).

Miller, J. B. (2003). *Telling the truth about power.* Wellesley, MA: Center for Research on Women.

Minor v. Happersett, 88 U.S. 162 (1874).

Minow, M. (1988). Feminist reason: Getting it and losing it. *Journal of Legal Education, 38,* 47–60.

Muller v. Oregon, 208 U.S. 412, 28 S. Ct. 324, 52 L. Ed. 551 (1908).

Personnel Administrator of Massachusetts v. Feeney, 442 U.S. 256, 273 (1979).

Reed v. Reed, 404 U.S. 71, 92 S. Ct. 251, 30 L. Ed. 2D 225 (1971).

Riedel, D. A. (2003). By way of the dodo: The unconstitutionality of the Selective Service Act male-only registration requirement under modern gender-based equal protection. *Dayton Law Review, 29,* 135–162.

Schlesinger v. Ballard, 419 U.S. 498, 510 (1975).

Siegel, R. B. (2002). She the people: The Nineteenth Amendment, sex equality, federalism, and the family. *Harvard Law Review, 115,* 947–1045.

Taub, N., & Schneider, E. M. (1993). Women's subordination and the role of law. In D. K. Weisberg (Ed.), *Feminist legal theory foundations.* Philadelphia: Temple University Press.

United States v. Anthony, 24 F. Cas. 829 (C.C.N.D.N.Y. 1873) (No. 14,459).

Weisberg, D. K. (1993). *Feminist legal theory foundations.* Philadelphia: Temple University Press.

Winkler, A. (2001). A revolution too soon: Women suffragists and the "Living Constitution." *New York University Law Review, 76,* 1456–1518.

CHAPTER THREE

Women, Work, and Discrimination

Nancy Lynn Baker, Ph.D., A.B.P.P.

T he context of work for women in the United States was radically altered in 1964. In that year, the U.S. Congress passed a historic civil rights act outlawing discrimination on the basis of race, sex, religion, and national origin. Title VII of that act is the basis for virtually all legal action against sex discrimination in the workplace, including sexual harassment, in the United States today. Interestingly, despite the history of women's rights activism in the United States, insertion of the term *sex* into Title VII of the Civil Rights Act was actually the cynical attempt of some southern lawmakers to block the passage of this legislation, which would protect the rights of black Americans and outlaw the system of segregation that codified discrimination against black Americans in many southern states. Before exploring the ongoing effect, however unintended, of that important legislation on working women and women's work in the United States, it is useful to examine the history of women's role in the workplace, especially in the United States, and the psychological issues involved in our understanding of sex and gender.

HISTORY

For as long as there has been work, women have worked. (The issue of at what point in the history of humanity meaningful or productive human activity became "work" is well outside the scope of this chapter.) However, the devaluing of women and women's work also has a long history. For example, Mednick (1982), quoting an article from the *Washington Post,* notes that "in the book of Leviticus, the Lord tells Moses what women are worth: three fifths as much as men" (p. 48). This tradition of counting women as less than men found its way into early American law handed down from English common law.

Although women have always worked, which women worked and the types of work that women have performed have changed over the ages. Furthermore, within a given historical period, the form of women's work has varied from location to location. Labor economist Francine Blau (1984) tells us that in colonial America, women and children were largely responsible for the making of thread, cloth, lace, clothing, soap, shoes, and candles. All of those activities, generally the province of craft guilds in Europe, were among the typical home work performed by women and children in the British colonies. By contrast, European women during the same time frame were more involved than colonial women in fieldwork and less involved in the production activities performed by European craft guilds. In addition, Blau reports that colonial women also worked as "tavern keepers, store managers, traders, speculators, printers, and publishers," in addition to the common roles of domestic servant, seamstress, and tailor (p. 298). Among colonial women, it is likely that only the wealthiest of women, with significant servant assistance, did not perform at least some productive labor. Furthermore, even those women were often the managers of the home, directing the productive activity of their domestic staff.

Later, during the industrialization of America, when production moved from the home into the factories, women continued to engage in productive work. Women were especially involved in the textile industries. The spinning, weaving, and clothing making that women had been performing in their homes was now conducted in the factory. By this time, work was increasingly the task of younger and less well-to-do women, especially black and immigrant women. By the late nineteenth century, as the frontier closed, the only groups of married women significantly participating in work outside the home were black and immigrant women. However, even in 1890, women still constituted 17 percent of the labor force, and 18.2 percent of women worked outside the home.

The appropriate tasks for women also decreased dramatically. By the end of the nineteenth century, black women typically performed the domestic work and fieldwork that black women had performed under slavery. Immigrant women and their children worked in the textile mills. This concentration of women in "traditional" domestic and "women's work" factory jobs continued with little interruption for many years. As late as 1960, the small percentages of women working in professional or technical jobs were concentrated in the roles of elementary school teacher, nurse, and social worker. Blau (1984) reports that in the 1975 census, half of all working women were employed in only seventeen of the four hundred job occupations listed by the Bureau of the Census, and a quarter of all working women were concentrated in only five occupations.

In 1960, four years before the Civil Rights Act of 1964 was passed, only 37.7 percent of women worked outside the home (Fullerton, 1999). There was no age group in which over 50 percent of women were employed outside the home. Furthermore, most women worked in a limited number of occupations and were seriously underrepresented in the ranks of upper management. Jobs were strongly sex and ethnicity segregated. Employment advertisements listed relatively few jobs as open to all candidates, with most being separated into men's or women's openings and often further split by ethnicity. When women worked in jobs that were primarily male occupations, they faced a wide range of discriminatory practices and policies. In addition, so-called protective legislation limited the times and the number of hours women could work as well as the weight they could lift. In other words, women's work participation was constricted by closed doors, narrow hallways, and glass ceilings.

The first effects of Title VII of the Civil Rights Act of 1964 on women's rights were in the reduction of the formal barriers to women's participation and equality in the workplace. The sex segregation of job advertisements was eliminated. So-called protective laws preventing women from working longer hours or lifting heavier weights were eliminated, in some cases because of legal challenges.

In the years since the Civil Rights Act of 1964, a variety of social and economic factors have greatly increased women's participation in the workforce. By 1998, the only age group of women over age sixteen with less than 50 percent participation in the workforce was the group of women over age sixty-five, with a participation rate below 10 percent at both time periods. The shift has been most dramatic for women in the child-rearing years, from ages twenty-five through sixty-four. By 1998, women's workforce participation in this age range had increased by roughly 40 percent over 1950 levels. However, the sex segregation of work, the underrepresentation of women in the upper ranks of businesses and professions, and the inequity of income between men and women have not disappeared.

This pattern of inequity is the context for claims of sex discrimination, including sexual harassment, in the workplace. Psychology's involvement in these issues developed from the psychological study of stereotyping, prejudice, and gender hostility and the manner in which those phenomena operate in the workplace. These issues are enmeshed in the individual and group claims of sex discrimination, including sexual harassment. In addition, psychologists address the psychological consequences, primarily at the individual level, of experiencing discriminatory acts in the workplace.

BASIS OF DISCRIMINATION

Underpinning discrimination against women in the workplace is a set of attitudes and beliefs about gender and work. People have stereotyped views about both the characteristics of women and the characteristics of particular jobs or job duties. They often have difficulty accepting that women can do work that requires the attributes normally ascribed to men, such as intelligence, decisiveness, strength, or aggressiveness. In addition, at least some people respond with hostility when individuals fail to conform to the standards expected for their gender. Finally, in many instances, the work environment does not eliminate, and may enhance, the general social power men have over women.

In an extensive review of the literature on stereotyping, prejudice, and discrimination, psychologist Susan Fiske (1998) describes a number of ways in which the cognitive properties of stereotyping create problems for women and other devalued groups. Psychological research has demonstrated that stereotypes, or preconceived expectations, affect the information that is sought (Kruger & Clement, 1994; Rusher & Fiske, 1990; Snyder 1984) and the degree to which it is remembered (Sekaquaptewa & von Hippel, 1994). Thus, an evaluator, supervisor, or hiring manager may fail to identify the stereotype-inconsistent abilities of women to perform "male" tasks and may forget about the evidence of effective performance that women demonstrate. Furthermore, the filtering effects of prejudice also affect the interpretation of information. For example, on "masculine tasks," men's successful performance tends to be attributed to ability, while women's positive performance is attributed to effort or luck (Swim & Sanna, 1996; Deaux, 1998).

Stereotyping and prejudice also constrain the way that behavior is interpreted. The finding that the same conduct, especially involving traditionally masculine characteristics such as strength, assertiveness, decisiveness, or goal rather than process orientation, is interpreted positively when performed by men and negatively when performed by women has been confirmed by multiple studies (Eagly, Makhinijani, & Klonsky, 1992). Thus, when women perform their workplace duties in the same manner that men perform them, the women tend to be negatively evaluated, creating quite a double-bind for women performing tasks where those "male" behaviors are necessary or desirable.

What makes the actions of stereotyping and prejudice even more problematic is that they can operate without conscious awareness (Dovidio & Gaertner, 1993). Furthermore, social psychologists have repeatedly demonstrated that stereotypes and prejudices become self-fulfilling prophecies, with the beliefs of the perceiver influencing the behavior of the actor in a manner consistent with the perceiver's original bias (Snyder, 1984, 1992; Word, Zanna, & Cooper, 1974). Finally, calling attention to the stereotype or prejudice does not necessarily inhibit the effect and can make matters worse (Macrae, Bodenhausen, Milne, & Jetten, 1994; Bodenhausen & Macrae, 1996).

Discrimination toward women in the workplace is and has been manifested in a wide variety of actions. Some of those manifestations involve direct discriminatory action, like being denied positions, opportunities, or training. Other manifestations include gender-based hostility and unwanted sexual attention. Many of the instances of discriminatory conduct that women, or members of other devalued and stigmatized groups, experience are not dramatic like the "men only" job signs of earlier years. They are instead what have been called microinequities and micro-aggressions (Pierce, 1970), seemingly minor slights, insults, and hostilities that form what has been labeled the minutia of sexism (Rowe, 1981). Because these events are, each by itself, almost trivial, it is difficult for an individual to protest them without seeming thin-skinned or petty. Yet in their cumulative weight, these small acts of omission and commission provide the fabric of a hostile or unwelcoming environment, creating barriers to women's participation and success in the workplace (Rowe, 1990).

One common manifestation of discrimination, whether based on unconscious stereotype or conscious plan, is the perpetuation of the gender segregation of work. Davison and Burke (2000), in a meta-analysis of studies that examined sex discrimination in employment over a thirty-year period, generally found that applicants applying for "opposite-sex" jobs received discriminatory evaluations. Although women now participate in many more than the seventeen job categories that accounted for most of women's work in 1960, numerous studies have found systematic differences in the work assignments of men and women even when their formal job titles were the same (Deaux & Ullman, 1983; Epstein, 1993; Reskin & Padavic, 1994; Reskin & Ross, 1992). As many have pointed out, one frequent pattern is for men rather than women to be assigned to the tasks and duties that improve their skills and prepare them for career advancement. This pattern of discrimination can be particularly difficult to address because the actual discriminatory effect can take years to accumulate. Furthermore, job assignment within a job classification is generally considered the purview of management rights, protected from intervention by union grievance or court scrutiny. Thus, all women and minority men are unable to effectively challenge the discriminatory practice until it has resulted in real differences of skills and experience, differences that can then be offered as a justification for differential rates of promotion or pay.

Some theorists (Glick & Fiske, 1996) have attempted to separate the discriminatory conduct by whether it is based on an overt endorsement of male superiority and female inferiority or on a more superficially benign endorsement of male and female difference. They label as hostile sexism the attitudes based on an endorsement of male superiority. A second set of attitudes, based on an endorsement of female superiority in such stereotypical female attributes as nurturance, congeniality, and patience, are labeled benevolent sexism. One problem with such distinctions is that although it is possible to develop scales that distinguish between the two attitudes, both are rooted in acceptance of categorical difference between males and females. All such beliefs overemphasize the stereotypical differences between males and females while ignoring the degree to which individual men or women frequently do not differ in the stereotyped direction on any particular attribute.

Other scholars have attempted to distinguish between behavior based on gender hostility and behavior based on sexual desire. Unfortunately, this is not as easy or clear a distinction as it might initially appear because of the intertwining of sex and sexuality with power, dominance, and hostility. As psychologist Kay Deaux (1998) notes, "Sexual harassment can be primarily sexual or primarily hostile, that is, its goal could be to secure a sexual liaison or to make life uncomfortable for a woman" (p. 812). Furthermore, as those working in the area of sexual assault frequently report (Koss et al., 1994), even acts that are designed to obtain sexual liaisons can be as much about power, dominance, and submission as about genital stimulation.

LEGAL ISSUES: LEGAL CONTEXT

The psychological processes described above, operating in the historical context of women's limited and devalued role in the work world, provide the context for the various complaints of discrimination that find their way into the legal system. As was noted previously, Title VII of the Civil Rights Act of 1964 is the principal foundation for most claims of sex discrimination in the United States. Prior to the passage of the Civil Rights Act, it was not unlawful to discriminate in employment on the basis of sex. Although some of the actions that can fall under the rubric of workplace sexual harassment, for example, sexual assault, were (and remain) crimes, they were not civil rights violations. Similarly, while pervasive or severe harassment may have been (and remains) the basis for common law tort claims of negligent or intentional infliction of emotional distress, assault and battery, false imprisonment, or invasion of privacy (Lindemann & Kadue, 1999), these did not fall under the banner of federal civil rights or employment law.

In the years since the passage of the Civil Rights Act of 1964, a number of changes have occurred. States and many local governments have passed employment rights laws that parallel and, in many cases, expand the federal protections against discrimination in the workplace. Legal actions have resulted in the abolition of various discriminatory practices such as sex-segregated employment advertisements, which provided formal barriers to women's full and equal participation in the workplace (Bergmann, 1986).

The legal actions brought under Title VII of the Civil Rights Act of 1964, as amended by the Civil Rights Act of 1991, can provide injunctive relief, forcing employers to rectify the discriminatory conduct. In addition, in some cases, monetary damages for lost wages and benefits, or even punitive damages, can also be awarded. However, monetary damages are generally awarded only when the discrimination has been intentional. Punitive damages are justified only when an employer acts with "malice or reckless indifference to the federally protected rights of an aggrieved individual" (Lindemann & Kadue, 1999, p. 317; for further discussion of damages, see EEOC Policy Guidance on Compensatory and Punitive Damages under the Civil Rights Act of 1991).

One of the many legal controversies developing from Title VII has involved the issue of "mixed motives," that is, situations where an employer takes an action in part because of "legitimate" reasons and in part because of discriminatory reasons. This issue is critical for legal actions concerning discrimination in the workplace because employment decisions are rarely justified purely on the basis of discriminatory factors. Instead, it is the discriminatory results of the psychological processes, like stereotyping and prejudice, that cause employers to discipline women more or more harshly for certain actions than they would men. One could describe the cognitive effects of prejudice as the mental equivalents of flypaper and nonstick coatings. Thus, there is generally some legitimate basis for the employer's action: the woman did make a mistake, use a curse word, or behave rudely, even though the same behavior has not received the same punishment when performed by a male employee because all of the woman's past transgressions were both noticed and remembered.

This mixed-motive issue was addressed by the U.S. Supreme Court in *Price Waterhouse* v. *Hopkins* (1989). In that case, evidence provided by psychologist Susan Fiske on sex stereotyping was cited by the Court in its decision supporting plaintiff Hopkins, who had been denied partnership because she was overly abrasive and advised by her employer to wear makeup and attend charm school. The Court recently affirmed and extended this decision in *Desert Palace, Inc.* v. *Costa* (2003). In that decision, the Court noted that the Congress, when it amended the Civil Rights Act in 1991, made it clear that it is unlawful for a company to use sex as a motivating factor in employment decisions even though other factors are also involved. This decision resolves almost twelve years of confusing case law concerning the proof a plaintiff must provide to establish that sex was a motivating factor. In *Desert Palace,* the Court stated that the plaintiff must establish only by a preponderance of evidence that sex was a factor in the decision. This was important because some courts had suggested that plaintiffs must present direct "smoking gun" proof in order to claim sex discrimination.

SEXUAL HARASSMENT: A SPECIAL CASE

Sexual harassment is a somewhat complex issue, with discussion made more difficult by the fact that while the phenomenon is quite old, the term itself did not exist when the Civil Rights Act of 1964 was passed (Bularzik, 1978; Farley, 1978; Baker, 1989). From the fictional stories of female servants to the documented reports by female slaves and wage workers, the narrative of women being pressured or forced into sexual acts in the context of work is an all-too-common report. What is newer is the social recognition that such conduct is wrong and the legal apparatus for complaints about it. As late as the 1980s, male managers and supervisors, when challenged by a government agency in California about demanding sex from women as a condition of employment, were "surprised in many cases that such behavior was against the law" (Coles, 1986, p. 91).

The legal system, even after the passage of the Civil Rights Act, took some time to recognize sexual harassment as an unlawful act. Quite early in the legal interpretations of the Civil Rights Act, the Equal Employment Opportunity Commission (EEOC) recognized that Title VII prohibits harassment. The courts supported the EEOC position that Title VII creates an affirmative duty for employers to provide a work environment free from harassment. Court decisions, initially on race issues, recognized that harassment created a climate of discrimination (*Anderson* v. *Methodist Evangelical Hospital,* 1972). The prohibited conduct includes, but is certainly not limited to, berating employees for mistakes, imposing extra duties, restricting privileges, or suggesting that a woman does not belong in the job when these actions are based on the employees' sex/gender (or any other of the categories protected under Title VII). In other words, Title VII requires employers to create an atmosphere where employees are not insulted or demeaned because of their "race, sex, color, religion, or national origin" (Equal Employment Opportunity Commission, 1992, sec. 615).

Although there was an early recognition that Title VII prohibited harassment, initially the courts did not view demands for sexual favors or other forms of sexual conduct as harassment. It was not until 1976 that a federal appellate court opined that a woman who had been fired because she refused the sexual advances of her male boss was the victim of sex discrimination (*Williams* v. *Saxbe,* 1976). The lower court had ruled that such conduct was the private and arguably natural behavior of a man toward a woman rather than an issue covered by employment law. However, the appellate court accepted the argument, developed largely by feminist legal scholars (MacKinnon, 1979), that this conduct was unlawful sex discrimination. The rationale is that the conduct is sex discrimination not because it involves sex but because it is conduct that is directed at a target because of her sex.

In 1980, the EEOC developed and published guidelines on sexual harassment that continue to be in use. The EEOC guidance on sexual harassment states:

Harassment on the basis of sex is a violation of Sec. 703 of Title VII (of the U.S. Civil Rights Act of 1964). Unwelcome advances, requests for sexual favors, and other verbal or physical conduct of a sexual nature constitute sexual harassment when:

1. submission to such conduct is made either explicitly or implicitly a term or condition of the individual's employment;

2. submission to or rejection of such conduct by an individual is used as the basis for employment decisions affecting such individual; or

3. such conduct has the purpose or effect of unreasonably interfering with an individual's work performance or creating an intimidating, hostile, or offensive work environment. [p. 74676].

In 1986, the U.S. Supreme Court, in *Meritor Savings Bank* v. *Vinson,* upheld the EEOC guidelines on sexual harassment. This case was particularly important because the Court upheld the concept of a hostile environment. In *Meritor,* the Court affirmed that the supervisor's demands for sexual favors created a hostile environment even though there was no direct threat of adverse job action.

Several important psychological issues are presented by the Court decision in *Meritor.* First, the standard for what constitutes a legally actionable situation was articulated as when the discriminatory conduct is severe enough to alter the conditions of employment. Second, the Court asserted that what matters is not whether compliance with the sexual demands was voluntary but whether it was welcomed. The issue of what distinguishes "welcome" from "unwelcome" conduct continues to evolve through case law and interpretation.

In addition, the Court addressed the question of when an employer is liable for the action of a supervisor. One position on this issue, the strict liability position, is that the employer is always liable for the actions of supervisors. The other position is that the employer should be held liable for the action of the supervisor only if the employer was negligent, meaning the employer knew about the supervisor's conduct or should have known about it and failed to take appropriate action.

For over a decade following the *Meritor* decision, the lower courts struggled with this issue. Finally, in 1998, the U.S. Supreme Court issued two opinions on the same day establishing clearer guidance on the issue of employer liability (*Burlington Industries, Inc.* v. *Ellerth*, 1998; *Faragher* v. *City of Boca Raton*, 1998). In these cases, the Court distinguished between situations where a tangible job action occurred and those where the issue was purely about the work environment or atmosphere. The Court stated:

> An employer is subject to vicarious liability to a victimized employee for an actionable hostile environment created by a supervisor with immediate (or successively higher) authority over the employee. When no tangible employment action is taken, a defendant employer may raise an affirmative defense to liability or damages, subject to proof by a preponderance of evidence. . . . The defense comprises two necessary elements: (a) that the employer exercised reasonable care to prevent and correct promptly any sexually harassing behavior, and (b) that the plaintiff employee unreasonably failed to take advantage of any preventive or corrective opportunities provided by the employer or to avoid harm otherwise. . . . No affirmative defense is available, however, when the supervisor's harassment culminates in a tangible employment action such as discharge, demotion, or undesirable reassignment [*Burlington Industries, Inc.* v. *Ellerth*, 1998, p. 765].

This decision appears to place employer liability for supervisors' actions when no adverse job action occurs in roughly the same category as the actions of coworkers.

Since these rulings, the issue of an affirmative defense has become a focus of considerable attention. Although there appears to be a tendency to equate the mere existence of a complaint procedure not used by the complaining party as evidence of an "unreasonable failure," psychological research may ultimately be important. In a recent article, psychologist Louise Fitzgerald and her colleagues (Bergman, Langhout,

Palmieri, Cortina, & Fitzgerald, 2002) present data that suggest reporting is often harmful to the complaining party. Their data also suggest that the likelihood of reporting is influenced by the way in which the complaint will be handled. Furthermore, other research suggests that the response of management to issues around sexual harassment affects the likelihood that victims will complain, with positive efforts to stop or eradicate harassment leading to more reporting and negative responses leading to less reporting (Offermann & Malamut, 2002). Unless this issue is adequately addressed, the actual effect of the "unreasonable failure" provision may be to reward employers for dealing with complaints so badly that victims do not complain.

The legal issues surrounding sex discrimination and including sexual harassment will continue to evolve, as they have since 1964. Both congressional action and case law will undoubtedly mold the landscape in new ways. The hope is that these changes will incorporate and reflect the information that psychological research can provide. Without that inclusion, victims will be penalized. For example, it has been important for case law to acknowledge the ubiquitous psychological research finding that experience is not gender neutral. Men and women experience and interpret behaviors relating to social interactions differently (Deaux, 1998; Rotundo, Nguyen, & Sackett, 2001). By emphasizing that the law's hypothetical "reasonable person" must be similarly situated (for example, of the same gender) as the actual victim, case law can incorporate the understandings that psychological research can provide.

SEXUAL HARASSMENT: WHAT ARE WE TALKING ABOUT?

One problem that occurs when discussing sexual harassment is that the experience is trivialized. Some have suggested that the prohibition against sexual harassment is like a code of civility for the workplace and complaints a matter of litigating bad manners. These suggestions miss two critical aspects of both the legal definition of sexual harassment and women's actual experience of it. To be legally actionable sexual harassment must be severe or pervasive (*Harris* v. *Forklift Systems,* 1993). For many women, it is both severe and pervasive.

Sexual harassment can include instances of rape, forced oral copulation, and other sexual assaults. Some of the most egregious cases reported by those working with women complaining of sexual harassment involve women who "consented" to have sex with supervisors as a condition of employment. While it may seem absurd that a woman would feel compelled to have sex just to hold on to a job, the women targeted by some of the more predatory harassers are extremely vulnerable. Consider, for example, the case of a young woman in a position with insurance benefits, whose husband did not have insurance through his job, who had recently given birth to a child with a chronic and severe medical condition that was expensive to treat. Even the less dramatic case of a single mother with limited skills in "the best-paying job I've ever had" faces a difficult dilemma.

Documentation of sexual assault as part of sexual harassment is not limited to anecdotal report. Large surveys of women's experiences in a variety of workplaces have included reports of both demands for sexual favors and attempted or successful sexual assaults (Fitzgerald et al., 1988; Fitzgerald & Ormerod, 1993). A 1995 survey of women in the military found that 6 percent reported rapes or rape attempts as part of their military experience (Hay & Elig, 1999). The psychological consequences of these assaults are significant. For example, one study of women veterans seeking treatment for stress-related disorders found that for 43 percent of them, rape or attempted rape during their military service was a significant factor in their need for treatment (Fontana & Rosenheck, 1998).

Other forms of harassment not directly involving sexual activity but directed at women violating gender norms either in their own personal appearance or by working in stereotypically male jobs can also be severe. Studies of blue-collar workers find between 20 and 40 percent of respondents in traditionally male occupations report attempts by their male coworkers to cause them physical harm (Baker, 1995). Anecdotal reports and individual cases of women in traditionally male occupations such as neurosurgery and investment banking include attempts either to cause physical harm or to sabotage their work product—and thus their professional standing or employment.

Of course, some harassing behaviors are not particularly egregious in isolation. As Mary Rowe (1990) so eloquently describes, they are the micro-inequities and micro-aggressions that gain power, like water dripping on granite, through endless repetition. Much of the early research on sexual harassment focused on delineating the extensive contours of the harassment experience. The early surveys by the U.S. Merit Systems Protection Board (1981, 1987) demonstrated that sexual harassment was a common and destructive phenomenon among federal employees.

In the late 1980s, Louise Fitzgerald and her colleagues introduced a measure that assessed almost thirty specific behaviors derived from theoretical constructs of sexual harassment (Fitzgerald et al., 1988). Their instrument, the Sexual Experiences Questionnaire (SEQ), with some modifications, is the most widely used and adapted instrument for the measurement of sexual harassment. Research using the SEQ and other instruments has established that the behaviors involved in sexual harassment occur with great frequency (Fitzgerald & Ormerod, 1993; Gelfand, Fitzgerald, & Drasgow, 1995) and that women generally report multiple forms of harassing experiences. Although the focus of sexual harassment research has shifted from documenting its existence to addressing antecedents and consequences, ongoing research continues to document the extensive nature of the experience (Schneider, Swan, & Fitzgerald, 1997).

In general, the behaviors comprising sexual harassment occur frequently. Some estimates suggest that as many as 50 percent of women will experience sexual harassment at some point in their life (Schneider et al., 1997). Furthermore, although there is a range of behaviors starting with offensive verbal behavior, sexual harassment includes physical and sexual assaults and pressure for sexual favors. Although there is some evidence that individual psychological factors are significant for perpetrators of sexual assaults and attempts to coerce sexual favors as a condition of employment (Bargh, Raymond, Pryor, & Strack, 1995), the work environment and the gender stereotype of the work are the critical factors in determining the overall level of sexual harassment in a workplace (Baker, 1995; Gruber, 1998; Schneider et al., 1997).

Women working outside the traditional female occupations have experienced the highest levels of sexual harassment, in both form of harassment and frequency of harassment (Baker, 1995; Harned, Ormerod, Palmieri, Collinsworth, & Reed, 2002). Their experiences can include daily occurrences of multiple forms of offensive conduct. In addition, the experiences of women working in stereotypically male occupations are more likely to include severe forms of nonsexual gender-based harassment. However, the data do not indicate that women in traditionally male jobs experience a differential rate of pressure for sexual favors as a condition of employment.

Feminist scholars and even the courts have recognized that sexual harassment is about power, not just about normal heterosexual behavior. At an almost axiomatic level, people cannot persist in unwanted behavior when those toward whom the behavior is directed have the power to make them stop. Conversely, research has found that structural changes that increase power inequities, such as the long-term use of temporary workers who lack standing as employees of the company, increase the likelihood that the less powerful workers will experience harassment (Rogers & Henson, 1997). Other factors that have been shown to influence the amount of harassment that occurs in a particular work setting are the number of men in the setting, the gender stereotype of the job, the gender ratio of the job, and the tolerance of harassment by the organization (Fitzgerald, Hulin, & Drasgow, 1994; Yoder & Aniakudo, 1996).

PSYCHOLOGICAL CONSEQUENCES OF SEX DISCRIMINATION

The issue of the psychological consequences of sex discrimination is complex because the variety of experiences that can occur as part of sex discrimination is vast. Sex discrimination can include everything from the experience of being not hired, not promoted, or not retained to the experiences of being insulted, assaulted, or physically injured. These experiences can occur individually but are often combined in a multifaceted pattern of discrimination. Furthermore, the experience of sex discrimination at work is compounded by both the general social devaluation of women and specific social issues such as vulnerability to sexual assault, domestic abuse, and poverty (Vasquez, Baker, & Shullman, 2003). Finally, many women also experience racism, another powerful source of discriminatory treatment.

There has been relatively little research on the specific psychological consequences of experiencing sex discrimination in the workplace. Perhaps this reflects the invisibility that accompanies a pervasive social phenomenon, the absence being more noticeable than the presence. Perhaps this reflects the difficulty of studying the effect of something so ubiquitous. Or perhaps the focus of attention has been on the extensive direct economic consequences rather than the psychological. Nonetheless, although it may have become fashionable to think of sex discrimination as something outlawed nearly forty years ago, it continues to exist.

It has been widely suggested that the violence associated with discrimination against women is a significant factor in women's depression, a position supported by the research on battered women and rape victims (Koss et al., 1994). One recent study that examined the psychological effects of discriminatory treatment based on sex found that women were more negatively affected by such experiences than were men (Schmitt, Branscombe, Kobrynowicz, & Owen 2002). One suggestion for this finding is that women experience the negative treatment as a confirmation of the pervasive discrimination against women rather than a random act. Each negative experience may serve as a warning of more to come. It may also be that current experiences of discriminatory conduct based on sex trigger memories of prior mistreatment based on sex, memories that women are immensely more likely to have than are men.

The negative consequences of sexual harassment have received somewhat greater research attention than sex discrimination in general. This may reflect the greater ease of studying a phenomenon that is more specifically focused. Or it may be that the legal attention to sexual harassment and the need to document damages caused by it has spurred research interest. Regardless, a number of studies document negative occupational and psychological outcomes as a result of experiencing sexual harassment (Glomb, Munson, Hulin, Bergman, & Drasgow, 1999). It is evident that the experience of sexual harassment decreases job satisfaction and increases the intent or desire to leave the job not just in the United States but in other countries and cultures where the effects of sexual harassment have been studied (Shaffer, Joplin, Bell, Lau, & Oguz, 2000; Wasti, Bergman, Glomb, & Drasgow, 2002).

Studies have found a variety of negative psychological and health outcomes as a result of sexual harassment. Women who have experienced sexual harassment involving sexual pressure are more likely than other women to be suffering from depression or posttraumatic stress disorder, even as long as eleven years after their harassment experience (Dansky & Kilpatrick, 1997). Other research has linked sexual harassment to a variety of psychological and health outcomes (Koss, 1990; Schneider et al., 1997), including increased nausea and headaches (Goldenhar, Swanson, Hurrell, Ruder, & Deddens, 1998) and eating disorders (Harned & Fitzgerald, 2002). More subtle psychological effects of harassment are also found, including reduction in self-confidence (Satterfield & Muehlenhard, 1997). Obviously, the experience of sexual harassment can be a significant stressor.

When the effects of race and ethnicity on the experience of sexual harassment have been examined, the picture has been somewhat unclear as to whether levels of sexual harassment increase, decrease, or remain the same across ethnic or racial groups. There is some indication that this may reflect the availability of multiple causal explanations for the harassing or discriminatory experiences of women in ethnic groups for whom racism is a common experience (Buchanan & Ormerod, 2002; Yoder & Aniakudo, 1996). Even when the behavior directed at a woman of color is explicitly sexual, it may be experienced as an outgrowth of racial prejudice or privilege, especially if the perpetrator is from the majority culture. Others have suggested that the instruments used to assess sexual harassment have not been culturally sensitive, thus failing to capture important information about the experiences of women not from the majority culture (Cortina, 2001). It is quite likely that both factors are important.

WHAT HAPPENS WHEN WOMEN COMPLAIN?

In a perfect or just world, sexual harassment would not occur. But if it did, it would certainly disappear when the targets of the harassment confronted it or complained about it. Unfortunately, both data and the anecdotal experiences of those who have experienced harassment provide painful evidence that we do not live in a perfect or even just world. The research to date suggests that the failure of most women to confront harassers or seek organizational relief may well reflect wisdom and a lack of real power rather than complicity or a lack of assertiveness (Bergman et al., 2002; Fitzgerald, Swan, & Fischer, 1995; Cortina & Magley, 2003).

While some early self-report data, from a time when there was less general awareness of the inappropriateness of making sexual remarks and advances in the workplace, suggested that telling the harasser to stop the behavior was generally associated with positive outcomes (U.S. Merit Systems Protection Board, 1987), more recent data suggest the opposite (Hesson-McInnis & Fitzgerald, 1997; Stockdale, 1998). Those who confront the harasser do not report improved outcomes and often experience worse outcomes. This may reflect problems with the original methodology, or it may reflect the effects of changing awareness. While an individual might have innocently believed that sexual remarks, innuendo, and requests for sexual favors were appropriate in the workplace of the 1980s, such behavior today represents a more conscious decision to ignore prohibitions against sexual harassment.

In a recent examination of the factors associated with better and worse outcomes, Fitzgerald and her colleagues found that it was not reporting itself that resulted in negative outcomes but the response of the organization to a report of harassment (Bergman et al., 2002). In organizations that are tolerant of sexual harassment, the outcome for those who report is likely to be worse. This quite probably reflects both the failure of the organization to take adequate steps to stop future harassment and a tolerance for retaliation against a complaining party. Working in a traditionally male job was also associated with a greater likelihood of negative consequences for reporting.

These findings are particularly important because the conventional wisdom is that women should confront harassers and complain if the initial confrontation is unsuccessful. The popular perception has been that the finding that most women do not confront their harasser and even fewer make formal complaints is a reflection of a failure or weakness. Organizational training generally encourages women to complain, and many organizational policies stress the importance of victims' making complaints. Even the courts, with the previously discussed standard allowing an affirmative defense for employers against harassment charges if women have not used complaint procedures, appear to be endorsing the expectation that women should confront and complain. Fortunately, the language of the court in requiring that women not unreasonably fail to make use of complaint procedures leaves the court with the opportunity to respond to the reality of the consequences for reporting in an organization where harassment is tolerated and retaliation condoned.

A HYPOTHETICAL CASE: STEP BY STEP

To understand some of the reasons and ways that reporting can make life more difficult for the targets of discrimination and harassment, it may be useful to follow the process step-by-step. Taking as a hypothetical example a woman in a blue-collar environment, let us follow her steps in confronting and complaining about harassment. Although this example is hypothetical, all of the facts are similar to actual situations.

First, our hypothetical victim may decide to tell her coworker that she is offended by his crude behavior. If, as is often the case, one reason for his conduct was his animosity toward the presence of women in his workplace, the information that she is upset by his conduct will increase it, not reduce it. Having failed to resolve the problem through direct confrontation, our victim now goes to the supervisor. If he takes no action or is dismissive of her complaint, she will feel more victimized, and her harasser may feel free to step up the harassment. If the supervisor takes disciplinary action but the work culture does not view harassment as a violation of the culture's code of conduct, the harasser and his coworkers may now view the victim as both a "wimp" and a "snitch." Harassment may not decrease, and retaliation, in the form of either hostile actions or social hostility and isolation, may occur. If there is hostility between the work group and management, both the likelihood and level of retaliation may be significant. Our victim is also in trouble if she is in one of the work cultures, like law enforcement, where complaining about a coworker is a serious violation of the informal work group ethic, that is, a code-of-silence culture.

Our victim now may find her situation becoming increasingly intolerable. The harassment may not have stopped, but retaliation is occurring. The supervisor may view her as a problem, since the turmoil may be interfering with the normal operation of his crew. This is especially likely if the supervisor does not view harassment as an important issue. Furthermore, since the supervisor failed to notice and stop the harassment before our victim found it necessary to complain, it is likely that he (or she) is tolerant of harassment.

Our victim now moves up the chain, complaining to human resources (HR). The pattern repeats, now at a higher level. If the HR representatives take no action or inadequate action, this again signals the supervisor and the work group that harassment is acceptable behavior. If HR takes action, then the potential for retaliation again increases. Unless the workplace culture really endorses the belief that what the harasser has done is not only wrong but a greater wrong than being a "snitch," then negative social consequences are the minimum reaction our victim can expect. Since most actions by HR will require an investigation to substantiate the victim's complaint, it is quite probable that the work group will close ranks to protect the harasser.

Our victim may now find her life becoming unbearable. Even if the original conduct has ceased to occur, she may find herself operating in an increasingly hostile environment. Her coworkers may ignore or insult her. Her every error and failing may be noticed, and the pressure of the social hostility may lead to an increase in her absenteeism and a reduction in the quality of her work performance. If this is a workplace where harassment is generally tolerated, she will be viewed as a problem. Her supervisor, now convinced that she is trouble, may begin to discipline her, perhaps even with the encouragement of upper management.

At this point, our victim may seek outside counsel and file a complaint. The organization, fearing large monetary damages, may now attempt to defend itself rather than step up its own efforts to correct the problem. Thus, efforts to end the harassment will stop, and efforts to prove that the company has done nothing wrong will begin or intensify. In many organizations, these attempts to prove that the organization has done nothing wrong will also include attempts to paint or portray the victim negatively. Her work performance may be degraded. There may be an effort to prove that she behaved in ways that show she welcomed any and all of the offensive conduct. Finally, especially if her legal claim includes any suggestion of psychological damages or if she has quit the job because of the harassment or retaliation, the employer may try to prove that she was emotionally unstable before the harassment began.

A review of this hypothetical example identifies several critical issues. First, and arguably most important, what is the organization's ethic about sexual harassment? This ethic is probably closely related to the organization's general view about women and about how people are to be treated. In an environment where women are viewed negatively and racism or other forms of prejudice and intolerance are condoned, the complaint, not the offensive conduct, is likely to be viewed as the problem. In such an environment, complaining is not likely to make the situation better. Second, and somewhat related, is the question of the relationship between the various levels and groups within the organization. In an organization where there is considerable hostility between front-line workers and management, or between the production and performance groups and HR (or, in police work, internal affairs), there is an increased probability that a complaint may get enmeshed in that conflict, with predictable negative consequences to the complaining party. Given the all-too-possible consequences, it is easy to understand why some harassment victims have described the decision of whether to complain as like trying to decide what to do on the sixteenth floor of a burning building, with the fire escapes already inflamed: Jump or burn?

CONCLUSION

The long history of discrimination at work has not been ended by the Civil Rights Act of 1964. Although blatant discrimination is less common than in the past, many subtle and not-so-subtle forms of discrimination against women continue. The segregation of work remains a problem, with some evidence that occupations become feminized, with men leaving, rather than gender neutralized once women enter those fields in significant numbers. Women continue to earn less than men do even when controlling for occupation and experience.

Yet the picture is not entirely gloomy. Certainly the situation for women in the workplace has improved in the forty years since the Civil Rights Act of 1964 was passed. There are many women alive today who do not realize that their mothers or grandmothers grew up in a world where they were not allowed to hold certain jobs—a world where women could be refused any job simply because the company wanted to hire a man. And there are companies and workplaces where sexual harassment is not condoned and where respecting the dignity of all is expected. However, as long as the categories of male and female are viewed as significant determinants of who should do what work, the problems of discrimination in the workplace are likely to persist.

References

Anderson v. Methodist Evangelical Hospital, Inc., 464 F.2d 723, 725 (6th Cir. 1972).

Baker, N. L. (1989). *Sexual harassment and job satisfaction in traditional and non-traditional industrial occupations.* Unpublished doctoral dissertation, California School of Professional Psychology.

Baker, N. L. (1995). The sex role construction of occupational roles: That's why they call it a man's world. In L. Brown (Chair), *Feminist forensic psychology.* Paper presented at the American Psychological Association Annual Convention, New York.

Bargh, J. A., Raymond, P., Pryor, J. B., & Strack, F. (1995). Attractiveness of the underling: An automatic power-sex association and its consequences for sexual harassment and aggression. *Journal of Personality and Social Psychology, 68*(5), 768–781.

Bergman, M. E., Langhout, R. D., Palmieri, P. A., Cortina, L. M., & Fitzgerald, L. F. (2002). The (un)reasonableness of reporting: Antecedents and consequences of reporting sexual harassment. *Journal of Applied Psychology, 87*(2), 230–242.

Bergmann, B. (1986). *The economic emergence of women.* New York: Basic Books.

Blau, F. D. (1984). Women in the labor force: An overview. In J. Freeman (Ed.), *Women: A feminist perspective* (3rd ed.). Mountain View, CA: Mayfield.

Bodenhausen, G. V., & Macrae, C. N. (1996). The self-regulation on inter-group perception: Mechanisms and consequences of stereotype suppression. In C. N. Macrae, C. Stangor, & M. Hewstone (Eds.), *Stereotypes and stereotyping.* New York: Guilford Press.

Buchanan, N. T., & Ormerod, A. J. (2002). Racialized sexual harassment in the lives of African American women. *Women and Therapy, 25*(3–4), 107–124.

Bularzik, M. (1978). Sexual harassment at the workplace: Historical notes. *Radical America, 12,* 25–43.

Burlington Industries, Inc. v. Ellerth, 524 U.S. 742 (1998).

Civil Rights Act of 1964, Pub. L. No. 88-352, 78 Stat. 253 (codified as amended at 42 U.S.C. 2000e to 2000e-17) (2000).

Civil Rights Act of 1964, Pub. L. No. 88-352, Title VII, 701, 78 Stat. 253 (codified as amended at 42 U.S.C. 2000e) (2000).

Coles, F. S. (1986). Forced to quit: Sexual harassment complaints and agency response. *Sex Roles, 14,* 81–95.

Cortina, L. M. (2001). Assessing sexual harassment among Latinas: Development of an instrument. *Cultural Diversity and Ethnic Minority Psychology, 7*(2), 164–181.

Cortina, L. M., & Magley, V. J. (2003). Raising voice, risking retaliation: Events following interpersonal mistreatment in the workplace. *Journal of Occupational Health Psychology, 8,* 247–265.

Dansky, B. S., & Kilpatrick, D. G. (1997). Effects of sexual harassment. In W. T. O'Donohue (Ed.), *Sexual harassment: Theory, research, and treatment* (pp. 152–174). Needham Heights, MA: Allyn & Bacon.

Davison, H. K., & Burke, M. J. (2000). Sex discrimination in simulated employment contexts: A meta-analytic investigation. *Journal of Vocational Behavior, 56,* 225–248.

Deaux, K. (1998). Gender. In D. T. Gilbert, S. T. Fiske, & G. Lindsey (Eds.), *The handbook of social psychology* (4th ed.). New York: Oxford University Press.

Deaux, K., & Ullman, J. C. (1983). *Women of steel: Female blue-collar workers in the basic steel industry.* New York: Praeger.

Desert Palace, Inc. v. Costa, 123 S. Ct. 2148, 2155 (2003).

Dovidio, J. F., & Gaertner, S. L. (1993). Stereotypes and the evaluation of intergroup bias. In D. M. Mackie & D. L. Hamilton (Eds.), *Affect, cognition, and stereotyping.* Orlando, FL: Academic Press.

Eagly, A. H., Makhinijani, M. G., & Klonsky, B. G. (1992). Gender and the evaluation of leaders: A meta-analysis. *Psychological Bulletin, 111,* 3–22.

Epstein, C. F. (1993). *Women in law.* Urbana: University of Illinois Press.

Equal Employment Opportunity Commission. (1980). Guidelines on discrimination because of sex. *Federal Register, 45,* 74676–74677.

Equal Employment Opportunity Commission. (1992). Policy guidance on compensatory and punitive damages under 1991 Civil Rights Act. 405 Fair Employment Practice Manual (BNA) 7091, 7093.

Faragher v. City of Boca Raton, 524 U.S. 775 (1998).

Farley, L. (1978). *Sexual shakedown: The sexual harassment of women on the job.* New York: McGraw-Hill.

Fiske, S. T. (1998). Stereotyping, prejudice, and discrimination. In D. T. Gilbert, S. T. Fiske, & G. Lindsey (Eds.), *The handbook of social psychology* (4th ed.). New York: Oxford University Press.

Fitzgerald, L. F., Hulin, C. L., & Drasgow, F. (1994). The antecedents and consequences of sexual harassment in organizations: An integrated model. In G. P. Keita & J. J. Hurrell Jr. (Eds.), *Job stress in a changing workforce: Investigating gender, diversity, and family issues* (pp. 55–73). Washington, DC: American Psychological Association.

Fitzgerald, L. F., & Ormerod, A. J. (1993). Breaking silence: The sexual harassment of women in academia and the workplace. In F. Denmark & M. Paludi (Eds.), *Psychology of women: A handbook of issues and theories* (pp. 553–582). Westport, CT: Greenwood Press.

Fitzgerald, L. F., Shullman, S. L., Bailey, N., Richards, M., Swecker, J., Gold, Y., Ormerod, M., & Weitzman, L. (1988). The incidence and dimensions of sexual harassment in academia and the workplace. *Journal of Vocational Behavior, 32,* 152–175.

Fitzgerald, L. F., Swan, S., & Fischer, K. (1995). Why didn't she just report him? The psychological and legal implications of women's responses to sexual harassment. *Journal of Social Issues, 51,* 117–138.

Fontana, A., & Rosenheck, R. (1998). Duty-related and sexual stress in the etiology of PTSD among women veterans who seek treatment. *Psychiatric Services, 49*(5), 658–662.

Fullerton, H. N., Jr. (1999, December). Labor force participation: Seventy-five years of change, 1950–1998 and 1998–2025. *Monthly Labor Review,* 3–12.

Gelfand, M. J., Fitzgerald, L. F., & Drasgow, F. (1995). The structure of sexual harassment: A confirmatory analysis across cultures and settings. *Journal of Vocational Behavior, 47,* 164–177.

Glick, P., & Fiske, S. T. (1996). The Ambivalent Sexism Inventory: Differentiating hostile and benevolent sexism. *Journal of Personality and Social Psychology, 70,* 491–512.

Glomb, T. M., Munson, L. J., Hulin, C. L., Bergman, M. E., & Drasgow, F. (1999). Structural equation models of sexual harassment: Longitudinal explorations and cross-sectional generalizations. *Journal of Applied Psychology, 84*(1), 14–28.

Goldenhar, L. M., Swanson, N. G., Hurrell, J. J., Ruder, A., & Deddens, J. (1998). Stressors and adverse outcomes for female construction workers. *Journal of Occupational Health Psychology, 3*(1), 19–32.

Gruber, J. E. (1998). The impact of male work environments and organizational policies on women's experiences of sexual harassment. *Gender and Society, 12*(3), 301–320.

Harned, M. S., & Fitzgerald, L. F. (2002). Understanding a link between sexual harassment and eating disorder symptoms: A mediational analysis. *Journal of Consulting and Clinical Psychology, 70*(5), 1170–1181.

Harned, M. S., Ormerod, A. J., Palmieri, P. A., Collinsworth, L. L., & Reed, M. (2002). Sexual assault and other types of sexual harassment by workplace personnel: A comparison of antecedents and consequences. *Journal of Occupational Health Psychology, 7*(2), 174–188.

Harris v. Forklift Systems, 510 U.S. 17-26 (1993).

Hay, M. S., & Elig, T. W. (1999). The 1995 Department of Defense sexual harassment survey: Overview and methodology. *Military Psychology, 11*(3), 233–242.

Hesson-McInnis, M. S., & Fitzgerald, L. F. (1997). Sexual harassment: A preliminary test of an integrative model. *Journal of Applied Social Psychology, 27*, 877–901.

Koss, M. P. (1990). Changed lives: The psychological impact of sexual harassment. In M. A. Paludi (Ed.), *Ivory power: Sexual harassment on campus* (pp. 73–92). Albany, NY: SUNY Press.

Koss, M. P., Goodman, L. A., Browne, A., Fitzgerald, L. F., Keita, G. P., & Russo, N. F. (Eds.). (1994). *No safe haven: Male violence against women at home, at work, and in the community.* Washington, DC: American Psychological Association.

Kruger, J., & Clement, R. W. (1994). Memory-based judgments about multiple categories: A revision and extension of Taifel's accentuation theory. *Journal of Personality and Social Psychology, 67*, 35–47.

Lindemann, B. T., & Kadue, D. D. (1999). *Sexual harassment in employment law. 1999 cumulative supplement.* Washington, DC: Bureau of National Affairs.

MacKinnon, C. A. (1979). *Sexual harassment of working women: A case of sex discrimination.* New Haven, CT: Yale University Press.

Macrae, C. N., Bodenhausen, G. V., Milne, A. B., & Jetten, J. (1994). Out of mind but back in sight: Stereotypes on the rebound. *Journal of Personality and Social Psychology, 67,* 808–817.

Mednick, M. T. (1982). Women and the psychology of achievement: Implications for personal and social change. In H. J. Bernardin (Ed.), *Women in the work force.* New York: Praeger.

Meritor Savings Bank v. Vinson, 477 U.S. 57 (1986).

Offermann, L. R., & Malamut, A. B. (2002). When leaders harass: The impact of target perceptions of organizational leadership and climate on harassment reporting and outcomes. *Journal of Applied Psychology, 87*(5), 885–893.

Pierce, C. (1970). Offensive mechanisms. In F. Barbour (Ed.), *The black 70s.* Boston: Sargent.

Price Waterhouse v. Hopkins, 490 U.S. 228 (1989).

Reskin, B. F., & Padavic, I. (1994). *Women and men at work.* Thousand Oaks, CA: Pine Forge Press.

Reskin, B. F., & Ross, C. E. (1992). Jobs, authority, and earnings among managers. *Work and Occupations, 19,* 342–365.

Rogers, J. K., & Henson, K. D. (1997). "Hey, why don't you wear a shorter skirt?" Structural vulnerability and the organization of sexual harassment in temporary clerical employment. *Gender and Society, 11*(2), 215–237.

Rotundo, M., Nguyen, D., & Sackett, P. R. (2001). A meta-analytic review of gender differences in perceptions of sexual harassment. *Journal of Applied Psychology, 86*(5), 914–922.

Rowe, M. (1981). The minutiae of discrimination: The need for support. In B. L. Forisha & B. H. Goldman (Eds.), *Outsiders on the inside.* Upper Saddle River, NJ: Prentice Hall.

Rowe, M. (1990). Barriers to equality: The power of subtle discrimination to maintain unequal opportunity. *Employee Responsibilities and Rights Journal, 3,* 153–163.

Rusher, J. B., & Fiske, S. T. (1990). Interpersonal competition can cause individuating impression formation. *Journal of Personality and Social Psychology, 58,* 832–838.

Satterfield, A. T., & Muehlenhard, C. L. (1997). Shaken confidence: The effects of an authority figure's flirtatiousness on women's and men's self-rated creativity. *Psychology of Women Quarterly, 21*(3), 395–416.

Schmitt, M. T., Branscombe, N. R., Kobrynowicz, D., & Owen, S. (2002). Perceiving discrimination against one's gender group has different implications for well-being in women and men. *Personality and Social Psychology Bulletin, 28,* 197–210.

Schneider, K. T., Swan, S., & Fitzgerald, L. F. (1997). Job-related and psychological effects of sexual harassment in the workplace: Empirical evidence from two organizations. *Journal of Applied Psychology, 82*(3), 401–415.

Sekaquaptewa, D., & von Hippel, W. (1994). *The role of prejudice in encoding and memory of stereotype-relevant behaviors.* Paper presented at the Sixty-Sixth Annual Meeting of the Midwestern Psychological Association, Chicago.

Shaffer, M. A., Joplin, J.R.W., Bell, M. P., Lau, T., & Oguz, C. (2000). Disruptions to women's social identity: A comparative study of workplace stress experienced by women in three geographic regions. *Journal of Occupational Health Psychology, 5*(4), 441–456.

Snyder, M. (1984). When belief creates reality. In L. Berkowitz (Ed.), *Advances in experimental social psychology, 18.* Orlando, FL: Academic Press.

Snyder, M. (1992). Motivational foundations of behavioral confirmation. In M. P. Zanna (Ed.), *Advances in experimental social psychology, 25.* Orlando, FL: Academic Press.

Stockdale, M. S. (1998). The direct and moderating influences of sexual harassment pervasiveness, coping strategies, and gender on work-related outcomes. *Psychology of Women Quarterly, 22,* 521–535.

Swim, J. K., & Sanna, L. J. (1996). He's skilled, she's lucky: A meta-analysis of observers' attributions for women's and men's successes and failures. *Personality and Social Psychology Bulletin, 22,* 507–519.

U.S. Merit Systems Protection Board. (1981). *Sexual harassment of federal workers: Is it a problem?* Washington, DC: U.S. Government Printing Office.

U.S. Merit Systems Protection Board. (1987). *Sexual harassment of federal workers: An update.* Washington, DC: U.S. Government Printing Office.

Vasquez, M.J.T., Baker, N. L., & Shullman, S. L. (2003). Assessing employment discrimination and harassment. In I. B. Weiner (Series Ed.) and A. M. Goldstein (Vol. Ed.), *Comprehensive handbook of psychology: Vol. 11. Forensic psychology.* New York: Wiley.

Wasti, S. A., Bergman, M. E., Glomb, T. M., & Drasgow, F. (2002). Test of the cross-cultural generalizability of a model of sexual harassment. *Journal of Applied Psychology, 85*(5), 766–778.

Williams v. Saxbe, 413 F. Supp. 654, 655–56 (D.D.C. 1976), vacated sub nom. Williams v. Bell, 587 F.2d 1240 (D.C. Cir. 1978).

Word, C. O., Zanna, M. P., & Cooper, J. (1974). The nonverbal mediation of self-fulfilling prophecies in interracial interaction. *Journal of Experimental Social Psychology, 10,* 109–120.

Yoder, J. D., & Aniakudo, P. (1996). When pranks become harassment: The case of African American women firefighters. *Sex Roles, 35*(5–6), 253–270.

CHAPTER FOUR

Sexual Harassment

The Organizational Perspective

Jay M. Finkelman, Ph.D., C.P.E.

Human resource (HR) management has two constituencies and a dual agenda when it comes to responding to sexual harassment allegations: it must protect employees from harassment and protect management from the potential liability associated with harassment. Although there is the inherent potential of a conflict, that should not preclude a professional HR department from adequately protecting the rights of all parties, including those of the alleged harasser. In fact, "doing the right thing" by the HR department is the best protection for everyone involved.

Following generally accepted HR management practices should ensure that any harassment is promptly stopped and precluded from recurring (as much as is reasonably possible), and that the accused harasser is warned against retaliation. It also should trigger an investigation designed to determine what, if anything, actually happened

---

The author of this chapter is not an attorney, and this chapter is not intended as legal advice. Readers should consult counsel regarding specific situations or problems.

and who is responsible. Nothing can be assumed or taken at face value. False accusations are as dangerous as lack of action. A professionally conducted investigation serves the interests of all of the participants: the organization, the alleged victim, and the alleged harasser.

An investigation is the best management defense and the best offense against both actual sexual harassment and false accusations of sexual harassment. For all these reasons, triggering a rapid neutral investigation of any alleged sexual harassment has become a significant management priority. An effective investigation is a critically important weapon in responding to allegations of sexual harassment.

THE DEFINITION OF SEXUAL HARASSMENT

Both the federal and state governments create and enforce laws covering workplace behavior such as harassment. For example, according to the Fair Employment and Housing Act in California, harassment because of sex includes sexual harassment, gender harassment, and harassment based on pregnancy, childbirth, or related medical conditions. The Fair Employment and Housing Commission regulations define sexual harassment as unwanted sexual advances, or visual, verbal, or physical conduct of a sexual nature. The Department of Fair Employment and Housing goes on to explain that the definition includes many forms of offensive behavior as well as gender-based harassment of a person of the same sex as the harasser.

CONDUCT PROHIBITED ON THE JOB

By way of example, the Department of Fair Employment and Housing in California is committed to preventing the following activities at work:

- Unwanted sexual advances
- Offers of employment benefits in exchange of sexual favors
- Reprisals made or threatened after a negative response to sexual advances
- Visual conduct such as leering, sexual gestures, display of sexually suggestive objects or pictures, cartoons, or posters
- Verbal sexual advances or propositions

- Verbal abuse of a sexual nature, graphic verbal commentaries about an individual's body, sexually degrading words used to describe an individual, suggestive or obscene letters, notes, or invitations
- Physical conduct such as touching, assault, impeding, or blocking movements

This is a rather comprehensive overview of some of the issues with which HR management professionals and experts must be prepared to respond to the challenges of sexual harassment allegations and the ensuing investigations. Although these are the specifics of the Department of Fair Employment and Housing in California, many of these concepts are more universal and generally reflected in equal employment opportunity commission guidelines as well.

WHAT DOES MANAGEMENT REALLY THINK?

Management believes that most allegations of sexual harassment are either bogus or the result of a misunderstanding between the parties, often emanating from consensual relationships "gone bad." It is rare that an executive today would knowingly tolerate actual sexual harassment. Yet managers tend to lose objectivity when they become involved in situations and relationships that may result in allegations of sexual harassment. From a corporate perspective, the situation is often compounded by the "strict liability" typically associated with sexual harassment by managers. The employer will be held legally responsible for the harassing behavior of managers, and the corporation will be required to pay any court-ordered compensation to the victim.

Given the prerogative, management would probably prefer that employees not engage in romantic (read sexual) relationships. But the reality is that they will, and nobody gets too excited about it until someone alleges sexual harassment or files an administrative complaint or lawsuit. The work environment constitutes the bulk of most people's lives, so it is not surprising that personal relationships do occur there. Also, most management efforts to preclude such activity are perceived as violating personal privacy, and they end in failure.

In general, these relationships are not a huge problem except when managers and subordinates are involved. That is why most organizations prohibit romantic relationships only between direct reports, although they often miss the point that strict liability might apply to anyone in a management capacity. However, a lot of effort may be expended in defining who is actually a manager from a legal perspective. At the very least, organizations should put these policies in writing and follow up and reinforce them through training.

WHO IS EXPLOITING WHOM?

The question of which party in a relationship is exploiting the other is tricky, and there is no consistently correct answer. Perhaps "it depends" is the right response. Certainly in the past, there was less ambiguity. While management may have preferred not to deal with sexual harassment, when it emerged as an issue, the accuser (then typically a woman) was generally honest and motivated primarily to end the harassment. Today things are less clear. Sexual harassment remains all too prevalent, but frivolous accusations are common as well.

Frivolous accusations encompass the continuum from misunderstandings and misinterpretation of conduct and motives to outright disingenuous charges designed to blackmail an organization for money or to avoid confronting genuine performance deficiencies. As an investigator, I believe that I have encountered each of these variations, along with instances of genuine harassment, of course.

From a management perspective (and not simply an HR management perspective) there is usually a strong desire to discourage sexual harassment because of the obvious consequences to the organization. But there is also a level of skepticism as to the legitimacy of many claims, often as a function of the prior experience of management in what appear to be similar situations. (This is how we all make judgments, including juries.)

When management is involved in the harassment, everything changes and the motivation to "do the right thing" becomes less clear. But enlightened management is even more vigilant in such circumstances because of strict liability as well as the obvious appearance issues.

ORGANIZATIONAL CLIMATE
AND TRAINING

Industrial-organizational psychologists and most managers recognize that company culture has a significant role in determining how various policies will be perceived, interpreted, and followed. Most companies truly want and expect that their HR management policies will be adhered to. However, there is a difference in the nonverbal communication that may be perceived as supporting—or undermining—the official policies.

It is rare that an organization deliberately sabotages its HR policies by its actions. But it is a common observation that companies may inadvertently shift the salience of their policies by the way that their managers conduct themselves in the presence of other employees and managers. That is why it is important for management (especially senior management) to be careful about its own behavior and vigilant about the behavior of others. An inappropriate casual remark by an influential manager may begin to subvert an entire program of formal training.

Training is usually an effective vehicle to reinforce the fundamentals of antiharassment and antidiscrimination policies. It is also an opportunity to influence organizational climate in a desired direction. To have maximum impact, it is useful to establish periodic reference points as to a company's culture and values. A dynamic, interactive, and perceptive trainer is a wonderful asset in shaping organizational climate.

It is still the informal culture of an organization that has the greatest impact on how women are regarded and treated in most organizations, and informal cultures are unfortunately quite resistant to change. That is why it is essential that management be committed to do the right thing over the long haul and not to accept compromise, even at an informal level.

DISCLOSURE AND "EQUAL OPPORTUNITY" HARASSMENT

Just as in the movie *Disclosure,* where the character played by Demi Moore harassed the character played by Michael Douglas, a female harassing a male does occur, though not with great frequency. Nevertheless, it is increasing as women gain organizational power and the perverse "perks" that are associated with that power.

In my own recent experience as an expert witness and HR management consultant, I note that same-sex sexual harassment is increasing even more rapidly in organizations today, typically, but not exclusively, male on male. Perhaps it is simply a function of greater reporting frequency, but that usually tracks the frequency of occurrence. Sometimes it appears as though it is confined to gay employees and sometimes appears to be triggered by the unilateral perception of the other party's being gay when in fact he is not. Not surprisingly, that misinterpretation is likely to trigger a sexual harassment complaint.

An even more troublesome issue from a management perspective is the use of a cross-complaint of sexual harassment as a proactive, though deceptive, defense against the original complaint. And in real organizational life, sexual harassment victims, such as that played by Michael Douglas in the movie, rarely get the fortuitous break that uncovers the truth that he received. Making life even more complicated, there often is ambiguity as to who may have initiated the contact or a proposed relationship.

Disclosure alludes to but does not fully address the situation in which a relationship is initiated consensually and then either party decides to end it unilaterally. Anyone has a right to do that, but it may have some unintended consequences in a corporate environment. Resentment by the spurned party may trigger a bogus sexual harassment complaint. Or the spurned party may not get the message and may continue to pursue the failed relationship, thus triggering a good-faith sexual harassment complaint, though perhaps one that was due to a legitimate misunderstanding.

What is the correct thing for management to do under these circumstances? It is not always clear other than the need to investigate any and all reported complaints of sexual harassment, to stop harassment that is determined to be occurring, and to attempt to preclude retaliation following a complaint.

THE RECKLESS MANAGER

Reckless managers—those that act rashly, impulsively, or irresponsibly—pose a serious risk to a company. It is too easy to ignore their behavior as immature and brush aside their comments as not to be taken seriously. But their colleagues and subordinates (and the courts) may not view it that way.

Most companies understand that they bear some level of responsibility for the conduct of their managers and supervisors. Depending on the circumstances, adequacy of responses, and jurisdiction, this may range from strict liability to no liability.

Reckless managers are often regarded and treated as "the life of the party." Sometimes they are respected for what is viewed as their "candor and directness"; that is, they say what they think. Unfortunately, this level of candor and lack of understanding is a double-edged sword. No one, especially the reckless manager, can correctly anticipate how individuals will react to others' language, gestures, and contact.

Reckless managers need to be exposed to the potential consequences of their behavior, which they may regard as innocent. And the organization may wish to document the exposure. Such sensitization can be accomplished in a variety of ways:

- Senior management must set a good example. Nothing undermines desired management behavior as much as senior management's violating it, even in jest.

- Establish and publish guidelines. Do not make anyone guess (or assume) how they are expected to behave.

- Train all staff in their responsibilities regarding appropriate behavior. Do not assume that good behavior is obvious. It is not. Encourage everyone to confront and report violations.

- Reinforce the training. Do not assume that training needs to take place only once. That may be adequate, but it may not be.

- Document the training and the participants. This obvious step can prevent having to scramble to respond to future claims that the company was negligent by not providing adequate training.

- Employ a multimodality approach to sensitization. Use training tapes, professional training, written antiharassment and antidiscrimination guidelines, management reinforcement, and appropriate discipline to support the message.

- Use management by walking around frequently and randomly. Never permit managers or supervisors to control access to those who report to them. Doing so could inadvertently encourage misbehavior.

- Practice a true open-door policy. This has tremendous utility in shaping good management behavior and constraining reckless behavior if practiced judiciously.

- Investigate alleged infractions. A professionally conducted investigation continues to be among the best defenses against sex and race discrimination and harassment claims.

- Confront violators immediately, and take appropriate action. Permitting misconduct to go unchallenged sends an inappropriate message to everyone.

- Protect employees against retaliation. All organizations are obligated to do whatever is reasonable to protect accusers and witnesses from the possibility of retaliation. The consequences of not guarding against foreseeable and demonstrated retaliation may be more serious than for the initial alleged harassment.

Reckless Managers and Egocentricity

The *Dictionary of Psychological and Psychoanalytical Terms* (English & English, 1966) defines egocentric as "concerned with oneself; preoccupied with one's own concerns and relatively insensitive to the concerns of others, though not necessarily selfish" (pp. 171–172).

Reckless managers tend to focus on themselves, not on how their behavior affects others. That is why they need coaching, mentoring, and perhaps discipline. They may have the leadership qualities needed to be effective, but they often come with considerable baggage. This situation must be dealt with in such a manner as not to intrude on these individuals' rights and privacy.

The risk problem is that egocentric managers are not likely to understand how their behavior is perceived by subordinates. Whether this is due to selective perception, selective listening, or simply arrogance and insensitivity as to how others react to their words and conduct, reckless managers proceed as though only they matter. It is management's task to try to control the destructive interpersonal consequences of someone's reckless conduct in order to mitigate liability in the workplace.

The 80/20 Rule

While reckless managers may constitute no more than 20 percent of all managers, they account for more than 80 percent of all HR liability and exposure in the workplace. (In fact, the ratio may be more like 90/10.) This means that a very small proportion of management and supervisory staff (typically only one person in a smaller company) will account for the overwhelming majority of interpersonal conflict, employee dissatisfaction, employee grievances, government agency complaints, legal and insurance costs, liability exposure, and senior management resources (a cost that is frequently overlooked).

It is ironic that the 20 percent of managers who are reckless may also be among the most productive managers (though they probably do not account for as much as 80 percent of overall managerial productivity and effectiveness). Even so, the corporate risk that they impose is certainly not worth retaining them in their reckless mode. However, their high-performance potential creates a strong reason to do everything possible to try to coach, correct, and, when possible, retain them.

Dealing with Risky Behavior

There are few absolute thresholds for reckless managerial behavior that automatically trigger the need for immediate termination. The rights of all parties need to be protected and balanced, but this should not be used as an excuse to retain reckless managers who engage in unacceptable behavior, especially after they have been warned.

A pattern of warnings followed by repetitive risky conduct may substantially increase the vulnerability to later litigation—frivolous or legitimate. It is almost always a professional HR management/legal judgment call. Managers should guide themselves accordingly. It is part of the challenge and responsibility of being in charge.

Examples of Reckless Management Behavior

A staffing manager did not pick up on a number of cues that his staff did not appreciate his interest in their personal affairs. He also had an unfortunate habit of making what he thought were innocuous comments about the attire of his female staff, despite being cautioned about the practice. He also was a "touchy-feely" sort of manager, and despite being repeatedly warned to avoid all physical contact, he was eventually terminated for touching the hair of one of his employees after she initiated a complaint against him. He truly believed that his conduct was innocuous.

A corporate manager repeatedly took advantage of his powerful position—and effective performance—to encourage women who reported to him to "entertain him" when he visited them during field trips. His misconduct was conveniently overlooked by other management because his operation was quite profitable. He had a history of similar difficulty with prior employers. He was eventually terminated after investigation of a documented complaint. He knew his conduct was inappropriate, but he probably thought he was too powerful and important to be held accountable.

SEXUAL HARASSMENT INVESTIGATIONS AND THE ROLE OF HR EXPERTS

The universal issue that appears on both sides of sexual harassment lawsuits is the timeliness and quality of the sexual harassment investigation that should have been triggered by the sexual harassment complaint. My experience is that the quality and timeliness of the investigation are among the most pivotal issues that courts consider in assessing the conduct of the company accused of sexual harassment. A professionally executed sexual harassment investigation is the most effective deterrent against frivolous litigation and the best defense against liability when harassment has actually occurred.

Preparation for the Investigation

In preparing for the investigation, management should review the written sexual harassment complaint, which should have been solicited at the beginning of an investigation. This will avoid accusations of conveniently evolving stories and circumstances in addition to obtrusive measurement error. (Obtrusive measurement occurs when an investigator changes the facts and circumstances by the very process of the investigation—obviously not a desirable outcome.)

Management should also determine whether the sexual harassment investigator has reasonably assessed the individuals privy to information about the alleged harassment before the actual investigation. They must be prepared to explain why any individual so identified might not have been interviewed for corroboration. Management may also need to comment about the nature of the investigation and interview team. A two-person team is ideal, though certainly not essential, for an internal investigation. If two interviewers are engaged, a male-female team is preferable.

Parties to the Investigation

Management should try to determine whether witnesses were told that there would be no retaliation for telling the truth or that their confidentiality could not be guaranteed. The experts should also be sensitive as to whether the complainant and witness information was shared only on a need-to-know basis. There is an obligation in an effective sexual harassment investigation to avoid defaming the accused harasser and unnecessarily embarrassing the complainant. It is always important to be aware that both parties have rights in a sexual harassment investigation.

Those conducting a sexual harassment investigation also have an obligation to protect the interests and reputations of all parties and should make no a priori assumptions as to motivation and fault. An HR management expert can be particularly effective in examining the facts and circumstances surrounding a sexual harassment investigation to make a determination as to whether the guidelines were followed. At trial, the expert may also be asked to comment about the wisdom of allowing the complainant to confront the accused harasser directly during the course of the investigation. In most circumstances, it is neither advisable nor necessary for the complainant to do this, although ideally, confrontation should have occurred prior to the initiation of a complaint.

The circumstances of any specific complaint may necessitate that the investigators interview other past or current employees who might have been exposed to harassment (if in fact it actually occurred). At trial, an HR management expert may be asked to second-guess the wisdom of those determinations (and the repercussions of the failure to do so).

Requirements of the Investigation

It is important that management understand that there is no single procedure that absolutely must be followed in conducting a professionally appropriate sexual harassment investigation. If, for example, a consultant has produced a guidebook outlining suggested steps for an investigation, it is unlikely that each step is an absolute requirement exactly as articulated. There is leeway in conducting appropriate sexual harassment investigations. Investigators must also consider whether an alleged incident is isolated or part of a pattern of harassment involving the complainant and possibly others. This may also be a legitimate area for expert inquiry in making a determination as to whether a pattern and practice exists.

Adverse Impact on Job Performance

A crucial issue in any employment situation is whether the conduct of the employer or its representatives had an adverse impact on job performance. That is a fundamental dimension of any assessment of harassment in the workplace. It is also understood to be an important motivating factor in the passage of antiharassment legislation. An expert should be prepared to comment about that issue and critique the measures used to make that determination.

Issues in the Investigation

An effective HR management expert needs to able to differentiate and explain to a jury the differences among insensitivity, tastelessness, and rudeness, which do not automatically reach the standard for determining that sexual harassment has occurred, unless other circumstances and conditions apply. An effective defense expert should be able to explain these differences to a jury.

The basic issues in most sexual harassment investigations boil down to whether the conduct in question was sexual in nature and whether the conduct was unwelcome in the sense that the complainant neither solicited nor incited it and also found it undesirable or offensive. These sensitive issues require care and finesse in understanding and interpreting. An expert may also be called on to determine whether the complainant or someone representing the complainant properly advised an alleged harasser in a hostile work environment situation that the behavior was unwelcome.

After a finding that sexual harassment has occurred, there are final issues in determining the appropriate discipline:

- Whether the complainant properly notified the alleged harasser
- The severity of harassment (obviously a judgment call, appropriate for expert testimony)
- The frequency of harassment
- Previous or concurrent harassment complaints

The conclusion of the investigation is also a subject for possible expert commentary, specifically with regard to sharing the response of the accused harasser as well as the outcome of the investigation with the complainant. An expert will be able to explain to the court that while the claimant should not be permitted to dictate disciplinary procedure or corrective action, if the claim is valid, the claimant's comfort with a particular outcome could be taken into consideration.

With regard to a sexual harassment complaint that is found to have merit, an expert may need to evaluate whether follow-up mechanisms were required or effective in ensuring that the harassment cease, with little or no probability of recurrence. Furthermore, an expert may be asked to assess whether corrective action was proper in order to stop the harassment, discipline the harasser, and reinforce that sexual harassment is neither acceptable nor tolerable.

Often the outcome of a sexual harassment investigation is inconclusive or disputed by one or another party. Management should be prepared to determine whether the investigation was concluded with any unresolved material inconsistencies between the parties. An expert may be asked to comment on whether actions taken within that investigation, such as separating the parties and minimizing their interaction, were appropriate. The expert may also be asked to provide an opinion as to whether such actions could have been accomplished with less detrimental impact on either party's position or reputation.

Liability in the Investigation

An expert's comments can be vital when reviewing the requirement of good faith and fair dealing that is entailed within a sexual harassment investigation, especially as it relates to the speed of such an investigation. When there is an attempt to achieve rapid resolution, an expert can determine whether greater speed might have compromised the integrity of the investigation, which is obviously not an acceptable outcome.

Retaliation

There is great sensitivity in HR to issues of retaliation or alleged retaliation. If that is part of the complaint, an expert may be asked to assess the behavior of the parties before and after the complaint to determine whether there was a change in conduct that might be reasonably determined to be retaliation or have the effect of retaliation.

Management must assess who initiated the change in conduct (the complainant or the accused harasser) and then determine whether the change was in response to objective performance-related issues in the workplace. Nothing is more critical than precluding the possibility of retaliation after a sexual harassment complaint has been lodged. The HR management expert must be prepared to address any lapses at trial.

PROACTIVE MANAGEMENT AND THE NEED TO CONFRONT WRONGDOING

There are few, if any, areas within HR management that are less tolerant of procrastination and delay than confronting implications—or certainly allegations—of sexual harassment. Although such encounters are awkward and unpleasant to deal with, it is nonetheless necessary to intervene quickly and aggressively to determine if harassment has taken place and to stop it if it has. This is the best possible approach to mitigating any ensuing liability and organizational damage. It should also be obvious.

What may be less obvious is the need to be proactive and confront wrongdoing—but with the utmost sensitivity to the feelings and vulnerabilities of all the parties in an alleged harassment situation. It is remarkable how everyone loses their composure and their perspective when there is an accusation of sexual harassment. This is not to minimize the seriousness of a sexual harassment complaint. But no one is immune to overreacting under these circumstances.

The alleged harasser typically encounters a range of strong emotions, only slightly as a function of whether this person is, in fact, guilty or innocent of wrongdoing. This apparent enigma is better understood when it is recognized that many harassers do not believe that they are guilty of harassment. If the accused harasser is innocent (or believes that he or she is innocent), the anticipated reaction is anger (at the accuser), embarrassment, and defensiveness. If the accused harasser is guilty, the anticipated reaction is still anger (at the accuser), embarrassment, and defensiveness.

The accuser also typically encounters a range of strong emotions. It often entails anger (at the harasser or the perceived harasser), embarrassment, and defensiveness (at possibly having invited or encouraged the harassment).

Witnesses may be initially reluctant to provide damaging information, especially if management is accused. And unless they are motivated to hurt someone, the typical reaction is annoyance at being asked or occasional indifference. Not surprisingly, it is almost always accompanied by embarrassment.

HR may appear excessively eager to assert its authority and confront the alleged harasser—or defensive about not having prevented the harassment in the first place. A weak HR manager may appear reluctant to confront senior management. Finally, HR may be conflicted about its dual responsibility (and loyalty) to protect employees as well as to protect management.

SETTING THE TONE

Management has the (negative) financial incentive to do the right thing when it comes to reining in sexually harassing conduct. It took a while to get there, but the financial consequences of failing to control inappropriate behavior were ultimately most persuasive. Organizations did not systematically condone harassment in the past, but it was not a high priority to be proactive and—perhaps intrusive—about confronting it.

A more laudable reason for confronting sexual harassment early is slowly emerging, and it probably reverts to the original rationale behind Congress's prohibiting it. Sexual harassment is a form of sex discrimination, and sex discrimination was correctly viewed as interfering with anyone's ability to be productive in the workplace. The real incentive may still be largely economic, and that is probably all right. Rather than interpret this as a condemnation of the capitalist system, it may be more accurate to view it as a serendipitous, self-regulating, and self-corrective feature of a surprisingly wise and enduring system.

Beyond crass motivation, management has an extraordinary ability to influence the behavior of subordinates by their own conduct and example. It is a subtle power but an awesome one. It has the ability to set the tone for future generations of effective and enlightened managers and productive employees. Senior managers should guide themselves accordingly.

Reference

English, H. B., & English, A. C. (1966). *Comprehensive dictionary of psychological and psychoanalytical terms.* New York: David McKay.

CHAPTER FIVE

Relational Practice

A Feminist Reconstruction of Work

Joyce K. Fletcher, Ph.D.

I t is recognized with increasing frequency that organizations—in theory, practice, and general discourse—are gendered, exemplifying, and in many cases reifying, stereotypically masculine traits (Acker, 1992; Collinson & Hearn, 1994; Ferguson, 1984; Mills & Tancred, 1992; P. Martin, 1995). Traditionally, this masculine bias, where noted, has been cast as problematic for women, inhibiting their career progress in organizational settings and contributing to what is commonly called the glass ceiling (Morrison, White, & Van Velsor, 1987). Recent organizational analysis from a feminist poststructuralist perspective, however, is beginning to broaden the implications of studying the gendered nature of organizing. Feminist poststructuralist critiques and rereadings of mainstream organizational theories, such as Mumby and Putnam's rereading of bounded rationality (1992), Martin and Knopoff's feminist critique of Weber (1995), and Barbara Townley's rereading of human resource management practices (1993), have begun to suggest that the gendered nature of these theories—the way they implicitly privilege stereotypically masculine attributes and devalue or ignore stereotypically feminine—is problematic in a more general sense.

That is, exploring the gendered nature of these mainstream theories has highlighted the way in which gendered assumptions are potentially problematic not only for women but also for men *and* for organizational effectiveness because they have resulted in narrow, conscripted understandings of organizational phenomena. Reworking these mainstream theories to include previously ignored or discounted perspectives is serving to challenge many of the organizational "realities" long accepted in the academy and to offer new ways of thinking about organizing.

The research summarized here is offered in this same spirit. It is feminist poststructuralist inquiry that seeks to expand the gendered definition of work by giving voice to a way of working—relational practice—that springs from a relational, or stereotypically feminine, belief system. Like other feminist poststructuralist rereadings of organizational phenomena, it argues that the current, commonsense definition of work in organizational discourse is not a passive concept; it is instead an active, although unobtrusive, *exercise of power* that silences and suppresses alternative definitions that might challenge the status quo (Clegg, 1989; Flax, 1990; Foucault, 1980; McNay, 1992; Weedon, 1987). Furthermore, it argues that this silencing results not only in certain elements of the experience of work being marginalized, but also in an undertheorized representation of these activities—and their impact on organizational output and effectiveness—in the organizational literature.

The study summarized here explores this phenomenon in two steps. First, it gives voice to an undertheorized aspect of the nature of work by making visible, giving language to, and building theory about relational activity as practice in organizations. Then, it explores the gender-power dynamic of the silencing process itself. That is, in addition to expanding the definition of work by detailing a way of working that springs from a relational belief system, this study explores the mechanisms—and the gender and organizational implications of the process—through which this way of working currently "gets disappeared" from commonsense definitions of real work.

THEORETICAL CONTEXT

The theoretical framing of this inquiry occurs at the intersection of three streams of thought. The first is poststructuralism, a form of postmodern philosophy that, with its emphasis on the relationship between knowledge, discourse, and power, establishes the context of the study and positions it as a challenge to commonsense definitions of work. The second is a feminist reading of the literature on the nature of work that suggests that these commonsense definitions are gendered because they are rooted in the social construction of the public-private dichotomy along gender lines. And the third is a particular type of feminist standpoint research, relational theory, that suggests what is likely to be invisible in these gendered definitions. The interplay of these three streams of thought as they relate to the research questions will be explored briefly.

Poststructuralism

Poststructuralism provides the theoretical context for this study. Of the many traits characteristic of poststructuralist thought, three distinguishing features are key to understanding this study, its design and methodology, and the way in which it positions itself as a challenge to commonsense definitions of work, competence, and skill. The first of these three features is that poststructuralist inquiry problematizes the process of knowledge production and conceptualizes it as an exercise of power where only some voices are heard and only some experience is counted as knowledge. That is, poststructuralist perspectives challenge the notion of transcendent or universalizing truth and assert that the very set of rules used to determine if something is "true" or "false" is ideologically determined and is itself an exercise of power intended to maintain the status quo and silence any serious challenge to it (Alvesson & Deetz, 1996; Clegg, 1989; Flax, 1990; Foucault, 1980; McNay, 1992; Weedon, 1987).

A second key feature of poststructuralist inquiry is that it emphasizes the role language plays in mediating the relationship between power and knowledge. It asserts that it is in discursive practice that social reality and its patterns of dominance are constructed. Indeed, there is no experience, there is no "knowing" self except that which is an effect of discursive practice (Collinson, 1994; Diamond & Quinby, 1989; Fairclough, 1989; Mumby, 1988; Weedon, 1987). From a poststructuralist perspective, then, textual representation is never neutral; instead, it is a powerful means of constructing an ideological worldview that furthers the interest of dominant groups.

This emphasis on textual representation is related to the third distinguishing feature of a poststructuralist perspective: the notion of resistance (Collinson, 1994; Clegg, 1989; Flax, 1990). The exercise of power in textual representation is not absolute but is "contingent, provisional, achieved not given" (Clegg, 1989, p. 151). Therefore, it can be resisted using destabilizing strategies, the most familiar of which is deconstruction (Jacobsen & Jacques, 1997). In other words, just as textual representation is used to construct social reality, it can be used to deconstruct this reality. Deconstruction entails challenging unexamined dichotomies in the text, revealing suppressed contradictions, and calling attention to what has been hidden, obscured, or invisible (Fairclough, 1989; Flax, 1990; J. Martin, 1990). Although this type of discourse analysis typically refers to written text, the same techniques have been applied to the spoken word (J. Martin, 1990) and to analyzing what Jacques (1992) calls "enacted text," that is, the practices and meaningful actions that precede and determine the printed text. Another destabilizing method is to focus on "subversive stories" that challenge the status quo. These usually take the form of personal accounts, emotional experience, or life stories of members of a marginalized group whose voice has been silenced or whose experience has not been counted as knowledge (Alvesson & Deetz, 1996; Ewick & Silbey, 1995; Harris, Bridger, Sachs, & Tallichet, 1995).

It is important to note that whatever method is used, this type of inquiry is not intended to replace one social reality with another or to claim one truth is preferable over another, but rather to disrupt taken-for-granted notions and make discussable what has been uncontested and assumed (Flax, 1990; Jacobsen & Jacques, 1997). The goal is to create what poststructuralists call discursive space, where new ways of thinking might surface. Creating discursive space means offering an alternative interpretation of reality that relaxes taken-for-granted assumptions, thereby creating—theoretically—a place where new things can be said and new social structures envisioned (Calas & Smircich, 1989; Clegg, 1989; Mumby, 1988).

These three features of poststructuralist inquiry outline the research terrain of this study. Its goal was to destabilize the definition of work in organizational discourse from a feminist perspective: it sought to problematize the masculine nature of the meta-narrative of knowledge production about work in organizational discourse by calling attention to the feminine as a voice that has been silenced or obscured. It sought to add this voice to the discourse, thereby momentarily relaxing taken-for-granted assumptions about the nature of work. And finally, by relaxing these assumptions, it sought to create discursive space in which new, less masculine ways of thinking about work, skill, and competence might be considered.

There are several methodological challenges in designing a field study covering this research terrain. These will be addressed in more depth in the methods section. But first, there are two additional theoretical positions that need to be established. The first is a rationale to support the claim that the current definition of work is gendered. The second is an identification of the marginalized voice that will be used to destabilize the definition of work and an explanation of how that voice can claim to represent the feminine.

The Definition of Work

Those studying the gendered nature of organizations, the social construction of skill, and notions of comparable worth (Acker, 1989, 1992; Bradley, 1989; Harding, 1986; Mills & Tancred, 1992; Smircich, 1985) suggest that the current definition of work in organizational discourse is a social construction premised on a gendered dichotomy between the public and private spheres of life. This dichotomy divides the world into two separate, gendered domains: a public work sphere where the dominant actor is assumed to be male and a private family sphere where the dominant actor is assumed to be female. While traditional conceptualizations of this public-private split posit the two spheres as complementary—separate but equal domains that function together for the good of society (Bellah, Madsen, Sullivan, Swidler, & Tipton, 1985; Parsons & Bales, 1955; Perrow, 1986)—these more recent conceptualizations problematize the split along two dimensions. The first has to do with the separateness of the two spheres and the second with the way in which they are gendered.

The problem in the separation of the two spheres is that knowledge production in each sphere proceeds independently, resulting in two separate discourses, each with certain "truth rules" and global criteria characterizing activity in its domain (Bailyn, 1993; Ferguson, 1984; Game & Pringle, 1983; Harding, 1986; Nicholson, 1990; Wadel, 1979). A summary of the characteristics generally identified with each domain is offered in Table 5.1.

From a poststructuralist perspective, the problem with the separation of the two spheres is that it is a social construction. Although subject positions operate in both spheres, often simultaneously, the discourse (social practice, structures and language) continues to create, reinforce, and textually represent them as separate and dichotomous (Bailyn, 1993; Bailyn, Rapaport, Kolb, & Fletcher, 1996; Bradley, 1993; Fletcher & Bailyn, 1996; Friedlander, 1994; Parkin, 1993). This

Public Sphere	Private Sphere
Work is something you have to do	Work is something you want to do
Money is the motivator	Love is the motivator
Work is paid	Work is unpaid
Rationality reified	Emotionality reified
Abstract	Concrete, Situated
Time span defined	Time span ambiguous
Output: marketable goods, services, money	Output: people, social relations, creation of community, attitudes, values, management of tension
Context of differential reward leads to focus on individuality	Context of creating a collective leads to focus on community
Skills needed are taught; work is considered complex	Skills needed are thought to be innate; work is considered not complex

Table 5.1.   Public and Private Spheres.

sets up a situation in which knowledge from one sphere is likely to be considered inappropriate to the other and thus unlikely to challenge its underlying narrative. As a result, public sphere attributes such as rationality, cognitive complexity, and abstract thinking are often absent from commonsense definitions of work in the private sphere (DeVault, 1990; Reverby, 1987; Roberts, 1990; Ruddick, 1989). By the same token, private sphere attributes, such as emotionality, caring, and community, are often invisible in commonsense definitions of work and competence in the public sphere (Fineman, 1993: Hall & Mirvis, 1996; Mumby & Putnam, 1992).

This brings us to the second dimension of the problem. If this separation is a social construction, how did it come to be, and what purpose is it serving? More to the poststructuralist point, what particular systems of power and inequity is it maintaining? Many feminists suggest that at least part of the answer to these questions lies in the gendered nature of the split and the way it reinforces patriarchal systems of power. For example, Harding (1986) suggests that the public-private dichotomy is rooted in the acceptance in Western thought of a more general gender dichotomy between culture and nature where men and masculinity are strongly associated with the public, cultural role and women and femininity with the private, natural role. The result is a gender split in which the notion of growth, effectiveness, and an ideal worker in the public work sphere is conflated with idealized masculinity and where, in the private sphere, these same notions are conflated with idealized femininity (Acker, 1990; Bradley, 1993; Collinson & Hearn, 1994; Gherardi, 1995; Lorber, 1991; P. Martin, 1995; Parkin, 1993). This suggests that assumptions about what is appropriate and inappropriate in each sphere are held in place not only by notions of separation but also, and perhaps more firmly, by deeply held images of masculinity and femininity that function to keep patriarchal systems of power in place (Acker, 1990; Cockburn, 1991; Connell, 1995).

This discussion of the public-private sphere split frames several important features of the study: it not only posits that the feminine is likely to be absent from organizational definitions of work, but also hints at the deeply interior power of a silencing process in which aspects of work that can be textually represented as congruent with idealized masculinity will be considered "real" work and those that are associated with idealized femininity will not (Bradley, 1993; Fletcher, 1994a; P. Martin, 1995). It also begins to give a sense of the way in which giving voice to private sphere, feminine knowledge could momentarily disrupt the gender-power dynamic inherent in the current definition of work in organizational discourse.

This brings us to the issue of what voice can be used to bring private sphere knowledge and its association with the feminine into organizational discourse and how this knowledge can be brought in as a destabilizing story, that is, with its inherent challenge to the discourse intact. To answer these questions, we move to a discussion of relational theory and its positioning as a feminine alternative to masculine theories of growth and development.

Relational Models of Growth, Development, and Achievement

First proposed by psychologists and psychiatrists at the Stone Center at Wellesley College (Miller, 1976; Jordan, Surrey, & Kaplan, 1991) and supported by the work of Carol Gilligan (1982), Sara Ruddick (1989), and others (Belenky, Clinchy, Goldberger, & Tarule, 1986; Brown & Gilligan, 1992), relational theory and its correlates were developed by listening for and to the experience of women. Although it draws on Chodorow's extension of object relations theory and gender differences in early life experience (1974), it makes no claim to speak for all women or to claim that only women subscribe to it. Nonetheless, it is a theory that positions itself as an alternative to the masculine bias in mainstream theories of psychological, intellectual, and moral growth (Miller, 1976; Gilligan, 1982) that underlie many societal structures.

Relational theory suggests that although the prevailing models of adult growth and achievement are based on public sphere characteristics such as separation, individuation, and independence, there exists an alternative model, called growth-in-connection, that is rooted in private sphere characteristics of connection, interdependence, and collectivity (Miller, 1986a; Jordan, Kaplan, Miller, Stiver, & Surrey, 1991). Unlike mainstream models that emphasize autonomy and the individuation process as central to personal growth and identity, growth-in-connection models emphasize the role of relational interactions in the development process. It is important to note that while both mainstream and relational theories of growth encompass both individual and relational processes, it is the preeminence of connection over individuation in the developmental process that gives relational theory its potential as a destabilizing alternative voice in organizational discourse and marks it as feminine (Fletcher, 1994a; Hall & Mirvis, 1996; Hall, 1996; Kram, 1996; Liou & Aldrich, 1995).

The basic tenet of relational theory, that growth and development occur best in a context of connection, is further delineated by the identification of specific characteristics of these growth-fostering connections. In other words, growth is conceptualized as occurring not in any engagement or relationship but through a specific kind of relational interaction. These growth-fostering interactions are characterized by mutual empathy and mutual empowerment, where both parties recognize vulnerability as part of the human condition, approach the interaction expecting to grow from it, and feel a responsibility to contribute to the growth of the other. The ability to develop relationally requires certain strengths: empathy, vulnerability, an ability to experience and express emotion, an ability to participate in the development of another, and an expectation that relational interactions will be sites of growth for both parties involved (Jordan, Kaplan et al., 1991; Miller, 1976). As Miller notes, however, the characterization of these attributes as "strengths" is itself a challenge to the dominant discourse, especially the psychological discourse in which giving preeminence to connection has traditionally been characterized as a weakness or psychological deficiency.

Although this model of growth does not presume to speak for all women, it does assert that there are strong forces operating simultaneously to discourage men and encourage women to enact it. These include internal forces based on early development (Chodorow, 1974) and external forces based on socialization and societal expectations of gender-appropriate behavior (Brown & Gilligan, 1992; Gilligan, 1982; West & Zimmerman, 1991). Indeed, Jean Baker Miller (1976) offers a radical view of these societal expectations, proposing that because men are socialized to deny in themselves the relational skills needed to survive psychologically, they rely on women to be the carriers of these traits in society. Thus, society assigns relational activity to women and it becomes "women's work," a phenomenon that has been noted in organizational settings (Huff, 1990; Kolb, 1992). These formulations suggest that enacting a relational model of growth is likely to be a site for the social construction of gender in the workplace, as it is one way of marking oneself "feminine." In summary, this discussion provides the rationale for using relational theory as a surrogate (one of many possible) for a feminist ideology from which to challenge the growth and effectiveness model underlying the organizational discourse on work.

RESEARCH PLAN

With this groundwork laid, it is now appropriate to detail the research plan of this poststructuralist field study. The first step in the plan was to collect a potentially destabilizing textual representation of work in an organizational setting. The ideal setting would gain its legitimacy from the extent to which it was an exemplar of public sphere characteristics and their underlying logic of growth and effectiveness. The ideal subject would be someone who stood at the "line of fault" (Smith, 1990) between the public and private spheres: that is, someone who was located in two particular and inherently contradictory subject positions in organizational discourse—"woman" and "worker"—and who would embody the contradictory expectations and predispositions attending these two subject positions (Gherardi, 1995; Harding, 1987; Morrison et al., 1987). The second step in the plan was to analyze the textual representation of work gathered from these subjects to reveal those practices that were motivated by tenets underlying relational theory. Relational theory had been selected on the basis of its legitimacy as representative of feminine, private sphere characteristics and their underlying logic of growth and effectiveness. The third step in the plan was to compare this alternative reality to the mainstream, commonsense definition of work in that particular organizational culture. It was expected that this comparison would reveal the differences between the two and the mechanisms by which the alternative representation of work was suppressed, invisible, or silenced in the dominant discourse. The last step was to take advantage of the discursive space created by destabilizing the commonsense definition of work in order to envision not only new ways of working but also new organizational structures to support them.

The following research questions guided the inquiry:

- Is there evidence that relational practice exists in this organizational setting? If so, what behaviors characterize it? What beliefs, assumptions, and values do these behaviors reflect?

- What are the mechanisms through which relational practice and the belief system underlying it are brought into the dominant discourse and subjected to the sense-making "truth rules" of that discourse?

METHOD

This study was an independent part of a larger action research project focused on gender equity that was conducted over a period of four years in a major high-technology company based in the northeastern United States. At the time the data analyzed in this study were collected, the research team had been on-site for two years, engaged in a process of cultural diagnosis that involved interviewing people at all levels of the organization, shadowing key employees, attending a wide range of technical and staff meetings, and analyzing company documents and policy statements (Bailyn et al., 1996).

The research questions for this portion of the study required three types of data. The first was a "potentially destabilizing textual representation of work" gathered by observing what Smith (1990) calls "line of fault" subjects; that is, people who live on the fault line between two competing subject positions, such as "worker" and "woman." These data were collected through a method of structured observation modeled on that used by Mintzberg (1973) in his study of managers and further refined by Jacques (1992) in his study of female knowledge workers. The design, as adapted for this study, entailed the intensive shadowing of six female design engineers. These six engineers were a sample of convenience, determined by organizational constraints. There were only seven female design engineers in the entire product development team who were available during the time frame. Six were shadowed and interviewed as planned. The shadowing of the seventh, who was in manufacturing design, was aborted after two hours because my presence on the shop floor was so intrusive that note taking was impossible.

The day-long shadowing produced a systematic unselective recording of each engineer's interactions with the environment: all encounters with people, objects, data, and systems. Each interaction was recorded in a log detailing the time, location, participants, and dialogue accompanying the event. At the end of the day, I taped my reactions, responses, and questions about the day's events. The following day, an intensive interview with the shadowee was held in which I walked her, minute by minute, through the previous day's events. This generated the second type of data—what is generally called contextualizing data—expected to yield the intentions, beliefs, assumptions, and values that comprise the participants' sense making around observed behavior (Alderfer & Brown, 1972; Spradley, 1979). In the interview, I asked an open-ended question for each interaction, such as, "What was this about?" or "What was going on here?" After the engineers got over their initial surprise at the level of detail in my notes, they grew quite comfortable with this contextualizing procedure, and I would just have to mention an incident with an uplift indicating a question, such as, "Then Dave came by?" and they would fill in the details.

These data were transcribed, encoded, and sorted into categories using The Ethnograph, an ethnographic software program. A list of potential categories was generated based on the attributes of relational theory. This initial list changed as unused categories were discarded and new ones were added as they emerged from the data. The resulting categories were refined using an iterative process described by Glaser and Strauss (1967, p. 101) as a "constant comparative" method of qualitative analysis. This method entails continually revisiting the underlying principle of each category as new incidents are added in order to refine the principles and allow theoretical precepts to emerge. When the categories had been integrated to the point where there was little overlap between them, a roundtable discussion with participants was held in which these still preliminary categories (now numbering six) were shared and reactions invited (Bougon, 1983). The format for the roundtable discussion was unstructured and straightforward. I simply listed the categories with examples of each and asked for reactions after all six were described. Data from the roundtable discussion, which had been recorded and transcribed, were used to integrate the categories further, resulting in the four described in the "Findings" section. A name for each category was selected to reflect what had emerged as its unifying property.

For the poststructuralist analysis, a third type of data was required: a representation of the current definition of work in that particular organizational setting. As a high-technology engineering firm, the setting met the criterion of being a potential exemplar of the gendered power-knowledge structures generally accepted as underlying organizational discourse (Ferguson, 1984; McIlwee & Robinson, 1992). Three other members of the research team and I gathered data used to represent the manifestation of the definition of work in this setting, using the cultural diagnosis process described briefly above and in more detail in Bailyn et al. (1996) and Perlow (1997). Data-gathering techniques for this cultural diagnosis paralleled those suggested by Levinson, Spohn, and Molinari (1972) for collecting interpretative data for organizational diagnosis and were informed by Schein's description of the elements of organizational culture (1985). For example, interview questions focused on eliciting organizational narratives that would help us understand the sense-making frameworks people used to understand things such as the formal and informal reward systems, the attributes of "ideal" workers, the commonsense definition of success, and the perception of the most pressing business problems facing the company. Along with the observational data noted earlier, these interview data were analyzed to reveal the assumptions and beliefs driving the way work got done in this environment. When the findings from the diagnosis were fed back to the organization, there was widespread agreement that they were representative of the current work culture in that group. Additional data representing the commonsense definition of work as understood by the line-of-fault subjects themselves were obtained by analyzing the interview and roundtable transcripts to reveal the inconsistencies, contradictions, and unexamined dichotomies between the hegemonic definition of work they embodied as members of the system and the subversive stories their observed behavior told.

FINDINGS

The findings from these three sources of data are reported next. First, we examine the basic components of relational practice. Then we look at the way in which relational practice was brought into the dominant discourse, subjected to the truth rules of that discourse, and ultimately "got disappeared" as work and got constructed as something other than work.

Components of Relational Practice

Analysis of the data collected to answer the first research question revealed four categories of activities constituting relational practice:

Preserving: These are relational activities associated with *task*. This category includes activities intended to preserve the life and well-being of the project.

Mutual Empowering: These are relational activities associated with an "*other.*" This category includes activities intended to enable or empower others to achieve and contribute to the project.

Achieving: These are activities associated with *self*. This category includes relational activities intended to empower oneself to achieve goals and contribute to the program.

Creating Team: These are activities associated with building a *collective*. This category includes activities intended to construct the social reality of "team" by creating an environment in which positive outcomes of relational interactions can be realized.

Selected examples of each type of activity are used to capture the essence of relational practice in the engineers' own words.

PRESERVING. The first category, Preserving, had to do with maintaining the well-being of the project through activities intended to foster its growth or protect it from harm. It encompassed three types of behavior: shouldering, connecting, and rescuing.

Shouldering refers to picking up on tasks that were outside the technical definition of the job. Examples included things such as taking on lower-level tasks—for example, soldering a board themselves if the technician was busy on something else—as well as things like this engineer's description of coming in on a weekend to prevent what she considered substandard products from going out the door: "I just could not *believe* Marketing was going to let those prints go out the door— I mean, I showed them to Tony [the copy quality person] and he just shrugged like 'whatever' and I just said to myself 'no way' . . . so Sara and I? We came in on Saturday and redid them, because, I mean, it had to be done."

Shouldering also included scanning the environment for information that needed to be passed on and then stepping out of a strict definition of the job and taking the initiative to pass it along. For those who did it, shouldering behavior was undertaken with an attitude of "if I don't do it nobody will." They appeared to consider it an essential part of the job and were hard on others who refused to work this way. As one subject put it, "What's wrong with picking up a soldering iron? Nothing. Your hands aren't going to fall off."

Connecting activities were those meant to keep the project connected to the people and resources it needed. For example, this engineer describes how she took the initiative to make sure that people who supply valuable resources to the project but have no reporting relationship to their team feel appreciated and valuable: "It's just that because I was more sensitive to it than Ned [the manager]. Like, if someone didn't feel that it was their job? and I might have sensed that they were getting to the point that they were going to get hurt or feel that they were being taken advantage of? Then I've put myself in that role and I've just said to Ned, 'Maybe we should send so-and-so a thank you' or whatever."

Other examples included a manager who sent one of the team to talk with someone she thought had "ruffled feathers" and another who "translated" one coworker's technical jargon for the rest of the team so his input would be included and not dismissed by those who considered him irrelevant and incomprehensible.

Another type of Preserving had to do with *rescuing,* or calling attention to problems. For example, one engineer, in describing the purpose of a meeting she had attended, explained that she had identified a problem she thought was serious. She had convinced her boss and her boss's boss that it was a problem and had arranged for a meeting with another division. She explained:

> If I am just one person going over there to them saying, "Look, we've got this terrible problem," . . . but if we've got someone at a higher level like Mike who can communicate to them that it's a problem [pause]. I mean if it was just me saying it . . . I mean, otherwise, they might not think it really is [pause], but I could tell. I thought it was a really good meeting because you don't see them that wound up about problems

that often, you know? They would rather dust them under the rug and say, "Look, if it's just one occurrence . . ."

At the meeting she had taken a back seat, deferring to her boss and letting him explain her data. Her description of the meeting indicated that this taking a back seat was a conscious decision she made to give the problem visibility.

What differentiated Preserving from other categories of relational practice was the focus on task and the relational representation of this focus as one of protection, nurturing, and connecting. In this way, Preserving activities were similar to what Sara Ruddick (1989) calls "preservative love," one of the three practices underlying maternal thinking. The engineers who engaged in these activities replicated the dependency relationship of mother and child in their adoption of an attitude of selfless giving, motivated not by love but by an apparent sense of responsibility. Taking on this responsibility for the whole appeared to be part of what it meant to these engineers to be effective workers, and they clearly expected others to do the same, holding in disdain those who refused to care for the project in this way.

Another belief underlying Preserving activity and the notion that everyone should put the needs of the project ahead of individual issues such as status or hierarchy was that such action would be seen as a sign of competence and commitment. In other words, the indirect nature and apparent invisibility of these activities was assumed to be characteristic of their effectiveness. Thus, the engineer who sacrificed an opportunity for self-promotion and deferred to her boss in order to give a problem visibility described her action with pride, as evidence of her competence: because of her action, they were now "wound up" about the problem.

The final dimension of the belief system underlying this practice was evidenced by the engineers' willingness to put effort into maintaining relationships they deemed critical to the project's health and vitality. Whether it meant sending thank-you notes to show appreciation, sending a peacemaker to smooth ruffled feathers, or protecting the project from the consequences of severed relationships, these activities implied a belief that keeping relationships in good working order was an important aspect of ensuring the life and well-being of the overall project.

Preserving required a certain set of skills, including the ability to think contextually, the ability to anticipate consequences, and the ability to sense the emotional context of situations in order to recognize and take action when, for example, someone "might be feeling like they're getting taken advantage of."

MUTUAL EMPOWERING. The second type of relational practice, Mutual Empowering, refers to behavior intended to enable others' achievement and contribution to the project. Although the term *empower* is used to describe this category, the behaviors included are quite different from those typically associated with an empowered worker in the management literature. The organizational definition of an empowered worker is one who has the information and authority to make decisions, structure and prioritize tasks, or improve process (Senge, 1990). The relational practice described here has less to do with authority and decision making and more to do with the act of enabling, or contributing to, the development of another. Nonetheless, the term *empower* with the modifier *mutual* was chosen to reflect the fact that the behavior in this category was intended to enhance others' power and was mutual in that both parties were expected to benefit.

The first practice associated with this type of empowering was *empathic teaching*—a way of teaching that took the learner's intellectual or emotional reality into account and focused on the other (What does she or he need to hear?) rather than on self (What would I like to say?). As one engineer said when explaining why she always talks someone through the process while she is fixing a computer file: "Look, the whole point is so they can do it without you next time, right?" Sometimes empathic teaching meant simplifying the information intellectually, like giving an everyday example of a statistical concept, and sometimes it meant modifying the emotional context of a teaching interaction. As one engineer put it, "Well, the way I work with Frank is a little different. You don't want to bruise any egos. I wanted Frank to feel comfortable, so that's why I sat down next to him and worked through stuff with him. . . . It's just a style thing."

This concern with minimizing the status difference inherent in a teaching interaction sometimes took the form of bracketing information with phrases like, "One of the things that might help . . ." or, "There may be lots of ways to do this but what I like to do is . . ." Often this collaborative language was marked by a self-deprecating tone that the engineers indicated they used intentionally because, as one noted, "you have to be careful not to intimidate." However, it appeared that making others feel comfortable was only part of the motivation to minimize the expert role. The other goal was to communicate an openness to learning and hearing other points of view. As another subject describes, "It sets my own learning and I always come away with something new." Implicit in this approach was an expectation that they, as teachers, were colearners in these enabling interactions.

The second practice associated with empowering was *protective connecting,* a practice that insulated people from their own lack of relational skill. For example, when the boss asked a coworker a question and he replied "That's not our job anymore; go ask Katie," the engineer I was observing jumped in and answered the question. The next day when I asked her about this incident, she explained:

> Oh, that was part of the problem I was explaining before . . . that we wanted that project and we lost it? [Our boss] lost it to that other group. So that was Sam using a little sarcasm there saying, "Hey, you guys; you didn't fight enough for it, so now you go talk to Katie about it. She's in charge of it." So that was the little zinger. But I could tell by Carl's voice that he was getting upset and Sam sometimes, like, grrrr [grinding noise], twists the knife in harder and harder. So I just jumped in and answered the question. Sam does that . . . if he really doesn't want to help you, he won't help you, END OF STORY. So I'm the middleman who goes, "Okay, this is the reason . . ." [pause] Sort of like a tension breaker, solving two problems at once I guess.

In summary, Mutual Empowering activities were those that enabled others to produce, achieve, and accomplish work-related goals and objectives. They were characterized by a willingness to put effort into what Cato Wadel (1979) calls embedded outcomes: outcomes embedded in other people, such as increased competence, increased self-confidence, or increased knowledge. What differentiated these activities from other types of relational practice was this focus on empowering an "other." Unlike the previous theme of Preserving, which is analogous to the dependency relationship in a mother-child model, this theme of empowering draws on a model of relational interaction characterized by interdependence and more fluid power relations. Mutual Empowering behavior appeared to be rooted in the belief not only that outcomes embedded in others were worth working for, but that everyone needs and should be able to expect this kind of help. As one subject described, "But everyone should feel like that. Because if everyone knew everything, we all wouldn't be here, you know? We all know something other people don't know, so it shouldn't be a big deal. . . . People should realize that . . . but some people don't, though."

Thus, Mutual Empowering appears to be based on a concept of power and expertise that is fluid, where dependence on others is assumed to be a natural but temporary state. Implicit is an expectation that others should adopt this same attitude and be willing to both give and receive help and that there are benefits to be gained in each role. This notion of mutuality was evident in the way the engineers spoke of enabling activities not as altruism, but as something that enhanced their own self-esteem and self-efficacy. In fact, it was part of what it meant to be good at a job: "I know I'm doing a good job when people think of me when they have a problem. I've succeeded when people think of me as someone who is (1) competent and (2) someone who will help. Most people around here only care about the first thing—competence—they don't care if they are seen as approachable. I do."

The people who enacted Mutual Empowering evidenced an ability to operate in an environment of fluid expertise, where power or expertise (or both) shifts from one party to the other, not only over time but in the course of one interaction. This required two sets of skills. One was a skill in empowering others: an ability to share—in some instances, even customizing—one's own reality, skill, knowledge, and other characteristics in ways that made it accessible to others. The other was skill in being empowered: an ability and willingness to step away from the expert role and minimize status differences in order to learn from or be influenced by the other.

ACHIEVING. The third type of relational practice, Achieving, refers to using relational skills to enhance one's own professional growth and effectiveness. It entailed three types of activities: reconnecting, reflecting, and relational asking. *Reconnecting* had to do with repairing potential or perceived breaks in working relationships. Those who engaged in this practice did things such as following up with someone they had disagreed with in a meeting or going out of their way to track someone down whose feelings they had hurt. What was striking about these activities was the distress and sense of urgency to "make things right" that accompanied many of these reconnections.

Reflecting, the second type of Achieving behavior, had to do with paying attention to the emotional overlay of situations in order to understand what was happening and what the most effective response should be. Sometimes this meant accessing one's own feelings as a source of data. For example, one engineer used "feeling bad" to understand the dynamics of getting recognized at meetings.

> I have been thinking about this a lot lately. This isn't true confessions but I came to a realization that I was being rude in meetings . . . a LOT . . . and I didn't like it because I didn't feel good. And I was pondering, Why am I doing that? Because it doesn't feel good, but I am still doing it. So there is something else rewarding me. . . . And it was the getting noticed. It was the easiest, fastest, simplest way to get noticed. And once you are noticed, you get heard. But since it doesn't feel good, I really want to find a different way that is still effective.

Sometimes reflecting meant assessing others' emotional contexts and modifying one's own behavior in response. For example, as we were sitting in the lab, an engineer came in and demanded, in an angry voice, to know what was going on. The engineer I was shadowing gave him some information about the problem she was working on and he turned and left. The next day she talked about the incident this way:

> Well, I told him about the problem because I think he feels a little territorial about it. He thinks of the lab as his area. Also, the meeting I have with him later is to get information from him that [our boss] wants me to document because she wants it documented in my style. Technically, this is his job, so I don't think he feels real comfortable with that, so he may be a little threatened and that may have something to do with his coming in here now and wanting to know.

This explanation indicates that her ability to understand how he might be feeling motivated her to share the information rather than withhold it. The sharing of the information appears to have been an intentional strategy to enhance her own effectiveness by increasing the chance that the meeting they have later in the day will go smoothly.

The third type of Achieving had to do with asking for help in a way that made it likely one would get the help needed. This *relational asking* called forth responsiveness in others. One engineer described it this way: "A lot of people around here will say something like: 'Katie, I'm in a position of leadership over you, and you have to do this for me. Make these files.' And I tend to like to say, 'Katie, can you show me how to do one of these?'"

It was not just the way of asking for help that was important; it was also the kind of help sought. As another subject said, "I know people don't mind helping me, because they know I'll share it with others in my group, so it's not like everyone will be coming to them." She contrasted her type of "empowering asking" with people who asked for help in an exploitative way. In noting why she refused to help someone who asked her to do a mundane part of his job, she commented, "He always does this. This is not real work for me because it's something he *could* do. I'm not adding any expertise to doing that part of it."

In summary, Achieving activities were those in which engineers used relational skills to enhance their own achievement. It was this focus on self, and the use of relational skills to strategize their own effectiveness, that differentiated Achieving from other categories of relational practice. Implicit in these activities was the belief that not just personal but professional growth is rooted in connection and that the long-term benefits of maintaining a relationship are worth the short-term costs. Relational theory suggests that the urgency to prevent or mend disruption is indicative of a belief that severed relationships have potentially negative effects that should be avoided (Brown & Gilligan, 1992; Jordan, Kaplan, et al., 1991).

Another belief had to do with the role of emotion. Spending time and effort reflecting on the emotional complexity of situations indicates a belief that emotions are an important source of information about oneself and about situations. Using these data enabled the engineers who engaged in this practice to develop what they perceived as more effective strategies in dealing with situations. Finally, the practice of relational asking implies a belief in a particular definition of interdependence, where asking for help is not a sign of weakness but an invitation to empower. The ability to differentiate it from other forms of asking suggests that this practice was a conscious decision, a strategy designed to increase the likelihood they would get the empowering outcome they sought.

In terms of skills, Achieving behavior required an ability to access emotional data and skill in understanding the complexity of these data. In addition, it required an ability to stay with contradictory information—feeling good about getting recognized, feeling bad about how it was done—so that a new strategy might evolve. Thus, it required an ability to blend thinking, feeling, and action in a way that bridged the rational-emotional divide.

CREATING TEAM. The relational practice of Creating Team had to do with working to create the background conditions in which group life can flourish. As differentiated from activities intended to create a particular team, these activities had less to do with managing group process (such as setting boundaries and defining who is "in" or "out" of the group defining task) and more to do with creating the experience of team. In other words, the activities in this category were those intended not to enhance one's personal relationships or to enable others (although they might have those effects), but to create the background conditions in which group life could flourish.

Creating Team entailed two types of activities: attending to the individual and attending to the collective. The first, attending to the individual, was expressed through practices that acknowledged others' unique preferences, problems, feelings, and circumstances. This included sending verbal and nonverbal messages of affirmation such as maintaining eye contact when others were talking and nodding, smiling, or making encouraging comments like, "Right," "Good point," "Okay, good" or even just "Yeah" and "Uh-huh." Pamela Fishman (1978) notes that this type of response during conversation is the maintenance work of conversational interaction and demonstrates an appreciation of and involvement with the speaker. Each of the engineers evidenced behavior of this sort in abundance.

Other ways of responding were associated with empathic responses to other's feelings, preferences, or particular circumstances. For example, this engineer, in explaining why she took time to listen to an older coworker "ramble about the good old days," goes on to say:

> The other thing is, because men joke around so much with each other, when a man does have something he wants to talk about, he won't go to another man . . . they'll go to a woman. I've had men who I know don't even like me use me to vent about really personal things. Like this one guy—I know he doesn't like me and I don't like him much— started to talk about the fertility problems he and his wife were having. I mean that's heavy stuff. And I've talked to several women who say that men come in and sit down and talk to them. You don't really have to say anything, just listen. They just want someone who will listen and not joke around about it. I feel bad when others are feeling bad or having a hard time, and I know it's not going to kill me to spend some time with them. And also, who else are they going to go

to? It doesn't cost me anything, really, just to listen. But sometimes it just feels like a big responsibility because even if you are not really in the mood, you HAVE to do it. I mean, if they are coming to you, it must be pretty bad, and where else can they go?

Clearly, she felt that this type of response was indeed work. At times it "just feels like a big responsibility," and she responded empathically even though she was fully aware that "he doesn't like me and I don't like him much." Nonetheless, she took it on herself to respond to him in a way that would validate and acknowledge his feelings. Rather than simple knee-jerk reactions, empathic responses such as this appeared to be motivated by a desire to create a certain kind of environment in the workplace. As another said, "The more team-spirited people are more effective in what they're doing. And I equate being conscious of other people's feelings with working in a team spirit. I think people are much more effective this way."

Relational theory supports this view and suggests that individuals who feel understood, accepted, appreciated, or "heard" are more likely to extend that same acceptance to others, leading to a kind of group life characterized by what Miller (1986b) calls a "zest" for interaction and connection.

Attending to the collective, the second type of behavior in this category, entailed creating conditions among people in order to create an environment that would foster collaboration and cooperation. Sometimes this meant creating the reality of interdependence by inventing structures that supported collaboration, such as one engineer who described creating a "liaison position" on her team. More commonly, it meant smoothing relationships between people or using collaborative rather than confrontational language in expressing ideas in a meeting—for example, saying things like, "What I like about Dave's idea is . . ." and then going on to add to it.

In summary, Creating Team appears to be characterized by a certain set of beliefs and assumptions about group life. First is the belief that individuals have a right to be noticed and that part of what it means to be a good coworker is to do the noticing. Second is a belief that team spirit and achievement depend on paying attention to others' feelings and preferences and that the intangible outcomes that result from these efforts—outcomes embedded in other people and in social relations—are things worth working for. Third, it was a practice that appears to be rooted in the assumption that a collective understanding of problems or situations, where others' ideas are fully explored and built on, is a good thing; that is, it is something that will enhance organizational effectiveness and lead to better decisions. It was this focus on creating a collective that distinguishes this category of activities from other types of Relational Practice.

In terms of skills, the behavior in this category required an ability to respond empathically to others and an ability to understand the emotional context in which they operated. In addition, it required a type of cognitive complexity not dependent on affect, one similar to what Irene Stiver (1991) calls "response/ability": the capacity to freely and wholeheartedly engage with another's subjectivity (that is, drawing out others' ideas), being able to acknowledge and affirm that reality while maintaining and being in touch with one's own to the extent that one could add to those ideas and create something new.

SUMMARY. The four types of relational practice are summarized in Table 5.2.

It should be remembered that the goal of this first phase of the analysis was to tell a subversive story by reading organizational text to reveal those practices that met a particular set of truth rules, those residing in relational theory. Thus, the answer to the first research question is intentionally selective. It focuses only on behaviors motivated by a belief in the preeminence of connection and highlights the relational skills required to enact them, such as empathy, mutuality, reciprocity, and a sensitivity to emotional contexts. In addition, it purposefully highlights the strategic intentions of the behavior, that is, the way in which it was motivated by a belief that operating in a context of connection was more effective, better for the project, and better for getting the job done. In describing the behavior from this relational perspective, the first phase of the analysis tells the story of relational practice as if it is the only plausible interpretation of the behavior and as if no tension exists between it and the current definition of work in organizational discourse.

Gender, Power, and "Getting Disappeared"

This brings us to the second part of the analysis. As noted earlier, a relational belief system—in which relational interactions are assumed to be sites of growth, achievement, and professional effectiveness—stands in sharp contrast to traditional organizational norms and beliefs about

Preserving
- Shouldering
   "Do whatever it takes"
   Scanning
- Connecting
   Preventive connecting
   Maintenance connecting
- Rescuing

Mutual Empowering
- Empathic teaching
   Modifying information
      Responding to emotional
      Responding to intellectual
- Protective connecting

Achieving
- Reconnecting
- Reflecting
   Self-reflection
   Reflecting on emotional context
- Relational asking

Creating Team
- Attending to individuals
   Responding/respecting
   Empathic listening
   Responding to preferences
- Attending to the collective
   Smoothing
   Envisioning and creating reality of interdependence

Table 5.2. Four Types of Relational Practice.

competence, effectiveness, and organizational success. The second stage of the analysis addresses the second research question of what happens to this relationally motivated behavior when it is practiced in an environment that is hostile to its basic assumptions. It explores the mechanisms by which relational practice is brought into organizational discourse and subjected to the truth rules of that discourse.

The poststructuralist framing of this study argues that all public sphere activity is implicitly subjected to general truth rules about the characteristics of real work, rules that are a reflection of the instrumental narrative underlying this sphere. Within this general framework in which all organizations reflect the instrumental values of rationality, abstraction, and linearity, a high-technology environment was intentionally selected as the research site (as opposed to, for example, a hospital, school, or social service agency) because it was assumed to be an exemplar of this power-knowledge structure. The cultural diagnosis conducted prior to the shadowing indicated that this was indeed the case (Bailyn et al., 1996; Perlow, 1997). This workplace was found to be similar to other environments in which design engineering is highly valued (McIlwee & Robinson, 1992). For example, an analysis of the organizational narratives gathered in the cultural diagnosis about the definition of success, the attributes of the ideal engineer, and the perception about what types of behaviors were likely to lead to promotions revealed that this was a work environment where autonomy, self-promotion, and individual heroics were highly prized, an environment where time was a surrogate for commitment and competence was measured by short-term results. Not only was technical competence highly valued and seen as the route to organizational power, but self-promotion was considered a display of competence. "Real" work was consistently defined as "solving problems," and engineers who moved on to supervisory positions even spoke of "no longer having a job" because all they did now was help other people do their work. It was a culture in which the definition of outcome was clear: outcomes were tangible, measurable, and concrete. In fact, in this environment, if something was not quantifiable, it was assumed to be of no consequence and often was eliminated as a variable.

When behavior motivated by a relational belief system (model of growth-in-connection) was brought into this organizational discourse, it "got disappeared" as work because by its very nature, it violated many of the truth rules mentioned above. By rereading the textual representation of work collected in the shadowing, interviewing, and roundtable discussion in order to surface inherent inconsistencies, contradictions, and dilemmas in the text, by observing and listening closely to how others responded to those who enacted relational practice, and by noting my own reactions to observing these activities, it was possible to identify the process by which relational practice "got disappeared" in this organizational setting. The following sections detail the disappearing of each relational practice.

DISAPPEARING PRESERVING. The practice of Preserving was rooted in a belief system that privileged context and connection. As such, it violated many of the truth rules in this engineering culture based on individualism and the hierarchical separation of specialization and connecting functions. For example, the engineer who attempted to pass information across functions by telling her manager that marketing would be sending out substandard prints was met with a shrug and a dismissive wave of the hand. The manager did not thank her for what she had done or give any verbal or nonverbal affirmation that this was an appreciated or expected piece of work. The nonverbal message appeared to be, "That's not your job; don't worry about it." In this culture of specialization, the willingness to put effort into taking responsibility for the whole seemed to mystify this manager, who appeared to be operating from a different belief system about what it means to be an effective worker. Another engineer who called her boss to warn of a possible duplication of effort was met with a similar response, one that seemed to suggest that such a warning was evidence of nitpicking or excessive devotion to detail.

Other types of Preserving were disappeared in a similar fashion. For example, being quietly competent or sacrificing an opportunity for self-promotion for the sake of the project violated some basic norms of behavior in this work culture, where competence was measured by an ability to self-promote, talk technical, and associate oneself with high-visibility problems. In fact, I found that even I, as an observer who was making an effort to view the engineers' behavior through a relational lens, "disappeared" this type of competence and constructed it as a personal aberration. When I observed the event described earlier of an engineer who took a back seat in a meeting and let her boss talk about her data, I at first coded this as evidence of her fear of power and success and wrote the word *meek* in the margins of my notes. I made sense of her behavior as some sort of personal aberration, assuming that she was uncomfortable with self-promotion or with being seen as an expert. It was not until later, as she spoke of the incident with pride and explained to me that it was an intentional strategy on her part to give the problem increased visibility and make sure it was taken seriously, that I began to realize that her behavior at that meeting could be understood differently and that I had been "disappearing" her work by labeling the behavior not only as inappropriate to the workplace and but also as evidence of her personal inadequacy.

DISAPPEARING MUTUAL EMPOWERING. The practice of Mutual Empowering also violated some truth rules in the dominant discourse that got it "disappeared" as work and constructed as something other than work. In a culture of independence and self-promotion, where individual achievement is what is prized, and competition means beating the other person out so you finish on top, voluntarily helping others achieve was puzzling behavior. Enacting a relational belief system in which interdependence is a natural state and enabling others is a source of self-esteem so violated professional norms that it seemed that the only way to make sense of the behavior was to attribute it to either powerlessness or naiveté. As one of the subjects notes: "If you try to nurture around here, they just don't get it. They don't understand that is what you are doing. They see it as a weakness and they use it against you. They don't see that you are doing it consciously . . . they think you have missed something or that they've gotten something over on you. So if you try to be nice, you end up doing other people's work."

Her experience suggests that in this environment, anyone who puts effort into achieving outcomes that are embedded in others apparently gets constructed not as someone working in a way that has the potential to enhance organizational learning and effectiveness, but rather as weak, naive, or exploitable. In her attempt to find organizationally strong language to represent what she is trying to do, she rejected the negative attribution of *weakness*. However, the more positive words she chose to describe the behavior—*nurture, being nice*—actually may have disappeared the work even more powerfully, as they tend to de-skill the practice, making it seem more like evidence of a personal attribute than conscious, intentional action.

She was not alone in trying to find organizationally strong language to describe enabling activity. Consider, for example, what this engineer said: "I've succeeded when people think of me as someone who is (1) competent and (2) someone who will help. Most people around here only care about the first thing—competence—they don't care if they are seen as approachable. I do."

It is clear that she is trying to describe an expanded definition of competence that includes a willingness and an ability to share and empower others. Having no organizationally strong language readily available to her to describe this kind of outcome—an outcome that would be embedded in another person—as evidence of competence, she uses *approachability* and *help*, words that are not nearly as strong and leave the definition of competence unchallenged. Ironically, her struggle with language actually ends up reinforcing the notion that enabling others is not part of competence but something separate.

Another subject described how taking several hours from her day to help someone from another unit gave her conflicting feelings. On the one hand, she felt proud that she had helped him "not reinvent the wheel," something "we should do more of around here." On the other, she felt that maybe she was naive to have helped and had been "taken down the garden path." She recognized that in this culture of individualism, the help she gave him was probably going to get disappeared from his achievement. As she said, "I don't have any trust that I am going to get anything back for that. He is going to look real good . . . and I don't think he should look as good as he is going to look!"

Interestingly, while many of the engineers struggled to enact and articulate a different definition of helping, they themselves often "disappeared" this work when it was done by others. For example, one subject spoke disparagingly of a contract employee in marketing as "O'Connor's little errand boy" because he did support work for that group. The implication was that as a contract employee, he had no power and therefore was reduced to being an errand boy. As if the message in that might not be clear enough, she added the adjective *little* to show what stature such a position confers.

DISAPPEARING ACHIEVING. In this engineering culture, where models of growth and achievement were based on individuation, independence, and autonomy, those who violated these truth rules by seeking growth-in-connection stood outside the discourse on achievement. As the following quotation indicates, subjects who put effort into connecting, reconnecting, and maintaining relationships in the service of their own achievement felt themselves to be understood as motivated by a need to be liked, that is, as seeking not growth but affection. As this subject indicates, it was difficult to articulate the possibility that achievement needs might be met through relational means. As she tries to transcend the achievement-affiliation dichotomy, she ends up going around in circles:

> So if I do get into a situation that is confrontational, not angry necessarily but even if we're just being very direct with each other and this person wants to do it one way and I want to do it another way, I'd be concentrating more on [pause, then little laugh] *winning* than on how they felt about it. I gave up a long time ago caring about how they felt about it, other than if how they feel about it is going to get in the way of getting it done. But if I don't perceive that their feelings are going to get in the way, then I kind of don't notice anymore [laugh]. So that's the only reason why I'm paying attention to their feelings. It isn't that I care

that much about their feelings. It's because if they feel threatened enough, I won't make any progress and not because [pause]. If I thought I'd win in spite of that, it wouldn't bother me at all. So it isn't that I'm terribly worried about whether the guys that I work with like me. I worry a lot about whether they respect me. *I don't really care if they like me or not* [emphasis added]. [laugh; pause] . . . I happen to think that usually those kind of end up going together, though. If you respect someone, you usually end up liking them, too . . . at the end of it all.

The contradictions and inconsistencies in this quotation give a good sense of the disappearing dynamic that occurs when relational practice is brought into the organizational discourse on work. She struggles to find language to represent her experience and is careful to distance herself from attributions of inappropriate motivation: she would be more concerned about winning, she wants me to know, than she would about someone's feelings. But then she gets entangled as she tries to describe her experience that these two things are not dichotomous. If feelings are going to get in the way of success, then of course she is concerned about them. If feelings were not real, that is, if she accepted the conventional wisdom that feelings are irrelevant to organizational phenomenon, she would not care about them at all because they would not stand in the way of winning. But she wants to make it clear that the reason she is concerned about feelings is not that she wants to be liked. She understands that this would be the "normal" attribution and wants to make sure I do not make it regarding her. So she falls back again into the dichotomy: she does not care if they like her as long as they respect her. Any language available to her to describe worrying about the effect of confrontation on the relationship, or to describe the possibility that behavior that gets her liked might also make her more effective, would risk the attribution of "needing to be liked," an attribution that would taint her as incompetent. Not having the organizational language to describe such a possibility *and* still be considered competent, she chooses to represent herself as competent. This reinforces rather than challenges the dichotomy, but it serves the purpose of making it clear that she is savvy enough to understand the difference between being liked and being respected. However, after giving me the party line, she recognizes the inadequacy of what she has said in trying to capture her experience so, after a slight pause and a little laugh, she undermines this dichotomous thinking: she happens to believe these two things go together—that being liked and being respected are not mutually exclusive.

Others went through similar verbal gymnastics to simultaneously reinforce and resist dominant sense-making schema about appropriate ways of working. For example, this engineer gives voice to the inviolate nature of the public-private split, carefully aligning herself with normative behavior: "I was talking to this guy the other day about it. And I said that you really have to be two totally different people: a businessperson who is really direct and then at home a different personality. So at home, sometimes I just withdraw, and they don't understand. And he said, 'Would you write that down and send it to my wife?' [laughs]."

Then, after a pause, she continued, subtly undermining this public-private dichotomy by offering an alternative that challenged it: "But really, I don't think . . . I think confrontation doesn't really work that well in the business place. Like all that women's lib stuff about demanding what you need? It doesn't work that way."

DISAPPEARING CREATING TEAM. The practice of Creating Team "got disappeared" through a similar process. Despite some organizational rhetoric about teamwork and collaboration, this was an environment in which individual heroism was the valued currency. Thus, it was understandably difficult to articulate or understand the motivation to engage in activity intended to create the conditions in which the benefits of group life could flourish. For example, this engineer has difficulty trying to describe her effort to use collaborative language to create an environment where ideas can be explored rather than attacked. She notes that if she uses this approach, rather than being seen as effective, she and her ideas disappear. In the roundtable discussion, she described this disappearing so vividly that the group laughs in recognition:

I think sometimes if you're in a meeting, and somebody states an idea. If I stand up and I say, "That's totally inappropriate, that's just plain stupid, this is what we should do" or if I stand up and say, "Well, that's a really good idea but another way of looking at it is this . . ." The person who stood up and was abusive about it is the person that people are going to remember as having come up with that idea later, when it's time to evaluate people. [This last sentence is said quite forcefully, and then after a slight pause and in a softer, more tentative voice she adds:] I think, lots of times [back to a more forceful tone, she continues] because even though it's a bad impression, you've made an impression. The other person, in being polite and a little self-effacing, has sort of melted into the background. . . . Sometimes if you're nice you'll say [pause]. I might be in a meeting and somebody will come up with an idea and I'll say, "Well, that's a really good idea, but I looked at it this way and this is what I came up with." And then [after you give your idea], they'll say, "Well, anyways . . ." [general laughter]. And because you haven't like stomped on them, *you're not even in the room* [emphasis in original].

What she recognizes is that if there is only one right way and discovering it makes her the winner, then building on others' ideas is likely to be considered inappropriate, or a sign that she has nothing new to add. Again, the private sphere language she uses to describe the behavior—*nice, polite, self-effacing*—tends to deskill and devalue it. This contributes to its near invisibility as a challenge to confrontational norms. Not having organizationally strong language readily available to describe it, she uses words that strongly associate it with femininity (*polite, nice*) and powerlessness (*self-effacing*). This belies her belief in it as a strategy that could make visible the reality of team, by, for example, creating a shared solution to a problem that transcends any one individual's ideas. This relational belief is buried in all the other sense-making schema vying for attention here:

> I see it as avoiding conflict. Because at least for me personally, I'm not somebody who feels very comfortable negotiating in an atmosphere of conflict. *I like to talk about things, explain why I think something, hear about what the other person thinks about something* [emphasis added]. But I know that there are some people that . . . they like to negotiate in a state of conflict, with voices raised, "That's NOT a good idea" instead of, "Why do you think that's a good idea?" So if I can keep it from ever getting elevated to that, then I can be working in an atmosphere that is more comfortable for me. I don't like yelling and screaming and accusations and the rest of that stuff.

SUMMARY: DISAPPEARING DYNAMIC. This description of the way in which the different types of relational practice were brought into the discourse suggests that there was a dynamic process in operation in which relational practice "got disappeared" as work and got constructed as something other than work. There were three specific aspects of this process evident in the data. The first had to do with the misattribution of the intention underlying relational practice, whereby it was seen as having been motivated not by a desire to work more effectively but by some sort of personal idiosyncrasy or trait. These included negative characteristics such as naiveté, powerlessness, weakness, and emotional need, as well as more positive attributions such as thoughtfulness, personal style, or being nice. What got disappeared in this construction of relational practice as personal aberration was the intentional strategy to enact a relational model of growth, achievement, and effectiveness as an alternative way of working.

It should be noted again that no claim is being made here about which interpretation of the behavior is more "true." Was the engineer who alerted her manager to the substandard prints being responsible or a nitpicking busybody? Was the engineer who helped someone from another unit a hero or a chump? Was the strategic intention to enhance effectiveness through relational practice actually realized? This study did not gather data that could answer these questions. Indeed, from the poststructuralist perspective of the study, these questions are beside the point. The interesting finding here is that the misattribution of motive tainted the behavior as inappropriate, thereby silencing the challenge that relational practice might have presented to organizational assumptions about achievement, success, and effectiveness. In poststructuralist terms, it filled in the discursive space that might have been created by acknowledging a different definition of work based on a model of growth-in-connection, thereby truncating the possibility of theorizing or envisioning alternative, relational strategies for success.

The second aspect of the disappearing dynamic had to do with the lack of organizationally strong language to represent this type of behavior as work. Many of the words the engineers used to describe relational practice (*helping, nurturing, nice, polite*) tended to associate it with the private sphere and femininity. This association gendered the behavior, diminishing its organizational relevance. At the same time, organizationally acceptable words that would have captured the unique belief system underlying this behavior—words like *outcome* and *competence*—had already been defined in this organizational discourse in ways that implicitly excluded relational aspects of work. Thus, the engineers seemed to have no way of describing the output of some relational activity as an achievement in its own right because, for example, outcomes embedded in people did not fit the organization definition of outcome and could not be claimed as "real work." As one of the engineers noted, "I don't do a lot of real work now. I do a lot of helping people understand what the problem is, *helping people believe they can do something on their own* [emphasis added]." In the same vein, the word *competence* could be used to describe only half of what made another engineer feel good about herself as a worker. She had to describe the other half as "approachability" even though it was clear that helping others was part of what defined competence in her mind.

The third aspect of the disappearing dynamic had to do with the social construction of gender. It was different from the first two aspects of "getting disappeared" because it had to do with how this way of working got conflated with images of femininity and motherhood. Thus, the first two mechanisms of disappearing—being labeled inappropriate and not having the language to describe these things as work—would perhaps operate on all who worked this way, regardless of gender. But when women enacted relational practice, something else happened. Because of gender roles, the female engineers felt they were expected to act relationally, to be soft, feminine, helpful, good listeners. In fact they did not seem to believe they had the option of acting any other way. As one said, "I try swearing, but I feel so stupid!" Another described what happened when she tried using confrontation to make a point:

> People notice that you said it, and it definitely gets the point on the table. But it certainly isn't good for your long-term relationships with that person. Especially, I think, if it comes from a woman to a man. I think that another man could do that, could say the exact same words, the exact same tone, and after the meeting it would just be over [pause]. I don't think it would be over if one of those players was a woman, even if it was over for the woman. I don't think it would be over for the man.

The conflation of gender expectations with relational practice was a powerful way of disappearing the motivation behind the behavior. It was difficult to articulate a relational way of working as an intentional choice when they sensed that they did not have a choice. As a result, the engineers often contradicted themselves or got hopelessly confused as they tried to capture the experience that they simultaneously resented being forced to use relational strategies *and* they believed these strategies were more effective.

Even more problematic for these line-of-fault workers in female bodies was that when they tried to enact certain elements of relational practice, such as Mutual Empowering, a practice characterized by mutuality and an expectation of reciprocity, they often were misinterpreted as enacting mothering, a practice characterized by selfless giving and little expectation of reciprocity. That is, they got responded to as women, not as coworkers. While they might have been willing to "do whatever it takes" to preserve the life and well-being of an inanimate object such as the project (with no expectation of reciprocal attention), it was clear they were not willing to be cast in this role permanently in their relationships with others.

For example, several of the engineers described being asked routinely to do support tasks by male engineers, things like copying, delivering papers to another office, or packing boxes. When they began to feel the lack of reciprocity and recognized that they were being taken advantage of, they would try to set some boundary around how much or what kind of help they were willing to give. As one said, "I mean really . . . you can't always give somebody your work. It's okay to do it once in awhile; that is not a problem. But you can't *always* do that." When she tried to limit her helping, however, she described being (jokingly) called things like "Tarantula Lady" or "Queen Bee." Getting called names for not being willing to help limitlessly makes visible the expectation that she, as a woman, should embrace this kind of helping behavior and do it willingly and gladly, with no expectation of reciprocity. To set limits, qualify, or differentiate among different types of help one was willing to give was to be called not unhelpful, but unfeminine, poisonous, arrogant.

Negative experiences such as this appeared to overwhelm the engineers' belief in this as an alternative way of working. Because they recognized the career implications of being exploited or seen as naive, in the roundtable they ended up simultaneously touting the value of this way of working and cautioning themselves and others not to do too much of it. As one said, "Although it might be good for the project, if you do it, you'll end up being a gopher your whole life."

In summary, it appears that these three aspects of the disappearing dynamic operated in concert, such that activity springing from a relational belief system "got disappeared" as relational practice (something new) and got constructed as something familiar (personal style, a natural expression of gender, private sphere behavior inappropriate to the public sphere, or something else). This set in motion a misunderstanding of the motivation underlying the behavior that silenced its potential challenge to the dominant organizational discourse on work. Thus, the disappearing dynamic was a sort of self-reinforcing cycle in which the behavior and its potential benefits were absorbed by the system, but the system itself was not challenged. The female engineers themselves were caught up in this cycle, wanting to work differently, unwittingly colluding in the "disappearing" of the behavior as work in the way they talked about it, cautioning each other about the negative effects of working this way but yet apparently unwilling to give up trying to enact this different, more relational way of working.

BROADER IMPLICATIONS

Discussing these findings and their broader implications presents a challenge. Although this was not framed as a sex differences study, the findings have compelling gender implications that raise sex differences questions. Readers can be forgiven for wondering what the male experience of these issues might be and wishing there were data to illuminate it. However, all the customary cautions about sample size and composition and the limits of generalizability to other populations and work environments apply here. Certainly it should be noted that, although tempting, it would be unwise as well as unwarranted to draw essentialist conclusions about men and women based on these findings. Rather, conclusions and implications must be drawn within the theoretical context and goals of the study, which were twofold. The first goal was to document the existence of a way of working in the public sphere that springs from a relational model of growth and development, a model conceptualized as marginal to public sphere thinking because of its association with the feminine. The second was to explore and explicate the power-knowledge forces acting to silence any challenge to the status quo that might be contained in this alternative way of working.

Within this theoretical context, there are a few interesting points for discussion. The first, which is related to the first goal of the study, has to do with the existence and detailing of relational practice as work. Although the findings cannot support a claim that relational practice exists and gets disappeared in all organizational settings, they certainly suggest that looking for relational practices—even in settings as unlikely as this engineering environment—is likely to yield expanded understandings of traditional organizational concepts. Thus, one contribution this study makes is that it identifies the extent of the gap in our knowledge about relational aspects of work and highlights the need to develop expanded models of organizational effectiveness and a new language of relational competence. It invites exploratory research that extends and further typologizes relational activity as work, making it an object of study rather than a taken-for-granted aspect of interpersonal relationships or process. For example, the findings suggest that the notion of helping in organizational settings may be a more complex concept than is generally accepted. These engineers clearly differentiated among types of helping interactions and, in the same vein, were able to categorize ways of asking, ways of teaching, and ways of encouraging collaboration. The variety of relational activity apparent even in this limited study suggests that the one-sided models of relational interactions currently used to understand these phenomena in the workplace (see, for example, Cammock, Nilakant, & Dakin, 1995) need to be expanded.

Exploring organizational phenomena from a relational, two-sided, or interdependent perspective could yield not only theoretical but also practical results. Take, for example, the concept of organizational learning. Adopting a two-sided focus to this concept has the potential to expand our understanding of the conditions that promote organizational learning by calling attention to the largely invisible task of continuous teaching. Conceptualizing workers not only as continuous learners but also as continuous teachers might raise some interesting questions for organizations to consider—for example: What are the conditions that promote, encourage, or support routine, continuous knowledge transfer within and across functional boundaries? What are the conditions that discourage or disappear this behavior? How might formal and informal reward systems need to change to promote both sides of relational interactions that lead to organizational learning? Expanding research on communities of practice (Seely-Brown & Duguid, 1991), knowledge workers (Nonaka, 1994), and multifunctional teams (Lipnack & Stamps, 1993; Slater, 1994) to include both sides of the relational interactions implicit in these concepts might yield more useful—and potentially more radical—suggestions for changes in organizational structures and systems to enhance organizational learning.

The second point for discussion has to do with the gender-power implications of the findings and their potential to challenge the organizational status quo. Detailing relational practice as *intentional action to achieve goals of achievement, growth, and effectiveness* momentarily reconstructs the definition of work by calling attention to the potential benefits to organizations of valuing relational practice and the variety of relational skills needed to enact it. This poststructuralist reconstruction is an act of resistance that challenges commonsense assumptions about work and competence, calls into question the hierarchical norms that support these narrow definitions, and creates discursive space in which new, perhaps radically different, practices, structures, and norms might surface.

It would appear that the organizational world would be eager to accept this particular challenge to the status quo. In the name of reengineering, reinvention, and organizational learning, organizations are routinely being encouraged—even warned—to move from traditional hierarchical structures to flatter, more collaborative entities in order to foster a new way of working. This way of working is remarkably similar to relational practice. Workers in new "boundaryless" organizations (Slater, 1994) are to be flexible and team oriented, not only continuous learners (Watkins & Marsick, 1993; Byham & Cox, 1994) but also emotionally intelligent (Goleman, 1995) systems thinkers, anticipating consequences, accepting ownership of problems, and working to solve them (Senge, 1990; Hammer & Champy, 1993).

What the findings from this study suggest, however, is that changing organizations in ways that might encourage the emergence of this kind of worker will not be so easy. Although the calls for radical change are real and the need may indeed be urgent, there appear to be powerful forces that silence and suppress just such challenges to organizational norms. In other words, the findings suggest that behaviors such as relational practice are not merely overlooked in organizations; they are systematically disappeared through a process in which they are coded as private sphere (feminine) activities that stand outside the definition of work and competence. What this means for organizations that are calling for team-oriented, less hierarchical, empowered workers is that they are unlikely to get them from current practice, regardless of calls for transformation. The inability to recognize the new behavior as evidence of competence, the lack of language to describe it as such, and the coding of such behavior as feminine are powerful dynamics undermining efforts to restructure work and the workplace in this way. Transformation will require far more than an exhortation to change organizational culture or reengineer the work process. Rather, it will require an acknowledgment of and an engagement with the complex gendered forces underlying current organizational norms. Without such an acknowledgment, efforts to disrupt these structures are likely to fail because, while calls for this radical change might appear benign, the way in which organizations would have to change in order to foster these changes are neither benign nor gender neutral.

Take, for example, the structural and practical implications of the suggestion that organizations value relational practice and encourage the development of relational skills in their workforce. The question of sex differences in relational competence aside, there is some evidence in the broader literature that many of the skills associated with this type of competence can be acquired in caretaking settings. The literature on the sociology of caring (Ruddick, 1989; Benner & Wrubel, 1989), for example, suggests that caring for others encourages a holistic approach to understanding and responding to events, an approach that develops an ability to integrate emotional, cognitive, and behavior data in forming a response. Interestingly, a recent study of service workers (Johansson, 1995) found that those who were able to assume this holistic approach, or what was called "total responsibility" for the work, were those who were involved in some sort of caretaking activity outside work, such as parenting, coaching, or being a team leader in a youth group.

This suggests that organizations intent on developing relational skills in their workers might do so through the systematic encouragement of all individuals to be involved in some sort of caretaking experience. Taking this a step further, developmental programs in organizations intent on transformation might even include some form of family or community involvement as a necessary condition of advancement or continued employment. Suggestions for meeting these developmental needs could include the use of "outside consultants" (children, elderly parents, members of shelters, schools, hospitals, and others) to assist in relational skills acquisition. This, of course, is radically different from the traditional view that employees who are involved in family or community are less committed or less valuable than those who focus only on work. Highlighting the organizational benefits of relaxing the boundary between work and family/community as a way of developing relational competence in workers has the potential to change the landscape of work-family interventions that organizations might consider.

The suggestion that organizations might want to relax the work-family boundary in order to develop relational skills in their workers may have been met with some form of skepticism or even amusement in the reader—a sense, perhaps, that the suggestion was naive or the connection far-fetched. This response highlights the most powerful implication of the findings: the suggestion that it might be in an organization's best interest to relax the work-family boundary is implicitly a challenge to organizational assumptions about the necessity of keeping a strict boundary between the public and private spheres of life. These assumptions manifest themselves in organizational norms, structures, and practices that reify that gendered separation, a separation that implicitly assigns one set of tasks and associated behaviors to women and another to men. Challenging these norms, then, challenges not only the separation but also the deeply held gender-linked assumptions that maintain that separation and reinforce a patriarchal pattern of male dominance in the public sphere.

What this points out is that the poststructuralist "act of resistance" inherent in reconstructing the definition of work in order to value the relational is not simply an act of resistance to hierarchy or other aspects of organizing. It is also, at a deeper level, an act of resistance to the way in which these ways of organizing create, recreate, and maintain a gendered dichotomy between the public and private spheres and to the power structure (patriarchy) that depends on this split. More specifically, it suggests that organizations intent on transforming will be unable to do so in any long-lasting way without engaging these patriarchal forces. One way to engage them is to begin to expose the gendered nature of the structures, norms, and practices that reinforce the public-private dichotomy at every level of analysis—from the deeply interior processes that privilege one source of self esteem and self-identify (public sphere accomplishments) over others; to the group level where structures, reward systems, and managerial practices support gendered, public-private split definitions of commitment, success, competence, and achievement; to the organizational level where work and family are constructed as separate and distinct spheres of life; to the societal level where the dissolution would mean counting both the public and private costs of doing business. Openly challenging the gendered nature of the public-private dichotomy at each of these levels has the potential to transform work and organizations for the next century in ways that go beyond superficial suggestions and calls for transformation. Indeed, challenging this dichotomy openly has the potential to highlight the more general, societal-level assumptions about gender that would need to change in order to respond to what are commonly represented as gender-neutral organizational calls to meet the challenges of this century.

References

Acker, J. (1989). *Doing comparable worth: Gender, class and pay equity.* Philadelphia: Temple University Press.

Acker, J. (1990). Hierarchies, jobs, bodies: A theory of gendered organizations. *Gender and Society, 4,* 139–158.

Acker, J. (1992). Gendering organizational theory. In A. J. Mills & P. Tancred (Eds.), *Gendering organizational analysis* (pp. 248–260). Thousand Oaks, CA: Sage.

Alderfer, C., & Brown, L. D. (1973). Designing an empathic questionnaire for organizational research. *Journal of Applied Psychology, 56*(6), 456–460.

Alvesson, M., & Deetz, S. (1996). Critical theory and postmodernism approaches to organizational studies. In S. Clegg, C. Hardy, & W. Nord (Eds.), *Handbook of organization studies* (pp. 191–217). Thousand Oaks, CA: Sage.

Bailyn, L. (1993). *Breaking the mold: women, men and time in the new corporate world.* New York: Free Press.

Bailyn, L., Rapaport, R., Kolb, D., & Fletcher, J. K. (1996). *Re-linking work and family: A catalyst for organizational change* (Working Paper 3892–96). Cambridge, MA: MIT Sloan School of Management.

Belenky, M., Clinchy, B., Goldberger, N., & Tarule, J. (1986). *Women's ways of knowing.* New York: Basic Books.

Bellah, R., Madsen, R., Sullivan, W., Swidler, A., & Tipton, S. (1985). *Habits of the heart.* Berkeley: University of California Press.

Benner, P., & Wrubel, J. (1989). *The primacy of caring.* Reading, MA: Addison-Wesley.

Bougon, M. (1983). Uncovering cognitive maps: The self-Q technique. In G. Morgan (Ed.), *Beyond method.* Thousand Oaks, CA: Sage.

Bradley, H. (1989). *Men's work, women's work.* Minneapolis: University of Minnesota Press.

Bradley, H. (1993). Across the great divide. In C. L. Williams (Ed.), *Doing women's work* (pp. 10–27). Thousand Oaks, CA: Sage.

Brown, L. M., & Gilligan, C. (1992). *Meeting at the crossroads.* Cambridge, MA: Harvard University Press.

Byham, W. C., & Cox, J. (1994). *Heroz.* New York: Harmony Books.

Calas, M., & Smircich, L. (1989). Using the "F" word: Feminist theories and the social consequences of organizational research. In *Proceedings of the Academy of Management.* Washington, DC: Academy of Management.

Cammock, P., Nilakant, V., & Dakin, S. (1995). Developing a lay model of managerial effectiveness: A social constructionist perspective. *Journal of Management Studies, 32*(4), 443–474.

Chodorow, N. (1974). Family structure and feminine personality. In M. Z. Rosaldo & L. Lamphere (Eds.), *Women, culture and society* (pp. 44–64). Stanford, CA: Stanford University Press.

Clegg, S. (1989). *Frameworks of power.* Thousand Oaks, CA: Sage.

Cockburn, C. (1991). *In the way of women: Men's resistance to sex equality in organizations.* Ithaca, NY: ILR Press.

Collinson, D. (1994). Strategies of resistance: Power, knowledge and subjectivity in the workplace. In J. M. Jermier, D. Knights, & W. Nord (Eds.), *Resistance and power in organizations* (pp. 25–69). London: Routledge.

Collinson, D., & Hearn, J. (1994). Naming men as men: Implications for work, organization and management. *Gender, Work and Organization, 1*(1), 2–22.

Connell, R. W. (1995). *Masculinities.* Berkeley: University of California Press.

DeVault, M. (1990). *Feeding the family.* Chicago: University of Chicago Press.

Diamond, I., & Quinby, L. (1988). *Feminism and Foucault.* Boston: Northeastern University Press.

Ewick, P., & Silbey, S. (1995). Subversive stories and hegemonic talks: Toward a sociology of narrative. *Law and Society Review, 29*(2), 197–226.

Fairclough, N. (1989). *Language and power.* New York: Longman.

Ferguson, K. E. (1984). *The feminist case against bureaucracy.* Philadelphia: Temple University Press.

Fineman, S. (1993). Organizations as emotional arenas. In S. Fineman (Ed.), *Emotion in organizations* (pp. 9–35). Thousand Oaks, CA: Sage.

Fishman, P. (1978). Interaction: The work women do. *Social Problems, 25,* 397–406.

Flax, J. (1990). *Thinking fragments.* Berkeley: University of California Press.

Fletcher, J. K. (1994a). Castrating the female advantage: Feminist standpoint research and management science. *Journal of Management Inquiry, 3*(1), 74–82.

Fletcher, J. K. (1994b). *Toward a theory of relational practice in organizations: A feminist reconstruction of "real" work.* Unpublished doctoral dissertation, Boston University.

Fletcher, J. K., & Bailyn, L. (1996). Challenging the last boundary. In M. Arthur & D. Rousseau (Eds.), *The boundaryless career* (pp. 256–267). New York: Oxford University Press.

Foucault, M. (1980). Truth and power. In C. Gordon (Ed.), *Power/knowledge: Selected interviews and other writings, 1972–1977, by Michel Foucault* (pp. 109–133). New York: Pantheon.

Friedlander, F. (1994). Toward whole systems and whole people. *Organization, 1,* 59–64.

Game, A., & Pringle R. (1983). *Gender at work.* Boston: Allen & Unwin.

Gherardi, S. (1995). *Gender, symbolism and organizational cultures.* Thousand Oaks, CA: Sage.

Gilligan, C. (1982). *In a different voice.* Cambridge, MA: Harvard University Press

Glaser, B., & Strauss, A. (1967). *The discovery of grounded theory: Strategies and qualitative research.* Hawthorne, NY: Aldine de Gruyter.

Goleman, D. (1995) *Emotional intelligence.* New York: Bantam Books.

Hall, D. T. (1996). Protean careers of the twenty-first century. *Academy of Management Executive, 10*(4), 8–17.

Hall, D. T., & Mirvis, P. (1996). The new protean career: Psychological success and the path with a heart. In D. T. Hall (Ed.), *The career is dead: Long live the career* (pp. 15–45). San Francisco: Jossey-Bass.

Hammer, M., & Champy, J. (1993) *Reengineering the corporation.* New York: HarperBusiness.

Harding, S. (1986). *The science question in feminism.* Ithaca, NY: Cornell University Press

Harding, S. (1987) *Feminism and methodology.* Bloomington: Indiana University Press.

Harris, R. P., Bridger, J. C., Sachs, C. E., & Tallichet, S. E. (1995). Empowering rural sociology: Exploring and linking alternative paradigms in theory and methodology. *Rural Sociology, 60*(4), 585–606.

Huff, A. (1990, May). *Wives—of the organization.* Paper presented at the Women and Work Conference, Arlington, TX.

Jacobsen, S., & Jacques, R. (1989, August). *Beyond androgyny: Future directions for gender research.* Paper presented at the Academy of Management, Washington, DC.

Jacobsen, S., & Jacques R. (1997). Destabilizing the field. *Journal of Management Inquiry, 6*(1), 42–59.

Jacques, R. (1992). *Re-presenting the knowledge worker: A poststructuralist analysis of the new employed professional.* Unpublished doctoral dissertation, University of Massachusetts.

Johansson, U. (1995, August). *Constructing the responsible worker: Changing structures, changing selves.* Paper presented at the Academy of Management meeting, Vancouver, BC.

Jordan, J., Kaplan, A., Miller, J. B., Stiver, I., & Surrey, J. (1991). *Women's growth in connection.* New York: Guilford Press.

Jordan, J., Surrey J., & Kaplan A. (1991). Women and empathy: Implications for psychological development and psychotherapy. In J. Jordan, A. Kaplan, J. B. Miller, I. Stiver, & J. Surrey (Eds.), *Women's growth in connection* (pp. 27–50). New York: Guilford Press.

Kolb, D. M. (1992). Women's work: Peacemaking in organizations. In D. M. Kolb & J. M. Bartunek (Eds.), *Hidden conflict in organizations: Uncovering behind the scenes disputes* (pp. 63–91). Thousand Oaks, CA: Sage.

Kram, K. (1996). A relational approach to career development. In D. T. Hall (Ed.), *The career is dead: Long live the career* (pp. 132–157). San Francisco: Jossey-Bass.

Levinson, H., Spohn, A., & Molinari, J. (1972). *Organizational diagnosis.* Cambridge, MA: Harvard University Press.

Liou, N., & Aldrich, H. E. (1995, August). *Women entrepreneurs: Is there a gender-based relational competence?* Paper presented at the American Sociological Association meetings, Washington, DC.

Lipnack, J., & Stamps, J. (1993). *The TeamNet factor: Bringing the power of boundary crossing into the heart of your business.* Essex Junction, VT: Oliver Wright Publications.

Lorber, J. (1991). Dismantling Noah's ark. In J. Lorber & S. Farrell (Eds.), *The social construction of gender.* Thousand Oaks, CA: Sage.

Martin, J. (1990). Deconstructing organizational taboos: The suppression of gender conflict in organizations. *Organizational Science, 1,* 1–21.

Martin, J., & Knopoff, K. (1995). The gendered implications of apparently gender-neutral theory: Re-reading Weber. In E. Freeman & A. Larson (Eds.), *Business ethics and women's studies.* New York: Oxford University Press.

Martin, P. Y. (1995, August). *Mobilized masculinities and glass ceilings.* Paper presented at the Academy of Management Meeting, Vancouver, BC.

McIlwee, J., & Robinson, J. G. (1992). *Women in engineering.* Albany, NY: SUNY Press.

McNay, L. (1992). *Foucault and feminism: Power, gender and the self.* Oxford: Blackwell Press.

Miller, J. B. (1976). *Toward a new psychology of women.* Boston: Beacon Press.

Miller, J. B. (1986a). *Toward a new psychology of women* (2nd ed.). Boston: Beacon Press.

Miller, J. B. (1986b) *What do we mean by relationships?* (Work in Progress No. 22). Wellesley, MA: Stone Center, Wellesley College.

Mills, A. J., & Tancred, P. (1992). Introduction. In A. J. Mills & P. Tancred (Eds.). *Gendering organizational analysis* (pp. 1–8). Thousand Oaks, CA: Sage.

Mintzberg, H. (1973). *The nature of managerial work.* Upper Saddle River, NJ: Prentice Hall.

Morrison, A., White, R., & Van Velsor, E. (1987). *Breaking the glass ceiling.* Reading, MA: Addison-Wesley.

Mumby, D. K. (1988). *Communication and power in organizations: Discourse, ideology and domination.* Norwood, NJ: Ablex.

Mumby, D. K., & Putnam. L. (1992). The politics of emotion: A feminist reading of bounded rationality. *Academy of Management Review, 17*(3), 465–486.

Nicholson, L. J. (Ed.). (1990). *Feminism/postmodernism.* New York: Routledge.

Nonaka, I. (1994). A dynamic theory of organizational knowledge creation. *Organization Science, 5*(1), 14–37.

Parkin, W. (1993). The public and the private: Gender sexuality and emotion. In S. Fineman (Ed.), *Emotion in organizations* (pp. 167–189). Thousand Oaks, CA: Sage

Parsons, T., & Bales, R. F. (1955). *Family, socialization and interaction process.* New York: Free Press.

Perlow, L. (1997). *Finding time.* Ithaca, NY: Cornell University Press.

Perrow, C. (1986). *Complex organizations* (3rd ed.). New York: Random House.

Reverby, S. (1987). *Ordered to care: The dilemma of American nursing, 1850–1945.* Cambridge: Cambridge University Press.

Roberts, J. (1990). Uncovering hidden caring. *Nursing Outlook, 38*(2), 67–69.

Ruddick, S. (1989). *Maternal thinking.* Boston: Beacon Press.

Seely-Brown, J., & Duguid, P. (1991). Organizational learning and communities-of-practice: Toward a unified view of working, learning and innovation. *Organization Science, 2*(1), 40–57.

Senge, P. (1990). *The fifth discipline.* New York: Doubleday.

Schein, E. (1985). *Organizational culture and leadership.* San Francisco: Jossey Bass.

Slater, R. (1994). *Get better or get beaten!* New York: Irwin.

Smircich, L. (1985, August). *Toward a woman centered organization theory.* Paper presented at the Academy of Management Annual Meeting, San Diego, CA.

Smith, D. (1990). *The conceptual practices of power.* Boston: Northeastern University Press.

Spradley, J. (1979). *The ethnographic interview.* New York: Holt.

Stiver, I. (1991). The meanings of dependency in female-male relationships. In J. Jordan, A. Kaplan, J. B. Miller, I. Stiver, & J. Surrey (Eds.), *Women's growth in connection* (pp. 143–161). New York: Guilford Press.

Townley, B. (1993). Foucault, power/knowledge and its relevance for human resource management. *Academy of Management Review, 18*(30), 518–545.

Wadel, C. (1979). The hidden work of everyday life. In S. Wallman (Ed.), *The social anthropology of work* (pp. 365–384). New York: Academic Press.

Watkins, K., & Marsick, V. (1993). *Sculpting the learning organization.* San Francisco: Jossey Bass.

Weedon, C. (1987). *Feminist practice and poststructuralist theory.* Oxford: Blackwell.

West, C., & Zimmerman, D. (1991). Doing gender. In J. Lorber & S. Farrell (Eds.), *The social construction of gender* (pp. 13–37). Thousand Oaks, CA: Sage.

CHAPTER SIX

Pregnancy Discrimination in the Workplace

Lisa Wilson, J.D.

T here are over 58 million women in the American labor force, and 85 percent of those women are expected to become pregnant at some point while they are working (U.S. Census Bureau, 2003; Jacobson, 1988). Given that the workplace is still fairly traditional in structure, it is not surprising that problems and discrimination surrounding pregnancy exist. In fact, complaints of pregnancy discrimination with the Equal Employment Opportunity Commission (EEOC) increased by 39 percent between 1992 and 2002 (Equal Employment Opportunity Commission, 2003).

Until 1978, discrimination against pregnant workers was widespread and usually legal. Employers could indulge in whatever stereotypes they had about pregnant women and act on their opinions as to what women should do once they became pregnant and after the birth of the child. Since then, the Pregnancy Discrimination Act and the Family and Medical Leave Act, as well as state and local laws, have changed the workplace dramatically for pregnant women and eliminated the most blatant and egregious forms of discrimination. However, these laws do not apply to all employees, and even when they do, they leave gaps in protection. Problems remain, and stereotypes persist.

This chapter briefly lays out the trajectory and current status of the law regarding pregnant workers. It covers the history of the treatment of pregnant workers, how and why the law changed to remedy that discrimination, and the problems with those laws and proposals to expand them. It also briefly reviews the efforts of states to supplement federal protections for pregnant workers and compares American policies to those of other nations.

LIFE BEFORE THE PREGNANCY DISCRIMINATION ACT

The history of the treatment of pregnant women, or even women who may become pregnant, in the workplace is not a pleasant one. Based on the idea that women, especially mothers, did not belong in the workplace, as well as the desire to reserve jobs for men, protective legislation for women was passed in the early part of the twentieth century (Strimling, 1989). This protective legislation is typified in the famous 1908 Supreme Court case of *Muller* v. *Oregon.* The state of Oregon had limited the number of hours per day that women could work but had passed no such limitation for men. The Court upheld this law, reasoning that it was women's "performance of maternal functions" (p. 421) that placed them at a natural disadvantage in life compared to men and that long working hours could injure women's fragile health, yet women needed to remain healthy in order to have healthy children. While a limitation of working hours today might be considered a reasonable and humane law, in the exploitative labor conditions at the turn of the twentieth century, legislation such as this deprived women of employment opportunities, which was its intended result.

This treatment was not just a phenomenon of the early twentieth century. Strikingly unequal treatment of pregnant women persisted into the 1970s, and during the 1950s and 1960s, some states even adopted new legislation that prohibited women from being hired for a specified period of time before and after childbirth (Caplan-Cotenoff, 1987). Employers routinely denied women disability benefits for pregnancy while providing coverage for many other temporarily disabling conditions. In some cases, employers forced pregnant women to take leave without assurance that their jobs would be there upon their return to work.

The women's movement of the 1970s aimed to change these practices, as well as other forms of discrimination against women. To address pregnancy discrimination in employment, women's advocates thought they already had the necessary legal tools. In *Reed* v. *Reed* in 1971, the Supreme Court first adopted the view that the equal protection clause of the Fourteenth Amendment prohibited differential treatment by the government based on sex. Feminists then argued that based on the clear connection between women's reproductive capabilities and societal discrimination, pregnancy discrimination was part and parcel of sex discrimination, and thus was covered by the equal protection clause. In 1974, the Court decided *Cleveland Board of Education* v. *LaFleur*. In *LaFleur*, the Supreme Court addressed two public school district polices that required teachers to take mandatory maternity leave for four or five months before the expected childbirth, which is long before most pregnant women would prefer to stop working. The lower courts that had previously heard these cases based their decisions on the equal protection clause, but the Supreme Court held that these polices violated the due process clause of the Fourteenth Amendment due to the burden they imposed on the fundamental right to bear children. Although this case advanced the rights of pregnant workers by invalidating these discriminatory policies, the rationale for the case focused on women in relation to reproduction, not sex discrimination (Strimling, 1989). The Court also later used this due process rationale to invalidate a Utah unemployment compensation statute, which had provided that women would get no benefits during unemployment in the third trimester of pregnancy or six weeks after childbirth because the state presumed a woman could not work then (*Turner* v. *Department of Employment Security*, 1975).

In addition, there was a federal statute protecting women in the workplace. Title VII of the Civil Rights Act of 1964, the foundation of modern employment antidiscrimination law, prohibited sex discrimination in employment, and it provided simply that discrimination based on sex was forbidden. But Title VII itself did not provide a definition of the term *sex*, and due to the unusual way in which the word was included in the act, the legislative history behind the inclusion of this term or what Congress considered it to cover was scant.[1] The EEOC stepped into this breach and began addressing to what extent the prohibition of discrimination based on sex applied to the treatment of pregnancy. Though it took eight years, the EEOC produced administrative guidelines by 1972 that clearly stated that Title VII prohibited differential treatment of pregnancy, including in disability and other benefits policies. This was at a time when the exclusion of pregnancy from such policies was routine. Thus, when women challenged policies that denied disability benefits for disability from pregnancy but not from other sources, including ones that primarily affected men, they met with success. Many federal district courts and several courts of appeals agreed that differential treatment based on pregnancy violated Title VII.[2]

However, this initial success was short-lived. The issue of whether pregnancy was included within the meaning of sex under the equal protection clause reached the Supreme Court in 1974 in *Geduldig* v. *Aiello*. At issue in *Geduldig* was the California State Disability Insurance Program, which provided disability payments to workers who were temporarily disabled by an illness but not eligible for workers' compensation funds. This plan specifically excluded disability based on pregnancy from coverage, while covering disability from almost every other cause. The Court examined this plan as it traditionally did other social insurance schemes, which meant it gave a wide berth to the policy choices of the state. The Court defined the policy of the state as excluding a benefit that would be expensive so as to keep employee contributions low and still keep the system solvent. The Court refused to see the exclusion of benefits for pregnancy as discrimination based on gender and stated in a line that later became famous (though it was relegated to a footnote in the opinion itself), "While it is true that only women can become pregnant . . . the program divides potential recipients into two groups—pregnant women and nonpregnant persons. While the first group is exclusively female, the second group includes members of both sexes. The fiscal and actuarial benefits of the program thus accrue to members of both sexes" (p. 497).

This seductively simple statement masks the reality of pregnancy discrimination, which feminists of the 1970s and today argue is that pregnant women are discriminated against because they are engaging in the reproductive role of women and that women are discriminated against in large part because they are the gender that is capable of bearing children. Justice William Brennan wrote a strong dissent to the *Geduldig* decision in which he examined pregnancy discrimination in a more thorough manner and concluded, "Such dissimilar treatment of men and women, on the basis of physical characteristics inextricably linked to one's sex, inevitably constitutes sex discrimination" (p. 501). Today, the *Geduldig* decision remains much criticized but valid law.[3]

Geduldig was a constitutional decision, but Title VII was statutory law that reached beyond the Constitution to regulate private employment and was not necessarily subject to the same analysis. So even after *Geduldig,* women continued to challenge the exclusion of coverage of pregnancy from disability policies under Title VII against private employers. And the lower courts hearing those cases found that the analysis in *Geduldig* did not necessarily apply in the context of Title VII and that pregnancy was included in the prohibition of sex discrimination in Title VII (*General Electric Co.* v. *Gilbert,* 1976).

The issue of whether pregnancy was included within the meaning of "sex" under Title VII reached the Supreme Court in 1976 in *General Electric Co.* v. *Gilbert.* Gilbert challenged a disability plan that was almost identical to the one in *Geduldig,* though offered through her employer, and the Court proceeded to analyze her challenge almost identically as well. The Court found that its analysis under the equal protection clause was applicable to Title VII and this time emphasized the "nonpregnant persons" language to state that the reason *Geduldig* rejected the feminist argument about the nature of pregnancy discrimination, and the Court was doing so again, was that neither plan in itself discriminated based on sex, since both men and women were the nonpregnant comparison group. However, Title VII also has a second avenue of liability that is not available under the equal protection clause: liability based on disparate impact. The theory of disparate impact liability is that a practice by an employer, even if neutral on its face, may be discriminatory if its negative effects fall disproportionately on a protected group. The Supreme Court in *Gilbert* recognized the possibility of applying this theory to the disability policy challenged, but it found the disparate impact theory not applicable to the case, reasoning that overall, the plan did not discriminate against women in that it covered them for many causes of disability. In so doing, the Court did not consider that the particular practice of excluding pregnancy, not the plan itself, was having the negative effect and that its sole effect was on women.

Justice Brennan also wrote a dissenting opinion in this case, and in that opinion he explored the context of sex discrimination at the company that provided the challenged plan. The company sued had "a history of . . . practices that have served to undercut the employment opportunities of women who become pregnant while employed" (p. 150), including scaling women's wages at two-thirds of men's and forcing employees to take maternity leave while not providing them with disability payments. That is, of course, the better way to see pregnancy discrimination: as part of a larger pattern of discrimination.

The reaction to the *Gilbert* decision in the feminist, union, and civil rights communities can be fairly described as livid. Critical discussions of the case immediately surfaced in legal articles, and feminists and others began a campaign to have Congress overrule the Court's decision, which it could do, since the Court's decision was interpreting a statute, not the Constitution.[4] It was called the Campaign to End Discrimination Against Pregnant Workers, and it offered, among other strategies, the testimony of prominent feminists to Congress (Strimling, 1989).

A year later, however, the Supreme Court issued a ruling that appeared to back off its stand in *Geduldig* and *Gilbert*. In *Nashville Gas Co. v. Satty* (1977), the Court found that a policy of forcing pregnant women to both take leave and forfeit their accrued seniority when they returned from leave, requiring them to compete with less senior people for their old jobs back, did violate Title VII. In distinguishing this situation from that in *Gilbert,* the Court used a benefit-versus-burden analysis to find that although employers did not have to extend maternity disability benefits to women that were inapplicable to men, they could not punish a woman by imposing on her the "substantial burden" (p. 142) of losing her seniority. This benefit-versus-burden analysis was briefly the law under Title VII, and at least two courts applied it to invalidate employer policies that did burden pregnant workers (*Zuniga* v. *Kleburg County Hospital,* 1982; *Mitchell* v. *Board of Trustees,* 1979).

THE PREGNANCY DISCRIMINATION ACT

Congress reacted quickly to the Supreme Court's decisions and the feminist campaign against them. After *Geduldig,* it amended the Internal Revenue Code to prevent the states from excluding pregnancy from their unemployment compensation programs. And in 1978, after *Gilbert,* Congress passed the Pregnancy Discrimination Act (PDA; P.L. 95-555) as an amendment to Title VII. Title VII already prohibited discrimination based on sex, and the PDA defined *sex* to include "pregnancy, childbirth, or related medical conditions." This amendment was passed specifically to reject the Supreme Court's interpretation of *sex* in *Gilbert,* and its legislative history makes this clear: "The Supreme Court's narrow interpretations of Title VII tend to erode our national policy of nondiscrimination in employment" (Prohibition of Sex Discrimination Based on Pregnancy, 1978).

With the PDA passed, the question for the courts (and advocates) was no longer whether the law covered pregnancy but the extent of that coverage. The PDA contains two clauses, the first of which is quoted above and the second of which states, "Women affected by pregnancy, childbirth, or related medical conditions shall be treated the same for all employment-related purposes, including receipt of benefits under fringe benefit plans, as other persons not so affected but similar in their ability or inability to work."

Under this law, it is clear that employers can no longer discriminate based on pregnancy. They cannot fire or refuse to hire pregnant women because they are pregnant, and they must offer coverage of pregnancy in any health and disability plans they offer that provide coverage of similarly disabling conditions. Mandatory leave is a clear-cut violation of the PDA, and voluntary leave around the time of childbirth is required under the PDA if the employer would allow such a leave for other reasons.

But because the PDA did not provide an "affirmative definition of gender equality" (Strimling, 1989, p. 189), what treatment of pregnant workers was allowed under the PDA and how best to remedy pregnancy discrimination became a defining issue in the "equal treatment" versus "special treatment" debate among feminists that was so prominent in the 1980s. Those who advocated equal treatment called for strict equality and neutrality in the law. They argued that laws explicitly based on pregnancy would only reinforce stereotypes of women as childbearers. Advocates of special treatment, however, contended that absolutely identical treatment of men and women resulted in inequality between the sexes where women's needs were different. Pregnancy, then, became a central part of this debate, as the capability to bear children is the defining biological difference between the sexes. Equal treatment proponents asserted that the PDA's equality approach was preferable, as it did not demand any treatment different from that which was available for similarly disabling conditions. They argued that any particular maternity policies smacked of the paternalism and sexism of the early twentieth-century protective legislation and would make women workers less attractive to employers, thus disadvantaging them in the workplace. Special treatment advocates countered that there was no condition similar to pregnancy and that it is simply a fact that women and men are different in this regard. To hold women to the same benefits as men perpetuated a male norm in the workplace. Only by providing for this unique condition of women would women actually be able to achieve equality in the workplace.[5]

The PDA creates equality of treatment only; it does not mandate any kind of treatment: time off, rehiring, or anything else. That is, an employer who offers no time off, no health insurance, or no disability insurance for its other employees need not offer those benefits just to pregnant employees. So while the mandate of equality in the PDA is essential, this bare requirement of equal treatment is also lacking: "Employers can treat pregnant women as badly as they treat similarly affected but non-pregnant employees" (*Troupe* v. *May Department Stores,* 1994, p. 738). Thus, while the PDA has been a great step forward for women in the workforce, it still leaves gaps in protection. Some states attempted to go further than the PDA and passed laws guaranteeing maternity leave or job reinstatement after a woman returns from maternity leave (or both). Such laws were seen as problematic to supporters of a strict equal treatment view, but were applauded by special treatment advocates.

The Supreme Court addressed the issue of whether these state laws were permitted under the PDA in *California Federal Savings and Loan Association* v. *Guerra* (1987). Although the case was decided on very narrow grounds of federal law preemption, as a practical matter it still answered the question of what states could and could not do to increase protections of pregnant workers. The Supreme Court upheld a California law that guaranteed new mothers four months of leave and reinstatement after the leave. The opponents of the California law, including some feminist organizations, argued this law was contrary to the PDA's second clause that mandated equal treatment only and would have the feared effect of making women stand out in the workplace as less desirable employees. The Court, however, agreed with proponents of the law, including other feminist groups (Strimling, 1989), that the PDA served only as a "floor" for the protection of pregnant workers. Since the California law and the PDA had the same goal—equality in the workplace for pregnant women—the state law was not preempted by the PDA. States are thus able, though not required, to provide greater protections for pregnant employees than are offered by the PDA, as some now do.

JOHNSON CONTROLS AND SPECIAL SUSCEPTIBILITIES DURING PREGNANCY

A particular quandary with regard to pregnant workers is the extent to which the physical changes during pregnancy make a woman more susceptible to any harm in the workplace. This can be a particular problem in industries in which workers are exposed to potentially harmful chemicals or other agents. There are two sides to this problem: the extent to which employers are allowed to mandate different treatment for pregnant employees and the extent to which employees are entitled to request different treatment. Within the framework of the PDA, employers are limited in what they can mandate for their employees, but employees have limited ability to request changes in their working environment.

In *International Union* v. *Johnson Controls* (1991), the Supreme Court addressed the legality, under Title VII, of an employment policy that prohibited all women of reproductive age, unless they could demonstrate infertility, from jobs that involved exposure to lead, due to concern about health risks to the fetus of any women who may become pregnant. The company's actual policy stated that women "capable of bearing children" would be forbidden from the jobs with exposure to lead, whereas there was no such limitation on the jobs available to fertile men. The Court held that this policy was a facially discriminatory one as fertile men were treated differently from fertile women, the only difference being sex. The express language of the PDA supported the Court's holding because the use of the phrase "capable of bearing children" thus "explicitly classifies on the basis of potential for pregnancy" (p. 199).[6] The employer's fear of liability suits for injured babies did not justify this facial discrimination. Thus, since *Johnson Controls,* women may not be singled out for different treatment in the workplace solely due to their potential to become pregnant, which was an increasingly common practice in industry until this ruling (Jason, 1990).

In *Johnson Controls,* the Court expressed approval of the approach of the Occupational Health and Safety Administration (OSHA) to regulating lead. That approach considers that lead is a potential danger to all employees; it prescribes a program of medical surveillance for all employees exposed to certain levels of lead and temporary removal of an employee from a job with exposure if he or she has a high blood lead level or on the recommendation of a physician. Physicians can recommend employees for removal based on any medical condition, including pregnancy. Pregnant workers, then, are protected from potential harm to their fetuses without being singled out for treatment different from other employees. This is an example of equal treatment combined with just a little bit of special treatment, as pregnancy is specifically mentioned as a temporary condition that may justify temporary job removal.

Johnson Controls did not, however, address whether pregnant employees have the right to request changes in their job conditions due to any increased level of danger to themselves or their fetuses. Again, under the PDA, employees are only guaranteed the same rights as others similarly able or unable to do their jobs. That means that if an employer generally allows changes in job structure or duties, or specifically does when a worker faces a new inability to do certain tasks, then that option must be made available to pregnant employees. But if the employer allows no such job alterations, then they need not be made just for pregnant employees. A well-known example is the case of a nurse who asked not to treat an HIV-positive patient due to her compromised immune system during her pregnancy. Her request was denied because an alteration of job responsibilities was not usually allowed. Accordingly, her resulting claim for pregnancy discrimination failed as well (*Armstrong* v. *Flowers Hospital, Inc.,* 1994). In another case decided under the District of Columbia Human Rights Act, which has language identical to the PDA, the court found a pregnant medical technician did not have the right to avoid work involving radiation exposure. As is discussed below, there is no right to reasonable accommodation in the PDA (Weirich, 2003).

LIMITATIONS OF THE PREGNANCY DISCRIMINATION ACT

Although the Pregnancy Discrimination Act represents an important milestone in the protection of women's legal rights in the workplace, it is based on a model of equality that also creates obstacles for pregnant women workers.

Limitations in What the PDA Covers

The PDA is the ultimate example of the equal treatment advocates' argument: pregnant workers are to be treated exactly like other employees who are similarly able or unable to perform their job duties—no better, no worse. However, that minimum of equality does not extend to behavior that is caused by or related to pregnancy, such as tardiness due to morning sickness or the need for frequent breaks to use the restroom or have snacks (Greenberg, 1998). Courts view such effects of pregnancy as actions standing alone, without considering that they are directly caused by the pregnancy. Lateness due to morning sickness is treated as the inability to be at work on time, not as the temporary result of the pregnancy (*Troupe* v. *May Department Stores*, 1994). There are even worse examples: employees have been laid off or fired while on maternity leave due to their absence. Courts nevertheless find that the reason for the dismissal was the absence from the workplace due to the leave, not that the pregnancy of the woman was the cause of the leave and thus the cause of the dismissal (*Crnokrak* v. *Evangelical Health Systems*, 1993). In addition to these limitations of coverage, not all employees are even covered by Title VII, which applies only to employers with fifteen or more employees. However, much smaller employers are often covered by state and local antidiscrimination statutes.

The lack of consideration of the effects of pregnancy, which vary from woman to woman, has led commentators on the law to propose that a model of reasonable accommodation should be applied to pregnancy. This model already applies to disabled workers under the Americans with Disabilities Act (ADA) and also to religiously observant workers under Title VII itself. Both the ADA and Title VII with regard to religion mandate that employers make reasonable accommodations in the workplace on an individualized basis in consideration of the employee's disability or religious observance, as long as the accommodation does not impose an undue burden on the employer. This model would provide coverage of many of the needs surrounding pregnancy, such as morning sickness, while taking into account that each woman's experience with pregnancy is different. However, pregnant women are not normally covered under the provisions of the ADA (Greenberg, 1998; Millsap, 1996) and reasonable accommodation is not a part of the PDA. But at least one state, Minnesota, currently provides reasonable accommodation of pregnancy in its state antidiscrimination laws (Greenberg, 1998).

The protection of the PDA does extend to the spouses of male employees (*Newport News Shipbuilding and Dry Dock Co.* v. *EEOC*, 1983). And the PDA explicitly covers "related medical conditions," which has been held to include insurance coverage for birth control pills but not for infertility treatment (*Erickson* v. *Bartell Drug Co.*, 2001; *Krauel* v. *Iowa Methodist Medical Center*, 1996). The Eighth Circuit Court of Appeals held that infertility is not covered under the PDA because infertility, unlike pregnancy and childbirth, is not limited to women and is different from the latter two conditions, which are postconception. Other courts, however, have disagreed with that position on infertility (Weirich, 2003). The PDA has also been held to prohibit discrimination based on whether a woman chooses to abort her pregnancy, though the language of the PDA itself specifically does not require employers to pay for insurance coverage of abortion (*Turic* v. *Holland Hospitality, Inc.*, 1996).

Difficulties with Pursuing a Lawsuit Under the PDA

For all employees who feel they have been discriminated against, taking a case to court is a difficult undertaking. Disparate treatment under Title VII must be intentional, and though the *McDonnell Douglas* burden-shifting procedure is designed to aid plaintiffs, such cases are still notoriously difficult, though of course not impossible, for plaintiffs to win.[7] In the case of pregnancy discrimination, the obstacles are, if anything, even greater. First, the prima facie case a plaintiff must prove to proceed with her case requires her to identify a similarly situated man (since pregnancy discrimination is a subset of sex discrimination) who was treated more favorably than she was. However, as numerous commentators have pointed out, there really is no other condition like pregnancy. It is not an illness, though it may have effects similar to some illnesses. It is necessarily of a limited and predictable duration, and the woman was likely not ill before her pregnancy and will not be ill after it. She probably does not consider herself ill. But without such a similarly situated person to compare herself to, most pregnancy discrimination plaintiffs' cases fail (Greenberg, 1998).

Second, the power that stereotypes still play is evident in the decisions of judges regarding so-called direct evidence of discrimination. A plaintiff with direct evidence of discrimination, usually a statement by the employer, should have a stronger case than one with only indirect proof. But some courts demand that for such a statement to be considered direct evidence, it must be close in time to and directly connected to the negative employment action, or the statement must be a bald one that the employer acted due to the employee's pregnancy (Greenberg, 1998; Magid, 2001; Millsap, 1996). However, employers have had experience with Title VII for forty years and the PDA for over twenty-five, and seldom make such incriminating statements. Rather, such comments are likely to come at more casual moments (Greenberg, 1998). Courts are unlikely to consider casual comments as indicating any discriminatory motive. Also, courts are likely to judge any comments about pregnant women other than "you're fired because you're pregnant" as insufficient evidence of motive. Examples include statements that women should not return to work after having a child and that pregnant women do not perform well in the workplace (Greenberg, 1998). Furthermore, as Greenberg argues in her article on the limitations of the PDA, judges may not accept such statements as discriminatory because they play into deep stereotypes of pregnant women: that they are and should be preoccupied with their families and that they are lazy or hysterical (or both). When stereotypes and assumptions are so deeply held, they are often difficult to see. But the persistence of these stereotypes makes it even more difficult for pregnancy discrimination plaintiffs to win lawsuits. Perhaps that fact is not unrelated to the increasing number of EEOC complaints of pregnancy discrimination (EEOC, 2003). However, one study found that verdicts for plaintiffs in pregnancy discrimination cases are substantially larger than those in other types of sex discrimination suits, such as sexual harassment and gender discrimination (Schultz, 2003). This suggests that although pregnancy discrimination is hard to prove, juries are especially outraged when it is proven.

THE FAMILY AND MEDICAL LEAVE ACT

The Family and Medical Leave Act (FMLA) acts as a supplement to the PDA that provides a positive mandate of treatment: leave from work for pregnancy, childbirth, and medical complications of either. This law was signed into effect by President Clinton in 1993 after years of advocacy by women's rights groups. The FMLA is a very technical law, and its coverage is limited: it applies only to employees of companies with fifty or more employees, who have worked there for at least twelve months and have worked at least 1,250 hours over those twelve months. The fifty-employee threshold means the FMLA's coverage is limited to 58 percent of employees in the private sector (Cantor et al., 2001). Covered employees are guaranteed up to twelve weeks of (unpaid) leave per year for qualifying events, including the birth of a child or a serious health condition of the worker. There is also guaranteed reinstatement to the same position or an equivalent one after the leave. Significantly, this is a strict liability statute, meaning that someone whose FMLA rights have been violated does not need to prove her employer violated her rights for any particular reason to prevail in a lawsuit, only that they were violated.

More important, this is a positive statute that creates a substantive entitlement to a particular amount of leave after the birth of a child or due to the health problems of the worker, which can include any pregnancy or childbirth-related problems if they are serious enough. This is a different type of remedy to the problems of pregnancy in the workplace, and one that is necessary for new mothers to avoid even more difficult choices than are inherent in both working and raising children. And it is an entitlement that many women are taking advantage of: in 2000, a Labor Department–sponsored survey of employees found that 7.9 percent of people taking FMLA leave, or 1.88 million women, had taken maternity-disability leave under the FMLA in the prior eighteen months and an additional 4.4 million people had taken leave to care for a new child (Cantor et al., 2001).

The women's rights community views the FMLA as a good start to meeting the needs of workers faced with conflicting demands between their jobs and their families. But it is only a start. Advocates would like to see leave allowed for more purposes, leave guaranteed for employees of smaller employers, and especially paid leave (National Partnership for Women and Families, 2002b). Advocacy for paid leave is taking place at both the federal and state levels and is having the most effect in the states. Paid leave would expand the practical impact of the FMLA enormously: 2.73 million workers in the Department of Labor survey did not take leave they needed because they could not afford to do so (Cantor et al., 2001).

A portion of the FMLA was recently challenged under the Eleventh Amendment: whether the FMLA can provide monetary damages for employees of state governments if they win a lawsuit under that law (there was never any doubt that the FMLA applied to the states as employers; the question was only about the type of enforcement).[8] In a ringing opinion in *Nevada Department of Human Resources* v. *Hibbs,* the Supreme Court in June 2003 held that the FMLA does properly authorize monetary damages against state governments, due to the fact that it addresses gender discrimination prohibited by the equal protection clause. This decision is important for many reasons, many of which have nothing to do with pregnancy discrimination. But it is vitally important for preserving the rights of millions of women who are employed by state governments, and it buttresses the interpretation of the equal protection clause that recognizes that stereotypes and expectations of women are a cause of discrimination and can be discriminatory themselves if applied to women.

STATE LAWS AND EMPLOYER POLICIES

Since the Supreme Court's ruling in *California Federal Savings and Loan Association* v. *Guerra* (1987), several states in addition to California have enacted legislative protection for pregnancy that exceeds that in the PDA. Many of those laws now are also state versions of the FMLA, which are often more generous than the federal law. State laws have the disadvantage of covering only workers in individual states, but they do expand protections for pregnant women in those states and can be "laboratories" (*New State Ice Co.* v. *Leibmann,* 1932) to provide positive examples and proof to counter arguments about costs to business used to argue against expanded federal protections.

Many states take the path that was affirmed in *California Federal Savings and Loan Association* v. *Guerra* and guarantee maternity disability leave. This leave is either for a set period of time, often six to eight weeks, or for the time of physical disability caused by pregnancy and birth, which is usually a similar period (Jacobson, 1988). As of 2004, twenty-one states have such maternity disability laws (Zintl, 2004). Those laws usually have a minimum number of employees an employer must have to be covered by the law, but that number is always lower than the high fifty-employee threshold in the FMLA. A few of the maternity disability laws (in Hawaii, New York, and Rhode Island) also give women a portion of their weekly wages while out on leave, a significant advantage over current federal law under both the PDA and FMLA. Several other states (some of which overlap with the maternity disability states) provide their own versions of the FMLA (U.S. Department of Labor, 2004).[9] Like the FMLA, these state laws are broader than maternity disability laws in that they cover other reasons for leave as well, but they always provide leave for childbirth and the postpartum period.

The latest frontier in this area of protections for pregnant employees is the idea of guaranteed paid leave. Although this idea is not new (Wilson, 1976–1977), it has only recently been seriously considered by state governments. California became one of the first states to provide paid FMLA-type leave for several reasons, including the birth of a child. Employees in California are guaranteed 55 to 60 percent of their wages for up to six weeks of leave per year. This program is an extension of the employee-funded State Disability Insurance system, the same one challenged in *Geduldig* v. *Aiello.* Eligibility for paid benefits under this program began in June 2004, when leave became a reality for millions of lower-income workers in California who could not otherwise afford to take the leave they or their families may require. Four other states have similar temporary disability benefit programs that could also be extended to cover maternity leave (National Partnership for Women and Families, 2002a). And in other states, paid leave study commissions have been set up or legislation has been introduced (National Partnership for Women and Families, 2002b). However, a different option for funding paid leave, apart from the expansion of existing disability payment systems, was recently eliminated. The Department of Labor had ruled in June 2002 that states could create "Baby UI" plans, programs by which states could choose to use their unemployment compensation funds to pay for leave due to the birth or adoption of a child. This was a significant step that opened up a realistic source of funding for this leave. However, no state implemented a "Baby UI" plan, and in the fall of 2003, the Department of Labor rescinded the rule allowing such programs.[10]

In addition to state laws, the *California Federal Savings and Loan Association* decision also allows employers to offer maternity policies that are much more generous than those required by any law (Lindemann, Grossman, & Cane, 1996). And many do: 24 percent of employers offer more than twelve weeks of unpaid leave per year, and 34 percent of all employers continue pay during maternity-related leave (Cantor et al., 2001). However, an admittedly unscientific poll by *American Baby* magazine in 2001 found that three out of four women are dissatisfied with the maternity leave offered by their employers, and almost half of women get no paid leave whatsoever from their employers ("Fifty Percent Increase in Women in the Workforce," 2001).

COMPARISON TO OTHER INDUSTRIALIZED COUNTRIES

The protection of pregnant workers in the United States, though increasing, is far less generous than international standards and the required leave and benefits for pregnant women in other industrialized countries. The International Labor Organization, a United Nations agency, has created a set of minimum standards for maternity leave: twelve weeks of leave, payment during leave of at least two-thirds of a woman's income, with such payments coming from a social security or insurance plan, not employers. The United States meets only the first of those standards, through the FMLA, and even that presumes that a woman has not had any other reason to use any of her total allotment of twelve weeks of leave per year. In contrast, other industrialized countries offer guaranteed maternity leave with some payment during that leave. And 140 countries around the world offer guaranteed maternity leave, although it is often not enforced in developing countries ("A Break for New Moms," 1996).

The European Union has a policy directive on pregnant workers that is binding on member countries. It directs its member countries to provide workers with at least fourteen weeks of maternity leave, including at least two weeks of compulsory leave around the birth itself; time off for prenatal medical care; protection that workers will not lose their jobs due to pregnancy or leave taking; and special procedures to protect pregnant women from potentially harmful chemicals in the workplace. Member countries must implement these provisions and are free to offer more generous leave, benefits, or protections if they desire. And many countries do. Some countries' policies originally had the nonfeminist purposes of encouraging childbirth and thus population growth (Hunt, Hsia, Smith, Martin, and Rosenwein, 1995) or were based on ideas that pregnant women should not work, but they are now based more on equality and general ideas of social welfare. All nineteen Western European countries[11] provide maternity leave job protection and paid parental leave, most of them offering benefits and protections that are far more generous than, though different from, those in the United States. For example, Germany guarantees mothers 100 percent of their wages for up to six weeks of leave before childbirth and eight weeks after it, with an additional sixty-nine weeks of leave at a flat rate. In France, parents are guaranteed sixteen weeks of leave at 100 percent of their wages and up to three years of unpaid leave with job protection. Perhaps more typical is the Netherlands, which offers sixteen weeks of paid leave and job protection for six months (Jordan, 1999). Those kinds of protections are obviously much more generous to new parents than current U.S. laws, and also better recognize the demands that new babies place on their parents. They allow parents the time they may wish to have with their children by making it economically feasible to take the time off. And they create a norm that parents do take significant time off from work after a child is born. Other industrialized countries are also ahead of the United States when it comes to maternity leave. Canada guarantees maternity leave, with the amount of leave up to the individual provinces. In Quebec the leave is for eighteen weeks, and in Ontario it is for seventeen weeks. There are also maternity leave benefits paid by the Federal Unemployment Insurance system (Invest in Canada, 2003; Glavinovich, 1996). New Zealand offers fourteen weeks of maternity leave and up to fifty-two weeks of extended parental leave, and in 2002 it initiated paid parental leave for twelve of those weeks (International Observatory of Labour Law, 2001; Thomas, 2002).

American policies, in contrast, have been described as "Third World" ("A Break for New Moms," 1996). But the policies of other nations inspired American advocates to work toward the PDA and FMLA initially, and they continue to inspire (and embarrass) advocates who want to continue to improve U.S. policies, especially toward paid leave (National Partnership for Women and Families, 2002b). European policies on maternity and parental leave differ in two other significant ways from American laws. First, seven countries restrict parental leave to women (Jordan, 1999). In the United States, though women do take more FMLA leave than men do (Cantor et al., 2001), the FMLA allows either parent to do so. As the Supreme Court recently recognized, opening parental leave to both men and women serves the simultaneous purposes of relieving gender discrimination against women and discouraging the stereotype that men are not involved in the care of children (*Nevada Department of Human Resources* v. *Hibbs,* 2003). Limiting leave to women may relieve overt discrimination, but it also may reinforce the already prevalent stereotype and profound expectation of mothers that they are the primary caregivers for their children. While many women embrace that role, it is not always possible or even preferred. Having achieved a gender-neutral leave law in this country, though, it is unlikely that the United States would then limit leave to women.

Nine European countries mandate that women take prenatal or postnatal leave (or both) from their jobs (Jordan, 1999), something that is not allowed under the PDA. There is an argument that compulsory paid leave, especially after the birth of a child, has the benefit of eliminating all pressure not to take the leave and stigma for taking it. However, mandated leave also deprives women of the option to choose for themselves how they want to handle the demands of both work and motherhood. And compulsory prenatal leave, regardless of the health status of the woman, deprives the many healthy and active pregnant women the option of working if they choose and reinforces the stereotype that pregnant women cannot or should not work.

Although generally other industrial countries provide pregnancy and parental leave policies that are far more generous than American ones, they sometimes do so in ways that are different from American policies and are not likely to be adopted here. The central policies of other nations with regard to maternity leave (longer leave and some pay during the leave) are clearly policies that the United States is slowing moving toward and may someday reach.

CONCLUSION

Pregnancy discrimination is an ongoing problem facing working women. Although the legislative achievements and judicial decisions of the past thirty years have greatly reduced the severity of such discrimination, it still exists and is difficult to prove. Advocates are pushing for, and many states are experimenting with providing, greater protections to pregnant workers, though a comparison to the law of other countries shows that it is possible to go much further.

Notes

1. The term *sex* was originally included in the draft legislation to defeat it, but then was championed by the few female legislators at the time. See "Comment: Sex Discrimination in Employment" (1968).
2. *Somers* v. *Aldine Independent School District* (1979) listed the number of courts that found pregnancy discrimination violated Title VII.
3. See Garner (2003) for a discussion of the consequences *Geduldig* could have today.
4. See Taylor (1978) for an example of a critical law review comment, and Recent Decisions: Civil Rights—Pregnancy Discrimination (1977), citing a contemporary *Ms. Magazine* article and press interview of ACLU spokesmen, union officials, and law professors against *Gilbert,* for examples of the more general critical response to the ruling.
5. This paragraph is a great simplification of the arguments offered by each of these positions. For more nuanced summaries of this debate and citations to the articles of the time, see Jacobson (1988), Strimling (1989), and Millsap (1996).
6. The only defense to a facially discriminatory policy under Title VII is whether the protected characteristic is a bona fide occupational qualification, which the Court held sex was not in this circumstance, as the ability to perform the jobs involving the lead exposure did not depend of sex.
7. Only 5 percent of potential plaintiffs are able to find an attorney. Then even if a court case is filed, 60 percent of employment discrimination claims are

dismissed on summary judgment for the employer. Furthermore, if the case proceeds to a trial, employees win only 40 percent of the time. See Howard (1995) and Maltby (1999).

8. In a simplified summary, the challenge to the law was under the Supreme Court's recent jurisprudence on the Eleventh Amendment that allows Congress to subject the states to monetary damages in a law if that law is based on enforcement of the Fourteenth Amendment and is supported by fact finding of discrimination by the states themselves and is a "congruent and proportional" response to that discrimination. See *Nevada Department of Human Resources* v. *Hibbs* (2003).

9. The states are California, Connecticut, Hawaii, Maine, Minnesota, New Jersey, Oregon, Rhode Island, Vermont, Washington, Wisconsin, and Washington, D.C.

10. The department concluded that this program was incompatible with the basic premise of unemployment insurance: that it is available only to people who are involuntarily unemployed and are actively seeking work, which is not necessarily true of people who are on maternity leave, and thus have jobs to go back to, or who have chosen to be full-time caregivers of their children

11. Andorra, Austria, Belgium, Denmark, England, Finland, France, Germany, Greece, Ireland, Italy, Liechtenstein, Luxembourg, Netherlands, Norway, Portugal, Spain, Sweden, and Switzerland. This group of countries is close to, but not precisely coextensive with, the European Union member states.

References

Armstrong v. Flowers Hospital Inc., 33 F.3d 1308 (11th Cir. 1994).

A break for new moms. (1996, Oct. 12). *Washington Post*, A24.

California Federal Savings and Loan Association v. Guerra, 479 U.S. 272 (1987).

Cantor, D., et al. (2001). *Balancing the needs of families and employers: The Family and Medical Leave surveys, 2000 update.* Washington, D.C.: U.S. Department of Labor.

Caplan-Cotenoff, S. A. (1987). Note and comment: Parental leave: The need for a national policy to foster sexual equality. *American Journal of Law and Medicine, 13,* 71–104.

Civil Rights Act of 1964, 42 U.S.C. §2000e-2(a) (2000).

Cleveland Board of Education v. LaFleur, 414 U.S. 632 (1974).

Comment: Sex discrimination in employment: An attempt to interpret Title VII of the Civil Rights Act of 1964. (1968). *Duke Law Journal, 1968,* 672–679.

Crnokrak v. Evangelical Health Systems, 819 F. Supp. 737 (N.D. Ill. 1993).

Equal Employment Opportunity Commission. (2003). Pregnancy Discrimination Charges EEOC and FEPAs Combined: FY 1992–FY 2003. Available at: http://www.eeoc.gov/stats/pregnancies.html.

Erickson v. Bartell Drug Co., 141 F. Supp. 2d 1266, 1276–77 (W.D. Wash. 2001).

Fifty percent increase in women in the workforce has not led to equivalent increase in maternity leave options; americanbaby.com survey shows parents demand issue receive national attention. (2001, Mar. 15). Available at: http://www.prnewswire.com.

Garner, B. (2003). Enforcing civil rights against the states: An analysis of the Pregnancy Discrimination Act of 1978 under the Court's Section 5 jurisprudence. *Review of Litigation, 22,* 711–758.

Geduldig v. Aiello, 417 U.S. 484 (1974).

General Electric Co. v. Gilbert, 429 U.S. 125 (1976).

Glavinovich, M. A. (1996). International suggestions for improving parental leave legislation in the United States. *Arizona Journal of International and Comparative Law, 13,* 147–174.

Greenberg, J. G. (1998). The Pregnancy Discrimination Act: Legitimating discrimination against pregnant women in the workforce. *Maine Law Review, 50,* 225–254.

Howard, W. M. (1995). Arbitrating claims of employment discrimination: What really does happen? What really should happen? *Dispute Resolution Journal, 50,* 40–45.

Hunt, L., Hsia, R. P., Smith, B. G., Martin, T. R., Rosenwein, B. H. (1995). Peoples and cultures from 1787 to the Global Age. In *The challenge of the West: Peoples and cultures from the Stone Age to the Global Age* (Vol. 30). Boston: Houghton Mifflin.

International Observatory of Labour Law. (2001). *National labour law profile: New Zealand.* http://ilo.org/public/english/dialogue/ifpdial/11/observatory/profiles/nz.org.

International Union v. Johnson Controls, Inc., 499 U.S. 187 (1991).

Invest in Canada. (2003). Other legislation impacting the employment relationship, subsec. 6. http://investincanada.gc.ca/ipc/cms. browse?IPC_Lang=e&IPC_PageAction=viewWebPage.

Jacobson, M. S. (1988). Pregnancy and employment: Three Approaches to equal opportunity. *Boston University Law Review, 68,* 1019–1045.

Jason, M. L. (1990). Note: International Union v. Johnson Controls, Inc.: Controlling women's equal employment opportunities through fetal protection policies. *American University Law Review, 40,* 453–502.

Jordan, L. (1999). *OLR research report: Background information on European and Canadian parental leave laws.* http:www.cga.state.ct.us/ps99/rpt/olr/htm/99-r-1214.htm.

Krauel v. Iowa Methodist Medical Center, 95 F.3d 674 (8th Cir. 1996).

Lindemann, B., Grossman, P., & Cane, P. W. (1996). *Employment discrimination law* (3rd ed.). Washington, D.C.: BNA Books.

Magid, J. M. (2001). Pregnant with possibility: Reexamining the Pregnancy Discrimination Act. *American Business Law Journal, 38,* 838–856.

Maltby, L. (1999, Fall). Employment arbitration: Is it really second class justice? *Dispute Resolution Magazine,* pp. 23–28.

Millsap, D. (1996). Reasonable accommodation of pregnancy in the workplace: A Proposal to Amend the Pregnancy Discrimination Act. *Houston Law Review, 32,* 1412–1450.

Mitchell v. Board of Trustees, 599 F.2d 582 (4th Cir.), cert. denied, 444 U.S. 965 (1979).

Muller v. Oregon, 208 U.S. 412 (1908).

Nashville Gas Co. v. Satty, 434 U.S. 136 (1977).

National Partnership for Women and Families. (2002a). *Establishing a state temporary disability insurance (TDI) program.* http://www.nationalpartnership.org/content.cfm?L1=8&L2=1&GuidesID=46&ArticleID=7.

National Partnership for Women and Families. (2002b). *State family leave benefit initiatives in the 2001–2002 state legislatures: Making family leave more affordable.* http://www.nationalpartnership.org/content.cfm?L1=8&L2=1&DBT=Guides&GSID=293.

Nevada Department of Human Resources v. Hibbs, 123 S. Ct. 1972, 1977, 1982 (2003).

New State Ice Co. v. Leibmann, 285 U.S. 262, 311 (1932).

Newport News Shipbuilding & Dry Dock Co. v. EEOC, 462 U.S. 669 (1983).

Pregnancy Discrimination Act. (1978). Pub. L. 95–555, 92 Stat. 2076 (codified as amended at 42 U.S.C. §2000e(k) (2000)).

Prohibition of Sex Discrimination Based on Pregnancy, H.R. Rep. No. 95-948, 95th Cong., 2d Sess. 2-3 (1978).

Recent decisions: Civil rights—pregnancy discrimination. (1997). 271, 282 n. 56.

Reed v. Reed, 404 U.S. 71 (1971).

Schultz, V. (2003). The sanitized workplace. *Yale Law Journal, 112,* 2061–2193.

Somers v. Aldine Independent School District, 464 F. Supp. 900, 902 (S.D. Tex. 1979).

Strimling, W. S. (1989). Comment: The constitutionality of state laws providing employment leave for pregnancy: Rethinking *Geduldig* after *Cal Fed. California Law Journal, 77,* 171–221.

Taylor, E. T. (1978). Comment: Differential treatment of pregnancy in employment: The impact of General Electric Co. v. Gilbert and Nashville Gas Co. v. Satty. *Harvard Civil Rights–Civil Liberties Law Review, 13,* 717–750.

Thomas, M. (2002). *Planning a family? Plan your parental leave.* http://www. prlaw.co.nz/news/empnews/parental.htm.

Troupe v. May Department Stores, Inc., 20 F.3d 734, 738 (7th Cir. 1994).

Turic v. Holland Hospitality, Inc., 85 F.3d 1211 (6th Cir. 1996).

Turner v. Department of Employment Security, 423 U.S. 44, 46 (1975).

U.S. Census Bureau. (2003). *Census 2000 brief: Employment status: 2000.* Washington, DC: U.S. Government Printing Office.

U.S. Department of Labor, Employment Standards Administration Wage and Hour Division. (2004). *Federal vs. state family and medical leave laws.* http://www.labor.gov/esa/programs/whd/state/fmla/.

Weirich, C. G. (2003). *Employment discrimination law 2002 supplement.* Washington, DC: BNA Books.

Wilson, C. S. (1976–1977). Note: Income protection for pregnant workers. *Drake Law Review, 26,* 389–422.

Zintl, A. (2004). How does your state measure up on maternity leave? *AmericanBaby.com.* Available at: http://www.americanbaby.com/ ab/story.jhtml?storyid=/templatedata/ab/story/data/1210.xml& catref=cat1840008.

Zuniga v. Kleburg County Hospital, 296 F.3d 986 (5th Cir. 1982).

CHAPTER SEVEN

Update on Abortion Law

Andrea Barnes, J.D., Ph.D.

I n the United States, the intensity of the discourse over abortion is frightening and frequently beyond reasoned debate. When physicians are murdered as a result of their abortion-related activities and clinics providing abortions require security precautions reminiscent of a prison system, it becomes difficult to imagine a middle ground. The goal of this chapter is not to revisit political and religious debates over whether abortion is right or wrong. Rather, it seeks to present a broader perspective. The reality of abortion has been acknowledged by the American legal system, with each Supreme Court decision redefining the line between a woman's legal right to make decisions about her own body and its reproductive functioning, and the limitations on that right as a pregnancy progresses and the viability of an unborn child outside the womb is more likely.

The evolution of American case law reflects the ongoing debate over the control of a woman's reproductive life, and it is often only in retrospect that we can see how unnecessarily intrusive a law has been. For example, until the Supreme Court began to discuss reproductive privacy in *Griswold* v. *Connecticut* in 1964, it was illegal in Connecticut for even married women to use birth control. Since then, case law has extended privacy to include a right to abortion (*Roe* v. *Wade,* 1973), but has continued to review the conditions under which this privacy can be exercised. It has examined the interests of a range of possible stakeholders in a woman's reproductive decisions (such as the spouse of an adult woman or the parents of a teenage girl), including the state and the unborn child. It has allowed constraints on access (funding, waiting periods) that make the right to abortion more theoretical than actual for many women. The politics of abortion have resulted in isolated rights for unborn children (twenty-six states have "fetal homicide" laws), while some legislators attempt to eliminate a pregnant woman's right to choose late-term abortion when her own life or health is at risk (the federal Partial Birth Abortion Act of 2003). The abortion debate has evolved to include moral judgments as well as moral loopholes: those who oppose abortion will generally allow it in the case of rape or incest; those who support abortion will tolerate Medicaid exclusions that make abortion effectively unavailable to poor women for financial reasons. This chapter reviews the legal reasoning underlying case decisions about abortion, as well as the psychological research on women's experience with abortion. It looks at current efforts to set limits on women's reproductive lives in what some have called "the new civil war" (Beckman & Harvey, 1998). It also looks at the efforts of a group of women who sought, if not reconciliation, then at least a mutual understanding in this "war" in the aftermath of the 1994 Boston-area shooting at a Planned Parenthood clinic by John Salvi.

HISTORY

Legislation and case law continue to struggle with two central issues: When do other people, including the state, have the right to make decisions about any individual's body? To what extent does a woman have the freedom to control her own reproductive activities? The abortion debate is partly about a woman's control of her own body and whether she is able to choose when and if she will get pregnant, and partly about a woman's control of the course of her life generally. For women, reproductive rights are not simply about access to abortion, but also include access to birth control and protections against discrimination once they become pregnant.

Historian Linda Gordon (1990) notes,

Because of the different interest of men and women in the practice of birth control, differences in birth-control techniques have social significance. Some techniques are more amenable than others to being used independently and even secretly by women; some give full control to men; others are more likely to be used cooperatively. Thus, it is important to be specific when considering birth control. For example, a list of the types of birth control might look like this: infanticide; abortion; sterilizing surgery; withdrawal by the male (coitus interruptus); melting suppositories designed to form an impenetrable coating over the cervix; diaphragms, caps, or other devices which are inserted into the vagina over the cervix and withdrawn after intercourse; intrauterine devices; internal medicines—potions or pills; douching and other forms of action after intercourse designed to kill or drive out the sperm; condoms; and varieties of rhythm methods, based on calculating the woman's fertile period and abstaining from intercourse during it. All these techniques were practiced in the ancient world and in modern preindustrial societies. Indeed, until the modern hormone-suppressing pill there were no essentially new birth-control devices, only improvements of the old [pp. 28–29].

In *Griswold* v. *Connecticut* (1965), the Supreme Court first addressed the issue of reproductive privacy when it overruled a Connecticut law banning the distribution or use of contraceptives, even within marriage. In writing for the majority, Justice William Douglas noted:

The present case . . . concerns a relationship lying within the zone of privacy created by several fundamental constitutional guarantees. And it concerns a law which, in forbidding the use of contraceptives rather than regulating their manufacture or sale, seeks to achieve its goals by means having the maximum destructive impact upon that relationship . . . . Would we allow the police to search the sacred precincts of marital bedrooms for telltale signs of the use of contraceptives? The very idea is repulsive to the notions of privacy surrounding the marriage relationship.

We deal with a right of privacy older than the bill of rights—older than our political parties, older than our school system. Marriage is a coming together for better or for worse, hopefully enduring, and intimate to the degree of being sacred. It is an association that promotes a way of life, not causes; a harmony in living, not political faiths; a bilateral loyalty, not commercial or social projects. Yet it is an association for as noble a purpose as any involved in our prior decisions [pp. 485–486].

ABORTION

Until relatively recently, abortion was treated like one of many methods of birth control and was not viewed as morally distinct from other methods. Law professors Sylvia Law, Jane E. Larson, and Clyde Spillenger reviewed the history of abortion in the United States in their amicus curiae brief submitted to the Supreme Court in *Planned Parenthood of Southeastern Pennsylvania* v. *Casey* (1992). They noted that at the time of the drafting of the federal constitution in the late eighteenth century, abortion was known and not illegal. In the nineteenth century, it became even more widely accepted.

> Through the nineteenth century, American common law decisions uniformly reaffirmed that women committed no offense in seeking abortions. Both common law and popular American understanding drew distinctions depending upon whether the fetus was "quick," i.e. whether the woman perceived signs of independent life. There was some dispute whether a common law misdemeanor occurred when a third party destroyed a fetus, after quickening, without the woman's consent. But early common law recognition of this crime against a pregnant woman did not diminish the woman's liberty to end a pregnancy herself in its early stages.
>
> Abortion was not a pressing social issue in colonial America, but as a social practice, it was far from unknown. Herbal abortifacients were widely known, and cookbooks and women's diaries of the era contained recipes for such medicines. Recent studies of the work of midwives in the 1700s report cases in which the midwives appeared to have provided women abortifacient compounds. Such treatments do not appear to have been regarded as extraordinary or illicit by those administering them. . . .
>
> In the late eighteenth century, strictures on sexual behavior loosened considerably. The incidence of premarital pregnancy rose sharply; by the late eighteenth century, one third of all New England brides were pregnant when they married, compared to less than ten percent in the seventeenth century. Falling birth rates in the 1780s suggest that, at the time of the drafting of the Constitution, the use of birth control and abortion was increasing. . . .
>
> Through the nineteenth century and well into the twentieth, abortion remained a widely accepted practice, despite growing efforts after 1860 to prohibit it. . . .

... The most common methods of abortion in the nineteenth century involved self administered herbs and devices available from pharmacists. Nonetheless, women also relied on professional abortionists: in 1871, New York City, with a population of less than one million, supported two hundred full-time abortionists, not including doctors who also sometimes performed abortions.

The late nineteenth century saw a movement toward professionalization across disciplines. This was a time when industrial and scientific developments were rapid, and meaningful progress was being made in the understanding of the basic sciences and their applications to medicine. At the same time, many workers perceived economic competition from both increased immigration and the increased levels of education (including professional education) becoming available to blacks and to women. The late 1800s saw the opening of the first women's colleges and the first black colleges, as well as some progress toward allowing these previously excluded groups to attend state universities.

As occupations such as medicine and law developed professional associations, they also created standards of training and licensure that were narrowly drawn and inevitably excluded women, minorities, and recently arrived immigrants. Law et al. (1992) note that between 1850 and 1880, the American Medical Association became the "single most important factor in altering the legal policies toward abortion in the country":

> The doctors found an audience for their effort to restrict abortion because they appealed to specific social concerns and anxieties: maternal health, consumer protection, discriminatory ideas about the properly subordinate status of women, and racist/nativist fears generated by the fact the elite Protestant women often sought abortions. Some of these doctors also sought to attribute moral status to the fetus.

Abortion regulation became a tool in the political and economics-driven process of defining who should be allowed to practice medicine and a means of excluding groups such as midwives and abortion providers who were not medical doctors. Law et al. (1992) note,

> Physicians were the principal nineteenth-century proponents of laws to restrict abortion. A core purpose of the nineteenth-century laws,

and the doctors in supporting them, was to control medical practice in the interest of public safety. . . . Anti-abortion laws would weaken the appeal of the competition and take the pressure off the more marginal members of the regulars' [regular physicians] own sect.

While physicians at the time argued that abortion regulation was for the purpose of protecting the safety and health of women, there is ample evidence of a general resistance to the increasing independence and self-determination of women. Similar arguments were waged at the idea of women receiving college educations, and women seeking education were warned that college would be both physically and socially damaging to them. Specifically, it would damage their ability to bear children and would certainly make them less attractive to potential husbands (Palmer, n.d.).

Law et al. (1992) argue that the enforcement of sharply differentiated concepts of the roles of men and women underlay efforts to regulate abortion and contraception in the nineteenth century:

Physicians persuaded political leaders (who were, of course, uniformly male) that "abortion constituted a threat to social order" and to male authority. Since the 1840s, a growing movement for women's suffrage and equality had generated popular fears that women were departing from a purely maternal role—fears fueled by the decline in family size during the nineteenth century. A central rhetorical focus of the woman's movement was framed by a new perception of women as the rightful possessors of their own bodies.

Opposition to abortion and contraception were closely linked, and can only be understood as a reaction to the uncertainties generated by changes in family function and anxieties created by women's challenges to their historic roles of silence and subservience. These challenges were critical factors motivating the all-male state legislatures that adopted restraints on women, including restrictions on abortion. In opposition to the feminist demand for control of reproduction, the federal government in 1873 took the lead in banning access to information about both contraception and abortion.

Law et al. (1992) argue that contraception and abortion regulation also reflected ethnocentric fears about relative birthrates of immigrant and white Protestants during a period of intense immigration at the end of the nineteenth century:

Beginning in the 1890s, and continuing through the first decades of the twentieth century, nativist fears coalesced into a drive against what was then called "race suicide." The "race suicide" alarmists worried that women of "good stock"—prosperous, white, and Protestant—were not having enough children to maintain the political and social supremacy of their group. Anxiety over the falling birth rates of Protestant whites in comparison with other groups helped shape policy governing both birth control and abortion.

Abortion became a focal point in the debate about women's lives. Interestingly, during the post–Civil War period, when the women's suffrage movement was gaining momentum and the first wave of feminism was attempting to redefine women's roles, there were feminists opposed to abortion. Mary Krane Derr, in a 1991 amicus curiae brief, notes:

> Early feminist opposition to abortion was deep-seated, and addressed the causes of abortion, not just the practice. In this way, it was distinguished from other anti-abortion efforts including those of the American Medical Association. Feminists documented that abortion was caused by, among other things, culturally enforced ignorance about sexual and reproductive physiology, especially family planning and fetal development; cultural construction of pregnancy as a pathological condition; a sexual double standard which permitted men to be sexually and parentally irresponsible; the social valuing of "legitimacy" over children's lives and women's well-being; and lack of social and economic support for mothers, especially single ones.

For women, the choices were never simple or free of stigma, but before 1973, upper- and middle-class patients with the right health care resources could obtain "therapeutic abortions" (Adler et al., 1992) if they declared themselves suicidal and received the appropriate documentation from one or two psychiatrists. In 1970, more than 98 percent of the legal therapeutic abortions were for mental health reasons (Adler et al., 1992).

LEGAL CASES

The Supreme Court has been the arena for promoting and challenging abortion in the United States. While *Roe* v. *Wade* (1973) established a woman's legal right to obtain an abortion, subsequent cases have addressed efforts to define and restrict that right.

Roe v. *Wade*: A Fundamental Privacy Right

In *Roe* v. *Wade* (1973), the U.S. Supreme Court described a woman's right to have an abortion as part of a fundamental right of privacy, similar to that in *Griswold,* and government interference with that right would be subject to strict judicial scrutiny.

Justice William Brennan, writing for the majority, noted that bans on abortion were relatively recent:

> It perhaps is not generally appreciated that the restrictive criminal abortion laws in effect in a majority of States today are of relatively recent vintage. Those laws, generally proscribing abortion or its attempt at any time during pregnancy except when necessary to preserve the pregnant woman's life, are not of ancient or even common-law origin. Instead, they derive from statutory changes effected, for the most part, in the latter half of the 19th century. . . .
>
> It is thus apparent that at common law, at the time of the adoption of our Constitution, and throughout the major portion of the 19th century, abortion was viewed with less disfavor than under most American statutes currently in effect. Phrasing it another way, a woman enjoyed a substantially broader right to terminate a pregnancy than she does today [p. 720].

He went on to describe the "person" for whom the Constitution was intended and then introduced the issue of "viability," or the point at which the state has a "compelling interest" in the unborn child:

> The Constitution does not define "person" in so many words. . . . But in nearly all these instances, the use of the word is such that it has application only postnatally. None indicates, with any assurance, that it has any possible prenatal application. . . . In short, the unborn have never been recognized in the law as persons in the whole sense.
>
> . . . We repeat, however, that the State does have an important and legitimate interest in preserving and protecting the health of the pregnant woman, whether she be a resident of the State or a non-resident who seeks medical consultation and treatment there, and that it has still another important and legitimate interest in protecting the potentiality of human life. *These interests are separate and distinct* [italics added]. Each grows in substantiality as the woman approaches term and, at a point during pregnancy, each becomes "compelling."

... The end of the first trimester mortality in abortion may be less than mortality in normal childbirth. It follows that, from and after this point, a State may regulate the abortion procedure to the extent that the regulation reasonably related to the preservation and protection of maternal health.

With respect to the state's important and legitimate interest in potential life, the "compelling" point is viability [p. 163].

Doe v. *Bolton*: Health of the Mother

In *Doe* v. *Bolton* (1973), the companion case to *Roe* v. *Wade*, the Supreme Court held that the decision of whether a woman requires an abortion for the health of the mother is a medical judgment to "be exercised in the light of all factors— physical, emotional, psychological, familial, and the woman's age— relevant to the well-being of the patient" (p. 212).

Hyde Amendment and *Maher* v. *Roe*: Medicaid Funding

Since *Roe* v. *Wade*, the Supreme Court has used abortion cases to refine its position and define the limits to a woman's access to abortion. As states have enacted increasingly restrictive abortion laws, the Supreme Court has had to determine the boundary between a state's legitimate interest and an unreasonable interference in access to abortion.

Federal regulations have also implemented limitations on access and funding of abortions. The Hyde Amendment, passed by Congress in 1976, excludes abortion from the health care coverage provided to low-income women through Medicaid, except when a woman's life is at risk (Lichtman, 2003). Congress later amended the Hyde Amendment to allow coverage for abortions in cases of rape or incest.

States enacted legislation with similar restrictions. In *Maher* v. *Roe* (1977), the Court was presented with the question of whether the right of access to abortion described in *Roe* v. *Wade* included an entitlement to Medicaid payments for abortions that are not medically necessary. At issue in *Maher* was a Connecticut welfare regulation under which Medicaid recipients received payments for medical services incidental to childbirth but not for medical services incidental to non-therapeutic abortions. The Court held that the constitutional freedom recognized in *Wade* and its progeny "protects the woman from unduly

burdensome interference with her freedom to decide whether to terminate her pregnancy" (pp. 473–474) such as the severe criminal sanctions at issue in *Roe* v. *Wade,* or the absolute requirement of spousal
consent for an abortion challenged in *Planned Parenthood of Central
Missouri* v. *Danforth* (1976), but did not prevent Connecticut from
being free to make "a value judgment favoring childbirth over abortion, and . . . implement that judgment by the allocation of public
funds" (p. 474):

> Although government may not place obstacles in the path of a wom-
> an's exercise of her freedom of choice, it need not remove those not of
> its own creation. Indigency falls in the latter category. The financial
> constraints that restrict an indigent woman's ability to enjoy the full
> range of constitutionally protected freedom of choice are the product
> not of governmental restrictions on access to abortions, but rather of
> her indigency [p. 478].

The Court stated that indigent women do not even have a right to
funding for a medically necessary abortion:

> Although Congress has opted to subsidize medically necessary services
> generally, but not certain medically necessary abortions, the fact re-
> mains that the Hyde Amendment leaves an indigent woman with at
> least the same range of choice in deciding whether to obtain a med-
> ically necessary abortion as she would have had if Congress had cho-
> sen to subsidize no health care costs at all. We are thus not persuaded
> that the Hyde Amendment impinges on the constitutionally protected
> freedom of choice recognized in Wade [p. 478].

The Hyde Amendment sets a floor, but permits states to use their
own funds to underwrite abortions for low-income women. As of February 2004, only four states (New York, Maryland, Hawaii, and Washington) have done this voluntarily. Thirteen other states have done so
under court order (Lichtman, 2003). Thirty-two states and the District of Columbia follow the federal standard and provide abortions
in cases of life endangerment, rape, or incest. One state, South Dakota,
pays for abortions only when necessary to protect the woman's life
(Alan Guttmacher Institute, 2004).

Congress has passed restrictions similar to the Hyde Amendment
affecting programs on which an estimated 20 million women rely for

their health care or insurance. According to the American Civil Liberties Union (2002), those denied access to federally funded abortion include poor women on Medicaid, Native Americans, federal employees and their dependents, Peace Corps volunteers, low-income residents of Washington, D.C., federal prisoners, and military personnel and their dependents.

New health initiatives are also being burdened by the legacy of the Hyde Amendment. The Children's Health Insurance Program, a program providing expanded health insurance for children aged nineteen or younger, includes a ban on the use of federal funds for abortions unless the pregnancy endangers the teenager's life or results from rape or incest. The Omnibus Appropriations Act for fiscal year 1999 also extended the Hyde Amendment to Medicare for the first time, prohibiting abortion coverage for disabled women, except in cases of rape, incest, or life endangerment (American Civil Liberties Union, 2002).

Planned Parenthood of Central Missouri v. *Danforth:* Spousal Consent

The Court held in this 1976 case that legislative bodies or courts could not properly determine the specific point in the gestational period when viability occurred, holding instead that such a determination varies with each pregnancy and should be left to the individual judgment of the attending physician.

Webster v. *Reproductive Health Services:* Use of Public Facilities and Public Personnel

In *Webster* v. *Reproductive Health Services* (1989), five state-employed health professionals and two nonprofit corporations brought a class action suit challenging Missouri's 1986 act. The act declared in its preamble that life begins at conception. It prohibited the use of public funds to counsel women to have an abortion unless necessary to save her life, and it prohibited the use of public hospitals or state employees for abortions unless necessary to save the woman's life. It also required physicians to perform viability tests on fetuses after twenty weeks' gestation. The Court articulated the position that a state may make a value judgment, as Missouri did in its preamble, which favored childbirth over abortion. The Supreme Court maintained that this act only restricted "a woman's ability to obtain an abortion to the extent she chooses a public facility" and did not examine the cost differences between a public and private facility, or the actual effect on access to abortion for poor women.

Planned Parenthood of Southeastern Pennsylvania v. *Casey*: Restrictive State Abortion Laws

In *Planned Parenthood of Southeastern Pennsylvania* v. *Casey* (1992), the Supreme Court reaffirmed the right to an abortion as part of a constitutionally protected right to privacy but simultaneously upheld a state's ability to pass restrictive abortion laws (Lichtman, 2003). It also lowered the standard of review for abortion legislation from "strict scrutiny" to "unduly burdensome," making it easier for such restrictions on abortion to be found constitutional.

Under a "strict scrutiny" analysis, legislation infringing on the right to privacy was treated with the most rigorous level of review, reserved for certain fundamental constitutional rights such as free speech, religious freedom, or freedom from racial discrimination. It is rare for legislation infringing on these rights to survive strict scrutiny. By lowering the standard of review to the more ambiguous "unduly burdensome," the Court opened the door to a number of restrictions that would make it more difficult for women to obtain abortions but did not go so far as to prohibit them.

At issue in this case were the provisions of the Pennsylvania Abortion Control Act of 1982, which

1. Required informed consent before an abortion and specified that certain information must be provided at least twenty-four hours before the abortion

2. Required consent of one of the parents of a minor seeking an abortion with the option of judicial bypass in certain circumstances

3. Required spousal notification by married women seeking abortions

4. Defined a "medical emergency" as a condition that necessitates an abortion to avoid death or serious, irreversible harm to the mother and exempted women in that condition from the above requirements

5. Imposed various reporting requirements for facilities that perform abortions

Justices Sandra Day O'Connor, Anthony Kennedy, and David Souter, writing for the majority, reaffirmed the essential holding of *Roe* v. *Wade*—a woman's right to an abortion before fetal viability—but rejected its trimester framework. The medical emergency definition and exemption, informed-consent requirement, parental consent requirement (with judicial bypass), and record-keeping provisions were upheld using an "undue burden" standard. The spousal notification requirement was held unconstitutional, because it imposed an undue burden on women who fear abuse from their husbands, as were the reporting requirements pertaining to it.

Public Policy Consequences of Restrictive Abortion Laws

Beginning with *Roe* v. *Wade*, the legal discussion of abortion has been one of physiology. A pregnant woman and her fetus are presented as two beings that happen to be temporarily interconnected. Becker, Bowman, and Torrey (1994) note "that the woman and her life are almost absent from the discussion of abortion in Roe v. Wade, which becomes instead the story of the fetus and the doctor . . . resulting from the fact that the Court typically reasons about reproductive regulation in physiological paradigms, seeing regulation as state action that concerns women's bodies rather than women's roles, despite the fact that the social role of women was clearly the central concern in the historical debate about abortion" (p. 378).

From the beginning of abortion case law, the Court introduced the idea that the interests of a pregnant woman and those of the "potentiality of human life" are "separate and distinct" (*Roe* v. *Wade*). This arguably artificial distinction between a pregnant woman and the child she carries encouraged a line of reasoning that would not be acceptable in other areas of the law. While discrimination based on pregnancy has been prohibited by legislation and case law, including discrimination in health insurance, the Court allowed exactly this discrimination in the Hyde Amendment by excluding insurance coverage when the pregnant woman needs an abortion, even when her life or health are at risk, which is surely the definition of "medically necessary."

Current legislation continues to set mother and unborn child against one another, and the value of the mother's life is explicitly disregarded. Before the movement to regulate abortion, when "quickening" was the criterion for a fetus's viability, it was the pregnant mother who determined whether she experienced evidence of life in the unborn child. Since *Roe* v. *Wade,* legislators have increasingly sought to regulate women as if they were simply vessels that happened to be physiologically connected to the unborn child.

Lichtman (2003) argues that states' restrictive abortion laws reduce access to abortions for low-income women and result in increases in unwanted births to low-income women and increases in the number of children needing and receiving public assistance. Underserved women are the first to lose their right to choose, because limitations on funding and access make abortion effectively unavailable to them. Lichtman compared three states: South Dakota, which has the most restrictive abortion laws and only one abortion provider in the entire state, and Vermont and Connecticut, which protect a woman's right to reproductive choice in their state constitutions. She found that by looking at indicators such as abortion rates, birthrates, child poverty levels, and public assistance caseloads, one can identify a link between abortion access and the number of unwanted births to underserved women. In contrast to Vermont and Connecticut, South Dakota has not been able to reduce its high number of children living in poverty. Lichtman states, "While motivations are both political as well as ethical, anti-abortion legislators and judges are imposing their own ethical beliefs on whomever they can control. In most instances, low-income women and minors are those with the least bargaining power and are thus easiest to control. If these anti-abortion legislators impose their moral beliefs about abortion on low-income women, by removing their access to abortion, these women's reproductive right to privacy is terminated" (p. 361).

CURRENT LEGISLATION

A series of legislative acts have emerged that illustrate the ongoing challenge to *Roe* v. *Wade* and abortion rights. Rather than trying to overrule the decision in *Roe,* opponents of abortion have used the strategy of incremental legislation, restricting abortion further and further until access is effectively unavailable.

The Partial-Birth Abortion Ban Act of 2003

The Partial-Birth Abortion Ban Act of 2003 represents the most recent challenge to *Roe* v. *Wade* and is a response to the 2000 Supreme

Court decision *Stenberg* v. *Carhart,* in which the Court struck down a similar state law in Nebraska.

In *Planned Parenthood* v. *Casey* (1992), the Court rejected the *Roe* trimester framework and held that the point of viability is the dividing line for determining when the state's interest in potential life outweighs a woman's interest in choosing whether to have an abortion. The *Casey* Court determined that the state's interest in potential life exists throughout pregnancy and thus a regulation on abortion is constitutional at any point during pregnancy so long as it does not place an "undue burden" on a woman's right to choose.

In *Stenberg,* the Court applied the *Casey* test to a Nebraska statute banning partial birth abortion. The statute in question banned partial birth abortion except when "necessary to save the life of the mother" (Holsinger, 2003). Though ostensibly aimed at prohibiting the abortion procedure known as "dilation and extraction" (D&X), the Nebraska law did not refer specifically to this procedure, and instead defined partial birth abortion as "an abortion procedure in which the person performing the abortion partially delivers vaginally a living unborn child before killing the unborn child and completing the delivery" (*Stenberg* v. *Carhart,* 2000, p. 922). The statute specifically prohibited the deliberate and intentional delivery "into the vagina a living unborn child, or a substantial portion thereof, for the purpose of performing a procedure that the person performing such procedure knows will kill the unborn child and does kill the unborn child" (*Stenberg* v. *Carhart,* 2000, p. 922).

The Court examined the Nebraska statute as it applied to pre- and postviability abortions and found that the statute's vague language rendered it unconstitutional with regard to previability abortions. In examining the definition of partial birth abortion, the Court found that the language applied to both D&X and to a different procedure "dilation and evacuation" (D&E). D&E is the most common procedure used for previability second-trimester abortions. Because the statute had the effect of banning the previability use of D&E, it constituted an undue burden on a woman's right to choose (Holsinger, 2003). In her concurrence in *Stenberg,* Justice O'Connor noted that if the Nebraska statute were limited to D&X and included a health exception, "the question presented would be quite different from the one we face today" (*Stenberg* v. *Carhart,* 2000, p. 950).

The language of the Partial-Birth Abortion Ban Act of 2003 is substantially the same as that of the Nebraska statute. The bill's drafters claim to have remedied one of the constitutional problems that plagued the Nebraska statute by defining partial birth abortion more precisely so as to exclude D&C procedures from the scope of the bill's prohibition (Holsinger, 2003). Holsinger argues that the bill easily could have been drafted to exclude D&E by specifically limiting the prohibition to either D&X or postviability procedures. Instead, like earlier versions, the bill employs nonmedical terminology to define the procedures prohibited under the bill. This intentional ambiguity is arguably intended to allow the broadest possible interpretation of the prohibition and thus to restrict abortion procedure by procedure.

Carhart v. Ashcroft

The Center for Reproductive Rights legally challenged the federal abortion ban. This case, known as *Carhart* v. *Ashcroft,* went to trial in 2004 in a Nebraska federal court. Representing doctors from Nebraska, New York, Virginia, and Iowa, the center argued that the ban on safe abortion procedures violates the U.S. Constitution and puts women's health and lives in serious jeopardy. To stop the federal ban from taking effect, a lawsuit was filed on October 31, 2003, on behalf of Dr. LeRoy Carhart, the lead plaintiff in the earlier Supreme Court case. When President Bush signed the new federal law, U.S. District Court Judge Richard G. Kopf, for the District of Nebraska, issued a temporary restraining order blocking enforcement of the abortion ban, allowing Dr. Carhart and the other physicians challenging the law to continue to perform abortions without fear of prosecution. Pending further legal decisions, the law was blocked by federal courts in Nebraska, New York, and California (Center for Reproductive Rights, 2004). In September 2004, Judge Kopf handed down a decision finding the Partial-Birth Abortion Ban Act of 2003 unconstitutional:

> After giving Congress the respectful consideration it is always due, I find and conclude that the ban is unreasonable and not supported by substantial evidence. In truth, "partial-birth abortions," which are medically known as "intact D&E" or "D&X" procedures, are sometimes necessary to preserve the health of a woman seeking an abortion. While the procedure is infrequently used as a relative matter, when it is needed, the health of women frequently hangs in the balance.
>
> Therefore, I declare the "Partial-Birth Abortion Ban Act of 2003" unconstitutional because it does not allow, and instead prohibits, the use of the procedure when necessary to preserve the health of a woman.

In addition, I decide that the ban fails as a result of other constitutional imperfections. As a result, I will also permanently enjoin enforcement of the ban. Importantly, however, because the evidence was sparse regarding postviability, I do not decide whether the law is unconstitutional when the fetus is indisputably viable [pp. 2, 5].

FACE: Freedom of Access to Clinic Entrances Act

Increased family planning and abortion clinic violence compelled Congress to pass the Freedom of Access to Clinic Entrances Act (FACE) in 1994, which prohibits the use of force, threats of force, and physical obstruction of clinic entrances. FACE appeared to be effective in decreasing the violent attacks on clinics. Although bomb threats, arson, death threats, and stalking still persist at 20 percent of clinics, the figure is down from 52 percent of clinics in 1994 (Smith, 2002).

While there have been challenges to FACE based on the First Amendment freedoms of speech and assembly, the U.S. Supreme Court has refused to hear these challenges. Lower courts have determined that the legislation is content-neutral and is thus is not biased against the expression of a particular viewpoint or political position. Courts have also determined that the First Amendment does not protect the types of activities that FACE seeks to prohibit (Smith, 2002). In May 2002, an en banc panel of the Ninth Circuit ruled that "wanted-style" posters and an Internet "hit list" identifying abortion providers are also threats under FACE. The court upheld the injunctive relief in the case, but remanded the case for further review regarding the size of the punitive damage award (Feminist Majority Foundation, 2004).

RU486

The violence that FACE tried to address also frightened away potential manufacturers of RU486, thereby denying American women a safe and more easily obtained early abortion procedure. According to Eric Schaff, M.D. (1999), the threat of physical violence is a major reason that potential manufacturers of RU486 are reluctant to step forward. Schaff notes that the escalating violence targeted at abortion providers and abortion facilities has decreased the number of physicians who are willing to risk their lives and careers to provide these services. Eighty-four percent of counties in the United States have no abortion provider. As a result, fewer services make it more difficult for women to access abortion, thus undermining their ability to control their fertility and health.

RU486, also known as mifepristone, represents a new class of medications that block the action of progesterone, a naturally occurring hormone produced by the ovaries. This causes a nonsurgical abortion in over 95 percent of early pregnancies. RU486 has also been shown to have many significant nonabortifacient-related benefits such as emergency contraception, once-a-month contraception, labor induction, and cervical dilation. It has also been used in the treatment of endometriosis, fibroids, meningioma, Cushing's syndrome, and progesterone-sensitive tumors such as some breast cancer, endometrial cancer, and prostate cancer (Schaff, 1999).

In November of 2003, the RU-486 Suspension and Review Act of 2003 was introduced by Sen. Sam Brownback (R-KS) and Rep. Mike DeMint (R-SC). This legislation was intended to prevent the use of mifepristone and called for a review of the process by which FDA approved the drug. It was not passed.

This legislation was viewed by many as blatantly antichoice politics, rather than reflecting a concern for women's health. The RU-486 Suspension and Review Act challenged the integrity of the FDA to determine the medical and scientific safety of the drugs it approves. In fact, the FDA has approved 557 new drugs since 1995, yet Congress has never attempted to impose such onerous and burdensome distribution requirements on any other drug. Legislating the approval or disapproval of any drug sets a dangerous precedent. The effort to restrict FDA approval of mifepristone on the basis of an antichoice viewpoint undermines the integrity of the drug approval process and prevents FDA's reliance on science as the sole determining factor in judging the safety of drugs. As is the case with all FDA-approved drugs, mifepristone was put through rigorous scientific research to determine its safety and efficacy (American Association of University Women, 2004).

Ideologically driven legislation such as this disregards other possible benefits of nascent medications and limits access both to safer means of abortion and to potentially effective treatments for other disorders, further undermining a woman's right to choose.

FETAL RIGHTS

The question of whether a fetus has rights independent of its mother has been the subject of political debate and has presented challenges to well-established rights of privacy, opportunities for valuable stem cell research, and the basic concept that a woman should have control over her own body. Issues of gender, race, and poverty discrimination are all raised in reference to the populations immediately affected by these policies.

In what has been referred to as a frontal assault on abortion rights, legislators at the state and federal levels have sought to define life as starting at conception, thus making abortion illegal as a form of murder. Congressman Duncan Hunter (R-CA) introduced a bill titled the "Life at Conception Act of 2003." Hunter's bill asserts that life begins at conception, and the California congressman hopes that if it ever becomes law, abortion supporters will have no legal leg on which to stand: "The only way that we're going to legislatively overturn Roe v. Wade is to establish personhood early on—and that is at conception," Hunter said (Tennessee Right to Life, 2003). Beyond abortion access, this type of legislation has implications for a woman to be held criminally accountable for the outcome of her pregnancy.

Ferguson v. *City of Charleston* (2001) accentuates the distinct problems behind conceptually separating a woman from her fetus for the purpose of law. Heard by the Supreme Court, *Ferguson* v. *City of Charleston* addressed matters of self-incrimination, right to privacy, and discrimination.

In 1989, in response to concern over the apparent increase in the use of cocaine by pregnant patients and "crack babies," the Medical University of South Carolina (MUSC) implemented a policy ordering drug screening to be performed on urine samples of pregnant women suspected of using cocaine. MUSC developed and implemented this policy in conjunction with local law enforcement officials. Police could be involved in one of two ways: identification of drug use during pregnancy and the identification of drug use after delivery. In the first way, the patient faced arrest only if she tested positive a second time or refused to enter and complete a substance abuse program. In the second way, the police promptly arrested the patient. Ten women who received care at MUSC were arrested after testing positive for cocaine. In *Ferguson* v. *City of Charleston,* they challenged the policy, stating that warrantless and nonconsensual drug tests conducted for criminal investigatory purposes were unconstitutional searches (Leslie, 2001).

The Supreme Court found that the state hospital's policy violated the constitutional rights of the women who were tested. It held that "a state hospital's performance of a diagnostic test to obtain evidence of a patient's criminal conduct for law enforcement purposes is an unreasonable search if the patient has not consented to the procedure" (Leslie, 2001, p. 95). The Court described the invasion of privacy in *Ferguson* as far more substantial than similar cases in that the hospital did not provide these pregnant women with an understanding about the purpose of the test, the potential use of the test results, or protections against the unauthorized distribution of the results to third parties. The Court noted that it was apparent that "the focus of the policy was on the arrest and prosecution of the drug-abusing mothers." While the ultimate goal of the program may have been substance abuse treatment for the women in question, the immediate goal of the searches was to generate evidence for law enforcement purposes. The Court found that the primary purpose of the Charleston program was to use the threat of arrest and prosecution in order to force women into treatment. Because of police involvement, the strictures of the Fourth Amendment should be strictly adhered. State hospital employees had a duty to inform patients of the potential ramifications of the urinalysis if the specific purpose for the test is to obtain evidence of potential drug abuse. The maternity patients should have been made aware that their urine drug tests were going to be reported to law enforcement if their urine tested positive for cocaine (Leslie, 2001).

The South Carolina case focused on women ingesting drugs or alcohol while pregnant, with the propensity for the women affected to be African American. Gagan (2000) reported that in a rehabilitation program generated for this "criminal" population, "forty-two women arrested under the program between 1989 and 1994 were black [all but one]. The single white woman allegedly had a black boyfriend, a fact which was noted on her chart" (p. 491).

Fried (1990) suggests that gender discrimination plays a role in these cases, in that a woman is being charged for criminal activities against the fetus while men who commit equal or greater degrees of violence are not prosecuted. Fried (1990) illustrates this in an example:

> While the behavior of pregnant women has, in some cases, led to criminal prosecution, there have been no prosecutorial efforts to arrest men for the damage that secondhand cigarette smoke may cause to a fetus; men have not been required to avoid exposure to drugs or chemicals known to cause damage to the sperm; nor have the male partners of pregnant battered women been targeted by prosecutors for their infliction of injury to the fetus in the course of physically abusing the woman [p. 265].

Efforts to legally establish fetal rights, and particularly life at conception, also threaten the possibility of scientific gains from embryonic stem cell research. Stevens (2003) emphasizes, "Because the Catholic Church, pro-life activists, and other religious groups believe that life starts at conception, they oppose embryonic stem cell research. These groups argue that benefiting from the destruction of a human embryo is 'no less a crime than abortion'"(p. 631).

Questions raised about the ethics of acquiring the embryonic stem cells must be matched with questions of the ethics of withholding possible medical treatments. Regardless of what stance is taken in this debate, medical advances that save lives are valuable.

PSYCHOLOGICAL AND CULTURAL PERSPECTIVES ON ABORTION

In 1969, the American Psychological Association (APA) Council of Representatives adopted a resolution that identified termination of unwanted pregnancies as a mental health and child welfare issue. It resolved that termination of pregnancy be considered a civil right of pregnant women, to be handled like other medical and surgical procedures in consultation with her physician (Adler et al., 1992).

In 1980, in response to governmental attempts to suppress research on abortion, the APA Council of Representatives passed a resolution supporting the right to conduct scientific research on abortion and reproductive health, stating that the APA "affirms the right of qualified researchers to conduct appropriate research in all areas of fertility regulation" (Adler et al., 1992, p. 1194).

In February 1989, the APA, wishing to improve the accuracy of the debate, convened a panel of experts to review the best scientific studies of abortion outcome. In August 1989, the APA Council of Representatives, concerned about the distortions of the research findings in the press, passed its third abortion resolution. This resolution, which cited the work of the panel, initiated a public awareness effort to correct the record on the scientific findings of abortion research (Adler et al. 1992).

Psychological Research on the Effects of Abortion

The psychological research on abortion has focused on postabortion emotional responses (Adler et al., 1992).

STRESS AND COPING. From the stress and coping perspective, an unwanted pregnancy is seen as an event that can be challenging or stressful. Stress has been defined as emerging from an interaction of the individual and the environment in a situation that the person appraises as "taxing or exceeding his or her resources and endangering his or her well-being" (Lazarus & Folkman, 1984, p. 19). Termination of an unwanted pregnancy may reduce the stress engendered by the occurrence of the pregnancy and the associated events. At the same time, the abortion itself may be experienced as stressful (Adler et al., 1992).

Research on the psychological effects of abortion has found that most women do not show any long-term harm after having had an abortion. According to Cozzarelli, Sumer, and Major (1998), "Although most women do not appear to experience severe, negative, postabortion psychological responses, abortion is perceived as an acute stressor by a large number of women." In general, individuals who feel efficacious have been found to handle stressful life events, including abortion, more effectively. Furthermore, self-efficacy beliefs have been found to mediate the positive effects of more global personal resources such as self-esteem, optimism, and locus of control on adjustment.

Adler et al. (1992) note the methodological difficulties in the psychological research literature on abortion, including researcher bias, too narrow a focus on pathological or negative outcomes of abortion, and questionable validity and reliability of outcome measures such as interviews. The varied quality of these studies makes it difficult to draw conclusions from the entire body of existing research literature. Many reports are clinical observations of small numbers of women. Some provide no data, or data are inappropriately or inadequately analyzed. Some studies report responses of women having illegal or therapeutic abortions rather than legal, elective procedures. Some studies, particularly those that are retrospective, may have a mix of women who had illegal, therapeutic, and elective abortions that are not analyzed separately.

In order to try to draw some conclusions from existing research, Adler et al. (1992) reviewed research that met the following minimum criteria: the study must be empirical (involving the collection of data subjected to statistical analysis) and use a definable sample. The studies used only samples of women who had abortions under legal, nonrestrictive conditions in the United States. The studies involved a range of medical settings, and the subjects covered a range of ethnicities and ages. The weight of the evidence was that legal abortion, as a resolution to an unwanted pregnancy, particularly in the first trimester, does not create psychological hazards for most women undergoing the procedure. In fact, psychological distress has generally been found to drop from before the procedure to immediately after and from preabortion or immediately postabortion to several weeks afterward.

SELF-ESTEEM. Russo and Zierk (1992) examined the relationship of abortion and childbearing to self-esteem in a national sample of 5,295 U.S. women interviewed annually from 1979 to 1987 in the National Longitudinal Study of Youth. Controlling for preexisting self-esteem, employment, income, and education, neither having one abortion nor having repeat abortions in the period from 1980 to 1987 was related to self-esteem. This study demonstrates that up to eight years following an abortion, no negative associations occur with self-esteem (Center for Human Resources Research, 1988).

DEMOGRAPHIC AND SOCIAL FACTORS. Younger and unmarried women without children were relatively more likely than those who were older and who had already given birth to experience negative responses. So too were women whose culture or religion prohibits abortions and those who attended church more frequently (Adler et al., 1992).

THE DECISION PROCESS. A number of studies have examined the relationship between aspects of the woman's decision process regarding abortion and her emotional response afterward. Most women do not have difficulty with the abortion decision. Osofsky, Osofsky, and Rajan (1973) found that 12 percent of 100 first-trimester patients stated the decision to have an abortion was difficult, and 7 percent reported initial indecision regarding continuation or termination of the pregnancy. Among 200 second-trimester patients in the study, 51 percent reported difficulty in deciding, and 36 percent reported initial indecision. Other correlates of difficult decisions or ambivalent feelings are being married and being Catholic (Adler et al., 1992).

Studies examining satisfaction with the abortion decision and postabortion emotional response consistently found that women who were satisfied with their choice or reported little difficulty in making the decision showed more positive postabortion responses. Greater difficulty in making the decision has been associated with higher negative postabortion reactions, including feelings of guilt, anxiety, and internally based negative emotions, such as regret and depression (Adler et al., 1992).

Women who initially want to be pregnant may react more negatively to abortion. Shusterman (1979) found an association between a woman's immediate affective response to learning that she was pregnant and her response to abortion. Women who reported the pregnancy as "highly meaningful" to them reported more physical complaints immediately after and anticipated more negative consequences from the abortion than did women who reported their pregnancy to be less meaningful (Adler et al., 1992).

Abortion in the Context of Culture

Catherine MacKinnon (1987) describes the aspect of abortion that the legal decision makers have chosen to overlook: that abortion is "inextricable from sexuality" and that men's and women's lives are very different for that reason:

> I first situate abortion and the abortion right in the experience of women. The argument is that abortion is inextricable from sexuality. . . .
> Most women who seek abortions became pregnant while having sexual intercourse with men. Most did not mean or wish to conceive. In contrast to this fact of women's experience, which converges sexuality with reproduction with gender, the abortion debate has centered on separating control over sexuality from control over reproduction, and on separating both from gender and the life options of the sexes.
> . . . Sexual intercourse, still the most common cause of pregnancy, cannot simply be presumed coequally determined. Sex doesn't look a whole lot like freedom when it appears normatively less costly for women to risk an undesired, often painful, traumatic, dangerous, sometime illegal, and potentially life-threatening procedure than to protect themselves in advance.
> In the context of a sexual critique of gender inequality, abortion promises to women sex with men on the same reproductive terms as men have sex with women [pp. 93, 94–96, 99].

Kathleen M. Sullivan and Susan R. Estrich (1989) noted,

> Abortion restrictions, like the most classic gender-based restrictions on women seeking to participate in the worlds of work and ideas, have historically rested on archaic stereotypes of women as persons whose

"paramount destiny and mission . . . [is] to fulfill the noble and benign office of wife and mother" (Bradwell v. Illinois, 1873). . . . Legislation prohibiting abortion, largely a product of the years between 1860
and 1880, reflected precisely the same ideas about the natural and proper
role of women as did the legislation of the same period—long-since
discredited—that prohibited women from serving on juries or participating in the professions, including the practice of law.

Abortion as an International Health Concern

The World Health Organization defined reproductive health as "complete physical, mental and social well-being in all matters related to the
reproductive system" (cited in Murphy, 2003, p. 205). It defined sexual
health as "a part of reproductive health that includes healthy sexual development, equitable and responsible relationships and sexual fulfillment, and freedom from illness, disease, disability, violence and other
harmful practices related to sexuality" (p. 205). Henry David (1994)
noted that the most significant development in reproductive behavior
over the past few decades has been the political commitment to the
worldwide expansion of more effective contraceptive practice:

> Historically, the human rights rationale emerged when women began
> to assert their rights as equal partners. A woman who lacks control
> over her fertility has considerable difficulty completing her education,
> maintaining gainful employment, and making independent marital
> decisions. The demographic rationale evolved in response to concerns
> about the negative effects of rapid population growth on socio-
> economic development and environmental degradation. The health
> rationale became the basis for advocating that pregnancy be delayed
> until the most appropriate time and for preventing high-risk unin-
> tended pregnancies [p. 344].

The human rights rationale is inextricably intertwined with a woman's role in decision making, cultural traditions, and access to education. In societies in which a woman's value is based on the number of
children she has, her ability to regulate and control her fertility will be
limited. Women in developing countries with seven or more years of
education tend to marry, on average, four years later and have two or
three fewer children than women with no schooling (David, 1994).

UNWANTED CHILDREN

One of the arguments in favor of access to abortion involves concern for the psychological and physical health of unwanted children, born because a woman did not have access to abortion. According to David (1994), unique circumstances combined to make available for detailed medical, psychological, and social assessment 110 boys and 110 girls born between 1961 and 1963 to Prague women twice denied an abortion for the same pregnancy: once on initial request to an abortion commission and again on appeal. In order to study the impact of being the result of an unwanted pregnancy, these 220 children were pair-matched with 220 children born to women who had purposely discontinued contraception or had accepted unplanned pregnancies. Matching criteria included age, sex, number of siblings, birth order, and school class. The mothers were matched for age, marital status, and socioeconomic status as determined by their male partner's occupation and presence in the home. All of the children were born into intact families, in which both the mother and father (or father substitute) were present.

The children were about nine years old at original assessment and have been followed over many years. Differences between the two groups of subjects widened over time, always to the detriment of those born from unwanted pregnancies. For example, at ages twenty-one to twenty-three, the subjects born to women twice denied abortion for the same pregnancy reported significantly more often than did the control subjects less job satisfaction, more conflict with coworkers and supervisors, less satisfying relations with friends, and more disappointments in love. A larger proportion had had sexual experience with more than ten partners, judged their marriages to be less happy, and more often expressed the desire not to be married to their current partner. There was considerable evidence that in the aggregate, being unwanted and subsequent compulsory childbearing had a detrimental effect on psychosocial development (David, 1994).

Romania represents the most striking failure of a coercive public policy designed to influence reproductive behavior, according to David (1994). After years of liberal abortion legislation and ready access to abortion services, on October 1, 1966, without prior warning, Romania severely restricted access to legal abortion, except for women over forty-five years or who met narrowly defined medical criteria, prohibited the importation of contraceptives, and threatened clandestine abortion providers with fines and imprisonment. The birthrate rose from 14.3 per 1,000 population in 1966 to 27.4 births in 1967, but gradually declined again to 13.8 in 1983. Public policy clashed deeply with societal values (David, 1994).

In 1986, President Nicolae Ceausescu proclaimed, "The fetus is the socialist property of the whole society. Giving birth is a patriotic duty . . . those who refuse to have children are deserters, escaping the law of natural continuity" (cited in David, 1994). To qualify for a legal abortion, a woman had to have five living children, all under the age of eighteen. The state required employed women to undergo periodic gynecological examinations and imposed special taxes on unmarried individuals over the age of twenty-five and on marital partners who were childless after two years. Modern contraceptives were available only on the black market. The World Health Organization reported a sharp increase in maternal mortality. It nearly doubled, from 86 deaths per 100,000 live births in 1981 to 169 per 100,000 in 1989, the highest rate ever recorded in Europe. After the overthrow of Ceausescu in December 1989, the new government, on its first day in office, revoked all prohibitions on abortion services and the availability of contraceptives. In 1990, the maternal mortality rate dropped by more than one-half from its previous peak and continues to decline (David, 1994; David, Dytrych, & Matejcek, 2003).

CONCLUSION

While the intensity of feelings associated with abortion makes conversation difficult, one group of women in Boston had the courage to talk directly to one another about their views. In response to the December 30, 1994, shootings of several Planned Parenthood clinics in Brookline, Massachusetts, by John Salvi, a group of six women began to meet privately. They were leaders in their community. Three identified themselves as prochoice and three as prolife. The Public Conversations Project, a Boston-based national group that designs and conducts dialogues about divisive public issues, consulted many community leaders about the value of top-level talks about abortion, and these six women began conversations that they discussed publicly only six years later. In a January 28, 2001, *Boston Globe* article (Fowler et al., 2001), they described their experience:

> These conversations revealed a deep divide. We saw that our differences on abortion reflect two world views that are irreconcilable.

If this is true, then why do we continue to meet?

First, because when we face our opponent, we see her dignity and goodness. Embracing this apparent contradiction stretches us spiritually. We've experienced something radical and life-altering that we describe in nonpolitical terms: "the mystery of love," "holy ground," or simply, "mysterious."

We continue because we are stretched intellectually, as well. This has been a rare opportunity to engage in sustained, candid conversations about serious moral disagreements. It has made our thinking sharper and our language more precise.

We hope, too, that we have become wiser and more effective leaders. We are more knowledgeable about our political opponents. We have learned to avoid being overreactive and disparaging to the other side and to focus instead on affirming our respective causes.

Since that first fear-filled meeting, we have experienced a paradox. While learning to treat each other with dignity and respect, we all have become firmer in our views about abortion.

We hope this account of our experience will encourage people everywhere to consider engaging in dialogues about abortion and other protracted disputes. In this world of polarizing conflicts, we have glimpsed a new possibility: a way in which people can disagree frankly and passionately, become clearer in heart and mind about their activism, and, at the same time, contribute to a more civil and compassionate society.

References

Adler, N. E., David, H. P., Major, B. M., Roth, S. H., Russo, N. F., & Wyatt, G. E. (1992). Psychological factors in abortion: A review. *American Psychologist, 47*(10), 1194–1204.

Alan Guttmacher Institute. (2004). *State facts about abortion: South Dakota.* http://www.agi-usa.org/.

American Association of University Women. (2004). *Mifepristone/RU486.* Retrieved Sept. 17, 2004, from http://www.aauw.org/takeaction/policyissues/ru486.cfm.

American Civil Liberties Union. (2002). *Public funding for abortion.* New York: ACLU/Reproductive Rights Freedom Project. Retrieved April 26, 2004, from http://www.aclu.org/library/funding.html.

Becker, M., Bowman, C. G., & Torrey, M. (1994). *Feminist jurisprudence: Taking women seriously.* St. Paul, MN: West.

Beckman, L., & Harvey, S. M. (1998). *The new civil war: The psychology, culture, and politics of abortion.* Washington, DC: American Psychological Association.

Bradwell v. Illinois, 83 U.S. 130, 141 (1873).

Bray v. Alexandria Women's Health Clinic, 113 S. Ct. 753 (1993).

Carhart v. Ashcroft, 300 F. Supp. 2d 921, 2004 U.S. Dist. LEXIS 18263 (D. Neb. 2004).

Center for Human Resources Research. (1988). *NLS handbook.* Columbus: Ohio State University.

Center for Reproductive Rights. *Carhart* v. *Ashcroft.* Retrieved April 27, 2004, from http://www.crlp.org/crt_pba.html.

Cozzarelli, C., Sumer, N., & Major, B. (1998). Mental models of attachment and coping with abortion. *Journal of Personality and Social Psychology, 74*(2), 453–467.

David, H. P. (1994). Reproductive rights and reproductive behavior: Clash or convergence of private values and public policies? *American Psychologist, 49*(4), 343–349.

David, H. P., Dytrych, Z., & Matejcek, Z. (2003). Born unwanted: Observations from the Prague study. *American Psychologist, 58*(3), 224–229.

Derr, M. K. (1991). Amicus brief of feminists for life in Bray v. Alexandria Women's Health Clinic, 506 U.S. 263 (No. 90–985).

Doe v. Bolton, 410 U.S. 179 (1973).

Feminist Majority Foundation. *Fact sheet on Freedom of Access to Clinic Entrances (FACE) Act.* Retrieved April 27, 2004, from http://www.feminist.org/news/newsbyte/uswirestory.asp?id=6536.

Ferguson v. City of Charleston, 121 S. Ct. 1281 (2001).

Fowler, A., Nichols Gamble N., Hogan, F., Kogut, M., McCommish, M., & Thorp, B. (2001, January 8). Talking with the enemy. *Boston Globe.* Retrieved April 27, 2004, from http://www.publicconversations.org/pcp/resources/resource detail.asp?ref_id=102.

Fried, M. G. (1990). *From abortion to reproductive freedom: A movement.* Boston: South End Press.

Gagan, B. J. (2000). Ferguson v. City of Charleston, South Carolina: Fetal abuse, drug testing and the Fourth Amendment. *Stanford Law Review, 53,* 491–518.

Gordon, L. (1990). *Women's body, women's right: Birth control in America.* New York: Grossman.

Griswold v. Connecticut, 381 U.S. 479, 85 S. Ct. 1678, 14 L. Ed.2d 510 (1965).

Holsinger, M. C. (2003). Note: The Partial-Birth Abortion Ban Act of 2003:

The congressional reaction to Stenberg v. Carhart. *New York University Journal of Legislation and Public Policy, 6,* 603–614.

Law, S., Larson, J. E., & Spillenger, C. (1992). Amicus brief of 250 American historians as amicus curiae in support of Planned Parenthood of Southeastern Pennsylvania v. Casey, 112 S. Ct. 2791 (Nos. 91–744 and 91–902).

Lazarus, R. S., & Folkman, S. (1984). *Stress, appraisal, and coping.* New York: Springer.

Leslie, H. C. (2001). Casenote: Ferguson v. City of Charleston: A limitation on the "special needs" doctrine. *Loyola Journal of Public Interest Law, 3,* 93–104.

Lichtman, J. (2003). Note: Restrictive state abortion laws: Today's most powerful conscience clause. *Georgetown Journal on Poverty Law and Policy, 10,* 345–362.

MacKinnon, C. A. (1987). *Feminism unmodified.* Cambridge, MA: Harvard University Press.

Maher v. Roe, 432 U.S. 464, 97 S. Ct. 2376, 53 L. Ed.2d 484 (1977).

Murphy, E. M. (2003). Being born female is dangerous for your health. *American Psychologist, 58*(3), 205–210.

Osofsky, J. D., Osofsky, H. J., & Rajan, R. (1973). Psychological effects of abortion: With emphasis upon immediate reactions and follow-up. In H. J. Osofsky & J. D. Osofsky (Eds.), *The abortion experience.* New York: HarperCollins.

Palmer, A. F. (n.d.). *Why go to college? Alice Freeman Palmer.* Retrieved on April 26, 2004, from http://womenshistory.about.com/library/etext/bl_palmer_alice_freeman.htm.

Planned Parenthood of Central Missouri v. Danforth, 428 U.S. 52, S. Ct. 2831, 49 L. Ed.2d 788 (1976).

Planned Parenthood of Southeastern Pennsylvania v. Casey, 505 U.S. 833, 112 S. Ct. 2791, 120 L. Ed.2d 674 (1992).

Roe v. Wade, 410 U.S. 113, 93 S. Ct. 705, 35 L. Ed.2d 147 (1973).

Russo, N. F., & Zierk, K. L. (1992). Abortion, childbearing, and women's well-being. *Professional Psychology, 23,* 269–280.

Schaff, E. (1999). Symposium: Redefining violence against women: The campaign of violence and the delay of RU486. *Temple Policy and Civil Rights Law Review, 8,* 311–324.

Shusterman, L. R. (1979). Predicting the psychosocial consequences of abortion. *Social Science and Medicine, 13A,* 683–689.

Smith, H. A. (2002). Comment: A new prescription for abortion. *University of Colorado Law Review, 73,* 1069–1097.

Stenberg v. Carhart, 530 U.S. 914 (2000).

Stevens, D. (2003). Embryonic stem cell research: Will President Bush's limitation on federal funding put the United States at a disadvantage? A comparison between U.S. and international law. *Houston Journal of International Law, 25*(3), 623–653.

Sullivan, K. M., & Estrich, S. R. (1989). Amicus brief of 274 organizations in support of Roe v. Wade in Turnock v. Ragsdale, 941 F.2d 501 (7th Cir.) (Nos. 88–790 and 88–805).

Tennessee Right to Life. (2003). *Congressional bill defines life's beginning at conception.* Retrieved April 27, 2004, from http://tennesseerighttolife.org/news_center/archives/02132003–01.htm.

Webster v. Reproductive Health Services, 492 U.S. 490, 494 (1989).

CHAPTER EIGHT

Insurance Coverage of Contraceptives

Narrowing the Gender Gap in Health Care Coverage

Judith C. Appelbaum, J.D.
Virginia S. Davis, J.D.

A ccess to safe and reliable contraception is an essential component of health care for women. Despite the fact that prescription contraceptives were first made available over forty years ago, many health insurance plans have a history of excluding coverage for prescription contraceptives even while covering other prescription drugs and devices and preventive care, as well as sterilization and abortion. This inequity did not get national attention until the mid-1990s, when a national survey of insurance coverage of reproductive health care revealed for the first time the extent to which women were being denied contraceptive coverage.

Shortly after the release of this study, Viagra, a drug used in treating male impotence, was approved by the Food and Drug Administration and was immediately covered by many insurance companies. The sharp contrast between insurance companies' willingness to cover Viagra and their reluctance to cover contraceptives, even in the face of studies demonstrating the need, captured the attention of the media and the public. Not surprisingly, the public broadly supported requiring contraceptive coverage. A 1998 Kaiser Family Foundation poll found that 75 percent of Americans believed contraception should be covered by insurers even if such coverage added to the cost of their insurance. This support has been steady. A 2001 poll found that 77 percent of Americans support laws requiring health insurance plans to cover prescription contraception (NARAL, 2001).

Energized by the increased awareness and support that developed in the mid-1990s, women's advocates and legislators began pushing for change and have had a great deal of success in challenging the denial of contraceptive coverage in a variety of ways. Since this problem came to the forefront just ten years ago, legislation has been adopted in twenty states across the country, and is being considered in Congress, to specifically mandate contraceptive equity in health insurance coverage. In addition, legal rulings have established the principle that singling out contraceptive coverage for exclusion from an otherwise comprehensive employee health plan is unlawful sex discrimination in employment. Although the battle for equity in health care coverage continues, the past ten years have witnessed a dramatic transformation in the legal landscape surrounding contraceptive coverage as this gender gap in health care coverage narrows.

WOMEN'S CONTRACEPTIVE NEEDS HAVE NOT BEEN MET

Despite public recognition of the importance of contraception to women's health and equality, health insurance has historically failed to provide adequate coverage of prescription contraceptive drugs and devices and related services. In 1994, the Alan Guttmacher Institute (AGI) released the first study establishing the extent to which women have been denied comprehensive insurance coverage. That survey showed that almost half of all fee-for-service large-group plans (those covering over one hundred employees) did not cover any form of contraception at all, and only one-third covered oral contraceptives, the most commonly used reversible contraceptive in the United States. Although managed care plans have typically provided better coverage than traditional fee-for-service plans, the study revealed that only 39 percent of health maintenance organizations routinely covered all methods of reversible contraception. Only 49 percent of large-group plans and 39 percent of small-group plans covered outpatient annual exams, which are essential for women using prescription contraceptive drugs or devices. In 2004, AGI released an updated study and found that coverage of contraceptives in employee health benefits plans is increasing. The percentage of plans routinely covering all methods of reversible contraceptives increased from 28 percent in 1994 to 86 percent (Alan Guttmacher Institute, 2004). But the fact that 99 percent of employee plans cover prescription drugs generally means that a contraceptive coverage gap remains (Kaiser Family Foundation/ Health Research Education Trust, 2003). These statistics indicate that although progress has been made in the fight to obtain full coverage of contraceptive drugs, devices, and services, many women are still not receiving the contraceptive coverage they require.

WHY CONTRACEPTIVE COVERAGE MATTERS

The gender gap in health care coverage that is created by the reluctance of health insurance companies to cover contraceptives affects women and their families adversely in several ways. Women who do not have health insurance coverage for contraception, but who nonetheless wish to avoid pregnancy, are often forced to use a less expensive, but also less effective, method of contraception (Darroch, 1998). A woman without insurance coverage also may not be able to afford to use the contraceptive method that is most appropriate for her medical and personal circumstances (Gold, 1998). For example, where oral contraceptives are contraindicated for medical reasons, an intrauterine device (IUD) or implant may be the most appropriate form of contraception, but these devices have the highest initial cost and therefore can be the hardest to pay for out-of-pocket.

Because pregnancy is a condition that is unique to women and because the only forms of prescription contraception available today are exclusively for women (oral contraceptives, injections like Depo Provera and Lunelle, implants like Norplant, IUDs, and barrier methods like the diaphragm and cervical cap), the exclusion of prescription contraceptives from health insurance coverage unfairly disadvantages women by singling out for unfavorable treatment a health insurance need that only women have. Failure to cover contraception forces women to bear higher health care costs to avoid pregnancy and exposes women to the unique physical, economic, and emotional consequences that can result from unintended pregnancy.

Pregnancy prevention is central to good health care for women. Most women have the biological potential for pregnancy for over thirty years of their lives. For approximately three-quarters of her reproductive life, the average woman is trying to postpone or avoid pregnancy (Alan Guttmacher Institute, 1998a). Nearly half of pregnancies in the United States are unintended, including 31 percent of pregnancies among married women (Henshaw, 1998). Access to contraception is critical to preventing unwanted pregnancies (and thus also to reducing the number of abortions).[1] It also enables women to control the timing and spacing of their pregnancies, which in turn reduces the incidence of maternal morbidity, low-birth-weight babies, and infant mortality (U.S. Office of Disease Prevention and Health Promotion, 2000; Alan Guttmacher Institute, 1998b).

Moreover, oral contraceptives are sometimes prescribed for health reasons other than birth control—for example, for medical conditions like dysmenorrhea and premenstrual syndrome or to help prevent ovarian cancer. Some insurance plans do not cover oral contraceptives even when they are prescribed for these purely medical reasons. Thus, in addition to the dangers to women's health presented by the failure of insurance to cover pregnancy prevention, the exclusion of contraception from insurance coverage causes other harmful consequences for women's health. For all these reasons, as a federal court declared, "the exclusion of prescription contraceptives creates a gaping hole in the coverage offered to female employees, leaving a fundamental and immediate healthcare need uncovered" (*Erickson* v. *Bartell Drug Co.*, 2001).

The lack of insurance coverage for contraceptives is also a matter of gender equity. When effective contraception is not used, it is women who bear the risk of unwanted pregnancy. When unintended pregnancy results, it is women who incur the attendant physical burdens and medical risks of pregnancy, women who disproportionately bear the health care costs of pregnancy and childbirth, and women who often face barriers to employment and educational opportunities as a result of pregnancy. These occur even today despite the fact that the law clearly prohibits this form of discrimination in the workplace and in educational institutions.

CLOSING THE GENDER GAP IN HEALTH CARE COVERAGE

Galvanized by the 1994 Alan Guttmacher Institute study revealing the common exclusion of contraceptives from health insurance plans, advocates for women's health and equity began pursuing a multitrack approach to ensure that women receive access to needed contraceptives.

At the federal level, this effort includes enforcing Title VII of the Civil Rights Act of 1964 as well as seeking passage of the Equity in Prescription Insurance and Contraceptive Coverage Act (EPICC). At the state level, efforts include both legislative and administrative approaches to establishing explicit legal requirements for contraceptive coverage. These approaches are complementary, and all are necessary.

The ability of women to obtain the contraceptive insurance coverage they need advanced significantly with two interpretations of the federal civil rights laws in 2000 and 2001. Both the Equal Employment Opportunity Commission (EEOC) and a federal court held that it is unlawful sex discrimination in the workplace under Title VII of the Civil Rights Act of 1964, and specifically the Pregnancy Discrimination Act of 1978 (PDA) that is incorporated in Title VII, for an employer covered by Title VII to exclude prescription contraceptive drugs and devices and related services from a health insurance plan provided to its employees, when the plan covers other prescription drugs and devices and preventive care generally.

Title VII prohibits all private employers with at least fifteen employees, as well as public employers, from discriminating on the basis of sex in the terms and conditions of employment, including fringe benefits. And as amended by the PDA, Title VII's prohibition against discrimination "on the basis of sex" includes discrimination "on the basis of pregnancy, childbirth, or related medical conditions." This language was enacted by Congress to overrule the decision in *General Electric Co.* v. *Gilbert* (1976), which held that excluding disabilities arising from pregnancy from an employee's disability plan did not violate Title VII. As the Supreme Court has held, the PDA now makes it clear that for purposes of Title VII, such singling out of pregnancy coverage is sex discrimination on its face (*Newport News Shipbuilding and Dry Dock* v. *EEOC,* 1982; *UAW* v. *Johnson Controls,* 1991).

The PDA, moreover, is not limited to discrimination based on pregnancy itself; it expressly applies to discrimination based on "pregnancy, childbirth, or related medical conditions." As the Supreme Court stated, "The 1978 Act makes clear that it is discriminatory to treat pregnancy-related conditions less favorably than other medical conditions" (*Newport News Shipbuilding and Dry Dock* v. *EEOC,* 1982, p. 684), and the EEOC has long interpreted the PDA to mean that "any health insurance provided [to employees] must cover expenses for pregnancy-related conditions on the same basis as expenses for other medical conditions" (Questions and Answers on the Pregnancy Discrimination Act, 2002).

Contraception—the prevention of pregnancy—is plainly pregnancy related. Moreover, contraception addresses a woman's potential for pregnancy, and the Supreme Court held in 1991 that an employer's classification of employees on the basis of potential for pregnancy is covered by the PDA's language. In *UAW* v. *Johnson Controls* (1991), the Court noted that an employer's policy barring fertile women from certain jobs was a classification on the basis of potential for pregnancy, and concluded that "under the PDA, such a classification must be regarded, for Title VII purposes, in the same light as explicit sex discrimination" (p. 199). The Court cited PDA legislative history to show that "this statutory standard was chosen to protect female workers from being treated differently from other employees simply because of their capacity to bear children" (p. 205).

In 1999, based on this analysis, sixty women's, civil rights, and health groups submitted a petition to the EEOC arguing that Title VII, as amended by the PDA, prohibits employers from excluding prescription contraceptive coverage from an employee health plan that otherwise covers prescription drugs and devices generally, as well as other preventive health care. The EEOC agreed, and in a ruling responding to two pending charges against employers, reasoned that Title VII's "prohibition on discrimination against women based on their ability to become pregnant . . . necessarily includes a prohibition on discrimination related to a woman's use of contraceptives" (U.S. Equal Employment Opportunity Commission, 2000). The commission issued a ruling that in order to be in compliance with Title VII:

> Respondents must cover the expenses of prescription contraceptives to the same extent and on the same terms, that they cover the expenses of [preventive] drugs, devices, and preventive care. . . . Respondents must also offer the same coverage for contraception-related outpatient services as are offered for other outpatient services. Where a woman visits her doctor to obtain a prescription for contraceptives, she must be afforded the same coverage that would apply if she, or any other employee, had consulted a doctor for other preventive or health maintenance services. Where, on the other hand, Respondents limit coverage of comparable drugs or services (e.g., by imposing maximum payable benefits), those limits may be applied to contraception as well.
>
> Respondents' coverage must extend to the full range of prescription contraceptive choices. Because the health needs of women may change—and because different women may need different prescription contraceptives at different times in their lives—Respondents must

cover each of the available options for prescription contraception. Moreover, Respondents must include such coverage in each of the health plan choices that it offers to its employees [p. 5].

Although the EEOC's decision was disposing of two specific pending charges, it constitutes a formal statement of commission policy and applies to all similarly situated employers. As the federal agency charged with administering and enforcing Title VII, the EEOC's interpretation of the law is authoritative.

The EEOC's ruling was followed by the court's decision in *Erickson* v. *Bartell Drug Co.* (2001). In *Erickson,* the U.S. District Court for the Western District of Washington cited the EEOC ruling favorably and found that the defendant's exclusion of prescription contraceptives from its otherwise comprehensive employee health benefits plan constituted a violation of Title VII. The court's decision, granting summary judgment to Jennifer Erickson and the plaintiff class she represented, was the first court decision ever to rule definitively on the merits of this issue. Other courts have subsequently ruled in favor of the plaintiffs in similar cases, denying the defendants' motions to dismiss and allowing the cases to proceed (*Cooley* v. *Daimler Chrysler Corp.,* 2003; *Equal Employment Opportunity Commission* v. *United Parcel Service,* 2001; *Wessling et al.* v. *AMN Healthcare and Medical Express,* 2001).

In the *Erickson* decision, the court carefully reviewed the legislative history of Title VII and the PDA, relevant precedents, the EEOC decision, and each of the arguments presented by the defendant. The court concluded:

Bartell's exclusion of prescription contraception from its prescription plan is inconsistent with the requirements of federal law. The PDA is not a begrudging recognition of a limited grant of rights to a strictly defined group of women who happen to be pregnant. Read in the context of Title VII as a whole, it is a broad acknowledgment of the intent of Congress to outlaw any and all discrimination against any and all women in the terms and conditions of their employment, including the benefits an employer provides to its employees. Male and female employees have different, sex-based disability and healthcare needs, and the law is no longer blind to the fact that only women can get pregnant, bear children, or use prescription contraception [p. 1271].

On this basis, the court ordered Bartell Drug Co., the defendant, to cover each of the available options for prescription contraception to the same extent, and on the same terms, that it covers other drugs, devices, and preventive care for its employees, as well as all contraception-related outpatient services.[2]

As a result of the EEOC and court rulings, all employers covered by Title VII are now on notice of their legal obligation to include coverage of prescription contraceptives if they are providing health insurance that otherwise covers prescription drugs and devices and preventive care. Some employers have responded by promptly adding this coverage to their employee health plans. Others have been more resistant to their obligations. In response, women have followed in Jennifer Erickson's footsteps and filed charges with the EEOC and Title VII suits against their employers for the exclusion of prescription contraceptives from their health plans. For example, one suit is currently pending against Wal-Mart Stores (*Mauldin* v. *Wal-Mart Stores,* 2001, 2002), and another suit has been filed against Union Pacific Railroad (Planned Parenthood of the Columbia/Willamette, 2004).

Many other women are demanding the contraceptive coverage to which they are legally entitled and hoping to obtain that coverage without embarking on formal legal action. Some have been successful. For example, after several female faculty and staff members at the University of Nebraska urged the university administration to add contraceptive coverage, the university regents agreed ("University Health Plan to Cover Birth Control After Vote," 2001). Dow Jones and Company also agreed to provide coverage for all FDA-approved prescription contraceptives and related medical services in all of its health plans for its employees, as part of a settlement of charges that had been filed with the EEOC by employees and their union (Planned Parenthood Federation of America, 2002b). In November 2003, Lenox Hill Hospital in New York City, in response to a demand for coverage by one employee, announced that it was adding this coverage for all employees. In addition, a number of unions have begun to press this issue on behalf of their members, spurred on by the Contraceptive Equity Project of the Coalition of Labor Union Women. A local council of the American Federation of State, County and Municipal Employees (AFSCME), for example, secured contraceptive coverage in the benefits package for employees of the city of Eugene, Oregon.

Students have begun to press for complete contraceptive coverage in their student health plans as well. They have argued that Title IX of the Education Amendments of 1972, which extends federal protection against sex discrimination to students at educational institutions that receive federal funds, must be interpreted, like Title VII, to prohibit the exclusion of prescription contraceptives from plans that include other prescription drugs and devices. This argument has proved successful. For example, in response to demands relying on this argument by several students, George Washington University added insurance coverage for prescription contraceptives to its student health insurance plan.

Employers sometimes resist adding contraceptive coverage to an employee health benefit plan on the grounds that it would raise employers' health care costs. As it turns out, however, as is true for other key forms of preventive health care, coverage of contraceptives actually saves money. For every dollar spent to provide publicly funded contraceptive services, an average of three dollars is saved in Medicaid costs alone for pregnancy-related health care and medical care for newborns (Forrest & Samara, 1996). In addition, studies by business groups and employer consultants have concluded that employers can save money by including contraceptive coverage in their employee health plans, thereby reducing unintended pregnancies and their associated costs, as well as promoting maternal and child health (Bonoan & Gonen, 2000; William M. Mercer, 2000). For example, the Washington Business Group on Health, which represents 160 national and multinational employers, has estimated that failing to provide contraceptive coverage could cost an employer at least 15 percent more than providing this coverage. This report concluded, "For health and financial reasons, employers concerned with providing both comprehensive and cost-effective health benefits ought to consider ensuring that they are covering the full range of contraceptive options" (Bonoan & Gonen, 2000, p. 7).

Moreover, any direct premium costs to an employer who adds contraceptive coverage to its benefits plan are at most extremely modest, and likely to be nonexistent. The experience of the Federal Employees Health Benefits Program (FEHBP) is most instructive. It showed that adding contraceptive coverage to the FEHBP caused no increase in the federal government's premium costs. When the FEHBP contraceptive coverage requirement was implemented, the Office of Personnel Management (OPM), which administers the program, arranged with the health carriers to adjust the 1999 premiums in 2000 to reflect any increased insurance costs due to the addition of contraceptive coverage. However, no such adjustment was necessary, and OPM reported that "there was no cost increase due to contraceptive coverage" (J. R. Lachance to M. D. Greenberger, Jan. 16, 2001). Another study found that on average, it costs a private employer only an additional $1.43

per month per employee to add coverage for the full range of FDA-approved reversible contraceptives (Darroch, 1998).

Of course, even if the cost of contraceptive coverage were substantial (which, as shown, it is not), such costs could not justify short-changing women or sacrificing their health. Cost is never recognized as a defense to discrimination, as has been noted by both the EEOC and the court in *Erickson.*

Erickson and the EEOC ruling are also influencing the interpretation of state employment discrimination laws. Almost every state has a law against sex discrimination in employment that is similar to federal law (Title VII). Given that Title VII has been interpreted as placing a contraceptive coverage requirement on employers who are covered by federal law, advocates have suggested that similar state laws should be interpreted the same way. In Wisconsin, the state attorney general issued an opinion that does just that (P. A. Lautenschlager to G. Moore, October 17, 2003). The opinion cites *Erickson* and the EEOC decision and finds that Wisconsin's Fair Employment Act should be interpreted, like Title VII, to require employers to include contraceptive coverage. In addition, the attorney general's opinion states that Wisconsin's law prohibiting sex (or pregnancy) discrimination in education applies the same principle to coverage for students by Wisconsin colleges and universities.

Advocates for women's rights and women's health are also pressing for the enactment of new legislation, at both the state and federal levels, to guarantee that all health insurance plans that provide coverage of prescription drugs include the same level of coverage for FDA-approved prescription contraceptives, as well as coverage for outpatient contraceptive services.

Maryland, in 1998, became the first state to enact a comprehensive contraceptive equity law (Maryland Insurance Code Annotated, 2003). Since that time, nineteen other states have passed laws requiring health plans that cover prescription drugs to include prescription contraceptives.[3] Similar legislation has been introduced in other states as well. In general, each of the state contraceptive equity laws provides that a health insurance policy that is issued in that state and provides coverage for prescription drugs generally must provide coverage for any prescription drug or device that has been approved by the FDA for use as a contraceptive. Most also direct that if an insurance policy provides coverage for outpatient health care services, it must provide coverage for outpatient contraceptive services, such as consultations, examinations, procedures, and other medical services. Most of the laws further provide that any deductible, copayment, or coinsurance that is applied to contraceptives may not be greater than the deductible, copayment, or coinsurance applied to other prescription drugs. Several of the laws mandate that the contraceptive coverage requirement apply to both the insured and the insured's covered spouse and other dependents.

Fifteen of the states with contraceptive equity laws have enacted religious refusal clauses, that is, exceptions to the contraceptive equity mandate for religious employers or insurers (or individuals enrolled in the plan) whose religious tenets prohibit the use of contraceptives.[4] These clauses vary in scope. About half of the states with religious refusal clauses require employers to cover contraceptives when they are used for noncontraceptive medical reasons. Two of the narrower religious refusal clauses are being challenged, so far unsuccessfully, by religiously affiliated employers in New York and California who are not covered by the exemption.[5]

At the federal level, advocates are urging passage of the EPICC, which has been introduced in the U.S. Senate and House with bipartisan support. EPICC does not require special treatment of contraceptives, only equitable treatment within the context of an existing prescription drug benefit. EPICC will extend protection to plans not provided by an employer to its employees, such as nonemployment group and individual plans, and to employer plans not covered by Title VII, thereby guaranteeing contraceptive coverage for the millions of women who receive their insurance from a source not covered by Title VII. Enactment of EPICC would represent an additional and important step forward for women's health.

CONCLUSION

It is long past time for health insurance plans to cover women's contraceptive needs when they cover other prescription drugs and devices. The evidence is clear that denying such coverage is harmful to women's physical and fiscal well-being. In the past few years, this persistent gender gap in health care coverage has begun to narrow, due to recognition of the need by the public and policymakers alike and new legal mandates. There is reason to hope that this momentum will continue and that women across the country will soon receive the contraceptive insurance coverage to which they are entitled.

Notes

1. For a general discussion of the consequences of unwanted pregnancies for women, men, children, and families, see Brown and Eisenberg (1995).
2. The parties subsequently reached an out-of-court settlement of the plaintiffs' claims for back pay (lost benefits), and Bartell dropped its appeal.
3. The states are Arizona, California, Connecticut, Delaware, Georgia, Hawaii, Illinois, Iowa, Maine, Maryland, Massachusetts, Missouri, Nevada, New Hampshire, New Mexico, New York, North Carolina, Rhode Island, Vermont, and Washington. For a more detailed discussion of each state's contraceptive equity law, see National Women's Law Center (2003).
4. The fifteen states with religious refusal clauses are Arizona, California, Connecticut, Delaware, Hawaii, Illinois, Maine, Maryland, Massachusetts, Missouri, Nevada, New Mexico, New York, North Carolina, and Rhode Island.
5. A challenge to the New York statute was dismissed on summary judgment (Catholic Charities of the Diocese of Albany v. Serio, 2003). The California Supreme Court recently heard oral argument in a challenge to California's statute in Catholic Charities v. Superior Court (2003).

References

Alan Guttmacher Institute. (1994). *Uneven and unequal: Insurance coverage and reproductive health services.* Washington, DC: Author. http://www.agi-usa.org/pubs/kaiser_0698.html.

Alan Guttmacher Institute. (1998a). *Facts in brief: Contraceptive use 1.* Retrieved November 12, 2003. www.guttmacher.org/pubs/fb_contr_use.html.

Alan Guttmacher Institute. (1998b). *Family planning improves child survival and health.* http://www.agi-usa.org/pubs/is20.html.

Alan Guttmacher Institute. (2004). *U.S. insurance coverage of contraceptives and the impact of contraceptive coverage mandates, 2002.* Washington, DC: Author.

Bonoan, R., & Gonen, J. (2000). *Promoting healthy pregnancies: Counseling and contraception as the first step.* Washington, DC: Washington Business Group on Health.

Brown, S. S., & Eisenberg, L. (1995). *The best intentions: Unintended pregnancy and the well-being of children and families.* Washington, DC: National Academy Press.

Catholic Charities v. Superior Court, S099822 (heard Dec. 2, 2003).

Catholic Charities of the Diocese of Albany v. Serio, Case No.

01–03–072905 (Sup. Ct. of New York, County of Albany, Nov. 28, 2003).

Cooley v. Daimler Chrysler Corp., 281 F. Supp. 2d 979 (E.D. Mo. 2003).

Darroch, J. E. (1998). *Cost to employer health plans of covering contraceptives.* Washington, DC: Alan Guttmacher Institute. http://www. agi-usa.org/pubs/kaiser_0698.html.

Equal Employment Opportunity Commission v. United Parcel Service, 141 F. Supp. 2d 1216 (D. Minn. 2001).

Erickson v. Bartell Drug Co., 141 F. Supp. 2d 1266, 1277 (W.D. Wash. 2001).

Forrest, J. D., & Samara, R. (1996, September–October). Impact of publicly funded contraceptive services on unintended pregnancies and implications for Medicaid expenditures. *Family Planning Perspectives, 28.* http://www.agi-usa.org/pubs/journals/2818896.htm.

General Electric Co. v. Gilbert, 429 U.S. 125 (1976).

Gold, R. B. (1998, August). The need for and cost of mandating private insurance coverage of contraception. *Guttmacher Report on Public Policy, 1,* 5–8.

Henshaw, S. K. (1998, January–February). Unintended pregnancy in the United States. *Family Planning Perspectives, 30.* http://www.agi-usa. org/pubs/journals/3002498.html.

Kaiser Family Foundation. (1998). *New national survey on contraceptive coverage: Americans support requiring insurers to cover contraceptives, even if premiums rise.* Menlo Park, CA: Author.

Kaiser Family Foundation/Health Research Education Trust. (2003). *2003 annual survey of employer-sponsored health benefits.* Menlo Park, CA: Author. http://www.kff.org/insurance/ehbs2003-10-set.cfm.http:// www.kff.org/insurance/ehbs2003–10-set.cfm.

Maryland Insurance Code Annotated. (2003). § 15-826.

Mauldin v. Wal-Mart Stores, Inc., U.S. District Court, Civ. Action No. 1:01-CV-2755-JEC (NDGA), filed Oct. 16, 2001.

Mauldin v. Wal-Mart, 2002 U.S. Dist. LEXIS 21024; 89 Fair Empl. Prac. Cas. (BNA) 1600; 90 A.F.T.R.2d (RIA) 6239.

NARAL. (2001). *America supports contraceptive equity for women, President Bush does not: New NARAL poll shows overwhelming support for contraceptive insurance coverage.* Washington, DC: Author.

National Women's Law Center. (2003, November). *Contraceptive equity laws in your state: Know your rights, use your rights.* www.nwlc.org/ pdf/ConCovStateGuide2003.pdf.

Newport News Shipbuilding & Dry Dock v. EEOC, 462 U.S. 669 (1982).

Planned Parenthood of the Columbia/Willamette. (2004). *Employee files suit against Union Pacific Railroad for failure to cover contraceptives in its health plan.* Press release. http://www.ppcw.org/news/news3.asp.

Planned Parenthood Federation of America. (2002a, May). *Equity in prescription insurance and contraceptive coverage.* www.plannedparenthood.org/library/BIRTHCONTROL/EPICC_facts.html.

Planned Parenthood Federation of America. (2002b, December 5). *Planned Parenthood successfully negotiates insurance coverage for contraceptives for Dow Jones employees.* Press release.

Pregnancy Discrimination Act of 1978. 42 U.S. Code §§ 2000e et seq.

Questions and answers on the Pregnancy Discrimination Act. 29 C.F.R. Part 1604, App. (2002).

UAW v. Johnson Controls, Inc., 499 U.S. 187, 199 (1991).

U.S. Equal Employment Opportunity Commission. (2000, December 5). *Decision on coverage of contraception.* http://www.eeoc.gov/docs/decision-contraception.html.

U.S. Office of Disease Prevention and Health Promotion. (2000). *Healthy People 2010* (Conference ed.). Washington, DC: U.S. Department of Health and Human Services.

University health plan to cover birth control after vote. (2001, April 7). Associated Press Newswires.

Wessling et al. v. AMN Healthcare and Medical Express, Inc., Case No. 01-CV-0757 W (S.D. Calif., Aug. 8, 2001).

William M. Mercer, Inc. (2000). *Women's health care issues: Contraception as a covered benefit.* New York: Author.

Women's Research and Education Institute. (1994). *Women's health insurance costs and experiences.* Washington, DC: Author.

CHAPTER NINE

Women and Depression

Jennifer R. R. Hightower

———

A s I sit to write this discourse, I glance out of my Venice Beach window and see a familiar face. There is a Mexican American woman whose name I have asked but never was able to understand because of her thick accent and my poor Spanish. She forages through the neighborhood recycling bins daily, collecting redeemable materials. Today, Super Bowl Sunday, she has brought her daughter. The girl cannot be more than ten years old, and the manner in which the young one bounces from bin to bin makes the task look more like a treasure hunt than labor that those of us watching million-dollar commercials would not tolerate. Does she not know her indigence, or has she just known nothing else? Or is it a matter of culture and familial foundation?

Mary Pipher (1994, p. 281) reminds us, "Properly faced, adversity makes us stronger." But what befalls the girls whom adversity overwhelms? What consequences of insufficient coping skills carry into womanhood and pass on to the next generation? Depression is one manifestation of these consequences, and cultural context plays an integral role in how depression is perceived, experienced, and expressed. The goal of this review of the research literature is to clarify some of the key issues that women encounter when coping with depression in the framework of specific cultural influences.

Women have endeavored throughout history to employ a voice of fortitude, faculty, and accord. The effects of poverty, abuse, discrimination, and restrictive gender roles extend beyond the social ramifications generated and into a woman's mental health. In an exposition written for the United Nations Division for Advancement of Women, Del Vecchio Good (n.d.) relates that "depression, hopelessness, exhaustion, anger and fear grow out of hunger, overwork, domestic and civil violence, entrapment and economic dependence. Understanding the sources of ill health for women means understanding how cultural and economic forces interact to undermine their social status" (para. 3).

A woman's willingness to seek aid for her symptoms puts her among the 12.4 million women reported by the National Institute of Mental Health (2002) to suffer from depression. The Depression and Bipolar Support Alliance (2004) reports that women experience depression at twice the rate of men, regardless of ethnicity. The majority of research conducted on women's depression has been on women of European descent, excluding other ethnic populations that need mental health care. The development of gender-sensitive services is an attempt to offer treatment that can distinguish between gender role expectations and those characteristics that leave women more vulnerable to depressive symptoms. The Department of Health (2002) published a strategy for the development of women's mental health that emphasized service characteristics such as providing women with a choice of type of treatment, creating a safe environment, and recognizing specific gender, religious, and cultural needs.

This chapter explores the distinctive features associated with depression among women in the African American, Latina, Caucasian, and Asian populations. The explanation of each ethnicity's experience of depressive symptoms will raise issues of diagnostic bias, discrepancy in symptom reports by different groups, misdiagnosis, treatment planning, and utilization of services. There are broad implications when labeling groups that include different cultural and religious factions. For the purpose of this chapter, the definitions provided by the National Women's Health Information Center (2002) are used. Latina women are of Cuban, Mexican, Puerto Rican, South or Central American, or other Spanish culture or race. African Americans have origins in any of the black racial groups of Africa, and Caucasians are descendants of Europeans, Middle Easterners, and North Africans. Finally, the Asian population entails those of the Far East, Southeast Asia, and the Indian subcontinent. Heeseung (2002) describes the "universal orientation" perspective of culture and mental health as one that considers both biological and cultural, or environmental, factors in human behavior. This perspective allows the clinician to integrate a range of therapies in treatment, providing more options to the client.

THERAPIST BIAS

Therapist or diagnostic bias complicates the accuracy of assessments and the proper treatment of specific populations. When cultural inconsistency exists between therapist and client, the client's expression of symptoms and the clinician's interpretation of that expression may result in inaccuracy in the perceived tendency of a population toward a specific mental illness (National Association for Mental Health, 2003). The experience of culture also includes common health concerns, similar educational opportunities in combination with socioeconomic level, family dynamics, religious inclinations, and worldviews. All of these factors influence a population's attitude toward mental health, which bears on how services are accessed and the effectiveness of treatments not culturally specified (VanderVoort & Skorikov, 2002).

An important component in considering a cultural view of depression is locus of control. Rotter (1975) describes locus of control as the individual's perception of life as experienced with an internal or external influence. The determination of the influence dictates an individual's type of coping mechanisms, worldview, and confidence in problem-solving skills (Sue & Sue, 2003). Religious affiliation can encourage the inclination to view external forces as destiny or fate, and in turn create opportunities for reflection and growth, but may hinder acceptance of personal responsibility (Ellison, 1993). Identifying locus of control is essential to determining the client's motivations, values, sense of personal responsibility, and relationship to society in treatment (Sue & Sue, 2003). The merging of these experiential components creates a unique cultural dynamic that has implications for a woman's experience of depression.

In this chapter, the review of literature will be done from the universal orientation perspective (Heeseung, 2002), beginning with broader gender and cultural issues and then exploring the specifics of each population. The function of gender roles, discrimination, and social status in the contribution to depression will be accentuated. In the review of these issues, the examination of racial, gender, and socioeconomic prejudice will be relevant in and outside the clinical setting in relation to depressive features. Next, research describing distinctions between cultural trends, perspectives, and the experience of depression is evaluated in terms of implications for treatment. Specific cultural dynamics of each population will be reviewed in relation to specific abilities to impose or prevent depression.

DISCRIMINATION AT THE ROOT: THE FOUNDATION OF DEPRESSION

Gender and culture play a large role in the formation of an individual's identity and life experiences, both in the way others respond to him or her, and in the way these encounters are interpreted, internally (as in depression) or externally (as in stereotyping and bias).

Gender Bias

Current research on gender and depression indicates that women suffer depressive symptoms at twice the rate of men (National Institute of Mental Health, 2002). There have been questions raised about the criteria on which the *Diagnostic and Statistical Manual of Mental Disorders* (DSM-IV-TR; American Psychiatric Association) diagnosis is based. McLaughlin (2002) notes that diagnostic bias has been defined as "an error in judgment that counselors make when they collect or interpret information . . . [and] as a differential prevalence of either false positive diagnosis . . . and/or false negative diagnosis" (p. 256). Joiner and Blalock (1995) elucidate three theories that may explain the increased diagnosis of women's depression: the artifact hypothesis, the biological theory, and psychosocial aspects (Joiner & Blalock, 1995).

The artifact hypothesis states that women are more likely to report symptoms of stress and depression (Joiner & Blalock, 1995). In combination with diagnostic criteria inclined to support the description of female depression, a disproportionate number of women diagnosed is not surprising. Gender-stereotyped behavior leads to a common diagnosis, whether or not based on valid observation (Cook & Warnke, 1993). Kopper and Epperson (1996) discuss the association of the expression of anger and depression. The results of their study suggest that "depressed women reported engaging in more verbal hostility than depressed men," and when under stress, they "were more likely to express their anger and feelings" (Kopper & Epperson, 1996). Cook and Warnke (1993) remind clinicians that gender differences in diagnostic criteria do not necessarily imply bias. This point emphasizes the role of the clinician's judgment as the ultimate determinant in bias.

McLaughlin (2002) discusses three important concepts of clinical bias: data availability and vividness, self-confirmatory bias, and self-fulfilling prophecy. Data availability and vividness implies that a clinician will diagnose a patient based on information most familiar to him or her and the characteristics that are regarded as obvious rather than the patient's actual presenting complaints. Self-confirmatory bias refers to a situation in which the clinician makes a diagnosis (possibly based on a stereotype or prejudice) and then notices only evidence that is consistent with that diagnosis. McLaughlin defines *self-fulfilling prophecy* as when a clinician responds to an individual in a way that confirms the clinician's expectations, in spite of incongruous evidence. These unconscious cognitive processes tend to confirm those beliefs and stereotypes that the clinician brought into the therapeutic encounter, regardless of the characteristics of the client. The merging of these factors creates the risk of gender and culture bias in therapy because of the strength and pervasiveness of gender and racial stereotypes throughout society.

Culture Bias

The factors that play the largest role in ethnocentric views of depression and cultural bias are issues of misdiagnosis, improper treatment, inequality and poverty discrimination, differences in exposure to physical and mental illness, and unequal access to care. The principal factor in these issues is the level of socioeconomic status. Furthermore, each of these factors is a contributor to the onset of depression. Myers et al. (2002) discuss the relationship between the rate of depressive symptoms in Latina, African American, and Caucasian women and socioeconomic status. Initially, more depressive symptoms were reported in the Latino population, but no significant difference was found when the affluent group was included (Myers et al., 2002). Andrew Solomon (2001), writing extensively on the cyclical epidemic of poverty and depression, points to the significance of parenting style: "Mechanisms by which one achieves positive change in life are incredibly basic, and most of us learn them in infancy in maternal interactions that demonstrate a link between cause and effect" (p. 350).

Finkelstein, Donenberg, and Martinovich (2001) concluded that the stringent parenting style, intended to cultivate coping mechanisms, of African Americans decreases susceptibility to adolescent depression. The Latino population has shown a high number of high school dropouts in addition to a lack of medical insurance. The 37 percent rate of Latino high school dropouts is two and four times more than in Caucasian and African American populations, respectively (Moore, 2001). In addition, Latina women are likely to be employed at low-paying jobs that supply a low social status (National Women's Health Information Center, 2002). Del Vecchio Good supports this statement by adding, "In the world of work, we find employment may bring self-esteem and independence; however, low paid or unpaid labor may contribute to oppression rather than independence" (n.d., para. 6). These low-paying positions are less inclined to offer job related health benefits, resulting in the 30 percent of the Latino population that remains uninsured (National Women's Health Information Center, 2002). Furthermore, policy that surrounds allocating funds to indigent populations is scrutinized for the lack of intended accuracy in who benefits. After speaking to members of Congress, Solomon remarked, "The question of whether [the community health programs] are serving the interest of the well is often examined; whether they are helping their target community seldom comes up" (2001, p. 377).

CULTURAL FEATURES AND DYNAMICS OF DEPRESSION

The diagnostic features of depression have historically been based on the symptoms displayed by Caucasians. As a consequence, treatment models have been assumed effective when applied across cultures (Sue & Sue, 2003). As mental health providers begin to accept the need for gender-specific treatment, the call for culturally sensitive services has emerged. Sociologist David Karp poses the important point that the question of culture "is a global question about what we owe to ourselves, what do we owe to others, and what do we think society owes us?" (2001, p. 235). Within each culture, the answer to this question is variable in terms of gender, but it is more prominently swayed by socioeconomic status. Asian, Latina, African American, and Caucasian women are highlighted as significant populations to be evaluated. The availability of research on each group differs, suggesting that a well-founded assessment of diagnostic basis, perception of culture by client and clinician, and realistic treatment options are necessary to develop effective interventions.

Asian Women and Depression

Contrary to the perception that Asian culture generates a healthy and "model" way of living, there is a disparity between reality and this perception that leads to what Sue and Sue (2003) describe as a myth of success. The depression rates reported by the National Asian Women's Health Organization (2003) illustrates this fact. Asian American girls exhibited the highest depression and suicide mortality rates across all ethnic groups considered. In addition, senior Asian women held the highest female suicide success rates amid all taken into account.

The Asian cultural attitude toward and experience of depression stems from facets of psychosocial, spirituality, and physical health elements (Cochrane & Hussain, 2002). In contrast to Western ideas of mental health, Eastern cultures take a holistic approach to illness (Cochrane & Hussain, 2002; Sue & Sue, 2003). This results in the incorporation of physical symptoms reported with mental health complaints. Asian Americans may experience culture-bound syndromes such as *hwa-byung* (American Psychiatric Association, 2000). *Hwa-byung,* or "suppressed anger syndrome," is characterized by symptoms such as constriction in the chest, palpitations, flushing, headache, dysphoria, anorexia, anxiety, and poor concentration. Studies by the Center for Asian-Pacific Exchange showed service utilization by 17 percent of the population (U.S. Department of Health and Human Services, 2001). While Asian Americans tend to postpone mental health treatment until a crisis because of shame and social stigma, once they are involved in treatment, typically the rate of success is very high. Hicks (2002) identified concerns about safety in reporting symptoms as one explanation of the low usage of public health care and specifically concerns that public health care utilization can threaten immigration status.

Spirituality may play a considerable part in treatment success in addition to physical healing. Techniques such as acupuncture and *qigong,* a Chinese breathing method combined with exercise, are looked to as viable alternatives to Western medicine (Solomon, 2001). The religious foundation of Asian culture teaches that answers are found within the individual experience. This is illustrated in a quotation from Buddha: "Be lamps unto yourselves" (Martin, 1999). However, because Asian society is collectivist, the locus of control tends to be one of externality (Sue & Sue, 2003). An effective psychotherapy must consider the complexity of social structures and religious factors that reinforce an external locus of control and a duty to family that is at odds with Western values of independence and autonomy.

Gender roles for Asian women are a significant factor in the onset of depression. Scattolon and Stoppard (1999) found that a woman's attempt to be consistent with the idea of a "good" woman was incorporated in the onset and alleviation of depression. Marital troubles or the inability to fulfill the role of the proper mother, daughter, sister, or wife creates family conflict (Cochrane & Hussain, 2002). Gordon (2003) points out the negative implications if a woman remains unmarried or resists the traditional marriage ideal. In turn, it is the prospect of fulfilling that role that will often aid in treatment motivation. Family cohesion, stability, and status are functions of an Asian woman's depression and recovery from which the malady originates. Regaining her "proper" role in the family increases status and social support, in addition to supplying a sense of worth that was otherwise absent (Cochrane & Hussain, 2002).

The issue of acculturation inconsistency between generational values is present when a woman's role is considered. Once a family has immigrated to the United States, the second generation of women is likely to pursue identification with a European American culture that clashes with traditional Asian values. Huang (1994) proposes identity development through biculturalism, which is the individual's amalgamation of dominant societal standards and traditional Asian values. Pipher's interview (1994) with an eighteen-year-old Vietnamese woman who had recently immigrated is an example of the complexity involved in biculturalism:

> She was dressed casually in a Garfield sweatshirt and jeans, but she was carefully groomed with long ice-blue nails and an elaborate hairstyle. Only her crooked teeth betrayed the poverty she must have experienced in Vietnam. . . . When we discussed American teenagers, Leah hesitated, clearly concerned not to appear rude. Then she said, "I don't like how American children leave home when they're eighteen. They abandon their parents and get into a lot of trouble. I don't think that's right" [pp. 87, 88].

When direct and indirect racial discrimination are incorporated, issues such as abuse, social isolation, and increased vulnerability to poverty emerge (Cochrane & Hussain, 2002). Cochrane and Hussain note that the locus of control that most Asian women experience is explained as a coalescence of the acceptance of depression and the function of kismet, or fate. Treatment implications involve the consideration of client participation in design and a deeper understanding of religious influences on behavior. Goal setting should be family inclusive, with consideration of acculturation in order to create a familiar support network and to process generational value conflicts (Sue & Sue, 2003). Ito and Maramba (2002) report a preference for the medicinal model of treatment by Asian American therapists, while remaining aware of the possible medication cure-all assumption by the client. An awareness of preexisting cultural ideas will prevent miscommunication and misdiagnosis and cultivate an encouraging and productive relationship between client and therapist.

Latina Women and Depression

There is a striking lack of information regarding Latina women's experience of depression across subcultures. If our scientific community functions at this limited level of awareness, then what expectations shall be held for the layperson? If the mental health community is to highlight culturally specific, gender-sensitive treatments and services, it is critical to have accurate and comprehensive information about the culture.

In comparison to the 75.1 percent of the Caucasian population, the Hispanic or Latino population accounts for 12.5 percent of the U.S. population (U.S. Census Bureau, 2000). This does not include the unauthorized Latino residents, estimated to number an additional 7.8 million (Bean, Van Hook, & Woodward-Lafield, 2001). The 1999 Surgeon General's Report estimated that fewer than one in eleven Latinos access mental health services, and fewer than one in five make contact with a primary care provider. Diversity among Latino populations is an important consideration, as each subpopulation varies in terms of use of health care facilities. Puerto Rican American women have higher rates of poverty than the larger Mexican American subgroup, but they access health facilities at rates similar to Caucasian women (NAWHO, 2003).

When faced with stressful life situations such as acculturation, poverty, and marital problems, the Latina woman is inclined to confer with family-approved religious resources such as an *Espiritistas* or *cu-*

randero (Heeseung, 2002; Stoeber, 2003; Sue & Sue, 2003). Stoeber (2003) attributes the preference of alternative treatments to a lack of concurrence in ethos between Latino culture and the traditional mental health provider. Religious or spiritually warranted services function with the dual purpose of healing and maintaining psychological health (Ramirez de Leon, 2002). Latino culture operates as a collective society, emphasizing commitment to family roles and relationships. Koss-Chioino (1999) observed the reaction of family shame to any display of aggressive behavior by Puerto Rican women. In place of the unapproved aggressive or assertive behavior, there are vindictive or malicious rumors circulated, a kind of indirect expression of aggression (Malgady, Rogler, & Cortés, 1996; Koss-Chioino, 1999). This is not to say that assertive behavior is discouraged in all circumstances within the Latino family structure. Pipher's interview (1994) with a sixteen-year-old Hispanic young woman, whose family had a long tradition of social activism, demonstrates the support available within the *familio,* or family unit:

> I wanted to fit in. I desperately tried to raise my coolness quotient. I even bought some Guess jeans, but they didn't help. The problem was my color. . . . Mom encouraged me to fight the pressure to be a certain way. She hates racism and elitism. [My brother] was a nonconformist and he teased me about those jeans. Later I did fight. . . . I was lonely and mixed up for awhile. I took everything personally, and I thought there must be something wrong with me. But [my brother] and my mom kept saying it wasn't me. They talked me into joining Amnesty International. . . . The people were great. Their friendship saved me [pp. 278, 279].

Similar to Asian culture, the theme of suppressed anger is identified in Latino culture as *obsesion simple,* the culture-bound syndrome that compares to depressive characteristics (Koss-Chioino, 1999). Another culture-bound syndrome, termed *nervios* by the DSM-IV-TR (American Psychiatric Association, 2000), shares the symptomatic characteristics of depression, as well as features of somatoform, adjustment, anxiety, dissociative, and psychotic disorders. The prominent identifiers of this culture-bound syndrome are the somatic indicia such as headaches, irritability, difficulty sleeping, and a tendency to weep. These somatic descriptors are an indicator of the manner in which most Latina women express and experience depression.

A noteworthy perception of variance between the mental illness of Mexican Americans and Puerto Ricans is accurately described by Lopez and Guarnaccia (2000), specifically the culture-bound syndrome *nervios*:

> Nervios among Mexican Americans and ataque de nervios among Puerto Ricans are similar in that the concept of nervios (nerves) reflects both a mental and physical state. The two concepts differ as well; for example, ataque de nervios is usually thought to have a sudden onset whereas nervios is more of a condition that befalls individuals who are thought to be weak or vulnerable [para. 7].

A collective society promotes an external control worldview that deepens the significance of relationships as coping mechanisms, but also promotes a pessimistic and fatalistic outlook of life events. Dent and Teasdale (1988) confirmed that the extent of negative self-perception displays a predictive correlation to the proportions of depressive features, but also aggravates the tendency to perceive a generalized negativity of the self and the environment. A negative perception of the self in combination with the collectivist external locus of control places emphasis on the feelings of helplessness that foster depression in women. Latina women place significant importance on their respective gender roles and the resulting functions. Specific emphasis is placed on the role of mother and wife, therefore intensifying the stressors of marital problems or family discord. Aranda, Castaneda, Lee, and Sobel (2001) drew from their study that the self-efficacy of a Mexican American woman is jeopardized by the family and marital stressors that may hinder her proficiency as a mother or wife. Self-sacrifice for the family unit is commended within the culture if the difficulties encountered are viewed as successfully surmounted by the woman (Koss-Chioino, 1999).

Jean Baker Miller (1976) describes the idea of self-sacrifice and service as an integral aspect of feminine identity. She explains further that vulnerability to "involutional depression" increases and often takes the form of somatic symptoms. According to Koss-Chioino's assessment of Puerto Rican women's dominant depressive symptoms (nervousness or intranquility, sleep disturbance or hallucinations, prolonged crying, and headaches or other bodily aches), the role of self-sacrifice draws on significant aspects of Latina identity. In contrast, when collectivist versus individualist groups were analyzed for salience in social connectedness and depressive features, VanderVoort and Skorikov (2002) controlled for level of income and found no significant difference in display of somatic symptoms. This indicates that it is possible that socioeconomic status accounts for the disparity in symptom expression. This assertion suggests multiple treatment implications that deemphasize cultural limitations and converge on economic and social facets. The restructuring of governmental policies that infringe on minority mental health will aid in the increased success of depression treatment.

African American Depression

Facts regarding depression in African American women are lacking or indecisive (HealthyPlace.com Depression Community, 2003). African American women join the rest of the American women in reporting depression at twice the rate of their male counterparts. The unique characteristic of the African American woman is her perspective on emotional stamina and the role personal perspective plays in depression. In Solomon's *Noonday Demon* (2001), Meri Danquah describes her experience of depression:

> Clinical depression simply did not exist within the realm of my possibilities, or that matter, in the realm of possibilities for any of the black women in my world. The illusion of strength has been and continues to be a major significance to me as a black woman. The one myth that I have had to endure my entire life is that of my supposed birthright to strength. Black women are *supposed* to be strong—caretakers, nurturers, healers of other people [p. 195].

The racism and discrimination endured by this population has created a sense of mistrust between African American culture and health care professionals. Sue and Sue (2003) regard historical hostility as a client's response to identification with present-day or past suffering due to discrimination. Solomon (2001) points out that "since the high rates of women's depression do not reflect a genetic predisposition that we can currently locate, we can say with some assurance that the rates of depression among women could be significantly reduced in a more equitable society" (p. 178).

Poverty, discrimination, and depression are potent reinforcers of one another. Individually, these social ills are arduous; when compounded, the burden created can overwhelm even a healthy individual, let alone

one who is already lacking resources and coping skills. The accessibility to and relationship with a familiar, trusted primary care provider is an important component in the diagnosis of depression, accuracy of treatment, and view of depression in the African American community. O'Malley, Forrest, and Miranda (2003) found that although fewer African American women than Caucasian women are diagnosed with depression, physicians who provided thorough medical services were more likely to inquire about and treat for depression. Myers et al. (2002) report that African American women have a lower level of trust than do Caucasian women, which also contributes to the amount of treatment offered to female African Americans. The nature of the physician and patient relationship is considered a contributing factor in how frequently a primary care provider is used and consequently how often a treatment is implemented. A respectful relationship between provider and patient sets an environment for open communication with a greater possibility for quality health care, illness prevention, and proper treatment of depression (O'Malley et al., 2003). The perception of the provider is also an issue of respect and trust that is present between the therapist and client. Sue and Sue (2003) explicate the importance of resolving any unease between client and therapist that would provoke the client to investigate the sincerity and integrity of the relationship beyond practical limits. Until this trepidation has ceased, the question of effective treatment taking place is at an impasse.

Similar to the collectivist natures of Latina and Asian cultures, the African American's cultural investment in religion can result in a view of predestination. The connection of spirituality and treatment is powerful in this community. "He [the Lord] brought me into the depression and out of there too. I done prayed to the Lord for help and he sent me Dr. Marian" (Solomon, 2001, p. 351). Finding support within church and community can be a coping mechanism, though when the community is ill, effective support is difficult to maintain. Bell and Doucet (2003) describe the limitations of a support system among women enduring similar circumstances, in which focusing on the shared stressors may be demoralizing and exacerbate feelings of powerlessness. Dependency among peers that may not be reliable sources of help can result in a continued sense of instability and isolation (Bell & Doucet, 2003). Solomon (2001) queries a young woman about her encounter with depression: "Since I think positive . . . I made it. Ain't nothing that bad you can't get through. . . . I say that loud with these people, they just dogs eating dog. And anyone can be saved. I had one woman, she drank, smoke, had been with my husband . . . but when she come round, I gonna help her, 'cause in order for her to get better she gotta have someone to help her" (p. 352).

In addition to helping individual women develop more effective coping skills, an emphasis on educating religious leaders in mental health skills may support the African American community from within the culture's unique dynamic. Taylor, Ellison, and Chatters (2000) explored the considerable influence of clergy on mental health care decisions, qualities, and access for their community. Clergy who establish trust within the community on a spiritual level and display personal investment by engaging in the community through advantages such as home visits create accessibility to mental health care unequaled by alternate sources (Taylor et al., 2000).

When exploring depression in specific populations, it is imperative to keep in mind that race is not equivalent to culture (Phinney, 1996). Cultural influence on a client's worldview dictates the extent to which problem solving is effective and the manner in which treatment is approached. An external locus of responsibility, or the propensity to identify with imposed discrimination and prejudice, is common among African Americans, which encompasses the impact of the history of slavery (Sue & Sue, 2003). The differentiating factor in the African American identity is the locus of control. Individuals who embody an internal locus of control tend to engender racial pride, while those who assume an external locus of control are more sensitive to outside influences (Sue & Sue, 2003). Martin and Hall (1992) ascertain an integral consideration of an African American woman's role prioritization in reference to the fortification of African Americans. Specifically important to account for in regard to treatment planning is the unique aspect of the inclination to forfeit power in the belief that it will strengthen racial solidarity.

Caucasian Women and Depression

The depression that a Caucasian woman experiences often stems from a lack of cohesiveness and the conflict formed when facing feminine socialization and ideals of American autonomy. Gender roles, the amount of value that is placed on them, and the woman's ability to fulfill those roles are significant factors across cultures. The non-Hispanic white woman seems to struggle with the lack of clarity and consistency within American gender roles. Karp (2001), in *The Burden of*

Sympathy, discusses the extent to which Americans have learned and prioritized self-interest and profit. He applies this to the concept of caring for the mentally ill and postulates that because there are no distinct cultural definitions and motivations, as a society we rely on outdated gender roles to create structure in caring. He relates this to women in the statement, "In a culture otherwise dedicated to expressive individualism, women—mothers in particular—often measure their morality through an ethic of care and willingness to subordinate self-interest to the greater good of the family" (p. 246).

Sullivan and Neale's meta-analysis of the genetic epidemiology of major depression (2000) provided evidence that genetics accounts for 40 percent of the risk in major depression. Depression within the family can complicate caretaking if none of those affected are being properly treated. Martha Manning (1994) speaks of her own undertaking with her grandmother:

> My grandmother sits at the kitchen table. . . . The lazy Susan spins in the center, with the host of prescription bottles, holy cards of dead people, Avon products, and napkins. . . . I watch the objects move as I circle my grandmother's depression. . . . Other people deal with it better than I. They have more distance. Her sorrow is not separate from me. It is in me too. I know it. I've known it all along. I have lived all my life with parallel visions of her: my magical creative wonderful grandmother who calls me golden and loves me like crazy, and the sad angry woman who gave up on life so long ago [pp. 26–28].

Women construct their identity on the equality of intimacy and relationships in their lives. Aspects that create a healthy identity, such as respect, meaningful work, safety, and loving relationships, may be misdirected or undeveloped, bringing vulnerability to depression (Pipher, 1994). A woman's adult identity dictates the quality of interpersonal relationships concerning family, spouse, and outside interactions. Uebelacker, Courtnage, and Whisman (2003) discovered that marital dissatisfaction was correlated with depressive symptoms in both men and women due to self-silencing. The significant factor in the women's depression was explained by the inability to express dissatisfaction with the marriage for fear of unsettling or compromising the relationship (Uebelacker et al., 2003).

The need to harmonize with outside relationships in addition to maintaining a cosmetically placid life creates stressors that are unique to women. Additional pressures of the worldview held by Caucasian women often accompany the consequence of self-silencing within and outside the home. American society generates an emphasis on production, ambition, and individuality (Sue & Sue, 2003). Self-blame is common when accountability is high in unrealistic goal setting, which is maintained by an internal locus of control and internal locus of responsibility (Sue & Sue, 2003). In addition to the pressures that women endure, there is an extension of the tendency to accept an ambitious, self-defining role without internalizing the relationship-dependent role and the autonomous role. Jean Baker Miller (1986) illustrates this as "paradoxical depression": "Such depressions may reflect the fact that the individual is forced to admit increased self-determination and to admit that [she], [herself], is responsible for what happens. [She] is not doing it for someone else or under the direction of someone else" (p. 92).

Miller postulates that the conflict of self-determination extends past accountability and into the basic issues of safety and love:

> If I can bring myself to admit that I can take on the determination and direction of my own life rather than give it over to others, can I exist with safety? With satisfaction? And who will ever love me, or even tolerate me, if I do that? Only after these questions are confronted, at least to some degree, can one begin to ask the even more basic question: what do I really want? And this question too, will not always be answered easily [p. 93].

Abuse and poverty are significant factors that impress on a woman's ability to cope with stressors. Physical, sexual, or emotional abuse that begins at an early age sets an interpersonal dynamic that is difficult to escape. Abuse from a dating partner is reported by 20 percent of women, which illustrates the commonalty in violence against women (Sue & Sue, 2003). Lack of educational resources and vulnerability to poverty leave women without the proper aids to divert depressive symptoms: the establishment of safe and equal relationships in treatment planning accompanied by access to basic resources. The relation between assessment of self-concept and the woman's ability to empower and problem-solve is essential to track progress: the creation of a "personal vision," as Miller (1986) describes it, and the search for the ideal authenticity that defines and determines "what we want."

CONCLUSION

Roosa, Dumka, Gonzales, and Knight (2002) state, "For interventions to be culturally competent, they must be designed and implemented in ways that not only fit the culture of the targeted group *but also* help the targeted group be successful in their context." Therefore, the emphasis in clinicians' service is conditioned on the character and capability of our empathy for the client. In order to do this, it is necessary that the key traits of a culture be kept at the forefront of considerations. Locus of control, the value of gender roles within that culture, and the client's extent of involvement in her culture are specific aspects that require attention. Without these considerations, the inconsistencies will continue to occur and the populations served will not benefit from the efforts put forth.

References

American Psychiatric Association. (2000). *Diagnostic and statistical manual of mental disorders* (4th ed.). Washington, DC: Author.

Aranda, M. P., Castaneda, I., Lee P-L., & Sobel, E. (2001). Stress, social support, and coping as predictors of depressive symptoms: Gender differences among Mexican Americans. *Social Work Research, 25*(1), 37–49.

Bean, F. D., Van Hook, J., & Woodward-Lafield, K. (2001). *Estimates of numbers of unauthorized migrants residing in the United States: The total, Mexican, and non-Mexican Central American unauthorized populations in mid-2001.* Washington, DC: Pew Charitable Trusts.

Bell, D., & Doucet, J. (2003). Poverty, inequality, and discrimination as sources of depression among U.S. women. *Psychology of Women Quarterly, 27*(2), 101–113.

Cochrane, R., & Hussain, F. A. (2002). Depression in South Asian women: Asian women's beliefs on causes and cures. *Mental Health, Religion and Culture, 5*(3), 285–312.

Cook, E. P., & Warnke, M. (1993). Gender bias and the DSM-III-R. *Counselor Education and Supervision, 32*(4), 311–323.

Del Vecchio Good, M. (n.d.). United Nations Division for the Advancement of Women, Department of Economic and Social Affairs, Commission on the Status of Women. *Women and mental health.* Retrieved February 27, 2004, from http://www.un.org/womenwatch/daw/csw/mental.

Dent, J., & Teasdale, J. D. (1998). Negative cognition and the persistence of depression. *Journal of Abnormal Psychology, 97*(1), 29–34.

Department of Health. (2002). *Women's mental health: Into the mainstream* (DH Publication No. 29433). London: Department of Health.

Depression and Bipolar Support Alliance. (2004, February 3). *Facts about depression.* Retrieved February 26, 2004, from http://www. dbsalliance.org/media/depressionfacts.html.

Ellison, C. G. (1993). Religious involvement and self-perception among black Americans. *Social Forces, 71*(4), 1027–1056.

Finkelstein, J. S., Donenberg, G. R., & Martinovich, Z. (2001). Maternal control and adolescent depression: Ethnic differences among clinically referred girls. *Journal of Youth and Adolescence, 30*(2), 155–171.

Gordon, P. A. (2003). The decision to remain single: Implications for women across cultures. *Journal of Mental Health Counseling, 25*(1), 33–45.

HealthyPlace.com Depression Community. (2003). *Examining depression among African American women from a psychiatric mental health nursing perspective.* Retrieved December 11, 2003, from http://www. healthyplace.com/Communities/Depression/minorities_8.asp.

Heeseung, C. (2002). Understanding adolescent depression in ethnocultural context. *Advances in Nursing Science, 25*(2), 71–86.

Hicks, M. (2002). Validity of the CIDI probe flow chart for depression in Chinese American women. *Transcultural Psychiatry, 39*(4), 434–451.

Huang, L. N. (1994). An integrative approach to clinical assessment and intervention with Asian American adolescents. *Journal of Clinical Child Psychology, 23*(1), 21–31.

Ito, K. L., & Maramba, G. G. (2002). Therapeutic beliefs of Asian American therapists: Views from an ethnic-specific clinic. *Transcultural Psychiatry, 39*(1), 33–73.

Joiner, T. E., & Blalock, J. A. (1995). Gender differences in depression: The role of anxiety and generalized negative affect. *Sex Roles. A Journal of Research, 33*(1/2), 91–110.

Karp, D. (2001). *The burden of sympathy: How families cope with mental illness.* New York: Oxford University Press.

Kopper, B. A., & Epperson, D. L. (1996). The experience and expression of anger: Relationships with gender, gender role socialization, depression, and mental health functioning. *Journal of Counseling Psychology, 43*(2), 158–165.

Koss-Chioino, J. D. (1999). Depression among Puerto Rican women: Culture, etiology and diagnosis. *Hispanic Journal of Behavioral Sciences, 21*(3), 330–351.

Lopez, S. R., & Guarnaccia, P. J. (2000). Cultural psychopathology: Uncovering the social world of mental illness. *Annual Review of Psychology, 51*(1), 571–599.

Malgady, R. G., Rogler, L. H., & Cortés, D. E. (1996). Cultural expression of psychiatric symptoms: Idioms of anger among Puerto Ricans. *Psychological Assessment, 8*(3), 1040–3590.

Manning, M. (1994). *Undercurrents: A life beneath the surface.* New York: HarperCollins.

Martin, J. K., & Hall, G. C. (1992). Thinking black, thinking internal, thinking feminist. *Journal of Counseling Psychology, 39*(4), 509–515.

Martin, P. (1999). *The Zen path through depression.* New York: Harper-Collins.

McLaughlin, J. E. (2002). Reducing diagnostic bias. *Journal of Mental Health Counseling, 24*(3), 256–269.

Miller, J. B. (1976). *Toward a new psychology of women.* Boston: Beacon Press.

Miller, J. B. (1986). *Toward a new psychology of women* (2nd ed.). Boston: Beacon Press.

Moore, K. A. (2001). Time to take a closer look at Hispanic children and families. *Policy and Practice of Public Human Services, 59*(2), 8–10.

Myers, H. F., Lesser, I., Rodriguez, N., Mira, C. B., Hwang, W., Camp, C., Anderson, D., Erickson, L., & Wohl, M. (2002). Ethnic differences in clinical presentation of depression in adult women. *Cultural Diversity and Ethnic Minority Psychology, 8*(2), 138–156.

National Asian Women's Health Organization. (2003). *Depression.* Retrieved December 18, 2003, from http://www.nawho.org/index. v3page;jsessionid=10qspsbnkgqus?ct=search&sr_pg=1&srmd=1.

National Association for Mental Health (MIND). (2003). *Information: Fact sheets, Diversity.* Retrieved December 18, 2003, from http://www. mind.org.uk/Information/?wbc_purpose=Basic&WBCMODE= PresentationUnpublished.

National Institute of Mental Health. (2002). *The numbers count: Mental disorders in America* (NIH Publication No. PB 01–4584). Bethesda, MD: Office of Communications.

National Women's Health Information Center. (2002). *Women of color health data book.* Retrieved February 14, 2004, from http://www. 4woman.gov/owh/pub/woc/toc.htm.

O'Malley, A. S., Forrest, C. B., & Miranda, J. (2003). Primary care attributes and care for depression among low-income African American women. *American Journal of Public Health, 93*(8), 1328–1334.

Phinney, J. S. (1996). When we talk about American ethnic groups, what do we mean? *American Psychologist, 51*(9), 918–927.

Pipher, M. (1994). *Reviving Ophelia.* New York: Ballantine Books.

Ramirez de Leon, A. (2002). An investigation of the relationship between spiritual well-being and psychological well-being among Mexican-American Catholics. *Dissertation Abstracts International, 63*(8), 3651B. (UMI No. 3060687)

Roosa, M. W., Dumka, L. E., Gonzales, N. A., & Knight, G. P. (2002). Cultural/ethnic issues and the prevention scientist in the 21st century. *Prevention & Treatment, 5*, Article 5. http://www.journals.apa.org/prevention/volume5/pre0050005a.html.

Rotter, J. (1975). Some problems and misconceptions related to the construct of internal versus external control of reinforcement. *Journal of Consulting and Clinical Psychology, 43*, 56–67.

Scattolon, Y., & Stoppard, J. M. (1999). "Getting on with life": Women's experiences and ways of coping with depression. *Canadian Psychology, 40*(2), 205–219.

Solomon, A. (2001). *Noonday demon.* New York: Touchstone.

Stoeber, J. (2003). Self-pity: Exploring the links to personality, control beliefs, and anger. *Journal of Personality, 71*(2), 183–220.

Sue, D. W., & Sue, D. (2003). *Counseling the culturally diverse: Theory and practice* (4th ed.). New York: Wiley.

Sullivan, P. F., & Neale, M. C. (2000). Genetic epidemiology of major depression: Review and meta-analysis. *American Journal of Psychiatry, 57*(10), 1552–1563.

Taylor, R. J., Ellison, C. G., & Chatters, L. M. (2000). Mental health services in faith communities: The role of clergy in Black church. *Social Work, 45*(1), 73–87.

Uebelacker, L. A., Courtnage, E. S., & Whisman, M. A. (2003). Correlates of depression and marital dissatisfaction: Perceptions of marital communication style. *Journal of Social and Personal Relationships, 20*(6), 757–769.

U.S. Census Bureau. (2000). *Census 2000 summary file 1.* Retrieved February 10, 2004, from http://factfinder.census.gov/servlet.

U.S. Department of Health and Human Services. (1999). *Mental health: Culture, race, and ethnicity: A supplement to Mental Health: A Report of the Surgeon General.* http://www.surgeongeneral.gov/library/mentalhealth/cre/.

U.S. Department of Health and Human Services. (2001, August). United States Surgeon General press release. Retrieved July 15, 2003, from http://www.surgeongeneral.gov/library/mentalhealth/cre/release.asp.

VanderVoort, D. J., & Skorikov, V. B. (2002). Physical health and social network characteristics as determinants of mental health across cultures. *Current Psychology, 21*(1), 50–68.

CHAPTER TEN

Intimacy and Injury

Legal Interventions
for Battered Women

Phyllis Goldfarb, J.D.

T he response of the law to the problem of violence in intimate relationships has not been swift. For centuries, legal actors neglected to notice or address the issue, an omission linked in large part to the broader problem of gender inequality deeply entrenched in the culture. Indeed, the common law of the Anglo-American world permitted the "master of the household" to "chastise" his wife using corporal punishment, as long as he did not inflict permanent physical injuries (Siegel, 1996).

Although American judges had explicitly rejected the doctrine of chastisement by the late nineteenth century, they began substituting for it a common law doctrine of family privacy that justified legal nonintervention in the marital relationship, despite evidence that a husband was subjecting his wife to physical abuse.[1] Since this shift in the

---

I am indebted to Jessica Baumgarten and Erin McFeron for research assistance; to Anne Marie Dolan, Donna Gattoni, and Jeannie Kelly for administrative assistance; and to Boston College Law School for research support.

justification for nonintervention coincided with the era of Reconstruction, it is not surprising that the understanding by which families were to be accorded privacy was racialized.[2] When the customs of racial hierarchy were threatened by the abolition of slavery,[3] intimate violence came to be understood as a problem of African American and poor immigrant men, such as those of German and Irish descent.[4] Legal sanctions, particularly the punishment of flogging, were imposed in some of these cases,[5] but not in instances of intimate violence committed by men of privileged classes.[6]

For most of the next century, intimate violence was treated as an occasion for social services to be brought to bear on women, with family courts sending marital violence cases to social workers, who used counseling and urged reconciliation (Siegel, 1996). The problem was understood as one in which women provoked violence.[7] When framed in this manner, the appropriate intervention became one of teaching women better habits to prevent their provocations.[8] Within this cultural framework, male violence receded from view. This notion of intimate violence as a private family dispute that women could be taught better skills to address extended late into the twentieth century.[9]

Due to this history of dramatic underenforcement of crimes of intimate violence against women, feminist activists and an influential victim's rights movement combined their energies to remove the cloak of privacy from the problem of intimate violence and put the issue on the public political agenda of the 1960s and 1970s. Their efforts were tremendously successful at local, state, and national levels. In relatively short order, they were able to alter the cultural understanding of the problem of intimate violence.[10]

Over the past three decades, battered women's advocates have established hundreds of battered women's hotlines, shelters, and victim's advocacy programs.[11] They have produced documentaries about battered women's experiences, generated a cross-disciplinary professional literature on the subject,[12] and in some instances, pioneered treatment programs for batterers (Adams, 1988). Medical schools have added course work about domestic violence to standard medical training, and a number of law schools now offer both classroom courses examining issues of domestic violence and clinical programs in which student-attorneys provide legal representation for battered women.[13] These extraordinary efforts have both reflected and promoted a growing cultural awareness of the nature, scope, and severity of the problem of violence between intimate partners.

These changing cultural attitudes have wrought many changes in law, particularly on the front lines of law enforcement. Many of these changes have involved toughening the criminal laws regarding violence between intimates and educating both law enforcement and judicial officials about the nature of the problem and the use of criminal laws to respond to it. Although the criminal justice system has been the primary locus of legal change on this issue, it has not been the exclusive one.

CONTEMPORARY LEGAL INTERVENTIONS

A variety of legal reforms have been undertaken to improve the responsiveness of law enforcement systems to victims of intimate abuse. Legal commentators have characterized domestic violence not just as a crime, but as a violation of human rights (Copelon, 1994; Culliton, 1993; Holt, 1994; Thomas & Easley, 1995), hate crime statutes (Copeland & Wolfe, 1991), and the prohibition on involuntary servitude found in the Thirteenth Amendment to the U.S. Constitution (McConnell, 1992). Consequently, courts have been deluged in recent years with a variety of cases brought on behalf of domestic violence victims.

Civil Protection Orders

The major way in which courts now seek to address the danger posed by intimate violence is through the provision of a process by which those who have suffered violence may obtain civil orders of protection, also known as restraining orders, against their batterers. Every American jurisdiction now has legislation by which courts can issue such orders to enjoin a batterer's abuse and threats (Finn & Colson, 1990). Different states have different procedural requirements by which victims may invoke the civil protection order process (Klein & Orloff, 1993; Kinports & Fischer, 1993).

Obviously, the effectiveness of the civil protection order process depends on how readily a victim of violence can access it and how willing local criminal justice officials will be to enforce it (Harris & Smith, 1996; Klein, 1996). Both of these are questions of resources. Jurisdictions vary as to how much outreach is provided to victims of intimate violence to assist them in using this process and in how many law enforcement resources are directed toward responding to it (Fischer &

Rose, 1995). These are significant issues: in some instances, the holder of a restraining order faces retaliatory actions and an escalation of intimate violence.[14]

Most states have enacted statutes criminalizing the violation of a restraining order, and others use criminal contempt laws to bolster the protection that a restraining order—a mere piece of paper—can provide (Zlotnick, 1995). In these jurisdictions, the restraining order process provides formal notice to the abuser that continued coercive contact with the person who obtained the order can be prosecuted as a crime. Although the crime is defined and punished in various ways depending on the jurisdiction, it has often been made a felony carrying the risk of years of imprisonment and significant collateral consequences (Epstein, 1999).

Arrest and Prosecution

Beyond the prosecution of violations of civil restraining orders, legal reforms have resulted in dramatic increases in the arrest and prosecution of batterers for the assaults and the batteries that they have committed. Some states prosecute intimate violence under their general laws against assaultive behavior, while others have enacted separate statutes with separate penalties for crimes of intimate violence (Hart, 1992).[15] States have also enacted statutes that define new crimes related to the circumstances of intimate violence. For example, every jurisdiction adopted an antistalking law in the 1990s (Jordan, Quinn, Jordan, & Daileader, 2000). While the first such statutes faced constitutional challenges due to the breadth and vagueness of the conduct they covered, newer antistalking legislation benefited from the more precisely worded model statute drafted in 1993 by the U.S. Department of Justice and other federal agencies.[16]

In most jurisdictions, the general rule is that police officers are forbidden to make arrests for misdemeanor offenses unless they first obtain an arrest warrant (James, 1994). Battered women's advocates worked to change this general policy, such that now most jurisdictions have statutes that permit arrests for the misdemeanor of assault and battery in domestic violence cases to be made without warrants (Zorza, 1992). Some locales also have mandatory domestic violence training for law enforcement officers (Gagné, 1998; Guinn & O'Dell, 1993).[17]

In responding to reports of intimate violence, police in some jurisdictions are permitted to exercise their discretion in making arrests, while other jurisdictions have removed that discretion. The 1984 publication of an experiment with mandatory arrest in Minneapolis spurred a number of states to adopt mandatory arrest statutes or policies.[18] These require police officers to arrest domestic violence suspects whenever the officers have probable cause to believe that a crime such as assault or battery has been committed. Other states have preferred discretionary arrest laws in these situations.[19]

Some jurisdictions have mandatory prosecution policies as well, such that prosecutors have no discretion to dismiss domestic violence charges once they are filed (Hanna, 1996). Even if the victim of the crime requests that the charges be dismissed and refuses to cooperate in pressing the charges, the prosecutor will be required to pursue the case nonetheless. In addition, most states have mandatory reporting laws that require medical professionals, and occasionally other social services workers, to file reports with police whenever they suspect that a patient's symptoms or injuries are caused by intimate violence (Mills, 1990).

Mandatory reporting, arrest, and prosecution are legal reforms intended to counter the long and notorious history of law enforcement's failure to respond to victims of intimate violence. Supporters of mandatory legal interventions believe that they provide powerful deterrents to batterers, demonstrating strong cultural condemnation of battering behavior and reducing the likelihood of discriminatory law enforcement. Therefore, they consider these policies the most effective available tool for reducing intimate violence (Hanna, 1996; Forum, 1997; Stark, 1996; Guinn & O'Dell, 1993; Zorza, 1994).

By contrast, opponents of mandatory interventions are deeply concerned when decisions to arrest and prosecute intimate violence are made without regard to the victim's wishes (Mills, 1990). They are concerned that especially when victims remain in relationship with abusers, as many do, mandatory criminal justice interventions can be harmful to the victim in a number of ways. These harms are compounded for women who come from communities with historically troubled relationships with law enforcement, immigrant women whose batterers may be deported, and women living on the edge of poverty (Fedders, 1997; Ruttenberg, 1994; Klein & Orloff, 1993; Crenshaw, 1993). Moreover, researchers are in dispute as to the long-term effectiveness of mandatory policies in reducing intimate violence (Zorza, 1994; Symposium on Domestic Violence, 1992).

A criminal conviction for a crime of domestic violence may in some instances result not in immediate incarceration, but in a sentence of probation with required conditions (Hanna, 1998). These conditions, enforced through the threat of future imprisonment for failure to comply, often require that the batterer enter individual counseling, an anger-management program, or other available social services (Adams, 1988; Harrell, 1991). In some jurisdictions, such as Boston, Seattle, and San Diego, there are therapeutic programs to which convicted batterers can be sentenced that are designed exclusively to treat men who perpetrate intimate violence (Rosenfeld, 1992).

Some commentators argue that encouraging and facilitating the use of therapeutic services in domestic violence cases would be more effective than mandating their use through the criminal justice system. They worry that the coercive qualities of criminal penalties impede the effectiveness of these services (Mills, 1990). Others suggest that in some cases, providing intimate violence victims with the material resources that many of them lack, such as independent housing and income, may be preferable to policies of punishing abusers through criminal justice sanctions (Coker, 2000).

While these controversies about the appropriateness of various kinds of legal interventions continue, there is no doubt that prosecutions of domestic violence cases have become features of the landscape in criminal courtrooms around the country. Some criminal courthouses hold specialized domestic violence sessions, and a handful of jurisdictions have established a court devoted exclusively to domestic violence (Keilitz, Efkeman, & Casey, 1997). The underlying rationale for the latter arrangement is that specialized domestic violence courts, overseeing all related civil and criminal matters, will more effectively address the complex issues—potentially involving divorce, property, child custody, and other issues—that may be implicated when efforts are underway to end an abusive relationship.

Civil Lawsuits

While far less common than criminal prosecutions, some victims of intimate violence have filed civil lawsuits, known as tort actions, against their abusers. Through these lawsuits, plaintiffs seek monetary compensation for the harms that they have suffered due to the defendants' abusive behavior (Scherer, 1992). The harms compensated need not be physical injuries alone, but might include the traumatic consequences of living under the coercive control of one's intimate partner. Many jurisdictions recognize a tort action for intentional infliction of emotional distress, and some commentators have suggested that claims based on this legal theory might be used as a source of redress for victims of intimate abuse in conjunction with tort actions for physical harms such as assault and battery (Scherer, 1992; Dalton, 1997).

Tort actions as a source of redress in these situations have some obvious constraints. First, victims will need the assistance of lawyers to pursue such actions, and there is a profound shortage of lawyers for those who are unable to pay for their services. Second, a batterer without sufficient financial means may be unable to pay a monetary judgment if it is imposed. Therefore, even in situations where plaintiffs are able to hire lawyers to file such suits and their claims are upheld by courts, the victories will be merely symbolic unless the defendants have significant resources. Hence, the deterrence picture provided by this legal remedy is a limited one, although there may be some individual cases where it is a viable avenue of redress.

Another kind of civil lawsuit that does not depend for its success on the resources of an individual defendant is a lawsuit against police departments and municipalities, alleging civil rights violations in the failure of police officers to respond to complaints of intimate violence. Evidence that the police had policies or practices of nonintervention in domestic violence cases led to a number of prominent lawsuits and multimillion-dollar judgments in the 1980s.[20] The prospect of liability at this level of financial magnitude encouraged police departments to increase their responsiveness to victims of intimate violence. Indeed, the fear of liability may well have led some communities to favor mandatory arrest programs (Dalton & Schneider, 2001).

The 1989 Supreme Court decision in *DeShaney* v. *Winnebago County Department of Social Services* seems to prohibit lawsuits against police departments and municipalities for failure to protect victims from private violence that the police could not control. Nonetheless, a plaintiff may still be able to prevail in such litigation on a claim that police enabled private violence (Borgmann, 1990) or engaged in discriminatory enforcement (Choundas, 1995). Although lawsuits of this sort may be advisable in particular situations, they are not a feasible approach in most cases of intimate violence.

Alternative Forms of Dispute Resolution

In cases involving family law, many courts prefer mediation as an alternative to litigation. This preference for mediation is sparked by a desire to reduce both case congestion and levels of antagonism in matters related to the family. Indeed, a number of states require mediation in cases involving child custody and visitation.[21]

The preference for mediation is controversial in cases involving intimate violence. Those who oppose mediation in cases of intimate violence argue that the posture of mediator neutrality prevents the mediator from giving the abused partner the support that she may need and inhibits any signaling of disapproval of the batterer's behavior. Consequently, mediation opponents fear that the ethos of mediation is such that it enables the batterer—and, even worse, the system—to overlook the extent of the harm that the batterer has inflicted and to avoid taking it into account in reaching agreements (Fischer, Vidmar, & Ellis, 1993; Cobb, 1997).

Supporters of mediation in at least some of the cases involving intimate violence believe that many of the opponents' concerns can be addressed through the manner in which the mediation setting is structured. The mediator can meet separately with the parties and can encourage the batterer to take responsibility for his behavior. This less adversarial mediation process is characterized as more potentially empowering to the battered woman than the formality of the courtroom setting (Joyce, 1997).

The controversies concerning the appropriateness of mediation in cases that entail intimate violence have influenced the legal regulation of access to mediation. Some of the jurisdictions that mandate mediation relinquish that requirement in cases where intimate violence has occurred. Some jurisdictions go so far as to ban mediation in these cases, whereas others permit the judge to make a discretionary judgment concerning the appropriateness of mediation in a particular case (Bartlett, Harris, & Rhode, 2002).

Mediation is not the only potential alternative setting for resolving disputes in cases that involve intimate violence. Coker (1999) has described the Navajo practice of peacemaking as a kind of forum that may provide assistance to battered women in some circumstances. Peacemaking processes may be initiated by the battered woman or by referral from the Navajo legal system. The peacemaker facilitates a conversation between the parties, those with a stake in the parties' lives, such as family and friends, and those with special expertise related to the pertinent issues. The group then works to try to create a plan for addressing the problem. This kind of model has been adopted by proponents of restorative justice programs, some of whom believe that these represent promising alternative interventions for at least a portion of the cases involving intimate violence.[22]

SELF-DEFENSE

Against the backdrop of the centuries-old reluctance to address the problem of intimate violence, all of these developments in the law were hard won and recently so. Nevertheless, attitudes often change more slowly than the law. As battered women's advocates have observed, legal decision makers' perceptions of battered women are often still plagued by stereotypes and misperceptions.[23] These problems manifest themselves acutely when the legal interventions detailed in the preceding section have not succeeded in preventing intimate violence and battered women find themselves on trial for killing their abusers.

In an intimate relationship that becomes violent, the violence may become lethal. When it does, the violence in the relationship has generally escalated to the extent that the abuser in the relationship kills the abused. Studies show that approximately one-third of female murder victims, compared to one-twenty-fifth of male murder victims, are killed by their intimate partners (Rennison, 2003).

Occasionally, lethality runs in the opposite direction from the pattern of abuse, such that a person who has suffered repeated and severe violence at the hands of her intimate partner responds by killing her batterer. Often these killings are charged as crimes, ranging from manslaughter to first-degree murder. A third of the women incarcerated for homicide have been convicted for killing an intimate partner. Research shows that a considerable percentage of these partners had histories of abusing the women who killed them (Browne, 1987).[24]

In such cases, the likely defense is self-defense. To meet the criteria of self-defense and thereby avoid conviction for acts of violence against a batterer, a defendant must convince a jury that she acted from a reasonable belief that she was in imminent danger of serious bodily harm or death (Gillespie, 1989). In other words, self-defense in this context entails a claim that the intimate violence had reached a point at which either the abuser or the abused would be maimed or killed. Stated more plainly, when the abused, now a criminal defendant, took the abuser's life, she did so to save her own.

Battered Woman Syndrome

Over the past three decades, psychologists have sought to understand more clearly the dynamics of abusive relationships, the experiences of battered women, and the psychological consequences of living for an extended period in an intimate relationship with a batterer. In the 1970s, psychologist Lenore Walker (1979) coined the term "battered woman syndrome," a subspecies of posttraumatic stress disorder, to explain the perceptions and behavior of women in such situations. Following the publication of Walker's research, lawyers representing women charged with violence against their batterers saw that prosecutors, judges, and jurors might learn more about how the world looks to women trapped in violent relationships and might view them more sympathetically if these decision makers were able to become better educated about battered women's lives.

Consequently, activists and lawyers for battered women developed a trial strategy of seeking to admit experts who could offer testimony to educate jurors about battering relationships and their consequences. Since "battered woman syndrome" had a scientific flavor, similar to other sorts of psychological and scientific testimony that experts were permitted to offer at trial, the educational process that occurred in the course of battered women's litigation took the form of admitting the expert testimony of psychologists. When permitted to testify, these experts would describe for the jury the nature of battered woman syndrome and explain how it might illuminate what occurred in the case at bar.[25]

Battered women's lawyers believed that through the admission of expert testimony about battered woman syndrome, which focused on the experiences, perceptions, and mental states of women caught in abusive relationships, jurors could come to appreciate how the defendant reasonably believed that she had to use violence to repel the imminent life-threatening violence of her batterer. In the absence of expert testimony, battered women's advocates feared that the law of self-defense would be applied in a gender-biased fashion, since judges and jurors might fail to apprehend the contextual conditions of battered women's lives (Schneider, 2000).

Initially, litigants' efforts to admit expert testimony of battered woman syndrome met with little success. Judges often refused the admission of such testimony, disputing its relevance, its scientific basis, or the notion that it would assist a jury. Battered women's advocates responded with campaigns to liberalize the evidentiary rulings to more readily allow for the admission of expert testimony in these cases. These campaigns yielded statutes adopted by some state legislatures that authorized the admission of such testimony[26] and case law from the highest court of many states that reached the same conclusion.[27] By the end of the 1980s, the admission of expert testimony on battered woman syndrome had become a far more commonly accepted practice in trials of battered women charged with violence against batterers.

When expert testimony of battered woman syndrome was admitted, it did not always work as battered women's advocates had hoped. Although some women whose self-defense trials featured testimony about battered woman syndrome did receive acquittals or convictions of lesser charges, many others were convicted of the crimes with which they had been charged.[28] Some argue that this pattern of results relates to inherent limitations in the concept of battered woman syndrome itself.

While testimony about battered woman syndrome can be a vehicle for educating jurors about battered women's relationships, perceptions, and experiences, it can also reinforce a view of battered women as mentally impaired.[29] Commentators observe that battered woman syndrome focuses attention on the psychology of the battered woman rather than on the batterer's pattern of coercive behavior. As a result, new stereotypes about battered women have been created, such that those who fail to meet the stereotypes are perceived to be less credible when they claim self-defense.[30] As several commentators have noted, the battered woman stereotype has worked to the particular disadvantage of black women, lesbians, women perceived to have assertive personalities, women with substance abuse histories, and others who for a variety of cultural reasons may not be as readily perceived to embody the passive virtues that fit constrained understandings of the battered woman profile.[31]

Success in court has been particularly elusive for battered women defendants who raise self-defense in cases in which the self-protective violence that they inflicted on their batterers did not occur in the middle of a threatening confrontation. Rather, the violence they inflicted may have been during a lull in the abuse, when the batterer was sleeping or otherwise off guard. While battered women's advocates have never contended that women should kill batterers in these nonconfrontational situations, they also suggest that it is not unreasonable in certain of these situations to view these women as acting in self-defense, similar in fashion to hostages overtaking their captors (Marcus, 1994; Cohen, 1996).

In cases in which the battered woman defendant had previously sought aid from police, courts, and social services, only to find them nonresponsive or ineffective in their efforts to protect her, a predicate may well be laid for an argument that she honestly and reasonably believed that she was able to protect her life from the batterer's impending lethal violence only by the assaultive actions for which she is now on trial. Indeed, decision makers would have no context within which to understand her actions and perceptions unless they heard extensive evidence of the violent dynamics in the relationship, the history of abuse, and prior efforts to escape or halt the violence. Nevertheless, women have not fared well in cases of nonconfrontational assaults, likely due to fears that if the imminent harm requirement of self-defense doctrine is stretched beyond confrontational episodes, battered women may be encouraged to take violent retaliatory actions and then claim self-defense.[32]

Problems in Representation of Battered Women as Defendants

Problems inherent in the interpretation and application of the concept of battered woman syndrome are not the only problems that battered women face as defendants in courtrooms. The failure of women who have defended their lives against their batterers to successfully defend themselves against criminal convictions has multiple causes. Sometimes it is related to inadequate representation, a problem that pervades the criminal justice system for those without access to considerable financial resources.[33]

Unfortunately, it is not an aberration to find practicing in criminal courtrooms around the country attorneys who are unschooled in the phenomenon of domestic violence, hold misconceptions or biases about battered women, or simply lack knowledge about the complexities of representing battered women and lack the desire to remedy this deficit.[34] Due at least in part to their misapprehension of the nature and the legal implications of the incidents underlying the charges, such attorneys may fail to effectively investigate the battered woman's claim of self-defense. They may fail to identify or interview potential defense witnesses such as family members or friends, find other sources of information such as medical records or employment records that corroborate the defense, or seek expert assistance to bolster an available defense.[35]

Attorneys who are not fully aware of the story of abuse that underlies the current charges may permit a biased jury to decide the case. This can happen when an attorney fails to properly question prospective jurors, through a procedure known as voir dire, about the misperceptions that they may hold of battered women.[36] It can also happen when the attorney fails to challenge the selection of jurors who reveal such biases. These attorneys may also fail to request that judges instruct jurors on how credible evidence of battering relates to a claim of self-defense.[37] In addition, attorneys may fail to develop relationships of trust with their clients, which when combined with the confusion and memory lapses that frequently plague battered women who have used lethal violence, may lead them to give poor advice to their clients regarding decisions to accept a plea bargain or to testify at trial.[38]

Despite the fact that the Sixth Amendment to the U.S. Constitution guarantees the effective assistance of counsel at a criminal trial, the Supreme Court has made it exceedingly difficult to overturn a conviction on the grounds of ineffective assistance.[39] This is so even when there is substantial evidence of significant inadequacies in representation. In a number of appellate cases, courts have refused to find that the ineffective assistance of trial counsel rose to the level of a constitutional violation, although counsel failed to develop a full evidentiary record of the history of battering in the defendant's relationship with a violent partner.[40]

Problems of Judge and Juror Bias

In addition to receiving inadequate representation, women raising self-defense claims have sometimes met judicial hostility. Judges unsympathetic to defendants generally, or to women raising self-defense claims in particular, have sometimes refused to admit evidence, expert or otherwise, proffered in support of self-defense on the grounds that it is not relevant or would not be helpful to the jury. In some instances, judges have refused to permit questioning of prospective jurors during the voir dire process to uncover specific attitudes that may bias them against a claim of self-defense in these circumstances. Judges may also refuse to instruct juries to consider self-defense in these cases (*State* v. *Norman*, 1989).

Recent case law and legislation in a number of jurisdictions requires the admission of evidence bearing on self-defense when a factual predicate can be established that the defendant on trial suffered a history of abuse at the hands of the person she is charged with assaulting or killing.[41] Nevertheless, judicial hostility remains an obstacle to fair trials in some instances, as judges still retain considerable discretionary authority over the presentation of evidence. After a careful study of appellate cases concerning battered women's claims of self-defense, Holly Maguigan (1991) concluded that the major obstacle to fair trials in these cases is error by the trial court judge in the application of self-defense doctrine to the evidence that the defense presents.

If the trial judges in these cases do not instruct jurors properly on self-defense, the jurors will be unable to determine the appropriate legal relevance of any evidence that the defense has been able to present. Yet even in the absence of judicial error or hostility, when jurors receive the evidence and are fairly instructed about how to consider it as bearing on self-defense, some juries, for a variety of reasons, reject it. Especially in situations of inadequate defense representation, these reasons may include the jurors' misconceptions of the nature of the abuse and its consequences, which may lead them to misinterpret as aggression or retaliation the self-defensive violence for which the battered woman is now on trial.[42]

After conviction, women in these circumstances may face severe penalties, ranging from a term of years, to life in prison with or without parole, to the death sentence. Sometimes the jurisdiction's statutory structure is set up such that the judge has no discretion about the sentence imposed after conviction on particular charges. In other circumstances, judges who have sentencing discretion and harbor misconceptions of battered women's situations have exercised it harshly.[43] An unduly stiff sentence imposed by a judge may result from inadequate defense representation, bias, or other factors that block the judge's apprehension of the mitigating features of the underlying events that were the subject of the trial. The penalties flowing from conviction involve not just the potential loss of life or liberty, but other serious collateral consequences, such as the loss of custody of children, future employment opportunities, and the right to vote (Mauer & Chesney-Lind, 2002).

THE EMERGENCE OF CLEMENCY PROJECTS

The nationwide difficulties that battered women encountered in receiving fair hearings on self-defense claims spawned another legal reform effort to address this injustice. In the 1990s, regional women's groups organized clemency projects around the country to seek a reduction in the penalties that battered women suffered after they were convicted of crimes against their batterers.[44] While the clemency movement has not concerned itself exclusively with battered women convicted of homicide, these are the cases to which the movement devoted its primary attention. Aided by the clemency projects, women imprisoned for killing their batterers sought executive clemency.

The Nature of Executive Clemency

Executive clemency refers to the discretionary power of the president of the United States or the governor of a state to reduce the severity of a criminal sentence. Clemency implies mercy, the application of a kind of forbearance or forgiveness of an unduly harsh sanction (Dorne & Gewerth, 1999). While a form of executive clemency has existed since ancient times and can be found in virtually every country's legal system (Moore, 1989), the prerogative to provide sentence relief on the part of the executive branches of state or federal governments is rooted in their respective constitutions.[45]

The clemency process as a means of ameliorating unduly harsh penalties varies from state to state. In many states, an advisory board, most frequently the state's parole board, considers petitions for clemency, gathers information to investigate the petitions, holds hearings in some instances, and makes recommendations to the governor about whether a pardon—signifying full absolution for the crime— or a commutation—signifying a reduction in sentence—should be granted.[46] Although they typically have independent decision-making authority, governors tend to heed the advice of their advisory boards. In a few states, a governor's decision to grant clemency may need to be approved by another administrative body as well. In Massachusetts, this body is the Governor's Council, established as a check on gubernatorial power.

Battered women who have petitioned for relief through the clemency process have rarely sought full pardons. Although the assertion in a clemency petition that a claim of self-defense was erroneously denied at trial establishes a legitimate ground for a pardon, battered women incarcerated for homicide, after making pragmatic assessments of the relative probabilities of success, have generally sought to have their sentences commuted or reduced in duration. In these instances, the petitioners were seeking recognition that the self-defensive aspects of their cases established the mitigating grounds for sentence relief.

From the petitioner's perspective, receiving a full pardon is a preferable remedy, in that it results in the petitioner's immediate release from prison as well as the erasure of the conviction and its attendant collateral disabilities. Nevertheless, a commutation provides substantial relief, as it can reduce a sentence to time served. In other words, receiving a commutation can also result in the petitioner's immediate release from prison—often the primary concern of the petitioner—even though in such an instance the conviction remains standing. Perceiving commutations to be more politically feasible and realizing that they too can result in grants of freedom from further incarceration, the battered women's clemency movement has focused primarily on sentence commutations.[47]

A request for a sentence commutation was especially compelling in a case where self-defense had not been asserted as well as it might have been at trial or where it had encountered some apparent bias on the part of the judge or jury. Another compelling feature of clemency claims was that many of the incarcerated women faced trial before cultural understandings about the lives of battered women had evolved, before significant services had been made available to them, and before legal reforms responsive to their situations had been incorporated. This was easily demonstrated in jurisdictions in which the incarcerated women were convicted prior to the enactment of laws that permitted the admission of expert testimony regarding battered woman syndrome and other types of evidence corroborating the extent and duration of the abuse the defendants had suffered at the hands of their batterers. Since these legal reforms were prospective in nature, applying only to cases not yet finalized, those already serving sentences had not received the more enlightened legal treatment that they would have received had their cases arisen later. Hence, sentence commutations came to be perceived as a form of equitable relief that substituted for the inability to retroactively apply legal reforms.[48]

The Ohio Experience: Leadership in Action

In the 1980s, issues of domestic violence were something of a *cause célèbre* for Governor Richard F. Celeste of Ohio, whose wife, Dagmar, had worked on these issues in the feminist community in Cleveland. In 1976, several women's groups in the Cleveland area had obtained a foundation grant to establish Ohio's first emergency shelter for battered women. At that time, when Richard Celeste was lieutenant governor, he and his wife provided their own home to serve as that shelter.

Celeste became governor of Ohio in 1982, and he was elected to a second term in 1986. During these years, Dagmar Celeste was provided an office and a staff in the statehouse and became an adviser to her husband's administration. Soon after his election, Dagmar Celeste began visiting the women's prison in Marysville, Ohio, learned that many of the incarcerated women had been victims of intimate violence, and generated support for recovery programs and other services to be made available to them. These experiences led her to propose to her husband that he undertake a wide-ranging review of the cases of incarcerated battered women to determine who among them might be deserving of gubernatorial clemency (Gagné, 1998).

The political prospects for clemency improved when the Ohio Supreme Court changed state law regarding the admission of expert testimony in trials of women charged with assaulting or killing their batterers. In 1981, just before Richard Celeste had become governor, the Ohio Supreme Court had decided *State* v. *Thomas,* upholding the murder conviction of a battered woman despite the trial judge's exclusion of expert testimony on battered woman syndrome. In March 1990, the court reversed itself. In the landmark case of *State* v. *Koss* (1990), the court overturned a battered woman's conviction for voluntary manslaughter against her batterer due to the exclusion of expert testimony concerning battered woman syndrome. Later in 1990, the state legislature adopted a statute permitting the admission of expert testimony about battered woman syndrome in the trial of a defendant who raised self-defense to charges that she committed violence against her batterer (Ohio Rev. Code. Ann. § 2901.06, 1990).

Governor Celeste was responsive to concerns that women tried before the passage of the legislation and the decision in the landmark case might have been unjustly convicted and sentenced. He understood arguments that they had been denied a fair opportunity to explain how battering and its consequences influenced their situations and supported their defenses. The first lady and her staff were undoubtedly helpful in formulating these arguments and urging them as a basis for political action. Consequently, the governor initiated a clemency process.

In November 1989, while the legislation was under discussion and the landmark case was pending, Governor Celeste instructed his staff to review the cases of battered women convicted of crimes against their batterers. He wanted to identify women whose crimes grew out of their victimization by a violent partner. After instructing the state correctional authority to cooperate in obtaining this research, the governor received a report recognizing over two hundred such women.

Many of them were serving sentences on the order of twenty-five years to life, and a few were under death sentence. The candidates for clemency were selected from among this group.

Over the course of a year, the governor's staff educated themselves and the Ohio Parole Board concerning battering, self-defense, and the trial process of those who had been convicted of violence against their batterers. The education process included meetings with the incarcerated women themselves. Since most of these women had been involved in support groups that the first lady's previous advocacy had helped to create, they were better able to articulate their experiences with both battering and the court system, and they were better able to advocate for clemency on their own behalf. After exhaustively reviewing the incarcerated women's case files, the governor's staff distributed applications for clemency to more than a hundred women. The women's groups in the prison and their supporters played a central role in disseminating information about the clemency process and in obtaining assistance for individual women in preparing their petitions.[49]

The governor and his staff reviewed over one hundred cases, seeking to document and verify the history of abuse described in the clemency petitions. After eliminating cases of women who had convictions for prior violence or records of disruptive prison behavior, the staff sought to identify the cases in which the women had been unable to defend themselves adequately at trial. They isolated a group of cases in which they were persuaded that had jurors been able to hear expert testimony about battered woman syndrome and evidence about a well-documented history of abuse, they may have decided differently. The Ohio Parole Board recommended clemency in eighteen of these cases (Gagné, 1998).

The national clemency movement was ignited when, in the winter of 1990, a few weeks before he left office, Governor Celeste exceeded the board's recommendations and commuted the sentences of twenty-seven women who had served or were serving sentences for violence, typically lethal violence, against their batterers. The governor pardoned a twenty-eighth woman who had already been released on parole. As a condition of their release from prison or from parole supervision, the women were required to perform two hundred hours of community service in a domestic violence context (Ammons, 1994).

An outcry immediately erupted in the media from those, most of them law enforcement officials, who opposed the governor's commutations. Others praised his courage, personal integrity, and sense of fairness.[50] Some petitioners who had shared support groups with the twenty-eight women who received clemency from Governor Celeste were devastated when they did not receive clemency as well, and some of their supporters believed that the governor would have been justified in granting an even greater number of petitions (Gagné, 1998).

Despite the controversies about whether Governor Celeste had done too much or too little, none of the cases in which he granted relief came back to haunt him in the future. Although a few of the battered woman he released were convicted of minor crimes later, recidivism proved a negligible problem. Of the few women who returned to the criminal courts, none returned for a crime of violence. Rather, in support of the view that Governor Celeste exercised his discretionary power cautiously, most of the women who were released after receiving clemency are living and working in their communities to this day (Ammons, 2003).

Events in Ohio caught the attention of feminist activists and battered women's advocates nationwide. Governor Celeste's precedent-setting grants of clemency to a group of battered women convicted of violent crimes against their batterers reverberated widely. Drawing on the strategies and experiences of those involved in the Ohio clemency project, a legal reform movement was born.[51]

The Maryland Experience: The Power of Narrative

In the 1980s, while litigation and legislation efforts on behalf of battered women were underway in Ohio and other states, battered women's advocates in Maryland were unsuccessful in obtaining legal rulings through the courts that authorized the admission of expert testimony on battered woman syndrome when battered women faced trial for violence against their batterers (*Kriscumas* v. *State,* 1987; *Friend* v. *State,* 1988). Responding to this failure, Maryland's battered women's advocates organized a powerful educational initiative. This initiative formed the backdrop to a larger project of law reform.

The public education initiative in Maryland drew from the consciousness-raising methods that had emerged in the feminist movement and from the related storytelling strategies that groups of women and other disempowered groups had been using to convey their all-too-often-ignored experiences. Exposure to these experiences was conceived as a vehicle for promoting insights that might generate social change. In furtherance of its educational strategy to promote this exposure, the coalition of advocates arranged a number of settings in which women convicted of violence against their abusers could tell the stories of their relationships, the abuse they had suffered, and the circumstances leading to their acts of violence against their intimate partners.[52]

In order to disseminate these gripping, poignant, and horrifying stories to a broader audience, the Maryland advocates produced a short film, *A Plea for Justice,* which was released early in 1990. In the film, four women serving sentences on the order of fifteen years to life for killing their batterers tell the stories of their experiences with their violent partners. The advocates' intentions were to create conditions under which viewers might experience vicariously the women's life-threatening predicaments and their suffering, fear, and isolation. Their hope was that the film would render battered women as sympathetic and their claims of self-defense—that they killed their batterers because they saw no other way to save themselves—credible and understandable.

Unlike Governor Celeste of Ohio, Governor William Donald Schaefer of Maryland had shown no prior interest in issues of domestic violence. Yet after he viewed the film with members of his staff, he requested a meeting at the Maryland women's prison with the women interviewed on video. The meeting was arranged, giving Governor Schaefer the opportunity to communicate in person with the women in the film and to hear from other similarly situated women as well. Later the governor told reporters that the meeting had altered his understanding of the problems that battered women face. Subsequently, he expressed interest in receiving petitions for clemency, promoted the adoption of state legislation to improve domestic violence training for judges, and supported legislation that required in appropriate cases the admission at trial of testimony about battering and its effects.

Many other state officials in the executive, legislative, and judicial branches of government viewed *A Plea for Justice.* The media covered the release of the film and the issues depicted in it as well. When battered women's advocates eventually prevailed in obtaining legislation that authorized the admission of evidence of battered woman syndrome in battered women's self-defense cases, this success was in no small measure due to the far-reaching persuasive power of the widely viewed thirty-minute video.[53]

Following their dramatically effective educational and legislative campaign, the coalition of battered women's advocates embarked on a clemency project. After identifying women who had suffered abuse and were incarcerated for crimes related to that abuse and notifying them about the possibility of filing petitions for clemency, thirty women requested interviews for clemency purposes. On January 23, 1991, after a process of interviewing and verification, the advocates filed a voluminous confidential report seeking clemency for twelve women serving extended sentences for violence against their batterers.

Relying on the increased awareness of the plight of battered women, the petitions detailed the individual experiences of each petitioner, her background, the abuse she suffered, and the events leading to the crime of which she was convicted. The request for clemency was rooted in the fact that much of this information had not been offered or considered prior to the verdict or the sentence in each of the cases. In selecting twelve women to recommend for clemency, the advocates decided to pursue relief in those cases most likely to win the governor's approval (Gagné, 1998).

On February 19, 1991, Governor Schaefer commuted the sentences of eight of the incarcerated battered women (Schneider, 1991). When he received further advocacy on behalf of the remaining four, he decided to grant early parole to two of them. The women's advocates helped those who had received clemency with the considerable transition difficulties—including housing, job placement, psychological adjustment, and media attention—that they would face upon reentering society. Through this assistance, the advocates hoped to facilitate the released women's social reentry and thereby reduce the potential political repercussions for Governor Schaefer (Gagné, 1998). By so doing, they would enhance the chances that other battered women might receive clemency in the future.

Fueled by its rapid success and national acclaim, the notion of clemency as a kind of partial justice for battered women incarcerated for killing their batterers had caught fire. With Governor Schaefer's clemencies in Maryland following so closely on the heels of Governor Celeste's path-breaking actions in Ohio, the national clemency movement took hold. Feminist activists and battered women's advocates organized clemency movements in many states and began requesting state governors to provide sentence relief to battered women incarcerated for crimes of violence against their batterers.

The Massachusetts Experience: The Framingham Eight

In the late 1980s and the early 1990s, eight women who were incarcerated in the women's prison in Framingham, Massachusetts, for having killed their batterers were meeting in a support and consciousness-raising group facilitated by a human rights activist. Due to similarities in their experiences, the incarcerated women took on a collective identity (Goldfarb, 1996). They called themselves the Framingham Eight, a name that implied solidarity among them and that, in part as a result of this implication, caught the media's attention. The battered women's advocates in Massachusetts consciously developed a media strategy to try to cultivate public understanding of battered women forced to defend their lives (Gagné, 1998).

By 1991, sympathetic stories prominently featured in the Boston press exposed the lethality of violence against women and linked cases of women killed by intimate partners to the cases of the Framingham Eight (Grossfeld, 1991; Kabat, 1991). In that year, the legislature addressed questions of legal protection for victims of intimate violence (Gagné, 1998). Subsequently, Governor William Weld, a socially moderate Republican who had also adopted a tough-on-crime persona, amended the guidelines for commutation of sentences to include "a history of abuse [that] significantly contributed to ... the offense" (Wong, 1994). This amendment was the first official action in the country that formally increased battered women's access to clemency relief.

In response to this perceived invitation, a coalition of women's advocacy groups recruited attorneys to represent each of the Framingham Eight in a quest for a commutation of her sentence.[54] On February 14, 1992, each of the eight respective defense teams filed a petition for commutation, detailing the petitioner's history of abuse and arguing that because each was tried before recent improvements in legal protections, she was therefore deserving of equitable relief (Locy, 1992a). Public hearings before the Advisory Board of Pardons and Parole were held in seven of the cases. Although some of the petitioners received other forms of relief, Governor Weld officially commuted just two of the sentences (Locy, 1993).

Before the clemency process in Massachusetts had concluded, the legislature had enacted a law that guaranteed the admission in appropriate cases of a history of abuse and expert testimony about battering and its effects (Mass. Gen. Laws, chap. 233, sec. 1, §23E). An independent film, *Defending Our Lives*, which featured interviews with four of the Framingham Eight, won an Academy Award as the year's best short documentary film (Biddle, 1994). The Framingham Eight had not only obtained some sentence relief, but their stories had received national attention as part of a public educational movement.

California: Many Requests, Little Relief

As in Massachusetts, the California clemency movement began with the formation of support groups for incarcerated battered women. In March 1991, members of the group that met in Frontera, the major women's prison in southern California, wrote to Governor Pete Wilson asking him to consider sentence commutations for all of the California women who were serving time for killing their batterers. Wilson responded by indicating that he would not conduct a statewide review of all of the cases of women incarcerated for killing their batterers, but that in the absence of any other requisite clemency protocols, he would consider the letter an application for clemency by the thirty-four women who had signed it. He proceeded to conduct a review of the signatories' cases (Gagné, 1998).

Inspired by the governor's apparent openness to considering such clemency requests, activists in California's battered women's movement decided to organize a large group of attorneys to prepare clemency petitions for all of the women incarcerated for killing their batterers. While they were engaged in the petition-drafting process, the California legislature considered a bill creating a right to introduce expert testimony on battered woman syndrome in appropriate cases (Gross, 1992). A number of legislators traveled to Frontera to hear the testimony of several incarcerated battered women who spoke about their abuse, their efforts to secure help, and their need to protect themselves (Morrison, 1991). When the battered woman syndrome bill was subsequently enacted, the petitioners had an additional argument for clemency, as all of them were convicted before the right to expert testimony was guaranteed.

In 1992, attorneys filed clemency petitions for thirty-four battered women, a group that contained only some of the signatories to the initial letter to Governor Wilson ("Thirty-Four California Killers Seek Clemency," 1992). In May 1993, Governor Wilson announced that he had reviewed six of these petitioners' cases and ten of those who had signed the letter. He reduced the sentence of two petitioners, one a seventy-eight-year-old inmate in failing health, and another, Brenda Aris, who after killing her abusive husband while he slept and failing to obtain relief through the courts, became eligible for parole a number of years earlier than her original sentence provided (Lucas & Moore, 1993).

Over the next several years, Governor Wilson denied either relief or review in virtually all other battered women's clemency cases. Although in 1992 he signed legislation that required parole commissioners to receive training concerning battered woman syndrome and domestic violence (Gagné, 1998), in 1993 he vetoed broadly supported bipartisan legislation that would have afforded battered women convicted before the guarantee of expert testimony an opportunity for review of their original trials (Baker, 1994). Despite a benefit showing of *Defending Our Lives* in California in 1994, combined with a concerted media campaign by incarcerated battered women and their supporters, Governor Wilson could not be moved to provide significant relief (Gagné, 1998).[55] With the base of his political support lying squarely among social conservatives, he apparently determined that his political future as a law-and-order politician was best protected by distancing himself from the movement to assist incarcerated battered women.

Governor Wilson's successor to office, Governor Gray Davis, borrowed the same political calculus. Seeking to bolster support among conservative voters, Davis vowed during the gubernatorial campaign to let no murderer go free during his term of office (Mydans, 1992). Under a new state law, however, the parole board was required to consider information regarding battered woman syndrome in any cases tried before such evidence had been rendered admissible. Although the parole board reviewed a few dozen cases, found battered woman syndrome to exist in a number of them, and recommended parole in eight of those cases, Governor Davis endorsed release on parole in only two of these cases (Warren, 2002).

Florida: Selective Advocacy

Florida has restrictive rules for seeking gubernatorial clemency. No one convicted in Florida may apply for a pardon until at least ten years after the completion of any sentence or parole conditions. No one may apply for a commutation without the consent of the governor, two cabinet members, and a recommendation of the Florida Parole Commission.

The first stage of battered women's clemency activism in Florida took the form of modifying these restrictions to enlarge the prospects for clemency ("Can Panels Blaze Legal Trail for Battered Women?" 1992). Aided by a media campaign, these efforts prevailed (Schweers, 1993). Effective January 1992, Governor Lawton Chiles revised Florida's clemency procedures to enable a woman who was incarcerated for killing her batterer and who could demonstrate a history of abuse to ask the Parole Commission to waive the usual application consent policies and refer her case to a panel of experts on issues of intimate violence. If the panel determined that the petitioner suffered from battered woman syndrome at the time of the offense, then the Parole Commission would recommend that the governor and the cabinet review the case for a possible commutation of sentence (Gagné, 1998).

In *Rogers* v. *State* (1993), the Florida Court of Appeals authorized the admission of expert testimony on battered woman syndrome in appropriate cases. Despite the new case and the new rules for clemency, Florida's battered women's activists chose to proceed cautiously, avoiding mass applications for clemency and recommending that each petitioner file an individual request for commutation. By the end of 1993, sixteen battered women had filed an individual application for clemency under Florida's revised procedures (O'Neal, 1993). After separate hearings, two women were granted clemency and released from prison in 1993 (Orlando & Willon, 1993). Seven others ultimately were granted commutations and released, but only after completing a prison work-release program (Gagné, 1998).

Given the potential for politicization of the clemency issue, battered women's advocates chose not to file additional clemency petitions during the Lawton Chiles–Jeb Bush gubernatorial campaign of 1994. After Chiles was reelected, efforts to obtain more commutations increased. Attorneys prepared and filed ten battered women's clemency petitions in 1996, focusing on the cases that had the greatest chance of success, and then submitted more petitions in 1998 (Gagné, 1998). After granting a couple of additional clemencies, Governor Chiles died late in 1998 ("Six Women Who Killed Abusive Men Are Granted Clemency," 1998).

When interim Governor Buddy MacKay took office, he granted the clemency petitions of six more women incarcerated for killing their batterers ("Six Women Who Killed Abusive Men Are Granted Clemency," 1998). The clemency prospects for incarcerated battered women in Florida were significantly diminished when Jeb Bush was elected governor in the next election. Battered women's advocates accuse Governor Bush of ignoring the legitimate claims to relief filed by battered women incarcerated in Florida's burgeoning prison system (Talan, 2000).

Illinois: Electoral Strategizing

After two Chicago defense attorneys obtained individual commutations for four incarcerated women, they decided to organize a broader clemency project, staffed by attorneys, activists, law professors, and law students. Founded in 1993, the Illinois Clemency Project conducted inmate outreach leading to the submission of twelve clemency petitions in 1994. After hearings before the Illinois Prisoner Review Board, which forwards its recommendation to the governor confidentially, Governor Jim Edgar granted four commutations in May 1994 (Gagné, 1998).

Governor Edgar's commutation decisions were likely influenced by his reelection strategy. His 1994 gubernatorial opponent was a liberal woman. As long as he could justify his decision to grant clemency to four battered women, he could capitalize on an opportunity to appeal to some of his opponent's potential supporters without risking the transfer of any of his conservative support to her (Gagné, 1998). Although the clemency petitioners had consciously avoided using the concept of battered woman syndrome in their requests for relief, based on concerns about the message that such psychological language conveys, Governor Edgar framed his justification for granting relief in those terms (Gagné, 1998).

In July 1995, the Illinois Clemency Project filed eighteen additional petitions for commutation. In this wave of applications, the petitioners included the language of battered woman syndrome, because the governor had previously favored granting relief on that basis. This time Governor Edgar decided to release one woman after she had served fifteen years of a twenty-nine-year sentence and to deny the seventeen other requests for commutation (Gagné, 1998).

Although additional commutation petitions were filed on behalf of incarcerated battered women during Governor Edgar's term of office, the governor granted relief in just a few more cases (Grunman & Kiernan, 1998). Without an election strategy to be advanced by his clemency decisions, Governor Edgar approved battered women's petitions for clemency on an extremely meager basis. His successor in office, Governor George Ryan, celebrated for his blanket commutations in death penalty cases, denied three requests for clemency by battered women but commuted the sentence of one (Brotman, 2003).

Kentucky: A Sympathetic Governor

In *Commonwealth* v. *Craig* (1990), the Kentucky Supreme Court embraced an expansive understanding of battered woman syndrome. Reversing prior law, the court indicated that battered woman syndrome was not a psychological condition about which only a mental health professional could attest, but one about which information on the dynamics of battering and its consequences was broadly relevant. After this case was decided, battered women's advocates filed a number of petitions for clemency. In December 1991, just before he left office, Governor Wallace Wilkinson pardoned one petitioner who had already served her prison term and denied relief to two other incarcerated battered women who had petitioned for clemency (Gagné, 1998).

In 1992, the Kentucky legislature enacted a law concerning battered women's self-defense that also established various reforms without relying on the concept of battered woman syndrome. Instead, the legislation reconceived the notion of imminent harm for purposes of battered women's self-defense. In self-defense cases involving domestic violence, the 1992 law permitted a defendant's asserted belief that danger was imminent to be supported by evidence that the victim had a history of serious and repeated abuse of the defendant (Kentucky Revised Statutes 503.010).

The 1992 act also amended certain requirements that violent felony offenders serve prison terms of a prescribed minimum duration, providing an exemption from these requirements for those convicted of killing their batterers. Finally, for offenders who had not previously had the opportunity to present evidence of their history of abuse, the act afforded a right to file motions to present such evidence in their original trial courts. This provision proved less consequential than it might have been, because few trial court judges complied. Their noncompliance apparently stemmed from their failure to appreciate the rationale for providing this admittedly unusual rehearing of a set of facts concerning a case in which the offender was already serving a prison sentence (Gagné, 1998).

These legislative changes became effective soon after Governor Brereton Jones took office. In 1993, he appointed Helen Howard-Hughes, who had expressed interest in domestic violence issues, to chair the Kentucky Parole Board. Howard-Hughes was responsive to the suggestions of battered women's activists that she review for clemency consideration the cases of women incarcerated for assaulting or killing their batterers (Gagné, 1998). In 1995, she arranged for all members of the Parole Board to receive training in domestic violence issues. Thereafter, the Parole Board reviewed a number of battered women's cases that had been identified by Howard-Hughes and developed for clemency by attorneys in the public defender's office ("Justice for Abused Women," 1995).

The Parole Board determined that fourteen incarcerated battered women should be considered for release on early parole. Five of these cases were scheduled for an early parole hearing, but under law, nine others were prohibited from early parole review until they had served a longer minimum prison sentence. Since these nine women had petitioned for clemency, the Parole Board recommended that the governor commute their sentences to a level at which they could receive hearings for early parole as well (Gagné, 1998).

Due to positive relations with the media that had been developed by battered women's advocates, the press became an ally in the quest for clemency. The media had shown particular interest in the life stories of the incarcerated women, especially in a quilt that they had made in their prison support group to depict their experiences with violence. Indeed, the governor had reportedly been moved on viewing the quilt in 1995 when it was displayed at the Kentucky State Fair. The governor had also received many letters describing and documenting these experiences from the women themselves, and some members of the Parole Board had viewed a video in which the incarcerated women described their experiences with violence (Ellers, 1996).

On December 11, 1995, Governor Jones granted the requested clemencies, resulting in the release of nine women in January 1996 on early parole. The governor also pardoned a woman who had already served her prison sentence (Ellers, 1995). The governor denied four subsequent clemency requests, but the Parole Board released other battered women who did not need clemency in order to be considered for parole (Gagné, 1998). In the course of a few years and with the help of a sympathetic governor, battered women's activists in Kentucky had achieved considerable success.

Clemency Nationwide

Before the 1990s had ended, hundreds of battered women had petitioned dozens of governors for clemency. In some cases, the clemency movement yielded significant victories, in others, searing disappointments. Across the country more than one hundred of the battered women who petitioned for clemency were successful in obtaining it.[56]

In addition to the clemencies in the states examined here, a limited number of battered women received sentence relief from several other governors. Governor Roy Romer of Colorado granted sentence commutations to four battered women at the same time that he denied clemency to four other petitioners (Mitchell, 1999). Governors George Pataki of New York, Steve Merrill of New Hampshire, Terry Brandstad of Iowa, and Barbara Roberts of Oregon each granted clemency to one battered woman who had petitioned for relief (Ammons, 2003). Even a law enforcer as harsh as U.S. Attorney General John Ashcroft reduced the sentences of two battered women when he was governor of Missouri (Young, 1992). Other governors who have granted clemency to battered women on at least one occasion are Fife Symington of Arizona, Charles Roemer of Louisiana, James Martin of North Carolina, and Gary Locke of Washington (Ammons, 2003).

Many of the governors defended their clemency decisions on the grounds that they believed the petitioners had been suffering from battered woman syndrome at the time of the crime, had been trapped in abusive relationships, and had been unable to offer a complete account of their abuse to a jury. Most used a rhetoric of justice and proportionality to support their decisions. Occasionally notions of mercy and compassion were invoked as well (Ammons, 2003).

CONTINUING CHALLENGES

Victims of Intimate Violence

As illuminated by the battered women's clemency movement and recent efforts to address the problems of intimate violence, the past generation's cultural support for battered women has both wrought tremendous changes and revealed profound challenges. Perhaps the most significant change is that groundbreaking legal and political developments have reconceived intimate violence as no longer a personal matter in a private relationship, but one of major social dimensions. Nevertheless, the problem of violence in intimate relationships remains frighteningly frequent and severe, and battered women's mortality rates remain tragically high.[57]

Battered women confront continuing problems, beyond the physical and psychological harm that they suffer and the disruption that their efforts to obtain help can entail. For a variety of reasons, some women may wish to remain in a relationship with their batterers and have difficulty finding interventions that are supportive of that choice and effective in reducing the violence that they suffer.[58] Some of these women resist the mandatory nature of criminal court involvement and resent the new reality that obtaining assistance during violent episodes is conditioned on an arrest and a prosecution that they may not support (Mills, 1990).

Many of those who wish to sever relationships with their batterers still find that the threat of violence actually increases with an attempt to end the relationship.[59] Moreover, even in these high-risk situations, legal and social services for battered women—just as for other needy populations who cannot pay for services—remain significantly underfunded and are especially vulnerable to further funding cuts in a declining economy.[60] This lack of material resources for programs and individuals makes independent living exceedingly difficult for many who try to leave their abusive partners (Coker, 2000). Those with children have an additional need for material resources and for negotiating continuing relationships with batterers in many circumstances, due to the requirements of child custody and visitation.

The law of child custody and visitation has formally acknowledged the problem of domestic violence.[61] Nevertheless, decision making in child custody cases is often insufficiently sensitive to the problems generated by intrafamily violence.[62] Moreover, a perceived failure to adequately protect children from witnessing or experiencing a partner's violence can jeopardize an abused parent's own liberty or custodial rights.[63]

Battered Women as Defendants

PROSECUTION. The extraordinary difficulties that battered women face even in an improved social and legal climate become more pronounced if she uses self-defense. In some respects, the perception that help is now available to her deepens her plight when she defends herself physically. Despite, or perhaps because of, public education concerning domestic violence, the reality that many battered women have greater recourse than in the past can turn the "Why didn't she leave?" question in any particular case into an even more haunting refrain.

When battered women are prosecuted for assault or homicide against their batterers, their accounts of underlying events continue to be regarded with skepticism. Criminal defendants in general tend to confront disbelief of their claims. The charges against them render their mitigating or exonerating accounts of events inherently suspect. Even when these accounts are truthful, they may be disbelieved because they are self-serving.[64]

Once charges have been filed, the adversary nature of the criminal justice system exacerbates skepticism, such that those who are allied with law enforcement feel professionally impelled toward disbelief of a battered woman's accounts. This disbelief carries a particular bite, as it often takes the form of an expression of support for battered women as a class, followed by an assertion that this defendant is not a member of that class.[65] The problem of intimate violence seems to have more credibility and visibility in the abstract than it does when particular human beings—imperfect as they are—in a particular context— factually complex as it will be—are said to embody the problem.

OVERSIMPLIFICATION. The adversarial legal system tends to reject complexity and insist that all human conduct be distilled into simple explanations.[66] Explaining that battering relationships are typically characterized not just by physical violence but by other manifestations of coercive control requires a more sophisticated analysis of the long-term dynamics of the relationship rather than descriptions of violent episodes.[67] Suggesting that a battering relationship may also include genuine forms of connection may be threatening to the listener— whether a judge, a jury member, or anyone else—because it invites comparison to one's own intimate relationships rather than facilitating the psychological distancing that makes sitting in judgment more comfortable.[68]

Women who take self-defensive measures during a lull in the abuse rather than during a confrontation with their abuser are especially vulnerable to the simple assertion that they acted in angry retaliation rather than in fear for their lives. Explaining how it can be reasonable to believe that they risk serious, imminent harm during a lull in the abuse requires considerable psychological and contextual knowledge (Willoughby, 1989). It is far easier to ignore or dismiss these complexities, and the adversarial legal system, built around the human desire for simplicity, facilitates this reaction.

GENDER STEREOTYPING. Despite significant social progress in coming to understand the problem of intimate violence, traditional notions of gender remain a powerful force in the assessment of any battered woman's self-defense claims. Actual women—diverse, flawed, and complex—often fall short of the cultural ideal and are found less credible. If understanding her situation requires understanding the long and psychologically complex dynamic of a relationship, the adversarial system is a poor forum for conveying that truth. The consequence is that many battered women are disbelieved. In these circumstances, disbelief can have dire consequences, including incarceration, injury, and even death.[69]

The more the accused diverges from the internalized cultural understanding of the good battered woman, the greater her credibility problems are. Perhaps not surprising, experience has shown that the features of the good battered woman stereotype are drawn from the traditional female stereotype to the extent that the less demure, docile, and deferential the battered woman is seen to be, the more credibility problems she has encountered.[70] Battered women's survival strategies, such as self-medication with drugs or alcohol, and previous instances of fighting back, may lead to a counterstory that she provoked intimate violence.[71] Women who are perceived to fall outside narrow and traditional gender role expectations of mainstream culture, whether by dint of personality (for example, independent, assertive) or identity (for example, lesbians, African American women), face particular difficulties in having their claims to have acted out of fear for their lives seen and heard.[72]

IMPEACHING CREDIBILITY. Battered women's credibility problems are exacerbated by the fact that the techniques routinely used by the legal system to assess credibility do not comport with psychological understandings of reactions to trauma. For example, a standard technique in the adversary system is to impeach a witness's credibility by showing that the witness made prior inconsistent statements about pertinent events, making it more likely that her current statements are manufactured.[73] Psychologists indicate that among the consequences of trauma are confusion, disorientation, and memory repression, such that soon after a violent event, a woman may provide the police an account that during a recovery process she comes to know as false or incomplete.[74]

A court's evidentiary system is organized around an understanding that contemporaneous accounts are more accurate than subsequent accounts. Therefore, battered women may confront a paradox. The memory complications that can flow from the violence that some battered women suffer are regarded as undermining the reliability of current accounts of that violence. Yet with respect to the psychological reality of the situation, initial memory problems may actually support a finding that she suffered significant trauma, and subsequent accounts may be the most accurate versions of events.[75]

EXPERT TESTIMONY. If a psychological expert's testimony on battered woman syndrome is admitted during such a case, the expert can address the impact of trauma on memory and try to mitigate the harm done by standard evidentiary practices. But the admissibility of expert testimony remains a double-edged sword in these cases. With its admission typically linked to the concept of battered woman syndrome, expert testimony can illuminate a battered woman's situation only to the extent that the features of the situation are understood as aspects of the syndrome.[76]

As many commentators have observed, viewing a victim of abuse as suffering from a syndrome deflects attention from the abuser and undermines an understanding that she conducted herself reasonably, albeit in desperate circumstances (Coughlin, 1994; Mahoney, 1991). This syndrome evidence, conjuring up images that the abuse victim suffers from pathology, can have an adverse impact on perceptions of her reliability. These adverse inferences can influence outcomes of legal proceedings and haunt other important efforts to achieve stability in her life as well.[77]

INADEQUATE DEFENSE SERVICES. Another challenge for battered women charged with crimes against batterers is that few locales have made significant progress in recent decades in improving the quality of indigent defense systems. In many jurisdictions, battered women charged with assault or homicide against their batterers still receive woefully deficient representation, particularly when they are represented by appointed counsel.[78]

Given the poor quality of representation for many who cannot afford to hire competent counsel, the progress of the domestic violence movement in enabling fairer trials for battered women remains hypothetical for a defendant whose counsel does not appreciate the nature and circumstances of the underlying events, the context of the defendant's relationship, the need for psychological expertise, or the prospects for raising self-defense issues during the course of the case. In these circumstances, the factual record that might support self-defense can remain underdeveloped and fair outcomes impeded. Until indigent defense systems provide reasonably competent counsel on a reliable basis, battered women who have assaulted or killed their batterers, a subset of indigent defendants, will not be guaranteed the benefit of the progress that has been made in obtaining fairer treatment in the legal system for battered women.

POSTCONVICTION RELIEF. Once a battered woman has been convicted of assault or homicide against her batterer, her chances for vindication through appeal, collateral attack, or executive clemency are low. Those who participated in obtaining the conviction often are institutionally invested in maintaining the original outcome and seek to preserve it. Decision makers with the power to overturn convictions or reduce sentences will naturally use this power quite sparingly.[79] For battered women, these phenomena have become even stronger, since our culture considers itself to have vastly improved its understanding and treatment of domestic violence. While this belief is partially true, it also generates limited interest in addressing the problems that remain.

Even for women who were convicted of crimes against their batterers before recent legal innovations, the clemency movement has achieved mixed success at best. Despite the approximately one hundred battered women across the nation who have received gubernatorial clemency, hundreds more have been denied. Many of these women have strong arguments for clemency, yet their petitions did not find a receptive audience at the statehouse. As a result, they serve the remainder of their sentences as originally imposed.

CONCLUSION

Intimate violence is linked to inequalities in perceptions and allocations of power within relationships. While any relationship can feature power disparities, women remain especially vulnerable to male violence in heterosexual relationships in a world of continuing gender inequality. As long as gender inequality persists, the problem of intimate violence will remain intractable, although public attention to the problem can partially alleviate the extraordinary harm that intimate violence creates.[80]

The battered women's movement has changed the world, creating many more options than previously existed for women who suffer intimate violence. Indeed, the considerable successes of the recent past create an especially challenging context for sustaining the energy of the movement today. Divisions within the movement about appropriate future directions can also drain its energies, and a difficult economic outlook makes competition for shrinking social services funds especially contentious.

The hope is that the many eyes that have been turned to the problem and the many voices addressing it will prove up to the task of mobilizing to face the challenges ahead and that the multiplicity of perspectives that high interest in the subject has generated will bring strength rather than fragmentation. The promise of a future containing far less intimate violence is well worth the struggle.

Notes

1. "During the antebellum era, courts began to invoke marital privacy as a supplementary rationale for chastisement, in order to justify the common law doctrine [of nonintervention] within the discourse of companionate marriage. . . . A judge reasoning about marriage as a companionate relationship could invoke values of marital privacy to justify giving wife beaters immunity from prosecution much as he could invoke authority-based conceptions of marriage to justify giving husbands a formal prerogative to beat their wives" (Siegel, 1996, p. 2151).

   An emerging doctrine of marital privacy not only prevented the imposition of criminal law sanctions in cases of marital violence, it also precluded lawsuits in tort brought by the victims of marital violence. See Siegel (1996, p. 2163): "Regardless of whether a husband beat, choked, stabbed, or shot his wife, all courts reviewing such claims initially rejected them, reasoning that spouses could not sue each other in tort—and buttressing this conclusion with justifications couched in the language of affect and privacy."

2. "A survey of criminal and tort law during the Reconstruction Era reveals that . . . chastisement law was supplanted by a new body of marital violence policies that were premised on a variety of gender-, race-, and class-based assumptions" (Siegel, 1996, pp. 2119–2120). One of the most commonly cited cases justifying criminal law's nonintervention in cases of marital violence is *State* v. *Rhodes* (1868). One of the first cases using a privacy rationale to justify a husband's immunity from tort liability for assaulting his wife is *Abbott* v. *Abbott* (1877).

3. After describing a number of nineteenth-century cases upholding a domestic violence prosecution against an African American man, Siegel (1996) writes that the court opinions "seem more interested in controlling African-American men than in protecting their wives" (p. 2136).

4. Statistics on arrests and convictions for wife beating in the late nineteenth century suggest that while criminal assault law was enforced against wife beaters only sporadically, it was most often enforced against immigrant and African American men. In northern states, members of immigrant ethnic groups (such as German Americans and Irish Americans) were targeted for prosecution; in the South, African Americans were singled out for prosecution in numbers dramatically exceeding their representation in the population.

5. By the 1880s, prominent members of the American Bar Association advocated punishing wife beaters at the whipping post and campaigned vigorously for legislation authorizing such a penalty. Between 1876 and 1906,

twelve states and the District of Columbia considered enacting legislation that provided for the punishment of wife beaters at the whipping post. The bills were enacted in Maryland (1882), Delaware (1901), and Oregon (1906).

6. "As courts addressed the regulation of marital violence in the wake of chastisement's demise, judges raised concerns about invading the privacy of the marriage relationship—most often, it would appear, when they contemplated the prospect of sanctioning wife beating in households of the middle and upper classes" (Siegel, 1996, p. 2153).

7. "Battered wives were discouraged from filing criminal charges against their husbands, urged to accept responsibility for their role in provoking the violence, and encouraged to remain in the relationship" (Siegel, 1996, p. 2170).

8. Stark (1995, p. 991) described how family courts treated cases involving "domestic trouble" as occasions for teaching wives better household habits.

9. Siegel (1996, p. 2170) writes, "The criminal justice system regulated marital violence in this 'therapeutic' framework for much of the twentieth century."

10. Elizabeth Schneider (2000), an attorney and activist who was involved with the feminist communities spearheading these efforts, describes this groundbreaking work.

11. The first shelter for battered women was opened in 1972 in Chiswick, England (Dobash & Dobash, 1988). The first shelter for battered women in the United States was established in 1974 in St. Paul, Minnesota (Schechter, 1982). By 1987, there were more than seven hundred shelters in the United States (Cherow-O'Leary, 1987).

12. For a sampling of the medical literature on domestic violence, see Abbott et al. (1995); American Psychiatric Association (1994); Brendtro and Bowker (1989); Council on Ethical and Judicial Affairs (1992); Hadley (1992); Jecker (1993); Kroll (1993); Loring and Smith (1994); "Domestic Violence" (1992); Sugg and Inui (1992); Tilden (1989); and "Doctors Are Advised to Screen Women for Abuse" (1992).

13. See Randall (1992). Attorney Mithra Merryman (1993) reports that Boston University School of Medicine has a four-year curriculum for medical students on family violence.

14. See Dalton and Schneider (2001): "All of us who read the papers also know the stories of women who have died at the hands of their abusers despite, and sometimes apparently because of, the restraining orders they secured" (p. 499). These attacks are one example of what Mahoney (1991) would call "separation assault."

15. Minnesota and California have enacted separate statutes defining a crime and a penalty specifically for domestic abuse. Minn. Stat. Ann. § 518B.01 (West 1990 & Supp. 1997); Calif. Penal Code § 273.5 (2000).

16. The Model Statute defines stalking as follows: "Any person who: (a) purposefully engages in a course of conduct directed at a specific person that would cause a reasonable person to fear bodily injury to himself or herself or a member of his or her immediate family or to fear the death of himself or herself or a member of his or her immediate family; and (b) has knowledge or should have knowledge that the specific person will be placed in reasonable fear of bodily injury to himself or herself or a member of his or her immediate family or will be placed in reasonable fear of the death of himself or herself or a member of his or her immediate family; and (c) whose acts induce fear in the specific person of bodily injury to himself or herself or a member of his or her immediate family or induce fear in the specific person of the death of himself or herself or a member of his or her immediate family; is guilty of stalking" (National Institute of Justice, 1993, pp. 43–44).

17. For examples of statutes that require domestic violence training for law enforcement, see Alaska Stat. § 18.65.240 (Michie 2002); Cal. Penal Code § 13519 (West 2000); Conn. Gen. Stat. Ann. § 7–29g (West 1999); D.C. Code Ann. § 16–1034 (2001); Fla. Stat. Ann. § 943.1701 (West 2001); Ky. Rev. Stat. Ann. § 403.784 (Michie Supp. 2002); Mass. Gen. Laws ch. 6, § 116A (2002): N.J. Stat. Ann. § 2C:25–20 (West Supp. 2003); N.Y. Exec. Law § 642(5) (McKinney 1996); R. I. Gen. Laws § 12–29–6 (2002).

18. Lawrence Sherman, coauthor of the first influential study on mandatory arrest (Sherman & Berk, 1984), has since urged the repeal of mandatory arrest laws. See also Schmidt and Sherman (1996).

19. In 1977, Oregon enacted the first mandatory arrest law, requiring an arrest when police had probable cause to believe that a crime of domestic violence had occurred. By the early 1990s, many other states had followed suit. Some states simply encouraged rather than required police officers to make arrests in these situations. See Dalton and Schneider (2001).

20. The most prominent case was *Thurman* v. *City of Torrington* (1984): a federal jury found that the police were liable for negligence in failing to respond to the plaintiff's repeated requests for protection from her abusive husband, awarding her $2.3 million in compensation for her injuries. Other related cases include *Hynson* v. *Chester* (1988; the mother and children of a woman killed by her boyfriend were permitted to sue police for refusing to arrest the boyfriend before the murder because the restraining order had expired), and *Watson* v. *Kansas City* (1988; the police department can be liable for failing to take action against an abusive husband who was a police officer, resulting in an attack on his wife and children).

21. Joyce (1997) discusses many state statutes.

22. Mills (2003) proposes the use of a restorative justice model as an alternative to a criminal justice model to address problems of intimate violence.

23. Mahoney (19991) describes stereotypical notions of women's experience that the term *battered woman* implies. Dowd (1992) describes images of "good" battered women and "bad" battered women that have emerged.

24. According to Browne and Williams (1989), 40 percent of 132 incarcerated women in Chicago were in prison for killing an abusive partner and all had sought help from police on at least five prior occasions. For more recent data, see the Web site of the Bureau of Justice Statistics (http://www.ojp. usdoj.gov/bjs), which contains considerable statistical information concerning crimes of intimate violence.

25. Schneider (2000) explores the strategic decisions that led to the effort to admit expert testimony at trial.

26. Statutes liberalizing evidentiary standards in cases involving battered women took a variety of forms. Some statutes explicitly permitted the introduction of expert testimony on "battered woman syndrome" or "battered spouse syndrome." Cal. Evid. Code §1107 (West 1995 & Supp. 2003) (enacted 1991); Md. Code Ann. Cts. & Jud. Proc. §10–916 (2002) (enacted 1991); Ohio Rev. Code Ann. §2901.06 (West 1997) (enacted 1990) (limited to self-defense claims); S.C. Code Ann. §17–23–170 (Law Co-op. 2003) (enacted 1995); Wyo. Stat. Ann. §6–1–203 (Michie 2003) (enacted 1993) (limited to self-defense claims).

Other statutes allow expert testimony on the effects of domestic violence; however, they avoid the "battered spouse syndrome" language: Ga. Code Ann. §16–3–21 (2003) (limited to self-defense claims); La. Code Evid. Ann. Art. 404 (West 1995) (enacted 1998); Mass. Gen. Laws Ann. ch., 233, §23F (West 2000) (enacted 1993) (limited to self-defense claims); Nev. Rev. Stat. Ann. 48.061 (enacted 1993), amended by 2003 Nev. Rev. Stat. 284; Okla. Stat. Ann. tit. 22, §40.7 (West 1992) (enacted 1992); Tex. Code Crim. Proc. Ann. Art. 38.36 (Vernon Supp. 2004) (enacted 1993) (limited to self-defense claims).

In comparison, other statutes have modified the standard for evaluating the defendant's mental culpability in cases involving evidence of domestic abuse: Ariz. Rev. Stat. Ann. §13–415 (West 2001) (enacted 1992); Ind. Code Ann. §§35–4–1–3.3, 35–41–3–11 (Michie 1998) (enacted 1997); Ky. Rev. Stat. Ann. §503.010 (Michie 1999) (amended 1992); Utah Code Ann. §76–2–402(5) (1999) (amended 1994).

27. Expert testimony on battering has been admitted in all fifty states in cases where battered women face trial on criminal charges. Most, but not all, of these cases involved claims of self-defense. See Dalton and Schneider (2001).

28. A 1995 study conducted by the National Clearinghouse for the Defense of Battered Women, commissioned by the U.S. Departments of Justice and Health and Human Services, found that 63 percent of convictions and sentences of battered women defendants were upheld on appeal, even though expert testimony was admitted in 71 percent of these. See Dalton and Schneider (2001) and Browne (1987), reporting only nine acquittals and one dismissal among forty-two cases of women charged with killing or injuring their partners.

29. Schneider (1986) argues that "battered woman syndrome" can be seen to reinforce stereotypes of women as passive, sick, powerless, and victimized. Coughlin (1994) claims that battered woman syndrome reinforces negative stereotypes of women.

30. Crocker (1985) notes that battered women on trial for killing their abusers do not benefit from expert testimony unless they fit a rigidly defined and narrowly applied definition of a battered woman.

31. Allard (1991) and Ammons (1995) argue that stereotypes of battered women who kill their abusers as passive, emotional, and dependent create problems for battered black women, who are not seen as fitting this image. Goldfarb (1996) argues that the narrow boundaries of the battered woman stereotype are rooted in traditional gender ideology and work to the particular disadvantage of women who diverge from that traditional ideology, most notably lesbians.

32. Maguigan (1991) observes that while women have not fared well in non-confrontational self-defense cases, most of the self-defense claims arise from confrontational situations, and evidence of bias exists even in the latter cases.

33. In *Gideon* v. *Wainwright* (1963), the U.S. Supreme Court held that the Sixth and Fourteenth amendments to the Constitution guarantee a defendant the right to counsel in criminal cases. Although the right to counsel was presumed to mean the right to *effective* counsel, commentators argue that due to underfunding and the lack of political will, the promise of effective counsel has gone largely unrealized for indigent defendants facing criminal charges. See Klein (1986) and Reed (2003).

34. From the number of claims of ineffective assistance of counsel based on faulty advice regarding plea bargains or the defendant testifying, and on attorney failure to present evidence and testimony that could have assisted the jury to understand and eradicate the very same misconceptions apparently held by counsel, it is apparent that attorneys are susceptible to misconceptions about battered women (Schneider, 2000).

35. An examination of postconviction cases in which battered women appeal their convictions or sentences on the grounds of ineffective assistance of

counsel reveals a variety of shortcomings in battered women's trial representation. Twenty-six of these cases are annotated in Sarno (1994).

36. For a proposed set of voir dire questions designed to address these misperceptions, see Lawrence and Kugler (1981).

37. See Schneider (2000): "Cases involving claims of ineffective assistance based on counsel's failure to offer jury instruction on battering suggest that many attorneys lack knowledge about the particular complexities of representing battered women" (p. 145).

38. A number of appeals by battered women concerning ineffective assistance of counsel at trial raise claims of inadequate advice, particularly relating to plea bargaining or testifying. See, for example, *State* v. *Zimmerman* (1991); *State* v. *Scott* (1989); *Larson* v. *State* (1988); and *State* v. *Gfeller* (1987). See also McMorrow (1993), who describes memory problems as a consequence of battering that can impair the communication of those consequences.

39. The U.S. Supreme Court established the standard of ineffective assistance as defective representation, unsupported by reason or tactics, that prejudices the defendant. See *Strickland* v. *Washington* (1983).

40. See, for example, *State* v. *Zimmerman* (1991); *Martin* v. *State* (1986); *Commonwealth* v. *Stonehouse* (1989); *Commonwealth* v. *Miller* (1993); *People* v. *Day* (1992).

41. See notes 26 and 27 and the accompanying text.

42. See notes 34 to 38 and accompanying text. Of course, jurors will be aided in their rejection of self-defense by a prosecutor who urges them to reach that conclusion.

43. See, for example, *Commonwealth* v. *Grimshaw* (1992), in which the defendant received an excellent "battered woman syndrome" defense by a noted trial attorney to a charge of murdering her abusive husband. When the jury failed to convict her of murder, convicting instead on the lesser charge of manslaughter, the trial judge sentenced the defendant to the maximum sentence for manslaughter. For more information about the harshness of the judge's actions, see Madden (1993) and Locy (1992b).

44. The organization of clemency projects in the 1990s is described in Gagné (1998).

45. Article II, section 2C1 of the U.S. Constitution states, "The President . . . shall have power to grant reprieves and pardons for offenses against the United States, except in cases of Impeachment." Many state constitutions contain provisions according a state governor parallel clemency powers over state convictions. Among them are the California Constitution (Article V, section 8: "The Governor . . . may grant a reprieve, pardon and commutation, after sentence"); the Illinois Constitution (Article V, section 12: "The Governor may grant reprieves, commutations and pardons, after conviction"); the

New York Constitution (Article IV, section 4: "The governor shall have the power to grant reprieves, commutations and pardons after conviction"); and the Virginia Constitution (Article V, section 12: "The Governor shall have the power . . . to grant reprieves and pardons after conviction").

46. See, for example, Mass. Gen. Laws ch. 127, § 154 (1992) and Mass. Regs. Code tit. 120, §§ 901.12(5)(1993), which empower the Advisory Board of Pardons, a special seating of the Massachusetts Parole Board, to make recommendations to the governor concerning pardons or commutations based solely on a written petition or upon a hearing of the petitioner's claim.

47. For a description of the kinds of strategic political decisions made by battered women's advocates for clemency, see Gagné (1998).

48. For an articulation of the justifications for clemency for incarcerated battered women, see Ammons (1994).

49. Linda Ammons was a member of Governor Celeste's staff and the primary staff member responsible for the clemency review in the governor's office. Ammons (1994) describes the Ohio clemency project in considerable detail.

50. For those who opposed the commutations, see Wilkerson (1990), Prendergast (1990), Sharkey (1990), "Celeste Defends Commutations" (1990), and Rooney (1990). For those who praised them, see "Justice and Battered Women" (1990) and Grey (1990).

51. Linda Ammons, executive assistant to Governor Celeste during the clemency review process, writes (2003): "Within days after the Ohio project was completed, I received calls from advocates from Maryland and New York. Weeks later I briefly consulted with persons, working with or for the late Governor Lawton Chiles of Florida. In the fall of 1991, I appeared before a California Assembly committee at Frontera Prison in California to talk about this issue in connection with an attempt to have Governor Pete Wilson review cases. Representatives working on behalf of battered women wanted to know how best to tell their clients' stories and what evidence would work best to persuade those who would make decisions about the women's fates" (p. 564).

52. Goldfarb (1991) describes consciousness-raising and storytelling strategies associated with feminism and how they have been used to promote social change.

53. This public education campaign in Maryland is described in Murphy (1993).

54. Greenwald and Manning (1994) describe recruitment by the Women's Bar Association's Framingham Project. I was one of the attorneys recruited.

Along with a defense team from Boston College Law School, I represented one of the members of the Framingham Eight.

55. Wilson did, however, provide limited additional relief. See "Wilson Commutes Sentence of Woman Who Killed Husband" (1998).

56. For information about battered women's clemency cases across the United States, see Ammons (2003).

57. While intimate violence against women appears to have decreased since 1993, data reveal that 1,247 women were killed by an intimate partner in 2000 (Rennison, 2003).

58. Schneider (2000) writes, "Many victims of domestic violence remain with their abusers, perhaps because they perceive no superior alternative" (p. 4).

59. This is a well-documented phenomenon. Hart (1990) cites data indicating that up to 75 percent of reported intimate violence occurs after the victim has left the batterer. More recent data (Tjaden & Thoennes, 2000) convey a disturbingly similar picture.

60. Schneider (2000) writes, "Although federal, state, and private resources devoted to these reform efforts have increased substantially, they are still minimal" (p. 27).

61. Most states have statutes requiring courts to consider domestic violence in child custody determinations, and some have adopted presumptions that batterers be denied custody and receive no more than supervised visitation. See Zorza (2001).

62. Studies show that psychologists who serve as custody evaluators often react adversely to women who alienate the child from the other parent by raising the issue of abuse (Zorza, 2001). Some family court judges misinterpret existing statutes, particularly regarding presumptions, and fail to give sufficient weight to the problem of intimate violence in adjudicating the issues of custody and visitation. See Levin (2000).

63. See, for example, *People* v. *Stancil* (1992; upholding the murder convictions of two women whose boyfriends fatally beat the women's children); In re *Glenn* G. (1992; a battered mother neglected her children by inadequately protecting them from father's abuse); *State* v. *Williquette* (1986; upholding the mother's conviction for child abuse based on her failure to protect children from father's abuse). See also Enos (1996), who claims that battered women who have failed to protect their children from the batterer in many cases lose custody.

64. See, for example, McMorrow (1993), who writes, "One common perception that defendants face is that a criminal defendant seeking release has every reason to stretch the truth or even lie. Unfortunately, this skepticism parallels the societal skepticism that battered women faced" (p. 226).

This skepticism is enhanced by the reality that many battered women cannot provide corroboration of their abuse. See, for example, Gelles (1987), and Greenwald and Manning (1994), who indicate that fear of retaliation, poverty, ignorance, and shame, among other reasons, can prevent battered women from revealing their abuse. The new regime of mandatory reporting, arrest, and prosecution may be another reason for failure to report abuse, as the abused partner may not support these interventions and may fear loss of control over the consequences of reporting. For further elaboration of the latter point, see Mills (2003).

65. Dowd (1992) writes, "The frontal assault on battered women as a whole has been replaced by the individual disqualification of certain women from the group" (p. 581). See also Goldfarb (1996) and McMorrow (1993).

66. Dowd (1992) writes, "The legal system pushes for simplicity in all cases" (p. 229).

67. Most commentators agree that coercive control, not episodic physical violence, is the most accurate description of a battering relationship. See, for example, Stark (1995) and Fischer, Vidmar, and Ellis (1993).

68. Schneider (2000) acknowledges that when battering is understood as lying on a continuum of uses of power that are characteristic of all intimate relationships, it threatens decision makers' capacities to distance themselves from the problem).

69. Goldfarb (1996) writes, "The obstacles faced by any actual woman, replete with the flaws and complexities of real human beings, in convincing decision makers that her life and her actions fall within the pinched boundaries of battered woman syndrome are high if not insurmountable" (p. 610).

70. Dowd (1992) notes, "'Good' battered women are passive, loyal housewives acting as loving companions to their abusers" (p. 581). Goldfarb (1996) writes, "Not surprisingly, the good battered woman is nothing more than a good woman, defined in traditional Victorian terms" (p. 608).

71. In *People* v. *Ciervo* (1986), the state challenged the defendant's claim of suffering from battered woman's syndrome by alleging that the defendant was an adulteress, a drug user, a neglectful mother, and a poor housekeeper, indicating that she had provoked the violence. McMorrow (1993) wrote, "If she ever fought back, then they argued that she was engaged in mutual combat and was not a battered woman. If she resorted to drugs or alcohol to escape the violence, she was 'druggie', [sic] not a battered woman" (p. 226).

72. See the sources cited in note 31.

73. Cleary (1984) describes the use of prior inconsistent statements to impeach a witness.

74. Walker (1992) describes memory difficulties as among the major symptom clusters associated with battered woman syndrome.
75. McMorrow (1993) notes memory problems that battering causes can be used to undermine a battered woman's claims when they are actually corroborative.
76. Raeder (1997) argues that a better practice would be to permit experts to give testimony about the general contextual features of domestic violence rather than about a psychological syndrome.
77. For example, these perceptions can undermine her efforts to achieve child custody. See notes 61 to 63 and the accompanying text.
78. See note 3 and the accompanying text.
79. Dalton and Schneider (2001) report the results of a 1995 study finding that 63 percent of convictions and sentences of battered women were upheld on appeal. Jordan (2000) reports statements by Governor Gray Davis that commutation is to be granted on "rare occasions."
80. Schneider (2000) writes, "The culture of female subordination that supports and maintains abuse has undergone little change" (p. 27).

References

Abbott v. Abbott, 67 Me. 304 (1877).

Abbott, J., et al. (1995). Domestic violence against women: Incidence and prevalence in an emergency department population. *JAMA, 273*(22), 1763–1767.

Adams, D. (1988). Treatment models of men who batter: A profeminist analysis. *Feminist Perspectives,* 176n15.

Allard, S. A. (1991). Rethinking battered woman syndrome: A black feminist perspective. *UCLA Women's Law Journal, 1,* 191–207.

American Psychiatric Association. (1994). Position statement on domestic violence against women. *American Journal of Psychiatry, 151,* 630.

Ammons, L. L. (1994). Discretionary justice: A legal and policy analysis of a governor's use of the clemency power in the cases of incarcerated battered women. *Journal of Law and Policy, 3,* 2–79.

Ammons, L. L. (1995). Mules, madonnas, babies, bathwater, racial imagery and stereotypes: The African-American woman and the battered woman syndrome. *Wisconsin Law Review, 1995,* 1004–1080.

Ammons, L. L. (2003). Why do you do the things you do? Clemency for battered incarcerated women, a decade's review. *Journal of Gender, Social Policy and Law, 11,* 533–565.

Baker, S. G. (1994). Deaf justice? Battered women unjustly imprisoned prior to the enactment of evidence code section 1107. *Golden Gate University Law Review, 24,* 99–129.

Bartlett, K. T., Harris, A. P., & Rhode, D. L. (2002). *Gender and law: Theory, doctrine, commentary* (3rd ed.). New York: Aspen.

Biddle, F. M. (1994, March 22). Award honors abused women. *Boston Globe,* p. 60.

Borgmann, C. E. (1990). Battered women's substantive due process claims: Can orders of protection deflect *DeShaney? New York University Law Review, 65,* 1280–1323.

Brendtro, M., & Bowker, L. H. (1989). Battered women: How can nurses help? *Issues in Mental Health Nursing, 10,* 169–180.

Bright, S. B. (1997). Neither equal nor just: The rationing and denial of legal services to the poor when life and liberty are at stake. *Annual Survey of American Law 1997,* 783–836.

Brotman, B. (2003, January 22). Woman's request for clemency denied. *Chicago Tribune,* p. 8.

Browne, A. (1987). *When battered women kill.* New York: Free Press.

Browne, A., & Williams, K. R. (1989). Exploring the effects of resource availability and the likelihood of female-perpetrated homicides. *Law and Society Review, 23,* 75–91.

Can panels blaze legal trail for battered women? (1992, December 13). *Ft. Lauderdale Sun-Sentinel,* p. 1E.

Celeste defends commutations. (1990, December 27). *Cleveland Plain Dealer,* p. 2B.

Cherow-O'Leary, R. (1987). *The state-by state guide to women's legal rights.* New York: McGraw-Hill.

Choundas, G. P. (1995). Neither equal nor protected: The invisible law of equal protection, the legal invisibility of its gender-based victims. *Emory Law Journal, 44,* 1069–1185.

Cleary, E. W. (1984). *McCormick on evidence* (3rd ed.). St. Paul, MN: West.

Cobb, S. (1997). The domestication of violence in mediation. *Law and Society Review, 31,* 397–440.

Cohen, J. M. (1996). Regimes of private tyranny: What do they mean to morality and for the criminal law? *University of Pittsburgh Law Review, 57,* 757–808.

Coker, D. (1999). Enhancing autonomy for battered women: Lessons from Navajo peacemaking. *UCLA Law Review, 47,* 1–111.

Coker, D. (2000). Shifting power for battered women: Law, material resources, and poor women of color. *U.C. Davis Law Review, 33,* 1009–1055.

Commonwealth v. Craig, 783 S.W.2d 387 (Ky. 1990).

Commonwealth v. Grimshaw, 590 N.E.2d 681 (Mass. 1992).

Commonwealth v. Miller, 634 A.2d 614 (Pa. Super. Ct. 1993).

Commonwealth v. Stonehouse, 555 A.2d 772 (Pa. Super. Ct. 1989).

Copeland, L., & Wolfe, L. R. (1991). *Violence against women as bias-motivated hate crime: Defining the issues.* Washington, DC: Center for Women Policy Studies.

Copelon, R. (1994). Recognizing the egregious in the everyday: Domestic violence as torture. *Columbia Human Rights Law Review, 25,* 291–368.

Coughlin, A. M. (1994). Excusing women. *California Law Review, 82,* 1–93.

Council on Ethical and Judicial Affairs, American Medical Association. (1992). Physicians and domestic violence: Ethical considerations. *JAMA, 267,* 3190–3193.

Crenshaw, K. (1993). Mapping the margins: Intersectionality, identity politics, and violence against women of color. *Stanford Law Review, 43,* 1241–1299.

Crocker, P. L. (1985). The meaning of equality for battered women who kill men in self-defense. *Harvard Women's Law Journal, 8,* 121–155.

Culliton, K. M. (1993). Finding a mechanism to enforce women's right to state protection from domestic violence in the Americas. *Harvard International Law Journal, 34,* 507–561.

Dalton, C. (1997). Domestic violence, domestic torts and divorce: Constraints and possibilities. *New England Law Review, 31,* 319–395.

Dalton, C., & Schneider, E. M. (2001). *Battered women and the law.* Westbury, NY: Foundation Press.

DeShaney v. Winnebago County Department of Social Services, 489 U.S. 189 (1989).

Dobash, R. E., & Dobash, R. P. (1988). Research as social action: The struggle for battered women. In K. Yllö & M. Bograd (Eds.), *Feminist perspectives on wife abuse.* Thousand Oaks, CA: Sage.

Doctors are advised to screen women for abuse. (1992, June 17). *New York Times,* p. A26.

Domestic violence [Special issue]. (1992). *JAMA, 267.*

Dorne, C., & Gewerth, K. (1999). Mercy in a climate of retributive justice: Interpretations from a national survey of executive clemency procedures. *New England Journal on Criminal and Civil Confinement, 25,* 413–467.

Dowd, M. (1992). Dispelling the myths about the "battered woman's defense": Towards a new understanding. *Fordham Urban Law Journal, 19,* 567–584.

Ellers, F. (1995, December 12). Jones grants women clemency: Nine inmates say abuse led them to commit crimes. *Louisville Courier-Journal,* p. 1A.

Ellers, F. (1996, March 15). Jones explains commuted sentences, governor, abuse victims on "Donahue." *Louisville Courier-Journal,* p. 9B.

Enos, V. P. (1996). Prosecuting battered mothers: State law's failure to protect battered women and abused children. *Harvard Women's Law Journal, 19,* 229–268.

Epstein, D. (1999). Effective intervention in domestic violence cases: Rethinking the roles of prosecutors, judges, and the court system. *Yale Journal of Law and Feminism, 11,* 3–50.

Fedders, B. (1997). Lobbying for mandatory-arrest policies: Race, class and the politics of the battered women's movement. *New York University Review of Law and Social Change. 23,* 281–301.

Finn, P., & Colson, S. (1990, March). *Civil protection orders: Legislation, current court practice, and enforcement.* Washington, DC: National Institute of Justice.

Fischer, K., & Rose, M. (1995). When enough is enough: Battered women's decision making around court orders of protection. *Crime and Delinquency, 41,* 414–429.

Fischer, K., Vidmar, N., & Ellis, R. (1993). The culture of battering and the role of mediation in domestic violence cases. *Southern Methodist University Law Review, 46,* 2117–2206.

Forum: Mandatory prosecution in domestic violence cases. (1997). *UCLA Women's Law Journal, 7,* 169–199.

Friend v. State, Md. Ct. Spec. App. 88–483 (December 12, 1988).

Gagné, P. (1998). *Battered women's justice: The movement for clemency and the politics of self-defense.* Woodbridge, CT: Twayne.

Gelles, R. (1987). *The violent home.* Thousand Oaks, CA: Sage.

Gideon v. Wainwright, 372 U.S. 335 (1963).

Gillespie, C. K. (1989). *Justifiable homicide: Battered women, self-defense, and the law.* Columbus: Ohio State University Press.

Goldfarb, P. (1991). A theory–practice spiral: The ethics of feminism and clinical education. *Minnesota Law Review, 75,* 1599–1699.

Goldfarb, P. (1996). Describing without circumscribing: Questioning the construction of gender in the discourse of intimate violence. *George Washington University Law Review, 64,* 582–631.

Greenwald, M. E., & Manning, M. E. (1994, March–April). When mercy seasons justice: Commutation for battered women who kill. *Boston Bar Journal,* pp. 3, 12–15.

Grey, L. (1990, December 30). Celeste's grants of clemency brought law, justice into accord. *Columbus Dispatch,* p. 3D.

Gross, J. (1992, Sept. 15). Abused women who kill seek a way out of cells. *New York Times*, p. A3.

Grossfeld, S. (1991, September 2). Love and terror: "Safer" and in jail: Women who kill their batterers. *Boston Globe*, p. M1.

Grunman, C., & Kiernan, L. (1998, Jan. 4). Edgar sets a battered wife free. *Chicago Tribune*, p. 1.

Guinn, C., & O'Dell, A. (1993). Stopping the violence. The role of the police officer and the prosecutor. *Western State University Law Review, 20*, 297–318.

Hadley, S. M. (1992). Working with battered women in the emergency department: A model program. *Journal of Emergency Nursing, 18*, 18–23.

Hanna, C. (1996). No right to choose: Mandated victim participation in domestic violence prosecutions. *Harvard Law Review, 109*, 1849–1910.

Hanna, C. (1998). The paradox of hope: The crime and punishment of domestic violence. *William and Mary Law Review, 39*, 1505–1584.

Harrell, A. (1991). *Evaluation of court-ordered treatment for domestic violence offenders.* Washington, DC: Urban Institute.

Harris, A., & Smith, B. E. (1996). Effects of restraining orders on domestic violence victims. In E. S. Buzawa & C. G. Buzawa (Eds.), *Do arrests and restraining orders work?* Thousand Oaks, CA: Sage.

Hart, B. J. (1990). Gentle jeopardy: The further endangerment of battered women and children in custody mediation. *Mediation Quarterly, 7*, 317–330.

Hart, B. (1992). State codes on domestic violence: Analysis, commentary, and recommendations. *Juvenile and Family Court Journal, 43*(4), 1-80.

Holt, R. (1994). Women's rights and international law: The Struggle for recognition and enforcement. *Columbia Journal of Gender and Law, 1*, 117–141.

Hynson v. Chester, 864 F.2d 1026 (3rd Cir. 1988).

In re Glenn G., 154 Misc. 2d 677 (N.Y. Fam. Ct. 1992).

James, N. (1994). Domestic violence: A history of arrest policies and a survey of modern laws. *Family Law Quarterly, 28*, 509–520.

Jecker, N. S. (1993). Privacy beliefs and the violent family: Extending the ethical argument for physician intervention. *JAMA, 269*, 776–780.

Jordan, C. E., Quinn, K., Jordan, B., & Daileader, C. R. (2000). Stalking: Cultural, clinical, and legal considerations. *Brandeis Law Journal, 38*, 513–579.

Jordan, H. (2000, October 28). Gov. Davis revising "no parole" policy as public opinion relaxes. *San Jose Mercury News*.

Joyce, H. (1997). Mediation and domestic violence: Legislative responses. *Journal of the American Academy of Matrimonial Law, 14,* 447–467.

Justice for abused women. (1995, June 17). *Louisville Courier-Journal,* p. B5.

Justice and battered women. (1990, December 27). *Chicago Tribune,* p. 18C.

Kabat, S. (1991, June 23). Battered women need help, not jail. *Boston Sunday Herald,* p. 23.

Keilitz, S., Efkeman, H., & Casey, P. (1997). *Domestic violence courts: Jurisdiction, organization, performance goals, and measures.* Williamsburg, VA: National Center for State Courts.

Kinports, K., & Fischer, K. (1993). Orders of protection in domestic violence cases: An empirical assessment of the impact of the reform statutes. *Texas Journal of Women and the Law, 2,* 163–276.

Klein, A. R. (1996). Re-abuse in a population of court-restrained male batterers: Why restraining orders don't work. In E. S. Buzawa & C. G. Buzawa (Eds.), *Do arrests and restraining orders work?* Thousand Oaks, CA: Sage.

Klein, C. F., & Orloff, L. E. (1993). Providing legal protection for battered women: An analysis of state statutes and case law. *Hofstra Law Review, 21,* 801–899.

Klein, R. (1986). The emperor Gideon has no clothes: The empty promise of the constitutional right to effective assistance of counsel. *Hastings Constitutional Law Quarterly, 13,* 625–694.

Kriscumas v. State, Md. Ct. Spec. App. 86–1072 (July 9, 1987).

Kroll, L. (1993). AMA family violence campaign. *JAMA, 269,* 1875.

Larson v. State, 766 P.2d 261 (Nev. 1988).

Lawrence, L., & Kugler, L. (1981). Selected voir dire questions. In E. Bochnak (Ed.), *Women's self-defense cases: Theory and practice.* Newark, NJ: Matthew Bender.

Levin, A. (2000). Comment: Child witnesses of domestic violence: How should judges apply the best interests of the child standard in custody and visitation involving domestic violence? *UCLA Law Review, 47,* 813–857.

Locy, T. (1992a, Feb. 15). Weld urged to free eight women. *Boston Globe,* pp. 15, 17.

Locy, T. (1992b, November 17). Jury chief urges pardon for convict: '89 sentence for woman called harsh. *Boston Globe,* p. 25.

Locy, T. (1993, Apr. 29). Woman's life sentence is commuted. *Boston Globe,* p. 1.

Loring, M. T., & Smith, R. W. (1994). *Health care barriers and interventions for battered women.* Washington, DC: U.S. Department of Health and Human Services.

Lucas, G., & Moore, T. (1993, May 29). Wilson grants clemency to two battered women: Petitions denied for fourteen other female petitioners. *San Francisco Chronicle,* p. A1.

Madden, A. M. (1993). Clemency for battered women who kill their abusers: Finding a just forum. *Hastings Women's Law Journal, 4,* 1–86.

Maguigan, H. (1991). Battered women and self-defense: Myths and misconceptions in current reform proposals. *University of Pennsylvania Law Review, 140,* 379–486.

Mahoney, M. (1991). Legal images of battered women: Redefining the issue of separation. *Michigan Law Review, 90,* 1–94.

Marcus, I. (1994). Reframing "domestic violence": Terrorism in the home. In M. A. Fineman & R. Mykitiuk (Eds.), *The public nature of private violence: The discovery of domestic abuse.* New York: Routledge.

Martin v. State, 501 So. 2d 1313 (Fla. Dist. Ct. App. 1986).

Mauer, M., & Chesney-Lind, M. (Eds.). (2002). *Invisible punishment: The collateral consequences of mass imprisonment.* New York: New Press.

McConnell, J. E. (1992). Beyond metaphor: Battered women, involuntary servitude and the Thirteenth Amendment. *Yale Journal of Law and Feminism, 4,* 207–254.

McMorrow, J. (1993). The power and limits of legal naming: A case study of "battered women syndrome." In R. Kevelson (Ed.), *The eyes of justice.* New York: Peter Lang.

Merryman, M. (1993). A survey of domestic violence programs in legal education. *New England Law Review, 28,* 383–452.

Mills, L. G. (1990). Killing her softly: Intimate abuse and the violence of state intervention. *Harvard Law Review, 113,* 550–613.

Mills, L. G. (2003). *Insult to injury: Rethinking our responses to intimate abuse.* Princeton, NJ: Princeton University Press.

Mitchell, K. (1999, January 12). Four killers win clemency: Romer cites abuse they endured. *Denver Post,* p. A01.

Moore, K. D. (1989). *Pardons, justice, mercy, and the public interest.* New York: Oxford University Press.

Morrison, P. (1991, September 18). Legislators listen to women who killed. *Los Angeles Times,* p. A3.

Murphy, J. C. (1993). Lawyering for social change: The power of narrative in domestic violence law reform. *Hofstra Law Review, 21,* 1243–1293.

Mydans, S. (1992, May 30). Clemency pleas denied in fourteen abuse-defense cases. *New York Times*, p. 21.

National Institute of Justice. (1993). *Project to develop a model anti-stalking code for the states: A research report*. Washington, DC: National Institute of Justice.

O'Neal, D. (1993, September 2). Clemency may be last hope for battered killers. *Orlando Sentinel*, p. B1.

Orlando, S., & Willon, P. (1993, July 15). Pinellas woman who killed husband goes free under new policy. *Tampa Tribune*, p. B1.

People v. Ciervo, 506 N.Y.S.2d 462, 464 (N.Y. App. Div. 1986).

People v. Day, 2 Cal. Rptr. 2d 916 (Cal. Ct. App. 1992).

People v. Stancil, 606 N.E.2d 1201 (Ill. 1992).

Prendergast, J. (1990, December 23). Reactions mixed to freeing women. *Cincinnati Enquirer*, p. B-1.

Raeder, M. S. (1997). The better way: The role of batterers' profiles and expert "social framework" background in cases implicating domestic violence. *University of Colorado Law Review, 68*, 147–187.

Randall, T. (1992). ACOG renews domestic violence campaign, calls for changes in medical school curricula. *JAMA, 267*, 3131.

Reed, S. L. (2003). A look back at Gideon v. Wainwright after forty years: An examination of the illusory Sixth Amendment right to assistance of counsel. *Drake Law Review, 47*, 47–70.

Rennison, C. M. (2003). *Intimate partner violence, 1993–2001*. Washington, DC: Bureau of Justice Statistics.

Rogers v. State, 616 So. 2d 1098 (1993).

Rooney, A. (1990, December 28). Celeste declares open season on Ohio men. *Columbus Dispatch*, p. 11A.

Rosenfeld, B. D. (1992). Court-ordered treatment of spouse abuse. *Clinical Psychology Review, 12*, 205–226.

Ruttenberg, M. H. (1994). A feminist critique of mandatory arrest: An analysis of race and gender in domestic violence policy. *American University Journal of Gender and the Law, 2*, 171–216.

Sarno, G. G. (1994). Ineffective assistance of counsel: Battered spouse syndrome as defense to homicide or other criminal offense. 11 *American Law Reports* 5th 871–905 (& 2003 Supp. 33–34).

Schechter, S. (1982). *Women and male violence: The visions and struggles of the battered women's movement*. Boston: South End Press.

Scherer, D. D. (1992). Tort remedies for victims of domestic abuse. *South Carolina Law Review, 43*, 543–580.

Schmidt, J. D., & Sherman, L. W. (1996). Does arrest deter domestic violence? In E. S. Buzawa & C. G. Buzawa (Eds.), *Do arrests and restraining orders work?* Thousand Oaks, CA: Sage.

Schneider, E. M. (1986). Describing and changing: Women's self-defense work and the problem of expert testimony on battering. *Women's Rights Law Reporter, 9,* 195–226.

Schneider, E. M. (2000). *Battered women and feminist lawmaking.* New Haven, CT: Yale University Press.

Schneider, H. (1991, February 20). Maryland to free abused women; Schaefer commutes eight terms, citing violence. *Washington Post,* p. A1.

Schweers, J. (1993, March 1). Battered woman syndrome defense raised. *Florida Bar News,* p. 14.

Sharkey, M. A. (1990, December 26). O, my darling clemency. *Cleveland Plain Dealer,* p. 8B

Sherman, L. W., & Berk, R. A. (1984), The specific deterrent effects of arrest for domestic assault. *American Sociological Review, 49,* 261–272.

Siegel, R. B. (1996). "The rule of love": Wife beatings as prerogative and privacy. *Yale Law Journal, 105,* 2117–2207.

Six women who killed abusive men are granted clemency. (1998, Dec. 31). *Miami Herald,* p. 6B.

Stark, E. (1995). Re-presenting woman battering: From battered woman syndrome to coercive control. *Albany Law Review, 58,* 973–1026.

Stark, E. (1996). Mandatory arrest of batterers: A reply to its critics. In E. S. Buzawa & C. G. Buzawa (Eds.), *Do arrests and restraining orders work?* Thousand Oaks, CA: Sage.

State v. Gfeller, 1987 WL 14328 (Tenn. Crim. App. 1987).

State v. Koss, 551 N.E.2d 970 (Ohio 1990).

State v. Norman, 378 S.E. 2d 8 (N.C. 1989).

State v. Rhodes, 61 N.C. 453 (1868).

State v. Scott, 1989 WL 90613 (Rel. Super. 1989).

State v. Thomas, 423 N.E.2d 137 (Ohio 1981).

State v. Williquette, 385 N.W.2d 145 (Wis. 1986).

State v. Zimmerman, 823 S.W.2d 220 (Tenn. Crim. App. 1991).

Strickland v. Washington, 466 U.S. 668 (1983).

Sugg, N. K., & Inui, T. (1992). Primary care physicians' response to domestic violence: Opening Pandora's box. *JAMA, 267,* 3157–3160.

Symposium on Domestic Violence. (1992). *Journal of Criminal Law and Criminology, 83,* 1–45.

Talan, S. (2000, August 15). Critics say Bush ignoring clemency. Capitol News Service, Tallahassee, FL.

Thirty-four California killers seek clemency, cite battered-woman defense. (1992, March 3). Columbus Dispatch, p. 8A.

Thomas, D. Q., & Easley, M. E. (1995). Domestic violence as a human rights issue. Albany Law Review, 58, 1119–1148.

Thurman v. City of Torrington, 595 F. Supp. 1521 (D. Conn. 1984).

Tilden, V. P. (1989). Response of the health care delivery system to battered women. Issues in Mental Health Nursing, 10, 309–320.

Tjaden, P., & Thoennes, N. (2000). Extent, nature, and consequences of intimate partner violence: Findings from the National Violence Against Women Survey. Collingdale, PA: Diane.

Walker, L. (1979). The battered woman. New York: HarperCollins.

Walker, L.E.A. (1992). Battered woman syndrome and self-defense. Notre Dame Journal of Law, Ethics & Public Policy, 6, 321–335.

Warren, J. (2002, April 11). Battered wife will get parole in murder; Prisons: Davis agrees for just the second time to free a killer. Los Angeles Times.

Watson v. Kansas City, 857 F.2d 690 (10th Cir. 1988).

Wilkerson, I. (1990, December 22). Clemency granted to twenty-five women convicted for assault or murder. New York Times, p. 1.

Willoughby, M. J. (1989). Rendering each woman her due: Can a battered woman claim self-defense when she kills her sleeping batterer? Kansas Law Review, 38, 169–192.

Wilson commutes sentence of woman who killed husband. (1998, Nov. 7). Orange County Register, p. A4.

Wong, D. S. (1994, March 4). Board urges clemency for two in cases tied to battered women's syndrome. Boston Globe, p. 35.

Young, V. (1992, Dec. 17,). Sentence cut for two who killed husbands. St. Louis Post-Dispatch, p. 1A.

Zlotnick, D. M. (1995). Empowering the battered woman: The use of criminal contempt sanctions to enforce civil protection orders. Ohio State Law Journal, 56, 1153–1215.

Zorza, J. (1992). The criminal law of misdemeanor domestic violence, 1970–1990. Journal of Criminal Law and Criminology, 83, 46–72.

Zorza, J. (1994). Must we stop arresting batterers? Analysis and policy implications of new police domestic violence studies. New England Law Review, 28, 929–990.

Zorza, J. (2001). Protecting the children in custody disputes when one parent abuses the other. In N.K.D. Lemon (Ed.), Domestic Violence Law. St. Paul, MN: West.

CHAPTER ELEVEN

Rape Resistance

Successes and Challenges

Patricia D. Rozee, Ph.D.

ape is widespread and persistent. It is one of the most prevalent and least recognized human rights issues in the world today (Heise, Ellsberg, & Gottemoeller, 1999; Rozee, 2000). Among industrialized nations. rape prevalence is estimated at 21 to 25 percent (Koss, Heise, & Russo, 1994). Among nonindustrial nations, it is estimated to occur in from 43 to 90 percent of cultures worldwide (Rozee, 1993). The United States has the highest rate of rape of any industrialized nation—four times that of Germany, twelve times that of England, and twenty times that of Japan. Research has shown little change in U.S. rape prevalence rates over time. A recent survey of rape prevalence studies found that the U.S. rape rate has remained at approximately 15 percent for the past quarter-century (Rozee & Koss, 2001).

This prevalence rate has not gone unaddressed by feminist scholars, activists, and individual women. There is a long and relatively successful history of women's resistance to sexual assault. The women's rights movement of the 1960s and 1970s spawned a powerful rape crisis movement that at its heart was a resistance movement. Like most other resistance movements, it sought changes at large-scale systems and institutional levels as well as at the individual level.

Resistance broadly defined includes challenging institutional, political, religious, judicial, legal, law enforcement, and medical establishments and their handling or interpretation of what is "real rape." This chapter addresses both the successes and continuing challenges of these efforts at each of the pertinent levels of intervention.

SYSTEMS-LEVEL INTERVENTIONS

Rape resistance at the systems level has occurred primarily in the way that legal systems define and prosecute rape.

Contested Definitions of Rape

One of the areas of contention in rape research concerns the definition of rape (Koss, 1992). Feminist scholars wrestle with the contradiction between the lived experience of rape survivors and the legal limits of prosecution. The legal definition of rape in the United States is so narrow as to severely limit the reporting, apprehension, prosecution, and conviction of perpetrators. In many states, forced penile penetration of the vagina of an unwilling victim is required to constitute rape. Yet many of the most violent rapes may not include penile penetration. Instead, penetration may be by fingers or other objects. Anal and oral penetrations are also common, as are penetration of a drugged or unconscious victim requiring no force. Feminist activists generally favor an expanded definition of rape that includes these other forms of violation, but many state laws use a more limited definition.

One of the most powerful effects of the resistance efforts of the rape crisis movement was on the definitions, legal and otherwise, of rape. Feminist scholarship and activism have transformed the analysis of rape and led to a paradigmatic shift away from rape as a crime against the father, husband, or other male relative of the victim to a crime against the woman herself. In addition, pressure from women's organizations resulted in the elimination in the 1970s of the "false accuser" jury instructions harking back to the seventeenth-century declaration by Sir Matthew Hale that rape accusations are easy to make but hard to prove and even harder to disprove (Sanday, 1996). The 1990s saw the overturn of the so-called spousal rape exemption that enforced Hale's view that a woman cannot retract her matrimonial consent to sexual union with her husband. Thus, a woman could not accuse her husband of rape since it was part of the matrimonial agreement. The effort to change this legal exemption for marital rapists was lengthy and was waged by feminists on a state-by-state basis over twenty years.

Rape Myths and the Consent Defense

Feminist rape critics have pointed to larger social stereotypes about rape that are existent in every rape courtroom in the country. Legal scholars were able to effect a change in courtroom procedure, called the *rape shield* law, which prohibited introduction of the sexual background of the victim into evidence under most circumstances. Formerly the strategy of exposing victim sexual history was used to show that she had had sex with other men, so her conduct with the defendant was likely consensual too. Despite the illogic in such a proposition, there has been an increasing reliance on a consent defense for rape perpetrators. This leads to the proverbial "he said, she said" scenario that rarely favors victims' rights. The consent defense strategy is effective because of the prevalence of a myriad of rape myths that are believed and acted on by juries of both men and women. Foremost among these is the widespread belief that many rape victims "ask for it" by their appearance, behavior, the situation in which they have placed themselves, or a combination of all three factors. This powerful myth persists despite the lack of research evidence to support it. An allied myth is that women secretly want to be forced or that many women like rough sex, despite women's protestations to the contrary. An additional rape myth is that men are basically unable to control their sexual impulses, especially if confronted with a particularly provocative female. This belies the fact that rape victims are on record from ages six weeks to up to ninety-five years old. In addition, most perpetrators have a legal source of sexual release with a wife or girlfriend and are not generally seeking a sexual outlet.

Juries are reluctant to convict if the victim is seen as somehow culpable in the assault. Ironically, the areas of culpability are basic to expected heterosexual dating behavior, such as voluntarily leaving a place of relative safety (such as a bar or restaurant) with the assailant, consenting to enter the home of her date, or consuming alcohol. What may be seen as typical dating behaviors becomes culpable behavior on the part of the victim when looked at through the lens of a rape trial. Victim blaming in rape cases is more extreme than in any other violent crime. Yet the predatory, manipulative, or coercive aspects of the assailant's behavior are of less concern in judicial procedures.

The consent defense often relies on evidence of victim resistance. Although feminist scholars were successful in removing the requirement of resistance to prove nonconsent, physical resistance is frequently relied on by juries in assessing consent (Krulewitz & Nash, 1979; Ryckman, Kaczor, & Thornton, 1992; Warner & Hewitt, 1993). This expectation flies in the face of common advice given to women that resistance is both futile and dangerous (Rozee, 2003). Only a small minority of consent defense rape cases result in convictions (Frazier & Haney, 1996).

RAPE: A GENDERED CRIME

There are two new areas of feminist legal scholarship that hold promise for future rape convictions. Both rely on the powerful finding of the gendered nature of rape. The examination of victim characteristics by numerous researchers has found that the only consistent predictor of being a rape victim is gender. In other words, women of all ages, appearance, and behavioral category and in all situations are raped. Rape is predominantly a crime against women that is perpetrated by men (Koss et al., 1994). The research finding of gender as a predictor of rape is the strongest contraindicator of the victim precipitation argument that is so prevalent in a consent defense. It requires us to examine the power relations between the sexes that both enable and condone rape and pass this information on to succeeding generations.

"No Duty" Rules

This reform method would erect additional barriers to admission of testimony regarding victim behavior. Ellen Bublick (1999) described the "no duty" rule, which insists that women should have the constitutionally guaranteed rights to freedom of movement, association, and expression in where they go, with whom, and how they dress and behave that men do. In other words, women have no duty to conduct themselves in fear of intentional rape, as if their every behavior will be judged as an indicator of a willingness to be raped.

"Reasonable Woman" Standard

The reasonable woman standard is consistently used in the prosecution of sexual harassment cases due to the vastly different experiences and perceptions of women and men. This standard is intended to recognize the structural inequalities that are inherent in gender relations, particularly involving the contested territory of women's bodies (Cahill, 2001). As noted by Joan McGregor (1994), gender stratification and gender inequalities render the perceptions of a reasonable woman as different from those of a reasonable man. This difference requires a change in rape law that would include "requiring affirmative consent and relying upon the standard of the *reasonable woman* as evidence in rape cases" (McGregor, 1994, p. 232). Similarly, Caroline Forell, a University of Oregon law professor, and Donna Matthews, a Eugene attorney, in their book, *A Law of Her Own: The Reasonable Woman as a Measure of Man* (2000), argue that a woman-centered standard should be applied to the behavior of perpetrators in circumstances where women and men differ on their experiences of sexual violence and women are overwhelmingly the victims of male violence. They contend that because men have traditionally defined what is lawful, if we hold men to a "reasonable woman" standard it may challenge unexamined biases in the law that fortify the systematic subordination of women (Forell & Matthews, 2000).

RAISING THE SOCIAL COSTS OF RAPE

Feminist legal scholars contend that raising the social costs to rape perpetrators is essential to the prevention of future rapes. Rapists must know that rape is not condoned by our society, that rape is not sex, and that all legal sanctions will be brought to bear to punish perpetrators. Committing rape must be seen as a costly endeavor for the rapist. Identifying and reporting rape is essential to raising the costs of rape to rapists.

However, narrow legal definitions of rape conflict with survivor declarations of rape. Because most researchers, activists, and even women themselves define "real rape" as a forceful attack by a stranger on an unwilling victim, many victims are reluctant to report rape (Estrich, 1987). This results in one of the lowest reporting rates for any violent crime, according to the Rape in America study (Kilpatrick, Edmunds, & Seymour, 1992). Only one in three rapes is reported, the lowest reporting rate since 1989 (Greenfield, 1997). The closer the relationship of the victim to the offender, the less likely she is to report the rape to authorities. Although date and acquaintance rapes are no longer the hidden rapes that they have been throughout history, they are still functionally condoned by social myth. This is evidenced by the relatively low conviction rate even though the perpetrator is typically easily identified.

Once reported, very few reported rapes ever reach the level of a trial (Gunn & Minch, 1992), and the few rapists who are tried rarely serve prison time.

Systems-level interventions are slow and difficult to achieve, but they can have a powerful impact on the successful outcomes of rape complaints for victims. The problem is multifaceted and will require resistance at multiple points.

INSTITUTIONAL-LEVEL INTERVENTIONS

Rape resistance efforts at the institutional level have taken place within those institutions having the most contact with rape survivors: medical providers, law enforcement, and educational institutions such as colleges and universities. The rape crisis movement resulted in the creation of dozens of rape crisis centers that have worked with local hospital and law enforcement professionals to enact changes in the initial handling of rape cases. A notably successful program in Long Beach, California, involved the creation of cooperative Sexual Assault Response Teams (SART). When police receive a rape call, they notify the SART, representing hospital, police, rape crisis victim advocates, and prosecutors. All members of the SART meet at a special wing of the community hospital that is dedicated to rape investigations. The rape unit is located away from the emergency room in a private area staffed with forensic nurses. There, the rape kit is prepared, and microscopic evidence is collected using specialized equipment. The victim/survivor tells her story only one time since all interested parties are present at the rape unit. Such programs illustrate the potency of institutional responses when territorial priorities take second place to serving victims.

Colleges and universities responding to requirements of the Violence Against Women Act of 1994 have conducted a wide range of rape education programs. These programs have occasionally been aimed at male fraternities or sports teams, but most rape prevention programs within both universities and communities have focused on avoidance strategies for women (Bachar & Koss, 2001). Although these programs have been effective in teaching women about personal safety, they lack information about precipitating perpetrator behavior and usually stop short of advocating physical self-defense as a prevention strategy for women (Rozee & Koss, 2001; Sochting, Fairbrother, & Koch, 2004). Bachar and Koss (2001), in a review of rape prevention programs, found that mixed-sex rape prevention groups are not as successful as single-sex groups due to the occurrence of gender polarization.

Only men can truly prevent rape; women can only avoid it. The prevalence of news reports regarding rape among organized male groups such as the military, sports teams, and fraternities communicates the desperate need to confront the distorted hypermasculinity among such groups and their negative effects on women. The few programs that have been evaluated focused mainly on developing victim empathy or reducing rape-supportive behaviors, with mixed results. It has been suggested that future male-focused programs be developed based on research on male cognitive, emotional, and behavioral indicators for risk of rape behavior, such as power motivation, power-sex associations, high dominance, calloused and adversarial sexual beliefs, hostility toward women, and a preference for emulating pornography (Rozee & Koss, 2001).

INDIVIDUAL-LEVEL INTERVENTIONS

Individual-level interventions have been the special focus of the rape crisis movement. Rape crisis centers, universities, and various community organizations have developed rape prevention and education programs offered in multiple settings in the community. Virtually all such programs are mixed-sex programs that deal with rape attitudes and myths. These programs often focus on information that is useful in avoiding rape by strangers. This strategy may be of questionable effectiveness given that estimates hold that 80 to 90 percent of rapes are committed by acquaintances. In addition, most women already have a long and quite sophisticated list of precautions that they practice daily (Rozee & Koss, 2001). As Cahill (2001) pointed out, most women continue to take these precautions because they believe that the risk of rape can be significantly reduced or even eliminated by correct behavior on the part of women.

Evaluations of rape prevention programs show a small but favorable attitude change that tends to decay or regress to pretest levels relatively quickly and no preventive effects on the occurrence of subsequent crimes (Bachar & Koss, 2001). Lonsway (1996) conducted a comprehensive review of all published rape education programs targeting women and men. Nearly all of them focused on attitude change, but only half actually decreased rape-supportive attitudes. Even among these, the change did not hold up in long-term follow-up.

Recent studies of programs that assessed rape reduction as an outcome measure found disappointing results. For example, Breitenbecher and Scarce (1999) found no reduction in the incidence of sexual assault despite an increase in knowledge about sexual assault. An in-depth review of empirical studies by Sochting et al. (2004) confirms these findings across studies. Most researchers in this area have concluded that there is no evidence for the effectiveness of current rape prevention programs in preventing rape.

Interestingly, self-defense training is not generally taught as part of standard rape prevention programs. However, when all the avoidance strategies fail, there has to be a fail-safe. The best answer to this is self-defense. The evidence is clear that women who fight back are less likely to be raped, and most women who do not resist are raped. Despite the fact that the research literature has supported this finding for nearly two decades, there is almost no mention of the facts of rape resistance in rape prevention programs. This is due in part to the prevalence of strong cultural myths that prevent women from resisting.

Myths About Rape Resistance

Most women have been taught that to fight back against a rapist is both futile and foolish (Rozee, 2003). One common myth is that it is un-likely that a woman who is accosted by a rapist will be able to escape or fight him off because of his greater size and strength. In truth, women are four times more likely to escape an attempted rapist than they are to be raped by him (Riger & Gordon, 1989). In addition, two literature reviews of research on rape resistance have found that women who fight back, and do so immediately, are less likely to be raped than women who do not (Furby & Fischhoff, 1986; Ullman, 1997). Self-defense is more a matter of technique and leverage than size and strength. In addition, women have a strong element of surprise since most rapists are not expecting resistance. Furby and Fischhoff (1986) found that these results held in both stranger and acquaintance rape situations and even in the presence of a weapon. There are fewer data on resistance in acquaintance rape situations, and this conclusion may require more research with more systematic definitions of resistance.

A second myth is that those who try to fight off an attacker are more likely to be injured. Injuries stemming from resistance tend to be minor, consisting mainly of cuts and bruises, with less than 3 percent suffering more serious injury such as a broken bone (Ruback & Ivie, 1988). Despite evidence that risks for serious injury are not high, women are led to believe that such injuries are common in rape cases when the woman resists.

Recent evidence clearly shows that women who fight back are no more likely to be injured than women who do not fight back (Ullman, 1997). Ullman's research demonstrated that reports of women being hurt when they fight back have the sequence backward: women fought back when they were being hurt, not the reverse. Physical self-defense often occurred in response to physical attack. Thus, it does a real disservice to women to dissuade them from resisting given that resistance is likely to prevent rape and result in no more injury than no resistance.

There are other advantages that can accrue to women who resist an attacker:

- Women who fight back experience fewer postassault symptoms (both physical and psychological) when their efforts prevent the completion of the rape (Koss, Koss, & Woodruff, 1991). It is important not to underestimate the injury of the rape itself.

- Women who fight back have faster psychological recoveries whether or not they are raped (Bart & O'Brien, 1985). This may be due to the sense of control that fighting back imparts, despite the outcome.

- Fighting back strengthens the physical evidence should the survivor decide to prosecute for rape or attempted rape.

Given the preponderance of evidence for the efficacy of physical resistance, it is perplexing that such information is so rarely presented to women as part of rape prevention and education programs.

Resistance to Resistance

Rape resistance in the form of physical self-defense is a controversial topic among feminist activists. There is often a split between activists who emphasize the need for physical resistance and those who think resistance is dangerous. It is notable that many rape activists have ignored the large body of empirical evidence on the effectiveness of physical resistance that has been in existence for nearly twenty years (Rozee & Koss, 2001). Martha McCaughey (1998) suggests that some are apathetic or uncomfortable, especially with physical resistance, because they identify violence as the symbol of patriarchy. It may be thought of as using "the master's tools" and there may be ambivalence about the "failure to honor nonviolence" (p. 278). The goal of self-defense courses is to deconstruct femininity, writes McCaughey: "Femininity, as it is socially defined, is precisely what women must overcome when learning to fight" (p. 281). If femininity is deconstructed and women are learning to fight, are they then becoming "like men"?

Other feminist authors have suggested that rape resistance training for women appears to make the assumption that stopping rape is primarily the responsibility of women (Lonsway, 1996; Bublick, 1999). Yet the same conclusion could be made about any kind of rape prevention strategies aimed at women instead of men. Indeed, it is easy to see where the focus on women's behavior by the legal system has taken us. Almost any conduct by a woman can put her at blame for rape. As Bublick (1999) puts it, "According to the defendants, she is forever doing the wrong thing when a man is trying to rape her. She does not run soon enough, or far enough or fast enough" (p. 1433).

Many feminists have been silent on the issue of resistance due to fears of putting even further burdens on women and limits on their individual liberty. Constant worries about self-protection exact a toll on women's ability to participate in the world freely. In making her case for the legal notion of "no duty" (women's legal entitlement to act on the assumption that others will not rape them), Bublick (1999) points out that women may have an interest in not taking constant precautions against rape since it requires them to give up more of their liberties than men do in order to gain the same legal protections. Care must be taken not to define rape prevention as the sole responsibility of women. However, until we are able to change men's behavior, the need for women's resistance remains.

We do women a disservice by not focusing more efforts in standard rape prevention education on rape resistance. The unfortunate truth is that after they are raped, many women enroll in self-defense classes (Huddleston, 1991). Feminist efforts to get this information to women sooner would be well rewarded.

Cognitive Resistance

It is important for researchers to be aware that the legal definition of rape is not the whole story. The legal confinements of rape often deny the experiences of rape victims and survivors. A phenomenological approach to defining rape resistance requires one to set aside legal definitions of rape that are nearly always at odds with women's experience. It also requires a focus only on the woman's experience of the unwanted sexual experience, expanding the parameters of what we label rape and what we label resistance.

Rape by its very definition implies resistance—psychological, if not physical. Women know when sex was not consensual and indeed may even declare it to be rape even if they did not resist or in any other way show a lack of willingness (Rozee, 1993). Ramos, Koss, and Russo (1999) illustrate this with the finding from their research with Mexican American women. Women in their focus groups reported that they consider it rape when husbands demand sex when she is not willing, even if she does not overtly indicate her unwillingness. Similarly, in my own research, many of the women described cognitive forms of resistance sometimes not evident to the rapist but nevertheless defining it as a rape for the victim. An examination of cognitive resistance requires us to think more creatively about what is and is not rape.

Several forms of cognitive resistance were described in the rape narratives of 253 rape survivors (Rozee, 2001). Cognitive resistance is the bedrock of women's self-definition of rape. It is the first line of defense against the bodily assaults of rape. During the rape, many women reported praying, as a strategy of cognitive resistance. Others reported that they concentrated on planning an escape, analyzing the risks, or memorizing details of the rapist for later description to the police. Many spent the time simply searching for explanations or reasons for the assault.

One of the most poignant forms of cognitive resistance involved various forms of *detachment:* a method of getting out of body and cognitively escaping the assault. One woman described this as follows: "I submitted myself, I neither wanted it nor did I fight it off. I mentally was very separate from myself physically. It was almost like I was looking at myself from above" (Rozee, 2001). Common descriptions involved out of-body experiences involving leaving the body and looking down at oneself as if at a stranger. Women also described feeling detached from what was happening, like an empty shell. As one woman describes it, "I was lying there like a dead person and I felt totally removed from the situation like I was somewhere else and that was just my body" (Rozee, 2001).

Many women fear rape at such an extreme level that they may offer no resistance whatsoever. This can best be described as *resignation.* Many women in my research reported that they simply submitted. They were resigned to "get it over with" and leave. Resignation can be a result of overwhelming force on the part of the perpetrator or overwhelming fear on the part of the victim. Resigned submission can also result from coercion. Strong coercion can result in unwanted sexual contact yet may appear as successful persuasion to the perpetrator. After repeatedly being raped by a family friend, one survivor recalled, "You put it out of your mind, when these things are happening, and you're not the person there that it's happening to" (Rozee, 2001).

These examples illustrate the vast separation between women's definition of rape and resistance and the legal definitions. They are presented here as a way of opening the discussion of women's perceptions of rape and resistance, outside the constrictive legal definitions of rape. The issue is much bigger phenomenologically than just the constricted world of legally defined rape.

CONCLUSION

The study of rape resistance is an area that requires considerably more thought among feminist scholars. Men and women live in different worlds when it comes to male violence against women. Laws that attempt to make rape gender neutral do a disservice to rape victims. Such laws assume that the experience of female victims and male victims is essentially the same. Although the trauma outcome may be similar, men do not experience the cultural context of fear in which women live. In fact, men are generally shocked when they learn about the cognitive worlds of the women with whom they are acquainted. I have seen male students sit in total disbelief when women students write on the chalkboard all the daily strategies they use to be safe from rape. One young woman reported to me that her boyfriend, who was also in the class, said to her, "Yeah, but you don't do all those things, do you?" She said, "Yes, of course I do." It is important for us to share our worldview and our internal experience with the men in our lives who care about us. This is an important strategy to change the ignorance that men have about the restricted freedoms of women in this society.

It is time to break the culture of silence that surrounds rape. Part of how a rape culture renews itself is by making sure that women stay silent about abuse. Many survivors blame themselves for the rape; shame and fear keep them silent. This is bad for the survivor's recovery and bad for society. African American women have termed the breaking of silence as "giving testimony" or "bearing witness," and these are important cultural ways of reaffirming our truths (West,

2002). This is a way to heal oneself and gather together with other supportive women to acknowledge violence against women and work together to make change. Speaking up and speaking out breaks the trauma. It is cathartic.

Change starts with each individual and ultimately affects the structural and institutional conditions that dictate the conditions of our lives.

References

Bachar, K. J., & Koss, M. P. (2001). From prevalence to prevention: Closing the gap between what we know about rape and what we do. In C. M. Renzetti, R. K. Bergen, & J. L. Edelson (Eds.), *Sourcebook on violence against women* (pp. 117–142). Thousand Oaks, CA: Sage.

Bart, P. B., & O'Brien, P. (1985). *Stopping rape: Successful survival strategies.* New York: Pergamon.

Breitenbecher, K. H., & Scarce, M. (1999). A longitudinal evaluation of the effectiveness of a sexual assault education program. *Journal of Interpersonal Violence, 14,* 459–478.

Bublick, E. M. (1999). Citizen no-duty rules: Rape victims and comparative fault. *Columbia Law Review, 99,* 1413–1490.

Cahill, A. J. (2001). *Rethinking rape.* Ithaca, NY: Cornell University Press.

Estrich, S. (1987). *Real rape: How the legal system victimizes women who say no.* Cambridge, MA: Harvard University Press.

Forell, C., & Matthews, D. (2000). *A law of her own: The reasonable woman as a measure of man.* New York: New York University Press.

Frazier, P., & Haney, B. (1996). Sexual assault cases in the legal system: Police, prosecutor, and victim perspectives. *Law and Human Behavior, 20,* 607–628.

Furby, L., & Fischhoff, B. (1986). *Rape self-defense strategies: A review of their effectiveness.* Eugene, OR: Eugene Research Institute.

Greenfield, L. A. (1997, February). *Sex offences and offenders: An analysis of data on rape and sexual assault* (Report NCJ163392). Washington, DC: U. S. Department of Justice, Bureau of Justice Statistics. http://www.ojp.gov/bjs/pub/pdf/soo.pdf.

Gunn, R., & Minch, C. (1992). Sexual assault in Canada: A social and legal analysis. In E. C. Viola (Ed.), *Critical issues in victimology: International perspectives* (pp. 166–173). New York: Springer.

Heise, L., Ellsberg, M., & Gottemoeller, M. (1999). Ending violence against women. *Population Reports, 27,* 1–43.

Huddleston, S. (1991). Prior victimization experiences and subsequent self-protective behavior as evidenced by personal choice of physical activity courses. *Psychology: A Journal of Human Behavior, 28,* 47–51.

Kilpatrick, D. G., Edmunds, C. N., & Seymour, A. E. (1992). *Rape in America: A report to the nation.* Arlington, VA: National Center for Victims of Crime.

Koss, M. P. (1992). The under detection of rape: Methodological choices influence incidence estimates. *Journal of Social Issues, 48,* 61–76.

Koss, M. P., Goodman, L. A., Brown, A., Fitzgerald, L. F., Keita, G. P., & Russo, N. G. (1994). *No safe haven: Male violence against women at home, at work, and in the community* (pp. 157–176). Washington, DC: American Psychological Association.

Koss, M. P., Heise, L., & Russo, N. F. (1994). The global health burden of rape. *Psychology of Women Quarterly, 18,* 509–537.

Koss, M. P., Koss, P. G., & Woodruff, W. J. (1991). Deleterious effects of criminal victimization on women's health and medical utilization. *Archives of Internal Medicine, 151,* 342–357.

Krulewitz, J. E., & Nash, J. E. (1979). Effects of rape victim resistance, assault outcomes, and sex of observer on attributions of rape. *Journal of Personality, 47,* 557–574.

Lonsway, K. A. (1996). Preventing acquaintance rape through education. What do we know? *Psychology of Women Quarterly, 20,* 229–265.

McCaughey, M. (1998). The fighting spirit: Women's self-defense training and the discourse of sexed embodiment. *Gender and Society, 12,* 277–300.

McGregor, J. (1994). Force, consent, and the reasonable woman. In J. L. Coleman & A. Buchanan (Eds.), *In harm's way: Essays in honor of Joel Feinburg* (pp. 231–254). Cambridge: Cambridge University Press.

Ramos, L. R., Koss, M. P., & Russo, N. F. (1999). Mexican-American women's definitions of rape and sexual abuse. *Hispanic Journal of Behavioral Sciences, 21,* 236–265.

Riger, S., & Gordon, M. (1989). *The female fear.* New York: Free Press.

Rozee, P. (1993). Forbidden or forgiven: Rape in cross-cultural perspective. *Psychology of Women Quarterly, 17,* 499–514.

Rozee, P. D. (2000). Sexual victimization: Harassment and rape. In M. Biaggio & M. Hersen (Eds.), *Issues in the psychology of women* (pp. 93–114). New York: Kluwer Academic/Plenum Publishers.

Rozee, P. D. (2001, February). *Conceptualizing cognitive aspects of rape resistance.* Paper presented at the Nag's Heart Conference on Feminist Dilemmas, Los Angeles.

Rozee, P. D. (2003). Women's fear of rape: Cause, consequences and coping. In J. Chrisler, C. Golden, & P. Rozee (Eds.), *Lectures in the psychology of women* (3rd ed.). New York: McGraw-Hill.

Rozee, P. D., & Koss, M. P. (2001). Rape: A century of resistance. *Psychology of Women Quarterly, Millennial Issue, 25*(4), 295–311.

Ruback, R. B., & Ivie, D. L. (1988). Prior relationship, resistance, and injury in rapes: Analysis of crisis center records. *Violence and Victims, 3,* 99–111.

Ryckman, R. M., Kaczor, L. M., & Thornton, B. (1992). Traditional and nontraditional women's attributions of responsibility to physically resistive and nonresistive rape victims. *Journal of Applied Social Psychology, 22,* 1453–1463.

Sanday, P. R. (1996). *A woman scorned: Acquaintance rape on trial.* New York: Doubleday.

Sochting, N., Fairbrother, N., & Koch, W. J. (2004). Sexual assault of women: Prevention efforts and risk factors. *Violence Against Women, 10*(1), 73–93.

Ullman, S. E. (1997). Review and critique of empirical studies of rape avoidance. *Criminal Justice and Behavior, 24,* 177–204.

Warner, A., & Hewitt, J. (1993). Victim resistance and judgments of victim "consensuality" in rape. *Perceptual and Motor Skills, 76,* 952–954.

West, C. M. (2002). *Violence in the lives of black women: Battered, black, and blue.* New York: Haworth Press.

CHAPTER TWELVE

Women's Human Rights Abuses in the Name of Religion

Shannon M. Roesler, J.D.

~~~

A woman remains in an abusive marriage because her husband refuses to consent to divorce. A young girl is forced to marry an older man with two other wives. A teenaged girl who is raped believes she is to blame because she kissed her date good-night. These three individuals live in different societies shaped by unique religious and cultural traditions, and yet all three suffer abuses justified in the name of religion. Although the global human rights and feminist movements have established gender equality as a fundamental human right, women continue to suffer gross human rights abuses that are frequently sanctioned by national governments as the free exercise of religion. Religion in its many forms has enriched cultures and communities throughout the world, but certain religious movements, often referred to as fundamentalist, have used religion to advance political agendas extremely detrimental to the rights of women.

A WOMAN'S PLACE:
THE FUNDAMENTALIST AGENDA

While fundamentalist religious movements are products of their own time and place, they share identifiable characteristics, especially regarding their attitudes toward women, gender, and sexuality.[1] These movements share a deep commitment to a separate-spheres ideology—a belief that although men and women may be spiritual equals, they have different roles and responsibilities in the physical world.[2] This belief system endorses a public-private division: men serve in the public sphere of work and politics, while women preside over the private, or domestic, sphere of family and home.

This artificial dichotomy is often reinforced by a belief in a divine hierarchy: men must obey God, and women must obey men in return for their protection and financial support. According to some fundamentalist ideologies, women require men's protection in large part because a woman's sexual virtue is a measure of the family's honor. Restrictions on women's dress and their movement, as well as their reproductive choices, are attempts to control women's sexuality, which is frequently portrayed as dangerous—as the evil responsible for the sin and imperfections of all human beings. As many human rights activists and scholars have noted, this separate-spheres ideology shields violations of women's human rights from outside intervention, hiding the continued subordination of women within their homes behind protectionist language.[3]

THE POLITICS OF RELIGION AND WOMEN'S RIGHTS

Fundamentalist religious movements are political movements.[4] That is, they seek to gain political power and frequently seek to change or preserve laws to reflect their particular religious ideology. Not surprisingly, they often focus on laws affecting women's status within the family and society generally. For example, conservative Christian organizations in the United States have invested substantial resources and time in securing the nomination and appointment of federal judges likely to limit or completely deny a woman's right to choose, as well as other fundamental rights.[5] In addition, these same groups have successfully lobbied Congress for laws and funds that support their agenda.[6] In 1996, Congress passed welfare legislation that allocated $50 million annually to abstinence-only sex education programs in public schools (Rose, 1999). These programs frequently provide adolescent students with misinformation or omit critical information concerning contraception and disease prevention in order to scare and shame students into abstaining from sex.

Moreover, at the heart of the abstinence-only curricula is the Christian fundamentalist message that girls and women are responsible for controlling the sexual behavior of men. In one publication, a chart designates the "prolonged kiss" as the "beginning of danger" and the point after which male sexual desire is aroused. Female sexual desire, however, is not so easily aroused, sending the message that girls are in a better position to control sexual desire and male behavior (Rose, 1999). Having heard this message, if a girl allows her date to kiss her and he then sexually assaults her, she will likely blame herself instead of recognizing sexual violence as a violation of her basic human rights. Furthermore, evidence does not support proponents' claims that these programs reduce teen pregnancy and sexually transmitted diseases. In fact, in countries with lower rates of teen pregnancy, social attitudes toward sexuality and sex education are typically more liberal, as is access to contraception and health care.[7]

Conservative Christian groups in the United States have not focused solely on domestic policy; they have successfully influenced the flow of U.S. foreign aid, to the detriment of women all over the world. Shortly after President Bush was elected in 2000, he reinstated the Mexico City policy, popularly known as the global gag rule, which bars any foreign organization receiving money from the U.S. Agency for International Development (2001) from providing or promoting abortion as a method of family planning. For example, when members of an organization in Zambia counseled young people that unprotected sex and unwanted pregnancies can lead to unsafe and even fatal abortions, the organization lost approximately $30,000 in essential U.S. aid. The chair of the organization emphasized the dire consequences of the loss: "I think they are killing these women, just as if they are pointing a gun and shooting. There is no difference" (Loder, 2003). Others would agree with her characterization. In the summer of 2003, the United States cut $50 million in funds to the United Nations Population Fund (UNFPA) in response to the Christian right's accusations that UNFPA resources were involved in coercive abortion practices in China. Because of the loss in funds, the UNFPA estimates that approximately "4,700 mothers, 77,000 infants and children, and 800,000 pregnancies will be lost" (People for the American Way, 2003). How the United States spends its dollars is truly a matter of life and death for women and girls.

Reproductive rights and access to safe abortions mean little if a woman is unable even to leave her home. In some societies, religious fundamentalism has resulted in severe violations of women's freedom of movement. The best-known example is the situation of girls and women under Taliban rule in Afghanistan: women could not leave their homes without a male chaperone and without being completely covered by a dark heavy garment called the burqa. They could not be properly examined by health care professionals, and they were denied the right to work. The Taliban promulgated decrees imposing draconian punishments on all those who violated these restrictions and justified them in the name of religion (Physicians for Human Rights, 1998). Although the Taliban's assault on women's rights is probably the best-known modern example, religion has been used in many other countries to restrict women's freedom of movement. For example, in some countries, the law requires that a woman secure permission from her father or husband before she can obtain a passport to travel.[8]

Even if a woman can leave her home, she may still feel she is a prisoner if laws and social practices prevent her from escaping an unhappy or abusive marriage. In several countries, certain interpretations of Islamic law are codified into discriminatory family laws that allow men to divorce their wives arbitrarily and unilaterally with no judicial supervision (Alami & Hinchcliffe, 1996; Mayer, 1999). Frequently, a man can effect a divorce simply by saying, "I divorce you," three times, leaving the woman with no financial support and often without custody of her children. This practice clearly discriminates on the basis of sex because women are not given the same access to divorce as their husbands. Although most Islamic family laws contain grounds for a wife to divorce her husband, they are often limited, and they always require judicial consent. In other words, if she is unable to prove one of the limited grounds, such as her husband's desertion or failure to support her, she may be unable to secure a divorce. And because the codes frequently codify—either explicitly or implicitly—the principle that a wife owes her husband her obedience in return for his financial support (Alami & Hinchcliffe, 1996; Heindel, 1999), domestic violence may be considered an acceptable means of correcting an "errant" wife rather than an acceptable ground for divorce, leaving her with no choice but to remain trapped in the marriage and suffering silently.

Religious family laws in many countries violate women's rights in other ways as well. For example, Islamic family laws often allow a man to marry as many as four women (Mayer, 1999). Although the first wife is sometimes granted the right to petition for divorce when her husband marries another woman (Esposito with DeLong-Bas, 2001), divorce may be an unattractive option if it leaves her with no financial support and without custody of the children (Heindel, 1999). Similarly, although the law may require a woman's consent to be married, in reality she may have little choice: in societies that restrict women's rights to work and own property, marriage may be the only realistic option for survival.

Furthermore, even when governments enact legal reforms that advance women's rights and gender equality in the public sphere (through affirmative action measures or antidiscrimination legislation), they frequently refuse to amend or repeal discriminatory family laws that are ostensibly based on religious law. For example, in Israel, a woman's access to divorce and other matters of personal status are governed by either Jewish, Muslim, or Christian law depending on the religion of her birth (Raday, 1999). Under Jewish law, a woman must obtain her husband's permission in order to obtain a divorce; if he refuses to give her a *get* (a divorce writ), she is not free to remarry, and if she has a relationship with another man, she may be labeled a "rebellious wife," jeopardizing her claims to alimony and child custody. Although the rabbinical courts have the power to order a husband to give his wife a *get,* if he chooses to disregard the order, his wife will remain married to him. This startling inequality exists alongside progressive secular laws advancing women's equality, such as laws on equal employment opportunity and equal pay for comparable work, comprehensive laws on sexual harassment, laws requiring affirmative action in the public sector, and laws recognizing women's right to participate in the armed services.[9]

Discriminatory family laws, such as those in Israel, have historical origins in religious practice. Under Jewish law in Israel, women do not have the same right to preclude their husbands' access to divorce; if a woman does not grant her husband's request for a divorce, the husband may nevertheless seek a rabbinical license to remarry (Raday, 1999). This inequality is rooted historically in the practice of polygamy. Because Jewish law once allowed men to marry more than one wife, the law continues to support a man who has multiple partners over time, while it condemns a woman who has more than one partner during her lifetime (Raday, 1999). In fundamentalist strains of Judaism, a separate-spheres ideology prevails; a woman has a religious duty to care for home and family, while a man must devote himself to religious study and ritual (Yuval-Davis, 1999). Despite claims that gender roles are different but equal, women are clearly considered inferior beings: they may not lead prayers, hold public religious positions, or testify in a religious court. Most telling, in his daily morning prayer, a man thanks God for not making him a woman, while a woman begins her day by thanking God for making her according to his will (Yuval-Davis, 1999).

WOMEN'S RIGHTS AND RELIGIOUS FREEDOM UNDER INTERNATIONAL HUMAN RIGHTS LAW

These discriminatory laws and practices clearly violate numerous human rights norms enshrined in national constitutions, international and regional treaties, and other international instruments. Widely ratified treaties, such as the International Covenant on Civil and Political Rights (ICCPR) and the Convention on the Elimination of All Forms of Discrimination Against Women (CEDAW), contain provisions prohibiting discrimination on the basis of sex and requiring that states reform laws and policies in order to prevent and eradicate gender discrimination. Regional treaties, such as the African (Banjul) Charter on Human and People's Rights and the American Convention on Human Rights, contain similar provisions. Moreover, comments and recommendations by treaty-monitoring bodies, such as the Human Rights Committee (CEDAW, 1981), which monitors compliance with the ICCPR, plainly establish that religion may not be used to justify otherwise discriminatory laws.

Moreover, the right to equality within the family enjoys special recognition in international human rights law. In addition to nondiscrimination and equal protection provisions, both CEDAW and the ICCPR contain articles (respectively, Articles 16 and 23) specifically requiring states "to take appropriate steps to ensure equality of rights and responsibilities of spouses as to marriage, during marriage and at its dissolution." Not surprisingly, several countries with religious family laws have entered reservations to Article 16(e) of CEDAW, which requires states "to eliminate discrimination against women in all matters relating to marriage and family relations." The subarticles elaborate on this general prescription, detailing important rights, such as the right "to decide freely and responsibly the number and spacing of children and to have access to the information, education and means" necessary to exercise these rights. Although the treaty does not specifically require states to provide access to abortion, this provision does suggest that girls and women have—at the very least—a right to comprehensive sex education, suggesting the Christian right's abstinence-only education is not enough. Unfortunately, in part because of strong opposition by Christian fundamentalist groups, the United States has yet to ratify CEDAW.[10]

Given the clarity of international human rights law (much of which is incorporated in national constitutions throughout the world), we may wonder why oppressive laws and practices continue to exist. From a legal perspective, fundamentalists often advance the argument that they have a right to these discriminatory laws and practices as a matter of religious freedom. But while human rights law certainly protects the freedom to practice one's religion of choice (ICCPR, Article 18), it does not do so at the expense of other rights and individual freedoms. Nondiscrimination clauses in various treaties place religion and sex on the same plane.[11] One may not be used to justify discrimination on the basis of the other. In fact, gender equality arguably occupies a privileged position. The ICCPR contains a separate article (Article 3) in addition to the general nondiscrimination clause requiring states "to ensure the equal right of men and women" to all rights in the treaty. Similarly, the UN Charter specifically notes the importance of gender equality in its preamble.

Furthermore, fundamentalists' claims to freedom of religion are dubious for another reason. Whose religion do they have the right to practice? No religion is monolithic or homogeneous; within every major religion, we find an abundance of interpretations, ideologies, and doctrines, each constantly contested and reinvented. When domestic laws codify religion, governments privilege one group's interpretation over another's, thereby endorsing one "right" religious view and marginalizing other religious views, which inevitably infringes on some people's freedom of religion. Moreover, even if a state allows each group to follow its own religious law, it cannot guarantee that all members of any given community participated in the creation of that law. In other words, if a state justifies its religious laws by claiming to defer to the wishes of each discrete religious community, we might ask how the state determines a "community." In fact, in response to the Indian government's "policy of non-interference in the personal affairs of any community," a women's rights organization asked this very question.[12] Before a community's religion becomes its law, women—who form at least half of the community—must have a voice in defining that religion and its practice. To exclude them is to violate their freedom of religion, in addition to their right to gender equality.

ADDRESSING THE PROBLEM: POTENTIAL CAUSES AND SOLUTIONS

But although international human rights law undoubtedly prohibits gender discrimination in the name of religion, eradicating such discrimination is a more complicated matter. Patriarchal attitudes and power structures do not change overnight. Before solutions are adopted, we must identify the causes and contributing factors to these movements and their misogynist doctrines. That is, we must first understand what fuels these movements in today's societies. Scholars and commentators have offered numerous explanations. Some believe recent fundamentalist movements are a response to modernity. In the wake of globalization, overwhelming poverty and exploitation give rise to a "genuine sense of despair and disorientation," leaving people searching for the comfort and sense of identity religion can provide (Yuval-Davis, 1999, p. 34). In addition, as communities of people historically fought for their right to self-determination, often in the context of colonial rule, "women were central to the definition of the cultural identity of a nation, and represented the spiritual sphere of the nation, away from colonial life and the public sphere" (Coomaraswamy, 1999). Colonial powers contributed to this public-private division, replacing local laws of business and commerce with their own laws but leaving family laws and other private matters to the indigenous population. In addition, colonial governments often attempted to codify local practices into law, imposing a rigid legal framework on what would otherwise be a dynamic social order more susceptible to change. Consequently, colonial codes shielded laws and customs harmful to women from the vicissitudes of social change and time (Benhabib, 2002).

The recent rise in fundamentalism might also be fueled by changes in the social order as a result of the women's rights movement. Men in many areas of society must now compete for power, wealth, and prestige in ways they did not previously: "When 'secondary-level' male elites are struggling to maintain male dominance in the middling areas of society where jobs are increasingly contested by women, they find that they can reassert themselves in the family, school, and church, which are the social institutions most accessible to them" (Rose, 1999, p. 19). This might in part explain the popularity of the recent evangelical men's movement called the Promise Keepers, which has filled U.S. football stadiums full of men in search of their Christian masculinity. In *Seven Promises of a Promise Keeper* (quoted in Rose, 1999),

Pastor Tony Evans characterizes the decline of the "traditional" family as a national crisis and identifies the "feminization of men" as the main cause for this crisis. In order to solve the problem, he exhorts men to fulfill their proper role as head of the family: "Unfortunately, however, there can be no compromise here. . . . Treat the lady gently and lovingly. But *lead*!" In this case, the fundamentalist belief in a separate-spheres ideology, in what is often termed "traditional family values," seeks to preserve male dominance in areas where it is losing ground.

Even a brief inquiry into potential causes and contributing factors demonstrates that although fundamentalist movements and ideologies share similar views regarding women and gender equality, they are situated in different political, historical, and cultural contexts. They therefore require individualized strategies for change. In addition, women's actual lived experiences in the context of different fundamentalist movements are different both across cultures and within cultures. The solution is to create spaces in which women can speak and are empowered to define their own religions and cultures, thereby changing laws and policies from within their societies.[13] By recognizing that women's lives are shaped by various factors and forces, advocates will be able to fashion strategies that respond to the specific contexts and to do so in partnership with the women and men directly affected.[14]

But this does not mean international activists and organizations have no role to play. The success of local advocacy frequently depends on international funds and resources. International actors can pressure domestic governments and intergovernmental organizations to fund local efforts that ensure women's equal participation in their communities and in the formation of domestic law and policy. International organizations can also facilitate the formation of networks and the provision of human rights resources and tools so that advocates may share strategies, successes, and frustrations and move forward in solidarity.

Notes

1. I use the term *fundamentalist* to denote conservative religious ideologies and groups that advocate the imposition of a divinely sanctioned social order that they claim is threatened by the evils of modern progress, including the feminist movement. Although I recognize that these groups do not always identify as fundamentalist, I use the term in order to connote the

similarities among the many political religious movements and in lieu of more pejorative terms, such as *extremist, radical,* or *militant.* Moreover, other terms, such as *revivalist* or *traditional,* suggest these groups are restoring or reviving the essence of an identifiable past tradition when they are often constructing new ideologies by claiming to restore a lost golden age.

2. Based on a review of the writings of activist religious women and academic scholars, Howland (1997) identifies several characteristics of a fundamentalist religious group: "These are that the group: believes that the group and society need to be rescued from the secular state; rejects Enlightenment norms, particularly individual rights and secularism; is committed to the authority of ancient scripture; holds a total worldview such that religious beliefs are inseparable from politics, law and culture; relies on an idealized past; is selective in drawing from the past for religious traditions and orthodox practice; centers that idealized past in a patriarchal framework mandating separate gender spheres and a 'pristine morality'; rejects outsiders and the concept of pluralism; and is committed to activism and fighting for changed social, political and legal order" (pp. 277–278).

3. See Bunch (1995). Of course, women's subordination within the home, or "private" sphere, also ensures their continued subordination in the public sphere: "When women are denied democracy and human rights in private, their human rights in the public sphere also suffer, since what occurs in 'private' shapes their ability to participate fully in the public arena" (p. 14).

4. Because this discussion is a brief and limited introduction to women's rights and religious fundamentalism, it contains only a few examples of the impact of religious fundamentalism on women's rights. Although the examples come from Christian, Islamic, and Jewish societies, fundamentalist movements and laws exist in virtually every society. Howland (1997) discusses the influence of religious fundamentalism on women's rights in several societies, including those with Buddhist, Hindu, and Shinto traditions.

5. Eagle Forum's Court Watch (http://www.eagleforum.org/court_watch) advocates a conservative Christian agenda. See generally Neas (2002).

6. These organizations, often referred to as the religious right or Christian right, include groups such as the Eagle Forum, Concerned Women for America, Focus on the Family, and Citizens for Excellence in Education (Rose, 1999).

7. According to the Committee on the Elimination of All Forms of Discrimination Against Women, gender-based violence violates several human rights, including the right to be free from torture, the right to health, the right to liberty and security of the person, and the right to equal protection under the law (CEDAW, 1981).

8. One example is Egypt. Egyptian law requires unmarried women under the age of twenty-one to secure permission from their fathers to obtain passports and travel (U.S. Department of State, 2003a). But recent Egyptian legislation allows women to apply to the courts for permission to travel abroad alone. See also Hassan (2000); U.S. Department of State (2003b), noting that women may not travel domestically or internationally without a male chaperone; and U.S. Department of State (2003c), noting that women must obtain the permission of their husbands or male guardians to travel abroad.

9. The secular courts have concurrent jurisdiction over matters of marital property and child custody, but religious courts have sole jurisdiction in determining whether to grant a divorce. But, not surprising, women often sacrifice property and custody claims they would otherwise have just to obtain their husbands' consent to divorce (Radday, 1999).

10. For articles and opinion pieces on CEDAW from a Christian fundamentalist perspective, see the Eagle Forum's Web site (http://www.eagleforum.org/topics/CEDAW/index.shtml).

11. For example, ICCPR, Article 2(1), states: "Each State Party to the present Covenant undertakes to respect and to ensure to all individuals within its territory and subject to its jurisdiction the rights recognized in the present Covenant, without distinction of any kind, such as race, colour, sex, language, religion, political or other opinion, national or social origin, property, birth or other status."

12. Landsberg-Lewis (1998) describes the advocacy of a women's rights group that petitioned the Indian Supreme Court for an order requiring the Indian government to state, in part, how it will ensure that women's voices are heard when determining what constitutes a "community" and its wishes.

13. Ahmed An-Na'im (1994) argues that "the only viable and acceptable way of changing religious and customary laws is by transforming popular beliefs and attitudes, and thereby changing common practice" (p. 178).

14. In other words, successful advocacy should proceed from a standpoint of intersectionality—that is, it should recognize that in addition to gender, various factors, such as race, nationality, sexual orientation, and economic status, shape women's lives. Given this reality, scholars and activists should acknowledge the many forces shaping a person's identity and experience through a more contextualized approach to scholarship and advocacy. See Wing (2000).

References

Ahmed An-Na'im, A. (1994). State responsibility under international human rights law to change religious and customary laws. In R. J.

Cook (Ed.), *Human rights of women: National and international perspectives.* Philadelphia: University of Pennsylvania Press.

Alami, D., & Hinchcliffe, D. (1996). *Islamic marriage and divorce laws of the Arab world.* Washington, DC: CQ Press.

Benhabib, S. (2002). *The claims of culture, equality and diversity in the global era.* Princeton, NJ: Princeton University Press.

Bunch, C. (1995). Transforming human rights from a feminist perspective. In J. Peters & A. Wolper (Eds.), *Women's rights, human rights: International feminist perspectives.* New York: Routledge.

CEDAW (Convention on the Elimination of All Forms of Discrimination Against Women). (1981, Sept. 3). G.A. res. 34/180, 34 U.N. GAOR Supp. (No. 46) at 193, U.N. Doc. A/34/46.

Coomaraswamy, R. (1999). Different but free: Cultural relativism and women's rights as human rights. In C. W. Howland (Ed.), *Religious fundamentalisms and the human rights of women.* New York: Palgrave Macmillan.

Esposito, J. L., with DeLong-Bas, N. J. (2001). *Women in Muslim family law.* Syracuse, NY: Syracuse University Press.

Hassan, H. (2000, March 28). Rights-Egypt: New law lets women divorce if they waive support. *Inter Press Service.* Retrieved February 2004 from http://www.ipsnews.net.

Heindel, A. H. (1999). Issues affecting Middle Eastern Muslim women: Self-determination and development in Turkey, Egypt, Iran, Iraq, and Saudi Arabia. In K. D. Askin & D. M. Koenig (Eds.), *Women and international human rights law.* Ardsley, NY: Transnational.

Howland, C. W. (1997). The challenge of religious fundamentalism to the liberty and equality rights of women: An analysis under the United Nations Charter. *Columbia Journal of Transactional Law, 35,* 271–377.

Landsberg-Lewis, I. (Ed.). (1998). *Bringing equality home: Implementing CEDAW.* New York: United Nations Development Fund for Women.

Loder, A. (2003, October 1). Global gag rule spurring deaths, disease. *WOMENSENEWS.* http://www.womensenews.org/article.cfm/dyn/aid/1539/context/archive.

Mayer, A. E. (1999). Issues affecting the human rights of Muslim women. In K. D. Askin & D. M. Koenig (Eds.), *Women and international human rights law.* Ardsley, NY: Transnational.

Neas, R. G. (2002, January). Ideology and the federal judiciary. *Insight Magazine.* http://www.pfaw.org/pfaw/general/default.aspx?oid=608.

People for the American Way. (2003). *House cuts funding for international family planning, White House played pressure role.* http://www.pfaw.org/pfaw/general/default.aspx?oid-11520.

Physicians for Human Rights. (1998). *The Taliban's war on women: A health and human rights crisis in Afghanistan.* Boston: Physicians for Human Rights.

Raday, F. (1999). Religion and patriarchal politics: The Israeli experience. In C. W. Howland (Ed.), *Religious fundamentalisms and the human rights of women.* New York: Palgrave Macmillan.

Rose, S. D. (1999). Christian fundamentalism: Patriarchy, sexuality, and human rights. In C. W. Howland (Ed.), *Religious fundamentalisms and the human rights of women.* New York: Palgrave Macmillan.

U.S. Agency for International Development. (2001, January 22). *Memorandum for the agency administrator from President George W. Bush, Subject: Restoration of the Mexico City Policy.* http://www.usaid.gov/bush_pro_new.html.

U.S. Department of State, Bureau of Democracy, Human Rights, and Labor. (2003a). *Egypt, country report.* Washington, DC: U.S. Government Printing Office.

U.S. Department of State, Bureau of Democracy, Human Rights, and Labor. (2003b). *Saudi Arabia, country report.* Washington, DC: U.S. Government Printing Office.

U.S. Department of State, Bureau of Democracy, Human Rights, and Labor. (2003c). *Sudan, country report.* Washington, DC: U.S. Government Printing Office.

Wing, A. K. (Ed.). (2000). *Global critical race feminism: An international reader.* New York: New York University Press.

Yuval-Davis, N. (1999). The personal is political: Jewish fundamentalism and women's empowerment. In C. W. Howland (Ed.), *Religious fundamentalisms and the human rights of women.* New York: Palgrave Macmillan.

CHAPTER THIRTEEN

Sexual Violence Against Women in War and Armed Conflict

Gretchen Borchelt, J.D.

Women remain uniquely vulnerable to violence and discrimination. War and armed conflicts compound this vulnerability, intensifying the violations women suffer. Not only are women in conflict situations murdered, tortured, and attacked along with men, they also are subjected to rape and other forms of sexual violence. Men also are raped during wartime, but evidence shows that women are the more frequent targets. International humanitarian law—the law of war—has long prohibited rape during war and armed conflict. Unfortunately, impunity for wartime rapists has just as long a history. Rape and other forms of sexual violence historically have not been condemned, investigated, and prosecuted with the same intensity and frequency as other war crimes. Recently, however, wartime rape has begun to receive the attention it deserves. The International Criminal Tribunal for the former Yugoslavia and the International Criminal Tribunal for Rwanda have convicted individuals of rape as a war crime, an instrument of genocide, and a crime against humanity. Decisions such as these are necessary steps in a movement to end a culture of impunity for wartime rapists. Despite these encouraging steps, there remains much work yet to be done to eradicate the pervasive culture of impunity protecting those who inflict sexual violence on women during war or armed conflict.

This chapter considers the subject of women and war, focusing on the ways in which the laws of war have dealt with sexual violence against women during war and armed conflict.

THE LAWS OF WAR

Two branches of law govern war. The first, jus *ad bellum*, defines the legitimate reasons a state may engage in war, focusing on the criteria for characterizing a war as "just." The second, jus *in bello*, regulates how a war is conducted, requiring warring parties to adhere to a set of basic principles. This body of law, also referred to as international humanitarian law, relies primarily on treaties, but also comprises customary law, or recognized practices of war. Unlike human rights law, which applies to all people at all times, international humanitarian law applies only during wartime and only to certain persons and situations. The principal documents that form the heart of international humanitarian law are the four Geneva Conventions of August 12, 1949,[1] and the two Additional Protocols of June 8, 1977.[2] The Geneva Conventions relate to protection and assistance for victims of conflicts: the First protects the wounded and sick, the Second the shipwrecked, the Third prisoners of war, and the Fourth civilians in times of war. Common to all four Geneva Conventions is Article 3, which establishes the minimum level of protection that must be provided in times of internal armed conflict. Common Article 3 applies to all parties to a noninternational conflict, including armed opposition forces. The Geneva Conventions codify many rules of the laws of armed conflict that were delineated in earlier treaties, and they are almost universally ratified. The First Additional Protocol completes and reinforces the provisions of the four Geneva Conventions. The Second Additional Protocol further regulates the protection of victims of noninternational armed conflicts, described in Common Article 3. It does not apply to situations of internal disturbances or tensions such as riots, which do not qualify as armed conflicts.

Various categories of crimes are prohibited during times of war and armed conflict. The Geneva Conventions codified one category of crime known as grave breaches. Grave breaches of the laws of war, as defined by the Geneva Conventions, include willful killing, torture or inhuman treatment, and willfully causing great suffering or serious injury to body or health. Because of the serious nature of these crimes, states are obligated to prosecute those accused of grave breaches or extradite them to another country that is willing to do so. The grave breaches provisions apply only in international armed conflict and to acts committed against protected persons, as defined by the Geneva Conventions.

Another category of crime is war crimes, which are defined in the Geneva Conventions and by customary law. War crimes are committed in times of war and are not subject to any statute of limitation. War crimes commonly include murder and ill treatment of the civilian population, killing of hostages, and murder or ill treatment of prisoners of war.

Finally, there are crimes against humanity. Crimes against humanity were first defined in the statute of the Nuremberg Tribunal, which was established to try members of the defeated armed forces after World War II.[3] Unlike war crimes, crimes against humanity are not limited to wartime; they can occur in times of war or peace. Crimes against humanity generally encompass acts that involve or occur in a context in which widespread or systematic killing or mistreatment of civilians is occurring. In other words, the killing of a single civilian in isolation would not constitute a crime against humanity but could constitute a war crime. Crimes against humanity, like grave breaches, are subject to universal jurisdiction, which means that they can be prosecuted by an international tribunal or by the domestic courts of any country.

These categories of crime—grave breaches, war crimes, and crimes against humanity—overlap but are distinct crimes, with specific definitions and legal elements. Historically, the international community has punished such crimes only on an ad hoc basis, establishing different international punishment mechanisms for each situation. Each mechanism consequently has yielded the formulation of different definitions of the crimes and different applications of the provisions of international humanitarian law. This has led to some inconsistency and inconclusiveness in the laws of war.[4] Fortunately, the international community is moving toward establishing more clarity in international humanitarian law. The establishment of the International Criminal Court (ICC) means an end to the ad hoc nature of international criminal justice. The ICC is the first ever permanent, treaty-based, international criminal court developed to punish the perpetrators of the most serious crimes of international concern.[5] Unlike the ad hoc tribunals for the former Yugoslavia and Rwanda, which were set up within the framework of the United Nations, the ICC is a new international organization that came into force on July 1, 2002. It has jurisdiction, when certain conditions are met, over individuals accused of war crimes, genocide, crimes against humanity, and the crime of aggression.[6] This jurisdiction extends only to crimes committed after the court came into existence. The ICC complements national judicial systems, prosecuting cases only if national courts are unwilling or unable to do so. By creating the ICC, the international community has clarified and codified crimes under international humanitarian law and indicated its intention to punish future perpetrators of those crimes.

RAPE AS A CRIME UNDER THE LAWS OF WAR PRIOR TO THE 1990S

The laws of war, both formal and customary, have prohibited rape for centuries. In 546 A.D. the Ostrogoth who captured Rome forbade his troops to rape Roman women (Brownmiller, 1975). Richard II's Ordinances of War, issued in 1385, prohibited the rape of women and stipulated that offenders were to be punished by death (Meron, 1998; Brownmiller, 1975). The 1419 Nantes Ordinances of Henry V drew on these rules and also proscribed the rape of women (Meron, 1998). English ordinances issued in 1639, 1640, and 1643 stated similar prohibitions on rape (Meron, 1998).[7] Several scholars, including the Italian Alberto Gentili (1552–1608) and Dutchman Hugo Grotius (1583–1645) advocated the prohibition of rape in wartime and peacetime (Askin, 1997; Meron, 1998).

More recently, the Lieber Code of 1863 explicitly prohibited "all rape" and punished its commission with death. In the trials of World War II war criminals, the Nuremberg Tribunal received reports of sexual assault (Askin, 1997; Tompkins 1995). In addition, under Article 2 of Control Council No. 10, signed in 1945 by the four occupying powers of Germany, rape was explicitly listed as a crime against humanity (Askin, 1997). Most notably, at the Tokyo Tribunal, rape was prosecuted successfully as a war crime under prohibitions against "inhumane treatment," "ill-treatment," and "failure to respect family honour and rights" (Askin, 1997). An unequivocal prohibition of rape was established in 1949 in the Fourth Geneva Convention, which characterizes rape as an attack on women's honor.[8] Additional Protocols I and II to the Geneva Conventions also protect women from rape, declaring that women deserve special respect and listing rape alongside other forms of attacks on dignity.[9]

Despite these prohibitions, soldiers and combatants have committed wartime rape with impunity for centuries. Indeed, the history of wartime rape reflects a tolerance for such actions. The founding of Rome began by the rape of the Sabine women. In ancient Greece, rape was "socially acceptable behavior well within the rules of warfare [and] an act without stigma for warriors." Christian rape and pillage of Muslims marked the Crusades (Brownmiller, 1975, pp. 33, 34). Similarly, it was accepted, from the Age of Chivalry (1100 to 1500) through the Age of Napoleon (1792 to 1815), that if a town was taken by siege, women could be raped (Parker, 1994; Rothenberg, 1994). And although Henry V sought to protect women and impose discipline among his soldiers by issuing ordinances banning rape, there is evidence that he knew his rules were being breached and that his desired protection for inhabitants "remained largely unaccomplished" (Meron, 1998).

Rape continues to be accepted as an inevitable by-product of war and armed conflict. Examples of mass rape abound in modern wars and armed conflicts: in the actions of the Germans in World War I; by the German, Japanese, and Russians during World War II; in Bangladesh during the 1971 armed conflict; by Americans during the war in Vietnam; and by the Indonesians in East Timor (Brownmiller, 1975; Meron, 1998; Tanaka, 1998; Habiba, 1998; Furusawa & Inglis, 1998). These crimes have gone largely unpunished, despite the written prohibitions and customs that penalize rape during war and armed conflict.

REASONS FOR THE CONTINUED EXISTENCE OF WARTIME RAPE

Although written and customary prohibitions of rape exist, they have not captured the true nature of this crime. Rather than identifying rape as a crime of violence, the prohibitions of rape classified it as an offense against women's honor. Defining rape in this way is problematic because it inextricably links a woman's dignity to her sexuality. This contrasts with other serious crimes like murder and torture, which are understood as violations of an individual's fundamental right to bodily integrity and security. Defining rape as a crime against honor means that "nowhere are the discriminatory and violent nature of the offence recognized" (Brunet & Rousseau, 1998; Erb, 1998). These definitions in international humanitarian law mischaracterize and obscure the crime of rape. Rape is more than merely a crime against a woman's honor, and it deserves the same condemnation and punishment as those war crimes that more commonly happen to men (Copelon, 1995). Unfortunately, because of the definition given rape in international humanitarian law, rape was placed on an unequal footing with other serious violations that occurred during war and armed conflict.

This insufficient definition of rape developed largely because of the absence of women's rights and perspectives within the framework of international human rights and humanitarian law. Feminists have decried international law as male dominated and reflective of a male point of view. One explanation for women's absence is that women's issues are seen as "private," whereas the "public" sphere "is regarded as the province of international law" (Charlesworth, Chinkin, & Wright, 1991, p. 625). Indeed, in international law, rape is often considered a private act by individual men, in contrast to the state violations of human rights, which are recognized and addressed at the international level (MacKinnon, 1993, 1994a).

Because sexual violations against women were not afforded equal status, they similarly received unequal punishment. For example, the 1907 Hague Convention Respecting the Laws and Customs of War on Land does not list rape as a violation but rather provides general protection for family honor and rights.[10] This provision has rarely been interpreted to cover rape (Meron, 1998). In addition, although evidence of rape and sexual assaults was presented to the Nuremberg Tribunal after World War II, defendants were never charged with rape as a war crime (Askin, 1997). In fact, neither the Nuremberg Charter nor the Tokyo Tribunal Charter enumerated rape as a crime against humanity (Meron, 1998; Askin, 1997). Likewise, the Fourth Geneva Convention (Article 147), despite establishing an unequivocal prohibition of rape, does not explicitly include acts of sexual assault within its provision on grave breaches, which are subject to universal jurisdiction (Meron, 1998). This failure to prioritize the punishment of wartime rapists created implied rules of war that permit, encourage, and condone sexual violence against women.

The willingness by states to tolerate sexual violence against women despite explicit prohibitions in international humanitarian law provides soldiers with a "license to rape because of their military association" (United Nations, (1993). They are shielded from prosecution and provided with impunity because rape has proven to be a valuable war strategy. Rape is used in war as a means of vengeance,[11] a tool of propaganda,[12] a way to signify power to the opposing side,[13] a reward for weary troops and a way to build morale,[14] and, increasingly, a strategic tool of ethnic cleansing or genocide.[15] Rape is an effective way to subjugate and terrorize a population and is a means of communication from conquering men to the conquered (Brownmiller, 1975; Mann, 1993). In this way, women as individuals are absent from the equation; their bodies are merely used to pass on a message or are seen as spoils of war.

The international community has finally begun to recognize the true nature of the crime of rape, signaling its intention to end the practice of using rape as a weapon of war by punishing the crime equally with other war crimes. This change came about largely as a result of the alarming prevalence of sexual violence inflicted on women in the former Yugoslavia and in Rwanda.

RAPE AS A WEAPON OF WAR: FORMER YUGOSLAVIA

The first rapes in the conflict of the former Yugoslavia occurred in 1991. They were thought to be isolated incidents and were largely ignored and disbelieved by the international community at that time.[16] Repeated stories of mass rape continued to emerge in 1992 (Stiglmayer, 1994b; Gutman, 1992), at the same time that Serbian aggression against Bosnia and Herzegovina began in earnest, and eventually, the mass rapes began receiving the attention they deserved. Estimates of the number of Bosnian Muslim rape victims range from twenty thousand to fifty thousand.[17] Not only were women raped in their homes and villages, but large numbers of women were forced into "rape camps" where they were held and raped repeatedly by various men.[18]

There is substantial evidence of the widespread use of rape as an instrument of ethnic cleansing in the former Yugoslavia (United Nations, 1993). Women were raped by men who taunted them with ethnic slurs and stated their intention to forcibly impregnate them. Because lineage is passed from the father, forcibly impregnating Muslim women meant that they would bear Serbian children, thereby "ethnically cleansing" the former Yugoslavia. In the context of rape as ethnic cleansing, "rape has been used not only as an attack on the individual victim, but is intended to humiliate, shame, degrade and terrify the entire ethnic group" (United Nations, 1993, para. 85). In the former Yugoslavia, it was rape with a particular political purpose; Serbs raped women publicly in front of friends, family, and neighbors, in a pattern of intimidation and abuse focused on forcing the Croatian or Bosnian population to flee (Ray, 1997; Amnesty International, 1993). This sent a clear message from Serbs that they were conquering the Muslim population and were leaving raped women as constant reminders of Serb domination. In fact, there is evidence that soldiers were ordered to rape Muslim women and could be subjected to castration or death for refusing to do so (Gutman, 1992; Askin, 1997).

In addition, Muslim women were raped with knowledge of the cultural significance of rape. In patriarchal Muslim society, "when a man knows that a woman has been raped, he treats her badly. . . . People think she must have given the man occasion to rape her. Her life could be ruined by that."[19] This sent another message to the community, since women who were raped brought shame and dishonor to their husbands and families. The rapes in the former Yugoslavia represent an example of women being targeted because of their multiple identities: as women, as Muslims, and as members of an ethnic group that was not dominant. By using rape to "ethnically cleanse" the Croatian and Bosnian population, the Serbian forces chose an effective and successful means of inflicting a reign of terror. The effect was the denigration of an ethnic group and the ostracism of raped women.

RAPE AS A WEAPON OF WAR: RWANDA

In 1994, genocide began in Rwanda.[20] From April to July, between 500,000 and 1 million Rwandans were slaughtered in a catastrophic effort to eliminate the Tutsi minority and moderate Hutu sympathizers.[21] Throughout that period, members of the Hutu militia groups known as Interhamwe, other civilians, and soldiers of the Rwandan Armed Forces subjected women to brutal sexual violence, including mass rape (Human Rights Watch/Africa, 1996). While it is impossible to determine the exact number of women who were raped, it is evident from survivors' testimony that the rapes were widespread and systematic (Human Rights Watch/Africa, 1996; United Nations, 1998). One estimate numbers anywhere from 250,000 to 500,000 rapes, based on the numbers of recorded pregnancies resulting from rapes.[22] Doctors working in Rwanda have confirmed the existence of high numbers of rape survivors (Human Rights Watch/Africa, 1996). Other observers believe that almost every woman and adolescent girl who survived the genocide was raped (Human Rights Watch/Africa, 1996).

Mass rapes of Rwandan women were strategically used as a tool of genocide calculated to destroy the Tutsi population.[23] This strategy was fostered by hate propaganda directed at Tutsi women, which "exhorted Hutu to commit the genocide [and] specifically identified the sexuality of Tutsi women as a means through which the Tutsi community sought to infiltrate and control the Hutu community" (Human Rights Watch/Africa, 1996, p. 2). The propaganda therefore encouraged sexual violence against Tutsi women as a way to subjugate and destroy the Tutsi population. As with the rapes in the former Yugoslavia, the Rwandan women were targeted because of the intersection of their ethnicity and gender. They were individually raped, gang raped, and raped with objects. These brutal rapes often were inflicted on women after they had witnessed the torture and killing of their relatives or after having been forced to kill their own children. A Rwandan women's rights activist explained, "Rape was a strategy. They chose to rape. There were no mistakes. During this genocide, everything was organized" (Human Rights Watch/Africa, 1996, p. 41).

LACK OF NATIONAL PROTECTION: FORMER YUGOSLAVIA

Although women were subjected to systematic rape as a weapon of war during the conflict in the former Yugoslavia, they were unable to access police protection and redress for the crimes perpetrated against them. In fact, after investigating the reports of rapes, a United Nations team of experts said that they "heard of no attempts made by anyone in a position of authority to try and stop the raping of women and girls" (United Nations, 1993, para. 48c). Human Rights Watch also claims that "there is no evidence that the Yugoslav Army or the Serbian Ministry of Interior made any attempt to apprehend or punish those responsible for the attacks" (Human Rights Watch, 2000, p. 3). Some women reported the rapes to local authorities, who either dismissed the women,[24] detained them,[25] told the women that although they knew what was happening, they could do nothing about it (Amnesty International, 1993), or told them that there "wasn't any kind of power or law that could control [the rapists]."[26] In this way, "practically speaking it was legal to rape Muslim women" (Stiglmayer, 1994a, p. 110). Indeed, the failure to punish rapists appears to be as consistent and widespread as the acts of rape. The local authorities were not just ignoring the mass rapes; some of those in power actively participated in them.[27] In the former Yugoslavia, the effective use of rape as a weapon of war was furthered by a lack of national prosecution or protection and by general impunity for rapists.

LACK OF NATIONAL PROTECTION: RWANDA

Women raped in the Rwandan genocide also faced a lack of intervention by authorities and tacit acceptance of the practice of mass rape as a tool of war. Despite laws on the books prohibiting rape and providing for its prosecution under Rwandan criminal law,[28] combatants used rape as a weapon with impunity during the genocide. In fact, those who orchestrated the genocide deliberately created and permitted an environment of lawlessness, in which "the government and military authorities gave the militias full license to commit egregious human rights abuses, including rape, with impunity" (Human Rights Watch/Africa, 1996, p. 40). Indeed, stories from survivors who were brutally raped by the militia are numerous and well chronicled (Human Rights Watch/Africa, 1996). The military also encouraged or condoned rape and violence by militia groups and others. In some cases, the soldiers or national policemen not only aided in attacks against the civilian population, but also were responsible for committing rapes themselves (Human Rights Watch/Africa, 1996). As a consequence of the involvement of the entire state apparatus and the militia of the ruling party in the genocide (United Nations, 1996), including rapes, it follows that the women would have had very little success had they tried to seek justice within the national system against their attackers. In this way, as in the former Yugoslavia, the weapon of rape was effectively used as a tool in armed conflict.

EFFORTS TO PROHIBIT WARTIME RAPE

Partly in response to the reports of mass rape that came out of the former Yugoslavia, public opinion mobilized around the issue of ensuring justice for victims of rape and other forms of sexual violence. At around the same time, the International Committee of the Red Cross (ICRC) adopted a broad construction of the existing Geneva Convention that had neglected to include rape as a grave breach. The ICRC determined that the grave breach of "willfully causing great suffering or serious injury to body or health" could include rape (Meron, 1998).

Soon after the ICRC issued its interpretation, the U.S. Department of State confirmed its belief that under customary international law and the Geneva Conventions, rape was considered a war crime or grave breach and could be prosecuted accordingly. The letter referred to the situation in the former Yugoslavia, stating that "in our reports to the United Nations on human rights violations in the former Yugoslavia, we have reported sexual assaults as grave breaches. We will continue to do so and will continue to press the international community to respond to the terrible sexual atrocities in the former Yugoslavia" (Meron, 1998, p. 208). It was within this framework—moving forward to punish wartime rape and increase the gravity with which rape was treated within international humanitarian law—that the stage was set for the creation of the international criminal tribunals for the former Yugoslavia and Rwanda.

THE INTERNATIONAL CRIMINAL TRIBUNALS

The specific intent to prosecute sexual assault crimes under the proposed International Criminal Tribunal for the Former Yugoslavia (ICTY) was evidenced by the 1993 report of the secretary general, who repeatedly condemned the systematic use of rape and urged liability for those responsible (Sellers & Okuizumi, 1997). Based on that report and strong public opinion, in 1993, the United Nations Security Council established the ICTY. The ICTY has jurisdiction over grave breaches of the Geneva Conventions of 1949, violations of the laws or customs of war, genocide, and crimes against humanity. Rape is specifically enumerated under Article 5 as a crime against humanity. The nonexhaustive list of the violations of the laws and customs of war (Article 3) also could permit the direct prosecution of rape. Since rape is not explicitly referred to in the grave breaches provision (Article 2) or in the genocide provision (Article 4), it cannot be explicitly and directly alleged as a violation of those articles. The ICTY's prosecutor, however, determined that acts of sexual assault could be prosecuted implicitly under all four types of crimes within the tribunal's jurisdiction (Sellers & Okuizumi, 1997).

On November 8, 1994, the United Nations Security Council, in Resolution 955 (1994) and acting under Chapter VII of the United Nations Charter, established the International Criminal Tribunal for

Rwanda (ICTR). The ICTR's jurisdiction covers genocide, crimes against humanity, and, because of its internal nature, violations of Article 3 common to the Geneva Conventions and of Additional Protocol II. As in the ICTY statute, the ICTR statute includes rape as a crime against humanity. The ICTR statute goes one step further by incorporating Additional Protocol II's explicit prohibition of rape into Article 4 of the statute.

Rape as Evidence of a Campaign of Terror

Although the first trial held by either tribunal was expected to be the first international war crimes trial to prosecute rape separately as a war crime, the prosecutor was forced to drop rape charges from two counts because the witness was afraid to testify (Askin, 1999; Marshall, 1996). The ICTY's decision in *Prosecutor* v. *Tadic* (1997) nevertheless offered some "absolute gems" in terms of prosecuting rape during wartime (Viseur-Sellers, 1998, p. 1509). One of these is the fact that the tribunal accepted testimony about the sexual violence that occurred and "the enormous pain and suffering endured by the women and girls and the community at large" from medical workers who did not witness the sexual violence (Askin, 1999, p. 102). The tribunal allowed this testimony under a hearsay exception and went on, in its decision, to quote that testimony at length. In addition, the tribunal interpreted testimony of rape as evidence of discriminatory intent ((Viseur-Sellers, 1998) and found that, based largely on the testimony of a rape survivor, "a policy to terrorize the non-Serb population . . . on discriminatory grounds is evident and that its implementation was widespread and systematic" (*Prosecutor* v. *Tadic,* 1997, para. 472). Although the prosecutor did not prove that Tadic himself had committed rape, Tadic was still held liable for participating in a general campaign of terror, manifested by rape and other forms of violence. This decision signifies that anyone—including nonstate actors and low-level participants such as Tadic, who was a civilian traffic officer—can be convicted of aiding and abetting crimes of sexual violence through knowing participation in or tacit encouragement of such crimes (Askin, 1999).

Rape as Genocide and a Crime Against Humanity

The ICTR decision in *Prosecutor* v. *Akayesu* (1998) has been hailed as historic in its treatment of rape within an internal conflict (Askin, 1999; Coalition on Women's Human Rights in Conflict Situations, 1998). It marked the first time an international court punished sexual violence in a civil war and the first time rape was found to be an instrument of genocide. Unfortunately, the rape allegations almost were ignored entirely.

When Jean-Paul Akayesu was charged in 1996, the indictment contained twelve counts, none of which included rape (Coalition on Women's Human Rights in Conflict Situations, 1998). It was largely due to a concerted effort and heavy international pressure from women's rights groups that sexual violence charges were added to the indictment (Coalition on Women's Human Rights in Conflict Situations, 1998; United Nations, 1998; Rosenberg, 1998; *Prosecutor* v. *Akayesu*, 1998). The ICTR acknowledged this in the final judgment: "The Chamber takes note of the interest shown in this issue by non-governmental organizations, which it considers as indicative of public concern over the historical exclusion of rape and other forms of sexual violence from the investigation and prosecution of war crimes. The investigation and presentation of evidence relating to sexual violence is in the interest of justice" *Prosecutor* v. *Akayesu*, 1998, para. 731)

It is important to note that at the time of the trial, there was no internationally accepted definition of rape. When considering this fact, the ICTR clearly departed from restrictive definitions of rape that exist in national law. Instead, the chamber defined rape "as a physical invasion of a sexual nature, committed on a person under circumstances which are coercive." This is a broad definition of rape, unrestricted to one gender or to particular body parts. In fact, the chamber stated that "the central elements of the crime of rape cannot be captured in a mechanical description of objects and body parts" (*Prosecutor* v. *Akayesu*, 1998, para. 597, 598). The chamber also found that force need not apply. Rather, coercive elements could include threats and intimidation.

In addition to providing a broad definition of rape, the ICTR indicated its understanding of the true nature of the crime. It moved away from the view formerly held in international humanitarian law that rape is a crime against honor. Instead, the ICTR looked to international definitions of torture. The ICTR declared that, like torture, "rape is used for such purposes as intimidation, degradation, humiliation, discrimination, punishment, control or destruction of a person. Like torture, rape is a violation of personal dignity" (*Prosecutor* v. *Akayesu*, 1998, para. 597). By reconceptualizing rape, the ICTR placed rape on equal footing with other serious violations that occur during armed conflict. These groundbreaking steps—broadening the definition of rape and assigning it equal status—allowed the tribunal to recognize sexual violence as a form of genocide and a crime against humanity and to prosecute the crime accordingly.

In its decision, the ICTR recognized sexual violence as an essential component of the genocide and found Akayesu guilty of genocide for crimes that included sexual violence. Although gender is not one of the enumerated groups protected from genocide, the ICTR found that when rape was used as a method to destroy a protected group by causing serious bodily or mental harm to the members thereof, it constituted an act of genocide.[29] The ICTR found that in the Rwandan genocide, sexual violence was intimately linked to genocide and meant to destroy the spirit and will to live of its victim and the collective group. As the trial chamber declared in its judgment, "Sexual violence was an integral part of the process of destruction, specifically targeting Tutsi women and specifically contributing to their destruction and to the destruction of the Tutsi group as a whole" (*Prosecutor* v. *Akayesu,* 1998, para. 731). The chamber also recognized rape and other forms of sexual violence as independent crimes constituting crimes against humanity. It found that the rapes had been systematic and carried out on a massive scale and that Akayesu had witnessed, and even encouraged, rapes of Tutsi women while serving as communal leader.

Akayesu was sentenced to three life terms plus eighty years. For genocide, he received a life term for each of the three counts. For rape as a crime against humanity, he received a fifteen-year sentence. This sentence was equal to sentences received for counts of murder, signaling the ICTR's recognition of rape as a crime of equal status to murder.

Through its broad definition of rape, its reconceptualization of the crime, its jurisprudence regarding genocide and crimes against humanity, and its sentencing, the ICTR began creating a paradigm shift concerning the crime of rape in war and armed conflict. Fortunately, the ICTY recognized the importance of this shift and carried it further in later decisions.

Rape as Torture

In the case of *Prosecutor* v. *Delalic et al.,* commonly referred to as the *Celebici* case, Zejnik Delalic, Zdravko Mucic, Esad Landzo, and Hazim Delic were charged with grave breaches and violations of the laws or customs of war, including torture. Some of the offenses charged were multiple rapes, public rape, gang rape, vaginal and anal intercourse, rape during interrogation, and multiple instances of rape. The judgment was rendered, in a nearly five-hundred-page document, on November 16, 1998. In considering the charge of rape as torture, the ICTY adopted the broad definition of rape provided by the ICTR in the *Akayesu* case.

In addition to accepting the ICTR's broad definition of rape, the ICTY also agreed with the ICTR's new understanding of the crime of rape. The trial chamber stated in its decision that it "considers the rape of any person to be a despicable act which strikes at the very core of human dignity and physical integrity. . . . Rape causes severe pain and suffering, both physical and psychological" (*Prosecutor* v. *Delalic,* 1998, para. 495). This signified a further shift away from understanding rape as a crime against women's honor and instead recognized it as a violation of integrity and a crime of violence.

In this way, building on the ICTR's *Akayesu* case, the ICTY recognized rape as torture (Askin, 1999). The tribunal stated that "there can be no question that acts of rape may constitute torture under customary law" (*Prosecutor* v. *Delalic et al.,* 1998). It then went on to find Hazim Delic guilty of rape as torture as both a grave breach of the Fourth Geneva Convention and a violation of the laws and customs of war. In its judgment, the principle of command responsibility also evolved; the tribunal found Zdravko Mucic, the camp commander, responsible for crimes committed at the camp, including gender-based crimes.

Rape as a War Crime

The trial of Anto Furundzija, a local military commander, gave the ICTY a chance to play an important role in the movement toward establishing rape as a serious violation of international humanitarian law. Furundzija was charged with a rape committed by his subordinate against a Bosnian Muslim woman during a single day of the conflict, which Furundzija witnessed and failed to disrupt or curtail (*Prosecutor* v. *Anto Furundzija,* 1998; Askin, 1999).

The trial chamber, which delivered its decision on December 10, 1998, admitted that it was not possible to discern the elements of the crime of rape from international treaty or customary law, from general principles of international criminal law, or general principles of international law. It therefore concluded that it was necessary to look to major legal systems of the world in order to find common principles of criminal law. After surveying municipal rape laws, the trial chamber found what it deemed a trend of broadening the definition of rape to include other forms of sexual assault. Although it did broad-en the definition of rape to include forced oral penetration, the trial chamber nevertheless delineated a surprisingly narrow and specific list of what it found to be the requisite elements of the offense of rape under international criminal law.[30] Some have seen the trial chamber's elaboration of the elements of rape as a regression from the broad def-inition established by the ICTR in *Akayesu* (Askin, 1999)

Nevertheless, the trial chamber in *Furundzija* agreed with the ICTR that rape and other forms of sexual violence must be recognized for the serious violations they are. In its decision, the chamber stated, "The essence of the whole corpus of international humanitarian law as well as human rights law lies in the protection of the human dignity of every person, whatever his or her gender" (*Prosecutor* v. *Anto Furund-zija*, 1998, para. 183). The trial chamber also affirmed, "It is indisput-able that rape and other serious sexual assaults in armed conflict entail the criminal liability of the perpetrators" (para. 169). The ICTY there-fore acknowledged the true nature of the crime of rape and the ne-cessity of punishing perpetrators accordingly.

The trial chamber went on to find Furundzija guilty, under Article 3 of the ICTY statute, of violating the laws or customs of war for torture and for outrages upon personal dignity, including rape.[31] He was sen-tenced to ten and eight years' imprisonment, respectively, which he was to serve concurrently. Although this was not a perfect decision,[32] *Fu-rundzija* nevertheless served to move the treatment of wartime rape along its progressive trajectory by recognizing the violent nature of rape, recognizing a single incident of rape as a war crime, and further-ing the liability of those who aid and abet wartime rape.

Rape as the Sole Charge

The decision of the ICTY was hailed as a groundbreaking case. When the indictment was issued, an article on the front page of the *New York Times* asserted, "This is a landmark indictment because it focuses ex-clusively on sexual assaults, without including any other charges. . . . There is no precedent for this. It is of major legal significance because it illustrates the court's strategy to focus on gender-related crimes and give them their proper place in the prosecution of war crimes" (Simons, 1996, p. 1).

Indeed, this case represents the first time that an international tri-bunal brought charges solely for crimes of sexual violence against women. The indictment charged all of the accused with various counts of violations of the laws and customs of war and crimes against humanity, and charged Dragoljub Kunarac and Zoran Vukovic with grave breaches, all stemming from crimes of sexual violence.[33]

In its decision, rendered on February 22, 2001, the ICTY took the opportunity to clarify the definition of rape in international law. It decided that part of the definition stated in the *Furundzija* decision was "more narrowly stated than is required by international law," in that it did not refer to factors other than coercion, force, or threat of force, "which would render an action of sexual penetration *non-consensual or non-voluntary* on the part of the victim." In order to develop a more appropriate definition of the crime in international law, the trial chamber determined that it must look to certain basic principles among the national legal systems. The trial chamber went on to say that the "true common denominator which unifies the various [national legal] systems may be a wider or more basic principle of penalising violations of sexual *autonomy*" (*Prosecutor* v. *Kunarac, Kovac, and Vukovic,* para. 438, 440).

The trial chamber then surveyed national legislation regarding three factors—force or threat of force; specific circumstances, which go to the vulnerability or deception of the victim; and absence of consent or voluntary participation—to make clear its point about autonomy. The trial chamber determined that these factors indicate that in international law, "serious violations of sexual *autonomy* are to be penalised" (*Prosecutor* v. *Kunarac, Kovac, and Vukovic,* para. 457). The judgment then offered a slightly broader definition of rape than in *Furundzija*.[34] This broader definition allowed for the rejection of Kunarac's claim that because one of the victims, D.B., took an active part in taking off his trousers and kissing him before having vaginal intercourse with him, she consented to sexual intercourse with him. Instead, the trial chamber found that D.B. did not in fact freely consent to any sexual intercourse with Kunarac, given the context of the surrounding circumstances, and that Kunarac had full knowledge that she did not freely consent. In so deciding, the court made clear that sexual autonomy is intrinsically connected to human dignity and bodily integrity (Boon, 2001), furthering the paradigm shift in international humanitarian law.

In addition, this was the first time the ICTY found rape and sexual enslavement to be crimes against humanity. The trial chamber was satisfied that rape met the elements of a crime against humanity: it was a widespread and systematic attack directed against any civilian population during an armed conflict. Notably, the trial chamber stated that no nexus between the acts of the accused and the armed conflict was required: the "armed conflict requirement is satisfied by proof that there was an armed conflict at the relevant time and place" (*Prosecutor* v. *Kunarac, Kovac, and Vukovic,* para. 413). There was found to be an armed conflict and the underlying crimes were related to the armed conflict. In considering the charge of rape under the provisions governing violations of the laws or customs of war, the trial chamber was satisfied that rape met the requirements for the application of Common Article 3 of the Geneva Conventions, including that it is a serious offense.

In its decision, the trial chamber convicted Kunarac, Radomir Kovac, and Vukovic of various counts of crimes against humanity and violations of the laws or customs of war for rape, torture, or enslavement and sentenced them to twenty-eight, twenty, and twelve years' imprisonment, respectively. According to prosecutor Peggy Kuo, the prosecution was "pleased with the court's decision because the sentences show that the court took the crimes very seriously" (Simons, 2001a, p. 1). The founder of a support group for women who have suffered trauma in war also praised the convictions: "I'm so glad, we've been waiting so long for such clear language and convictions" (Simons, 2001b, p. A1).

EFFECT OF THE TRIBUNALS' DECISIONS

These decisions from the ICTY and ICTR recognize the nature of sexual violence in armed conflict and signal that these crimes deserve unrelenting investigation and prosecution.

Giving Rape Equal Status and Equal Punishment

One important component of these decisions is the international definition of rape, which, due to the *Foca* decision, now links rape to a violation of women's autonomy. In this way, the international community has acknowledged finally that rape should not be seen as a violation of a woman's honor and thereby inextricably linked to her sexuality. Instead, the definition is cast from the victim's perspective, with rape as a violation of bodily integrity. This represents a major legal development as well, since prior to these cases, there was no standard definition of rape in international law. The definitions developed by the ICTY and the ICTR will have a normative effect, informing other tribunals grappling with crimes of sexual violence during war and armed conflict. The *Foca* decision, which explicitly condemned rape and sexual violence and established, in clear and compelling language, that rape can constitute a war crime, genocide, and crime against humanity, will lead the way.

Aside from the definition of rape, the tribunals' decisions also are remarkable for moving away from the idea of women as property to be taken as spoils of war. These decisions represent a paradigm shift in international humanitarian law. They indicate the international community's willingness to consider sexual violence where it belongs, on a par with other serious violations of individuals' rights. The elevation of rape and other sexual violence to the level of other war crimes means that there should be no further uncertainty about how to handle evidence of rape during war and armed conflict. Rape is not to be ignored or tolerated as a tool of war. Rather, its thorough investigation and prosecution should occur with the same frequency as other serious crimes committed during war.

This progress regarding the treatment of wartime rape is seen clearly in Sierra Leone, which currently is attempting to grapple with crimes committed during its decade-long conflict, which has been marked by an extraordinary level of brutal human rights abuses, including widespread sexual assault of women. Physicians for Human Rights (2002) estimates that approximately fifty thousand to sixty thousand internally displaced Sierra Leonean women may have suffered war-related sexual assaults. The Special Court for Sierra Leone, which was set up jointly by the United Nations and Sierra Leone, began its work in June 2002. The statute of the special court explicitly includes gender-based violence in its definition of several categories of crimes that the court has power to prosecute. Rape, sexual slavery, enforced prostitution, forced pregnancy, and any other form of sexual violence are listed in the article delineating crimes against humanity (Special Court for Sierra Leone, 2000). The court also expressly includes rape, enforced prostitution, and any other form of indecent assault as violations of humanitarian law as enshrined in Common Article 3 and Additional Protocol II. The court has shown its willingness to treat rape and other forms of sexual violence as deserving of investigation and prosecution alongside other serious violations of humanitarian law. By the end of 2003, crimes of sexual violence were included in ten of the thirteen indictments issued. The court also has two full-time gender crimes investigators and has conducted gender sensitivity training for all of its investigators (Jefferson, 2004).

Incorporating Women's Rights into International Humanitarian Law

Through the tribunals' decisions, the international community has become aware of gender-based atrocities in situations of war and armed conflict. This has helped not only to bring women's issues to the forefront but also to make women's voices audible. Indeed, the "opportunity to present rape in an international forum with the attendant media and world scrutiny offers women an unprecedented opportunity to try to tell the story of wartime rape from women's point of view" (Tompkins, 1995, p. 851). Once people listen to accounts of rape and the harm that accompanies such violations, they are more likely to understand the violation and seek to end the impunity that has served men so well in wars for centuries. One journalist eloquently described the impact of the *Foca* decision as "justice being done, but justice being played in a new, female key; painted in new, female colours that depicted rape as a tool of war and crime against humanity" (Vulliamy, 2001, p. 27). Women have largely been absent from international law. The tribunals' decisions indicate a change in the opposite direction. It was women's groups that encouraged rape to be pursued in the tribunals to the extent documented in this chapter.[35] Women's voices and concerns are now beginning to be heard and taken seriously in the international arena.

Indeed, this integration of women's rights into the international arena is seen clearly in the ICC. The statute of the ICC incorporates a gender-based perspective to ensure not only that women who are victims of crimes during war and armed conflict receive justice, but also that women play an active role in the court itself. The ICC statute explicitly recognizes rape and other forms of sexual violence as a crime against humanity and a war crime.[36] It also clarifies the definition of rape as a war crime and a crime against humanity, providing definitions both broad enough to recognize other forms of sexual assault and coercive circumstances and specific enough to ensure that future perpetrators have advance notice. The ICC statute further incorporates a gender-based perspective by requiring that the prosecutor and registrar, when hiring staff, take into account the need for fair representation of men and women, and that they appoint advisers with legal expertise on sexual and gender violence (Article 44[2]). It demands the same of states when electing judges (Articles 36[8a, 8b]). Out of the first eighteen judges elected to the court in 2003, seven are women. In this way, the international community has demonstrated its intention to clarify the crime of rape within international humanitarian law, place rape on an equal footing with other serious crimes, end impunity for perpetrators of wartime rape, and ensure gender equality and sensitivity within the ICC itself.

Further Challenges

Although the tribunals' decisions undoubtedly have led to an increased awareness of women's rights in international humanitarian law, it is important to examine how the decisions translate into the lives of women survivors of wartime rape.

ENSURING THE SAFETY OF VICTIMS AND WITNESSES. One of the most immediate issues is the safety of survivors. In Rwanda, for example, there have been consistent and increasing attacks on genocide survivors who might serve as witnesses at trial ("'Survivors' Tell of Rwanda Revenge Killings," 1994; "Hutus May Be Targeting Witnesses," 1994; "Family of Six Assassinated," 1997; "Extremists Said Killing Witnesses to Genocide," 1997). Part of the problem is that many perpetrators are still free. The tribunals cannot hold hearings in absentia and have no power to force other states to turn over their citizens for trial (Atlas, 1994). Rather, the primary responsibility for seeking out and arresting war criminals rests with the national states (Schiller, 1996). Unfortunately, states have not been forthcoming in the arrest of their national criminals, so perpetrators remain at large, mixing with the citizen population that may include their prior victims. In the *Foca* case, for instance, of the eight men originally indicted, three were still at large when the decision came down (Human Rights Watch, 2001). In fact, shortly after the indictment was issued and had been hailed for its progressive view on punishing wartime rape, a journalist reported that the victims in the case "have little cause to celebrate the legal gain. If they returned to their hometown of Foca, they could not go to a grocery [store] or enter a café without the risk of bumping into the men they have accused of repeatedly raping them" (Ricchiardi, 1998). In Rwanda, one victim "moves from place to place, frightened of meeting some of the other perpetrators who are still wandering around freely" while at the same time being "threatened and perse-cuted" by the family of one person she testified against (United Na-tions, 1998). As long as those who are indicted remain at large, the women live in fear, and impunity for rapists remains.

Witnesses also fear reprisal because of their testimony. Unfortu-nately, the tribunals offer protection to witnesses only during their in-volvement at the tribunal. If someone is intent on retribution, the small period of protection might prove insufficient. For example, some Rwandan rape survivors told the UN special rapporteur on violence against women during her visit that they were afraid to travel to the ICTR to testify because they did not believe they would be adequately protected (United Nations, 1998). Witnesses in Rwanda voiced con-cern to the special rapporteur that the danger was not actually in Arusha, Tanzania, where the ICTR sits, but in Rwanda, where the wit-nesses returned after testifying. Because Arusha is remote from Rwanda, most feel that it is not possible for the ICTR to effectively protect wit-nesses on their return (United Nations, 1998). This has proven true; in 1997, a Hutu woman who had testified before the ICTR against Jean-Paul Akayesu was killed along with her husband, four of their own chil-dren, and three other children who were in the house at the time of the attack (Walsh, 2000; Softline Info., 1997; Woodruff, 1997).

This problem is no different at the ICTY, which sits in The Hague, a considerable distance from the atrocities in the former Yugoslavia. Witnesses travel to and from the ICTY without protection; the pro-tection offered by the ICTY begins only once the witnesses arrive in The Hague.[37] Before arriving in The Hague or after leaving, a witness is dependent on the country of residence for protection. The ICTY, however, does not have reliable lines of communication with local po-lice in other countries. In addition, it has no legal enforcement au-thority within territories of other states and no practical means of implementing any measures of safety for victims and witnesses even if it wanted to do so.

Furthermore, the protection offered to witnesses at the tribunals is lacking in many respects. The special rapporteur found that "despite the enormous threat to women victims of violence and women witnesses, the ICTR has not really developed procedures concerning witness incog-nito" within the courtroom (United Nations, 1998). There have been similar problems with the ICTY. In fact, in the *Tadic* case (*Prosecutor* v. *Tadic*, 1995), there was a decision on the prosecutor's motion request-ing protective measures for victims and witnesses, which dealt with the issue of witness protection by means of confidentiality or anonymity. One witness eventually had to withdraw from the case because of threats made against her and her family, causing the prosecutors to drop rape charges against the accused (Askin, 1999; Marshall, 1996). Another problem is the leaking of identities of witnesses despite nondisclosure orders.[38] In one case, information was leaked to the public; in another, the list of prosecution witnesses, including protected witnesses, was published in a newspaper alongside an interview with one of the accused. In neither case was the defense penalized (Murphy, 1999). It was not until April 2003 that the ICTY finally took action against someone for revealing the identity of a secret witness.[39] Fortunately, the statute and rules of the ICC attempt to address many of the problems that witnesses at the two ad hoc tribunals face (see Articles 42, 43, 54[1][b], 57, 64, 68, 87[4]). As the ICC begins its work, the international community needs to guarantee the protections and services provided for in these articles and rules.

PROVIDING SERVICES TO SURVIVORS OF SEXUAL VIOLENCE. Another difficulty facing women survivors of wartime rape is the lack of counseling and medical services available to them. An abstract verdict in an international tribunal concerning rape as a crime against humanity may not mean much for a woman who is trying to resume life after enduring rape. Women survivors of sexual violence need access to medical services, which can include screening for sexually transmitted diseases (STDs), access to abortion, and obstetrical and gynecological services. Unfortunately, these services are not readily available in countries trying to recover from the devastation of war or internal conflict. In Rwanda, for instance, despite large numbers of rape survivors and the massive injuries to reproductive organs that many of them endured, there were only five gynecologists in the country in 1998 (United Nations, 1998). Similarly, in the former Yugoslavia, "women are not being provided with the necessary gynaecological and STD screening that should be part of their overall care following rape" (United Nations, 1993, para. 36). Many victims of rape and other forms of sexual violence were infected with HIV and need access to HIV/AIDS testing, counseling, and treatment.

In addition to medical traumas, victims sustain psychological traumas, which may be ignored or hidden as a result of the stigma attached to rape and the prioritizing of other war injuries. Survivors of sexual violence need access to mental health services in order to address the trauma to which they have been subjected. Unfortunately, because of the shame and disgrace associated with rape, especially in Rwandan and Muslim cultures, women may be reluctant to seek help (United Nations, 1993, 1998). Those living with HIV face increased ostracism and alienation. Accessible, affordable psychological services and programs are critical for the healthy resumption of victims' lives.

Because of the stigma attending sexual violence, many victims will find themselves in need of basic necessities, such as shelter and food. In the Balkans, "most of the rape victims have been cast out of their homes and left to fend for themselves . . . in battle zones without food, warm clothing or shelter" (Williams, 1992, p. A1). Humanitarian assistance in the form of economic assistance is necessary. Shelters, job training skills, and other forms of economic opportunities can help these women ensure their continued livelihood and assist their reintegration into society.

CONTINUED LACK OF POLITICAL WILL TO END IMPUNITY FOR WARTIME RAPE. The prohibitions against rape are now firmly developed in international humanitarian law, and jurisprudence around these issues has developed from the decisions of the ICTY and the ICTR. Statutes and jurisprudence condemning wartime rape and sexual violence will be effective, however, only if those in power use them in the future to prosecute perpetrators, thereby ending impunity. Unfortunately, the political will to proceed with prosecutions of wartime rapists is lacking. Instead, combatants in conflicts around the world continue to effectively use rape as a weapon of war. In Liberia, for example, "more than 14 years of fighting . . . has made rape as common as looting or gunshot wounds" (Wax, 2003a, p. A16). There is no punishment for perpetrators. Similarly, in the eastern Congo, rapes have been widespread, systematic, and brutal. Some aid groups estimate that one in every three women is a victim (Wax, 2003b). Unfortunately, as in the former Yugoslavia and Rwanda, in the Congo, rape was turned "into a primary weapon of war. . . . Rape has even been encouraged by commanders as a way to gain control of such scarce resources as food, water and firewood, intimidating the women on a continent where women do nearly all the labor in the fields. . . . With Congo lacking a functioning court system, no one has been punished" (Wax 2003b, p. A17). This underscores the fact that international courts cannot exist in a vacuum; they must be complemented by strong national systems. The international community must ensure that national institutions receive the proper instruction in prosecuting rape as a violation of international humanitarian law, and receive gender-sensitivity training in order to allow them to do so in a way that respects the rights of survivors.

The lack of political will to prosecute rape is not only a domestic problem. It has plagued the ad hoc tribunals themselves. Since the initial effort to investigate and prosecute sexual violence in the former Yugoslavia and Rwanda, the commitment of the tribunals to end impunity for wartime rapists has waned. According to Human Rights Watch, the tribunals do not have an effective long-term prosecution strategy that acknowledges the degree of wartime sexual violence suffered by women (Jefferson, 2004). At the ICTR, for example, only one conviction involving sexual assault—that of Jean-Paul Akayesu—has survived appeal.

CONCLUSION

While the tribunals' indictments and decisions have begun to shape the future prosecution of gender-based violence by affording rape equal status and providing equal punishment, the tribunals cannot cease to continue prosecuting such crimes. Instead, all courts prosecuting crimes committed during war and armed conflict—including the ICTR and ICTY, other ad hoc tribunals, the ICC, and national courts—must continue to ensure that the protections that have developed against rape are real and effective, rather than theoretical and illusory, for women victims. These courts must prioritize the prosecution of rape and redress its commission, thereby ending impunity for wartime rapists. If this occurs alongside an effort to create gender equity in international and national institutions, the practice of rape during war and armed conflict may cease altogether.

Notes

1. These are the Convention for the Amelioration of the Condition of the Wounded and Sick in Armed Forces in the Field, including Annex 1, August 12, 1949, 6 U.S.T. 3114, 75 U.N.T.S. 31; Convention for the Amelioration of the Condition of the Wounded, Sick, and Shipwrecked Members of Armed Forces at Sea, August 12, 1949, 6 U.S.T. 3217, 75 U.N.T.S. 85; Convention Relative to the Treatment of Prisoners of War, including Annexes I–V, August 12, 1949, 6 U.S.T. 3316, 75 U.N.T.S. 135; Convention Relative to the

Protection of Civilian Persons in Time of War, August 12, 1949, 6 U.S.T. 3516, 75 U.N.T.S. 287 (hereafter referred to as the Fourth Geneva Convention).

2. These are the Protocol Additional to the Geneva Conventions of 12 August 1949 and Relating to the Protection of Victims of International Armed Conflicts, June 8 1977, 1125 U.N.T.S. 3 (hereafter referred to as the Additional Protocol I); Protocol Additional to the Geneva Conventions of 12 August 1949, and Relating to the Protection of Victims of Non-International Armed Conflicts, June 8, 1977, 1125 U.N.T.S. 609 (hereafter referred to as the Additional Protocol II).

3. This is the Charter of the International Military Tribunal, Agreement for the Prosecution and Punishment of the Major War Criminals of the European Axis, August 8, 1945, 82 U.N.T.S. 280–311 No. 251, art. 6(c).

4. One important gray area is whether to classify conflicts as internal or international. This classification determines which provisions of international humanitarian law apply. For example, if a conflict is internal, then the grave breaches provisions of the Geneva Conventions do not apply. See Allison and Goldman (1999).

5. See the International Criminal Court home page, at http://www.icc-cpi. int/php/show.php?id=home.

6. See Rome Statute of the International Criminal Court, U.N. Diplomatic Conference of Plenipotentiaries on the Establishment of an International Criminal Court, U.N. Doc. A/Conf.183/9 (1998), reprinted in 37 I.L.M. 999 (1998) (hereafter referred to as the ICC Statute).

7. These detail the 1639 Lawes and Ordinances of Warre, for the Better Government of his Majesties Army Royall, in the Present Expedition for the Northern Parts, and Safety of the Kindome, under the Conduct of . . . Thomas Earl of Arundel and Surrey; the 1640 Lawes and Ordinances of Warre Established for the Better Conduct of the Service in the Northern Parts issued by the Earl of Northumberland; and the 1643 Articles and Ordinances of War for the Present Expedition of the Army of the Kingdom of Scotland, by the Committee of the Estates [and] the Lord General of the Army).

8. "Women shall be especially protected against any attack on their honour, in particular against rape, enforced prostitution, or any form of indecent assault." Fourth Geneva Convention, Article 27.

9. Additional Protocol I, Article 76: "Women shall be the object of special respect and shall be protected in particular against rape, forced prostitution and any other form of indecent assault." Additional Protocol II, Article 2(e): prohibiting "outrages upon personal dignity, in particular humiliating and

degrading treatment, rape, enforced prostitution and any form of indecent assault."

10. The Convention Respecting the Laws and Customs of War on Land and Annexed Regulations, October 18, 1907, 36 Stat. 2277, Article XLVI, states that "family honor and rights, the lives of persons . . . must be respected."

11. Brownmiller (1975) writes, "Rape was a weapon of revenge as the Russian Army marched through Berlin in World War II" (p. 32). See also Tompkins (1995).

12. Brownmiller (1975) describes the use of rape as propaganda in World War I. MacKinnon (1994b) describes Serbian propaganda of actual rapes of Muslim and Croatian women by Serbian soldiers that were made to look like Serbian women being raped by Muslim or Croatian men and were then broadcast over the news.

13. Brownmiller (1975) writes, "Rape was a weapon of terror as the German Hun marched through Belgium in World War I" (p. 32), and "A simple rule of thumb in war is that the winning side is the side that does the raping" (p. 35).

14. Nietzsche instructed that "men should be trained for war and woman for the recreation of the warrior" (Brownmiller, 1975, p. 48). MacKinnon (1994b, p. 75) writes, "In a war crimes trial in Sarajevo in March 1993, Borislav Herak, a Serbian soldier, testified that the rapes he committed had been ordered for 'Serbian morale.'" Stiglmayer (1994a) provides a transcript of an interview with Borislav Herak.

15. See Tompkins (1995). MacKinnon (1994a) states that the Nazis required Eastern European women to get special permission for abortions if impregnated by German men. Stiglmayer (1994a) relates the story of a rape survivor who was told by the Serbians who raped her and other women that "if you could have Utasha babies, then you can have a Chetnik baby, too." The survivor also reports that those women who got pregnant were forced to stay in the "rape camp" for seven or eight months "so that they could give birth to a Serbian kid" (p. 119). See generally Human Rights Watch/Africa, Human Rights Watch Women's Rights Project, and Fédération Internationale des Ligues des Droits de l'Homme (1996), describing the rapes in Rwanda as a tool of genocide.

16. See Stiglmayer (1994a). Mann (1993) explains that Catharine MacKinnon, eventually retained to represent Muslim and Croatian victims of sexual assaults by Serbian forces, "did not believe the reports of mass rapes when they first surfaced in mid-1991."

17. Stiglmayer (1994a) cites twenty thousand as the estimate by the European Community and fifty thousand as the Bosnian Ministry of the Interior's

estimate. See also Kohn (1994). Although there are cases of Serbian women being raped, the majority of the rape victims were Muslim women.

18. Stiglmayer (1994a) details rapes of women in "rape camps." See also MacKinnon (1994a).

19. Rodrigue (1993, p. A1), quoting Dr. Muhamet Sestic at Zenica's main hospital. Ray (1997) relates that after journalists visited a group of women in a refugee camp and recorded their stories of rape, seven of the women committed suicide, presumably due to the acute sense of shame attached to rape in Muslim culture.

20. For a description of the history of Rwanda and the events leading up to the 1994 genocide, see Prunier (1995). See also United Nations (1998), describing the two schools of thought as to the history of the conflict.

21. See Human Rights Watch/Africa (1996). United Nations (1998) states that 500,000 to 1 million people were killed, but giving the time period as April to December 1994.

22. Human Rights Watch/Africa (1996) cites United Nations (1996). Rosenberg (1998) cites a U.N. estimate of at least a quarter-million women raped in Rwanda.

23. Human Rights Watch/Africa (1996, p. 35) states that there was an overall pattern of sexual violence showing that acts of rape were "carried out with the aim of eradicating the Tutsi." Rapists mentioned their intent to destroy the Tutsi population and their use of sexual violence to help achieve that end.

24. Stiglmayer (1994a, pp. 124–125) relates the testimony of rape survivor Muniba's mother, who says that she went to the police station every day after her daughters were taken away and raped by Serbs but was told "there was nothing they could do about it."

25. Amnesty International (1993, p. 8) relates the story of G, who was raped by three Serbian men and reported the incident to the police in town. "After an initially sympathetic response she was accused of possessing arms and a radio receiver and detained for two days in a corn-store."

26. Stiglmayer (1994a) provides testimony of two rape survivors, Mirsada and Azra.

27. United Nations (1993, para. 48c) writes, "One example for this was given by a Muslim woman living in a Serb-occupied town. She reported being taken by an ethnic Serb policeman to a private home where she was presented" to a strong political figure in the region and raped. Rodrigue (1993) relates the story of Besima, who was raped every day, sometimes by the local police chief.

28. According to Human Rights Watch/Africa (1996, p. 36), "Rwandan law provides for the prosecution of rape under its criminal law. . . . Rape is a crime under Article 360 of the 1977 Rwandan Penal Code, and is punishable by five to ten years imprisonment."

29. The protected groups are national, ethnic, racial, or religious groups. Convention on the Prevention and Punishment of the Crime of Genocide, entered into force January 12, 1951.

30. The trial chamber defined rape (*Prosecutor* v. *Anto Furundzija*, 1998, para. 185) as:

    "(i) the sexual penetration, however slight:

      (a) of the vagina or anus of the victim by the penis of the perpetrator or any other object used by the perpetrator; or

     "(b) of the mouth of the victim by the penis of the perpetrator,

    "(ii) by coercion or force or threat of force against the victim or a third person."

31. Statement of the Trial Chamber at the Judgement Hearing, *Prosecutor* v. *Anto Furundzija* (December 10, 1998). Although Article 3 of the statute does not explicitly list rape as a war crime, the trial chamber determined that the article is an "umbrella article" and covers "any serious violation of a rule of customary international humanitarian law entailing, under international customary or conventional law, the individual criminal responsibility of the person breaching the rule." *Prosecutor* v. *Anto Furundzija*, Judgement, No. IT-95–17/1-T, para. 132–133 (December 10, 1998). The trial chamber found that Additional Protocol II's prohibition on outrages against personal dignity, including rape, was covered by the broad scope of Article 3. See note 9 and accompanying text.

32. The return to a narrower definition of rape and the fact that Furundzija was to serve the sentences concurrently makes this decision less than ideal with respect to prosecuting rape as a war crime.

33. The grave breach charges were subsequently dropped. The indictment was amended on July 13, 1998, to eliminate all charges of grave breaches, among other things. According to Askin (1999), this was "a reaction to the *Tadic* appeals chamber decision on jurisdiction in which the majority ruled that grave breaches apply only to international armed conflicts and only when committed against persons or property protected by Geneva Conventions" (p. 121).

34. "The sexual penetration, however slight: (a) of the vagina or anus of the victim by the penis of the perpetrator or any other object used by the perpetrator; or (b) of the mouth of the victim by the penis of the perpetrator;

where such sexual penetration occurs without the consent of the victim. Consent for this purpose must be consent given voluntarily, as a result of the victim's free will, assessed in the context of the surrounding circumstances. The *mens rea* is the intention to effect this sexual penetration, and the knowledge that it occurs without the consent of the victim" (*Prosecutor* v. *Kunarac, Kovac, and Vukovic*, February 22, 2001, para. 460).)

35. As Justice Richard Goldstone (2000) describes: "Soon after I arrived in The Hague, I was besieged by thousands of letters and petitions signed by people, mostly women, from many countries, urging me to give adequate attention to gender-related war crimes. They pointed to the many reports of systematic mass rape in Bosnia and to the glaring inadequacies of humanitarian law in dealing with that crime. I was grateful to those people and organizations, who made me more sensitive to the issue and more determined to do something about it. It led, among other things, to my appointing Patricia Sellers . . . as my special adviser on gender, both in our office and in relation to investigations and indictments. I believed that if we failed to deal appropriately with gender matters within the Office of the Prosecutor, we would be ill equipped to deal with them properly in our investigations and indictments" (p. 85).

36. ICC Statute, Article 7(1)(g), defines "crime against humanity" to include "rape, sexual slavery, enforced prostitution, forced pregnancy, enforced sterilization, or any other form of sexual violence of comparable gravity." Article 8(2)(b)(xxii) defines "war crime" to include "committing rape, sexual slavery, enforced prostitution, forced pregnancy, . . . enforced sterilization, or any other form of sexual violence also constituting a grave breach of the Geneva Conventions."

37. In rare circumstances when the court has determined that the witness is at extreme risk, the Dutch police or the police of the country of the victim's residence may travel with the witness. The expenses are paid by the country that provides the police escort.

38. Murphy (1999) describes leaks during the Blaskic and Celebici cases.

39. The ICTY indicted a newspaper editor from Montenegro who revealed the name of a secret witness in the trial of former Yugoslav president Slobodan Milosevic. The witness had been subjected to death threats since the identity was revealed. "It was the first time the International Criminal Tribunal for the Former Yugoslavia has taken action against someone for revealing the identity of a secret witness" ("Editor Indicted for Identifying Milosevic Witness," 2003, p. A13).

References

Allison, E., & Goldman, R. K. (1999). Gray areas in international humanitarian law. In R. Gutman & D. Rieff (Eds.), *Crimes of war: What the public should know.* New York: Norton.

Amnesty International. (1993, January). *Bosnia-Herzegovina: Rape and sexual abuse by armed forces.* London: Amnesty International.

Askin, K. D. (1997). *War crimes against women: Prosecution in international war crimes tribunals.* Boston: Brill Academic.

Askin, K. D. (1999). Developments in international criminal law: Sexual violence in decisions and indictments of the Yugoslav and Rwandan tribunals: Current status. *American Journal of International Law, 93,* 97–123.

Atlas, T. (1994, January 30). UN will pursue war crimes trials for Bosnia rapes war crimes. *Chicago Tribune,* p. 1.

Boon, K. (2003). Rape and forced pregnancy under the ICC statute: Human dignity, autonomy, and consent. *Columbia Human Rights Law Review, 32,* 625–675.

Brownmiller, S. (1975). *Against our will: Men, women and rape.* New York: Simon and Schuster.

Brunet, A., & Rousseau, S. (1998). Acknowledging violations, struggling against impunity: Women's rights, human rights. In I. L. Sajor (Ed.), *Common grounds: Violence against women in war and armed conflict situations.* Manila, Phil: ASCENT.

Charlesworth, H., Chinkin, C., & Wright, S. (1991). Feminist approaches to international law. *American Journal of International Law, 85,* 613–645.

Coalition on Women's Human Rights in Conflict Situations. (1998). *Rwanda: Akayesu sentencing a victory for women's rights.* www.essex.ac.uk/armedcon/story_id/000054.pdf.

Copelon, R. (1995). Women's rights as international human rights: Women and war crimes. *St. John's Law Review, 69,* 61–68.

Editor indicted for identifying Milosevic witness. (2003, April 9). *Washington Post,* p. A13.

Erb, N. E. (1998). Gender-based crimes under the draft statute for the Permanent International Criminal Court. *Columbia Human Rights Law Review, 29,* 401–435.

Extremists said killing witnesses to genocide in Rwanda. (1997, April 11). Deutsche Presse-Agentur.

Family of six assassinated in Rwanda. (1997, April 1). Deutsche Presse-Agentur.

Furusawa, K., & Inglis, J. (1998). Violence against women in East Timor under the Indonesian occupation. In I. L. Sajor (Ed.), *Common grounds: Violence against women in war and armed conflict situations.* Manila, Phil: ASCENT.

Goldstone, R. J. (2000). *For humanity: Reflections of a war crimes investigator.* New Haven: Yale University Press.

Gutman, R. (1992, August 23). Serbs' rape of Muslim women in Bosnia seen as tactic of war. *Houston Chronicle,* p. A1.

Habiba, S. U. (1998). Mass rape and violence in the 1971 armed conflict of Bangladesh: Justice and other issues. In I. L. Sajor (Ed.), *Common grounds: Violence against women in war and armed conflict situations.* Manila, Phil: ASCENT.

Human Rights Watch. (2000). *Kosovo: Rape as a weapon of "ethnic cleansing."* New York: Human Rights Watch.

Human Rights Watch. (2001, February 22). *Bosnia: Landmark verdicts for rape, torture, and sexual enslavement.* New York: Human Rights Watch.

Human Rights Watch/Africa, Human Rights Watch Women's Rights Project, & Fédération Internationale des Ligues des Droits de l'Homme (1996). *Shattered lives: Sexual violence during the Rwandan genocide and its aftermath.* New York: Human Rights Watch.

Hutus may be targeting witnesses of Rwandan genocide for death. (1994, December 12). *Chicago Tribune,* p. 4.

Jefferson, L. R. (2004). In war as in peace: Sexual violence and women's status. In *World Report 2004* (pp. 341–342). New York: Human Rights Watch.

Kohn, E. A. (1994). Rape as a weapon of war: Women's human rights during the dissolution of Yugoslavia. *Golden Gate University Law Review, 24,* 199–203.

Lieber, F. (1863). *Instructions for the government of armies of the United States in the field, Article 44.*

MacKinnon, C. (1993). Crimes of war, crimes of peace. *UCLA Women's Law Journal, 4,* 59–86.

MacKinnon, C, (1994a). Rape, genocide, and women's human rights. *Harvard Women's Law Journal, 17,* 5–17.

MacKinnon, C. (1994b). Turning rape into pornography: Postmodern genocide. In A. Stiglmayer (Ed.), *Mass rape: The war against women in Bosnia-Herzegovina.* Lincoln: University of Nebraska Press.

Mann, J. (1993, January 13). Rape and war crimes. *Washington Post.*

Marshall, T. (1996, May 8). International court opens Bosnia war crimes trial. *Los Angeles Times,* p. A1.

Meron, T. (1998). Medieval and Renaissance ordinances of war: Codifying discipline and humanity. In T. Meron (Ed.), *War crimes law comes of age.* New York: Oxford University Press.

Murphy, S. D. (1999). Progress and jurisprudence of the International Criminal Tribunal for the former Yugoslavia. *American Journal of International Law, 93,* 57–97.

Parker, G. (1994). Early modern Europe. In M. Howard, G. J. Andreopoulos, & M. R. Shulman (Eds.), *The laws of war: Constraints on warfare in the Western World.* New Haven, CT: Yale University Press.

Physicians for Human Rights. (2002). *War-related sexual violence in Sierra Leone.* Washington, DC: Physicians for Human Rights.

Prosecutor v. Akayesu, Judgment, No. ICTR-96–4-T (1998).

Prosecutor v. Anto Furundzija, No. IT-95-17/1-T (1998).

Prosecutor v. Delalic et. al. ("Celebici"), Statement of the Trial Chamber at the Judgement Hearing (Nov. 16, 1998). http://www.un.org/icty/pressreal/cel-sumj981116e.htm.

Prosecutor v. Delalic, Judgment, No. IT-96–21-T (1998).

Prosecutor v. Tadic, Opinion and Judgment, No. IT-94–1-T (1997).

Prunier, G. (1995). *The Rwandan crisis: History of a genocide.* New York: Columbia University Press.

Ray, A. E. (1997). The shame of it: Gender-based terrorism in the former Yugoslavia and the failure of international human rights law to comprehend the injuries. *American University Law Review, 46,* 793–840.

Ricchiardi, S. (1998, June 15). Women say NATO won't arrest rapists; war crimes suspects live openly in Bosnia, while troops pay no attention; problem "is lack of political will." *St. Louis Post-Dispatch,* p. A8.

Rodrigue, G. (1993, May 5). Politics of rape. *Dallas Morning News,* p. A1.

Rosenberg, T. (1998, April 5). New punishment for an ancient war crime. *New York Times,* 4:14.

Rothenberg, G. (1994). The age of Napoleon. In M. Howard, G. J. Andreopoulos, & M. R. Shulman (Eds.), *The laws of war: Constraints on warfare in the Western World.* New Haven, CT: Yale University Press.

Schiller, B. (1996, February 25). Judge: "No one beyond reach." *Toronto Star,* p. F6.

Sellers, P. V., & Okuizumi, K. (1997). Symposium. Prosecuting international crimes: An inside view. Intentional prosecution of sexual assaults. *Transnational Law and Contemporary Problems, 7,* 45–80.

Simons, M. (1996, June 28). U.N. court, for first time, defines rape as war crime. *New York Times*, p. A1.

Simons, M. (2001a, Feb. 23). Serbs guilty of wartime sex crimes, court rules. *International Herald Tribune*, p. 1.

Simons, M. (2001b, Feb. 23). Three Serbs convicted in wartime rapes. *New York Times*, pp. A1, A7.

Softline Info. (1997, February 4). Hutus begin new wave of terror in Rwanda: Killing of three Europeans renews world concern over plight of Rwanda. *Weekly Journal* [Montreal].

Special Court for Sierra Leone. (2000, August 14). *Statute of the Special Court for Sierra Leone.* http://www.sc-sl.org/.

Stiglmayer, A. (1994a). The rapes in Bosnia-Herzegovina. In A. Stiglmayer (Ed.), *Mass rape: The war against women in Bosnia-Herzegovina.* Lincoln: University of Nebraska Press.

Stiglmayer, A. (1994b). The war in the former Yugoslavia. In A. Stiglmayer (Ed.), *Mass rape: The war against women in Bosnia-Herzegovina.* Lincoln: University of Nebraska Press.

"Survivors" tell of Rwanda revenge killings. (1994, August 19). Press Association Newsfile.

Tanaka, Y. (1998). Rape and war: The Japanese experience. In I. L. Sajor (Ed.), *Common grounds: Violence against women in war and armed conflict situations.* Manila, Phil: ASCENT.

Tompkins, T. L. (1995). Prosecuting rape as a war crime: Speaking the unspeakable. *Notre Dame Law Review, 70,* 845–890.

United Nations. (1993). *Report on the situation of human rights in the territory of the former Yugoslavia submitted by Mr. Tadeusz Mazowiecki, special rapporteur of the Commission on Human Rights, Pursuant to Commission Resolution 1992/S-1/1 of 14 August 1992.* New York: United Nations.

United Nations. (1996). *Report on the situation of human rights in Rwanda submitted by Mr. René Degni-Segui, special rapporteur of the Commission on Human Rights, under paragraph 20 of the resolution S-3/1 of 25 May 1994.* New York: United Nations.

United Nations. (1998). *Report of the special rapporteur on violence against women, its causes and consequences, Ms. Radhika Coomaraswamy, addendum, report of the mission to Rwanda on the issues of violence against women in situations of armed conflict.* New York: United Nations.

Viseur-Sellers, P. (1998). Emerging jurisprudence on crimes of sexual violence. *American University International Law Review, 13,* 1509.

Vulliamy, E. (2001, March 4). The Observer profile: Carla del Ponte: Avenging angel. *Observer,* p. 27.

Walsh, C. (2000). *Witness protection, gender and the ICTR. International Centre for Human Rights and Democratic Development.* http://www.ichrdd.ca/111/english/commdoc/publications/womtrirw.html.

Wax, E. (2003a, August 29). Soldiers with dolls and blue hair gel: Rape and despair turn Liberian girls into armed fighters. *Washington Post,* p. A16.

Wax, E. (2003b, October 25). A brutal legacy of Congo war: Extent of violence against women surfaces as fighting recedes. *Washington Post,* pp. A1, A17.

Williams, C. J. (1992, November 30). Balkan war rape victims: Traumatized and ignored. *Los Angeles Times,* p. A1.

Woodruff, J. (1997, January 16). *Rwandan woman and her family murdered after testimony regarding the 1995 genocide.* CNN Worldview, Transcript 97011603V18.

CHAPTER FOURTEEN

Women and the Military

Catherine Toth

W omen in the military face many issues that are unique to the military environment and that are specifically gender related. Women in the military are in a traditionally male environment, which can be simultaneously a source of pride and a source of discouragement. Every advance that women make in the military is a significant achievement for the equality of all women. Equality between the genders depends on equality in all areas of life, including education, access to health care, and legal protection. This chapter is a discussion of the lack of equality in the military, both historically and today.

THE U.S. MILITARY

Regardless of the specific role any individual women have played in war, women were always present in and part of warfare. "Evidence of institutionalized warfare enters the record of the human past suddenly in about 4000 BC. . . . Slavery, subordination of women, and the organization of warriors into professional armies appeared simultaneously" (De Pauw, 1998, pp. 35–36). In the six thousand years since the institutionalization of warfare, the male-dominated military culture had been so deeply ingrained in history that it seems as though men are naturally warlike and protective, while women are naturally nurturing and in need of protection. Women who preferred to hold a position in the military that was not characterized as nurturing or supportive of the men were treated as abnormal, mentally impaired, or morally corrupt, while nurses were readily accepted into the ranks.

Civilian female nurses were employed during the American Revolution and the Civil War, but the criteria reflected the "social practices of the times rather than the rigors of wartime nursing. To serve as a nurse, a woman had to be over thirty, very plain looking, and wear plain brown or black dresses. No previous nursing experience was required. . . . The only criterion was a 'willingness to work'" (Holm, 1992, p. 8). When wartime ended, the women were not allowed to continue their work with the military. Men who were unable to take part in battles—too old, too young, or too disabled—replaced female nurses and took care of wounded soldiers until 1898, when the United States entered the Spanish-American War. The military recognized that there were not enough men to care for all of the casualties, and civilian female nurses were hired once again. It was expected that once the war was over, these women would go back to being housewives and would be glad to do so. However, the contribution of these hard-working and dedicated women convinced the decision makers that they needed nurses as a permanent part of the medical services branch of the military. Holm (1992) describes the sequence of events that militarized the nursing profession:

> In 1901, Congress established the Nurse Corps as an auxiliary of the Army. In this ambiguous quasi-military status, nurses still had no military rank, equal pay, or other benefits normal to military service such as retirement or veterans' benefits. Seven years later, on 12 May 1908, the Navy followed the Army's example. . . . The Marine Corps did not begin to recruit women until August 1918. . . . Although full military status would have to wait until 1944, the nurses were officially recognized as a necessary and permanent part of the Army and Navy [pp. 9, 12].

The era of industrialization created great demands for skilled workers. Women began to be hired in many fields previously closed to them, working as typists, factory workers, and telephone operators and doing clerical work. As men began preparing for World War I and began leaving the industrial labor force en masse, women were accepted as employees into the higher-paying, traditionally male areas such as in shipyards, steel mills, and aircraft plants (Holm, 1992). As office work became classified as "women's work," the military allowed many women to fill clerical and secretarial jobs in the military. The U.S. Navy began to recruit women in 1917 to work in clerical positions and as translators and radio operators in order to free up men for the front lines of the Great War (Worth, 1999). As America prepared to enter another world war in 1941, the military projected that even more men than in the previous war would be needed for combat. "And the need for men to fight in Europe and the Pacific was so great that more women served in the armed forces than ever before" (Worth, 1999, p. 21). Women were also injured in the armed forces more than ever before.

Congresswoman Edith Nourse Rogers became interested in lobbying for military status for women after "she became involved in legislation to obtain financial relief for women who had lost their health as a result of war service but who, because they had no military status, were not entitled to veterans' gratuities or care" (Holm, 1992, p. 22). The result was not exactly what Rogers had envisioned. Since the men opposed giving women full status in the military, a compromise was struck: a small auxiliary corps was established in 1941 where highly educated, technically qualified women would be used as unskilled labor. Not only did this compromise mean that women were held to higher standards than men for doing the same job, but, as Holm (1992) describes, tension between the sexes was also created because, from the men's perspective, the women were doing less of a job than the men while getting equal pay and benefits:

Men's attitudes were also determined by their desires or fears about going to sea or into combat. The recruiting themes for all the women's components were variations of "release a man for sea" or ". . . to fight." Early in the war, the military naively assumed that all able-bodied military men wanted to see action. In reality, many preferred the relative safety of stateside non-combat jobs and bitterly resented the idea of being replaced by a woman to go off to fight. Their resentment naturally focused upon those responsible—the military women [p. 51].

This well-intentioned compromise, which was meant to protect women from dangerous situations while making the military more efficient by freeing up men from clerical jobs to do the necessary fighting, may have set the stage for the sex discrimination and sexual harassment that military women still experience today. It makes sense that if men were given the same pay, benefits, and entitlements as the women while the men were also being told to risk life and limb for no other reason than their sex, the men would come to resent the women solely for their sex. Naturally, the men would use this difference between them—sex—as a way to discriminate against and harass these women who were taking their "safe" jobs in the United States and forcing the men into combat positions overseas.

Sexual Harassment in the Military

In the early years that women spent in the military, there was little to no legal protection from gender discrimination or sexual harassment. Title VII of the Civil Rights Act, which protects workers from discrimination based on sex, was not passed until 1964. Only as recently as 1986, in *Meritor Savings Bank* v. *Vinson,* did the Supreme Court make clear that sexual harassment is also a violation of Title VII. Even if there had been legal protection, the women probably would not have thought to use it and risk jeopardizing the opportunity to serve. Elizabeth McIntosh, a recruit of America's World War II intelligence agency, the Office of Strategic Services, noted that "most of the women in the early days . . . theorized that the intrigue and excitement were worth the occasional discrimination they encountered with the 'old boy net'" (McIntosh, 1998, p. 242).

There was more than occasional discrimination, as a comparison of statistics will reveal. A survey of female military veterans residing in New York by Rose (2002) has shown that 62 percent of the respondents reported experiencing repeated sexual harassment experiences during their military service years, and 81 percent of the veterans under the age of fifty-five reported exposure to military-related sexual harassment. The numbers of women in the military experiencing sexual harassment are much larger than their civilian counterparts. Research conducted by Fitzgerald and Shullman (1993) has shown that 50 percent of civilian women will experience sexual harassment at some point in their time at work. Culbertson and Rosenfeld (1994) surveyed approximately six thousand enlisted women in the navy and report that 6 percent experienced completed or attempted rape while on duty during a one-year survey period. According to Martindale (1991), in a study of over twenty thousand men and women serving in the U.S. military, 5 percent of women experienced either completed or attempted rape by a military coworker over a period of eighteen months.

Research in this area is especially important in terms of learning how to prevent sexual harassment and assault. Experience has shown that women who undergo this type of trauma experience more than hurt feelings and a hostile work environment. Skinner et al. (2000) conducted a survey of a nationally representative sample of women veterans on military sexual assault that revealed that 23 percent of the women reported being sexually assaulted while in the military. Their survey asked questions about health status, military experiences, use of health care services, current medical conditions, life events, and social support. The respondents who reported military sexual assault scored lower in health status than the respondents who reported no military sexual assault. Victims of sexual trauma, when compared to nonvictims, have been found to have significantly worse health (Martin, Rosen, Durand, Knudson, & Stretch, 2000; Koss, Koss, & Woodruff, 1991; Leserman, Drossman, Zhiming, Toomey, & Nachman Glogau, 1996; Frayne, Skinner, Sullivan, & Freund, 2003). A random sample of 3,632 women veterans surveyed by Frayne et al. (2003) discovered that obesity, smoking, problem alcohol use, sedentary lifestyle, and hysterectomy before age forty were found to be more common in women reporting a history of sexual assault while in the military than in women without such history.

It appears that the military's policy of "Don't ask, don't tell" applies to more than just homosexuality. Rose (2002) reports that only 10 percent of respondents recalled ever being screened for exposure to sexual harassment. Female veterans had to wait until 1992 for Congress to require the Department of Veterans Affairs to provide treatment to veterans traumatized by sexual assault experienced during active military duty (Suris, Davis, Kashner, Gillaspy, & Petty, 1998). These findings have serious implications for women's long-term health and suggest that clinicians should consider mandatory screenings for all women in the military for histories of sexual assault (Skinner et al., 2000).

Minimizing Sexual Harassment in the Military

In addition to screening women for exposure to sexual harassment, the screening of male recruits for indicators of the tendency to rape is imperative. Merrill, Thomsen, Gold, and Milner (2001) investigated the impact of childhood physical abuse and childhood sexual abuse on male naval recruits' likelihood of raping women. Results of the survey indicate that males who experienced childhood physical abuse or sexual assault are 200 percent more likely than nonvictims to rape women. Male recruits who experienced both physical and sexual abuse in their childhood were 400 to 600 percent more likely to rape women. Merrill et al. (2001) also found a relationship between alcohol problems, number of sexual partners, and men's propensity to rape women, which they had anticipated based on previous research of convicted rapists. Researchers have found that sex offenders are likely to report large numbers of sexual partners (Kanin, 1984, 1985) and to report earlier sexual experiences than non–sex offenders (Rubinstein, Yeager, Goodstein, & Lewis, 1993).

Convicted rapists are often intoxicated at the time of the assault and exhibit alcohol abuse or dependence. Alcohol may increase a man's arousal, anger, and aggression, and then these men use the intoxication as a rationalization for antisocial behavior. Men are also more likely to misinterpret a woman's intentions at a time when their inhibitions against violence, including sexual violence, are reduced (Hillbrand, Foster, & Hirt, 1990; Abbey, 1991; Crowell & Burgess, 1996; Johnson, Gibson, & Linden, 1978; Koss, Gidycz, & Wisniewski, 1987; Muehlenhard & Linton, 1987; George & Marlatt, 1986; Tedeschi & Felson, 1994; Koss & Gaines, 1993; Barbaree, Marshall, Yates, & Lightfoot, 1983; Kanin, 1984, 1985).

This is not to say that men in the military who drink alcohol are going to rape women; nevertheless, many sexual assaults in the military are found to be alcohol related. Unfortunately, military men have acquired a reputation for being "always one beer away from a sexual assault, no more able to control their violent impulses than an attack dog" (Quindlen, 2003). In reality, the discipline and structure of the military environment may help to curb the sexually violent impulses of the majority of male military recruits. More recently, sexual harassment and assault in the military have been highly publicized, and steps are being taken to minimize these incidents. The attitude of a particular organization within the military structure can have an impact on instances of sexual harassment in that organization. By making efforts to enforce policies and procedures related to sexual harassment, publicizing the services provided to harassment victims (counseling, offices for complaints, hotlines), and providing sexual harassment training to every member of the organization, the leadership can create an atmosphere that is less tolerant of sexual harassment than the military has been in the past (Hunter Williams, Fitzgerald, & Drasgow, 1999). With education, screening, and a zero-tolerance atmosphere, sexual harassment and assault can be minimized in the military, resulting in increased productivity and better work performance overall, as well as happier and healthier women.

THE U.S. MILITARY ACADEMIES

In the early years of women in the military, women were not allowed to serve in combat, so money was not allotted for training and preparing them for combat, which included educating women in the military academies. The promotion policies that were in place to promote officers from O-6 (colonels and naval captains) to O-7 (generals and naval admirals) favored officers who had combat experience: "Candidates . . . in non-combat fields were still expected to have a firm professional foundation in the business of war" (Mitchell, 1998, p. 12). The military academies provided such a foundation for academy cadets. While women were barred from performing combat service and sea duty, it did not make sense for the federal government to pay for educating women who would be prohibited by law from putting their knowledge to use.

Opening the Academies to Women

Several factors came together in the late 1960s and 1970s that resulted in the decision to open the academies to women. The Equal Pay Act of 1963 (Public Law 88–38) provided that employees would not receive different rates of pay based solely on sex. The passage of this act helped to pave the way for future measures both protecting and advancing women in the workforce. Title VII of the Civil Rights Act of 1964 (Public Law 88–352) prohibited employment discrimination based on race, color, religion, national origin, and sex. Unfortunately, this law did not include employment with the U.S. government, including the military, but it did stimulate the movement toward equality for the sexes in the military. As the trouble was heating up in Vietnam and more men were needed for combat, draft-age men began fleeing the country, enrolling in college, or avoiding the draft by other legal means. Possibly in an effort to "lighten the burden of the draft on the nation's men" (Mitchell, 1998, p. 15), President Johnson signed the Act of November 8, 1967 (Public Law 90–130), which opened promotions for women to O-6 (colonels and navy captains) and above, as well as removed the restrictive 2 percent cap on the number of women allowed to serve on active duty.

In 1971, the air force was the first branch of the military to change its recruiting rules to allow women with children to enlist. Title IX of the Education Amendment was passed in 1972, as well as the Equal Employment Opportunity Act. The Reserve Officers Training Corps opened to women in 1972, but graduates from the military academies had the first choice of jobs and assignments, still leaving women at a disadvantage. When the draft ended in 1973, the military became an all-volunteer force. Fewer men volunteering for duty put the pressure on the services to make the military a viable career choice for more women. The movement toward equality was strengthened when August 24, 1974, was declared National Women's Equality Day and all of 1975 as International Women's Year. Finally, in 1975, Public Law 94–106 was signed into law, admitting women into federally funded military academies with the provision that all of the standards for women would be the same as for men except for any necessary changes in the physical requirements.

Changing Attitudes

It would take more than laws to change the attitudes that initially barred women from the academies. The first class of female air force cadets entered the Air Force Academy in 1976 and had to pass by the slogan on the wall, "Bring me men." This slogan remained posted until early 2003, a full twenty-six years after women were first admitted to the school and thirty-one years after Title IX of the Education Amendment had been passed. In 1996, the first year that female cadets were allowed to enter South Carolina's state-run military academy, the Citadel (there were only four women that year), two of the female cadets were splashed with nail polish remover and set afire (D'Amico & Weinstein, 1999). On the day that the first females (thirty in all) were beginning their initiation at the Virginia Military Institute, thirty dead laboratory rats were found on the parade grounds along with a sign reading, "Save the Males" ("Dead Rats," 1997).

The initiation that underclassmen go through in all the academies is intended to reveal weaknesses and strengthen character in a relatively safe environment. To go into battle and discover that loud noises and people screaming at you cause one to forget important steps in loading a rifle, for example, could lead to physical injury and possibly death. It is better to discover these weaknesses in the academy in order to overcome them or make the decision to choose another career path. The extreme environment of the U.S. military academies might be called hazing in other colleges, but it is considered necessary when training leaders for war.

Upper-class cadets, known as first-years and second-years, are in charge of the incoming freshmen, known as fourth-years or doolies. When the first female cadets were admitted, there were only male cadets available to initiate them.

"Scandals at the academies cut close to the national quick, especially the abuse of America's best and brightest daughters by America's supposedly best and brightest sons" (Francke, 1997, p. 186). Several of the federal academies faced scandals in the early 1990s: a cheating scandal at West Point, a series of rapes reported in 1993 at the Air Force Academy, and drug dealing and handcuffing of female cadets scandals at Annapolis.

The army and navy themselves also faced very public sex scandals in their active duty populations as well. The Tailhook Convention in Las Vegas in 1991, where female officers were groped and forced to run a gauntlet through male officers, was a public and embarrassing scandal for the navy. When it was revealed in 1996 that a military training instructor was coercing female trainees in his care to have sex with him at Aberdeen Proving Grounds, the army took notice, implementing drastic changes in training programs and opening a telephone line specifically for reporting sexual harassment. These very public and very embarrassing scandals within the army and the navy prompted changes to an environment that had previously been tolerant of sexual harassment. The changes made enough of a successful impact that the Pentagon allowed the charter for a panel that addressed sexual assault throughout the military to expire in February 2002. Apparently the Defense Advisory Committee on Women in the Services was no longer needed in its full capacity because women had been fully integrated into the military. A new charter was issued reducing the number of committee members by over half.

Predictably, a major scandal began late in 2002 when the report came out regarding a thirteen-year-old girl being raped by a cadet at a sports camp held at the Air Force Academy. A female cadet then e-mailed senators and the news media in December 2002 regarding numerous counts of sexual harassment and rape being covered up at the academy. One of the Colorado senators, Wayne Allard, opened an investigation based on these two incidents, and approximately sixty other female cadets have since come forward with further allegations of sexual harassment and rape. Since the academy is federally funded, when problems arise, it must answer to Congress as well as the commander in chief of the military: the president of the United States. Because of the public nature of the scandal, as well as the public nature of congressional hearings and investigations, the air force made sure to publicize how and when changes would be made. The first change was the removal of the "Bring Me Men'" sign from the walls of the academy in March 2003.

The Military Academy Environment

The military academies are not like other colleges and universities. The environment is unique and should be examined prior to any discussion of where to place the blame for these unfortunate incidents. The military academies are among the most selective in the country, comparable to Ivy League schools. The acceptance rate of the U.S. Air Force Academy for the class of 2007 was 12 percent, with women making up 17 percent of the total class size ("Class of 2007 Profile," 2003a). The acceptance rate at West Point for the class of 2007 was 10 percent, with women making 14.6 percent of the total class size ("Class of 2007 Enters Academy," 2003). The Naval Academy accepted only 8.7 percent for an appointment, with women making 16.7 percent ("Class of 2007 Profile," 2003b). The acceptance rate of the class of 2007 at Yale University was 11 percent ("Class of 2007 Has Arrived," 2003) and at Harvard University just 9.8 percent ("Class of '07 Selected," 2003) with women making approximately 50 percent of the total class size at both schools.

Those who are admitted to the military academies are without doubt among the best and brightest students in the nation. Candidates are evaluated on their academic performance, demonstrated leadership potential, and physical fitness. Candidates must meet the medical qualification and age requirements, and they must not be married, pregnant, or have a legal obligation to support a child or children. Candidates must receive a nomination from the vice president, either U.S. senator from his or her state, or his or her U.S. representative. There can be as many as ten applicants for every one nomination available. It is recommended that potential applicants start preparing in junior high school for the academy. The proportion of men to women in the academy is similar to the proportion of men to women in the military, approximately four to one, with women comprising only 20 percent of the academies' students. This is unlike civilian colleges and universities, which more closely approximate the gender ratio of the general population, or roughly fifty-fifty.

Candidates who are selected must attend basic cadet training over the summer prior to the fall classes. Congressional funding pays for the education; the military pays for food, clothing, housing, and medical and dental care. Cadets receive a small monthly allowance that helps them to pay for hair cuts, dry cleaning, toiletries, and other necessities. Cadets who drop out within the first two years incur no financial obligation; leaving during the third or fourth years requires paying back the government a significant portion of the cost of attendance. Graduates are obligated to serve on active duty for at least five years and may apply for a deferment to attend graduate school.

Students who attend the military academies did not simply choose the school closest to their home. They are not attending the military academies because they want to attend "party" schools, and they are definitely not looking for an easy college education. Applicants who are chosen display the qualities needed for the long-term commitment required: a dedication to service, honor, integrity, and loyalty. Students who attend the academies are a highly motivated, self-sacrificing, driven group of people who are dedicated to the ideals of "service before self" and "excellence in all we do." As one graduate summed up his academy experience, "It is a hard place to be in, but a great place to be from" (personal communication, December 1994).

The first year at the academy is meant to test and strengthen these qualities in cadets. In order to be a good leader, it is believed that a person must first be a good follower, able to take orders without complaint. A first-class cadet could order a doolie to hand over a personal belonging, such as a watch, and the doolie must demonstrate unquestioning loyalty by handing it over, with no expectations of seeing that personal belonging again. The cadets must adhere to a myriad of rules and regulations that might seem ridiculous and overbearing to many seventeen-year-olds, but are a necessary part of the process of developing great leaders. Many seem harmless enough, such as a rule about not driving motor vehicles until after spring break of the junior year, even when home on leave. However, this is the most common honor code violation. Cadets who disregard this rule without recourse may become complacent toward other rules as well, such as the rule about no sexual activity in the dorms. Discipline for infractions of the honor code is administered mainly through first-years, or senior cadets. Cadets who feel the rules do not apply to them may abuse their role as leaders and mistreat members of the lower classes through the guise of discipline.

The first-year cadets dictate the majority of the moves the doolies may make. First-class cadets determine whether doolies eat at meals and are extended extra study time for an exam or whether doolies spend time washing the laundry of every squadron member and scrubbing floors. Doolies are stripped of personal belongings including their civilian clothes and hair upon entering basic cadet training. They are away from family and any peer support they may have had in high school. The isolation, extreme physical and academic duress, and the power differential that doolies experience in relation to first-class cadets create the climate that led to so many reports of sexual harassment and assault.

The Military Justice System

In addition to following the rules at the academy, as officers in training, cadets also fall under the jurisdiction of the federal Uniform Code of Military Justice (UCMJ). Article 120 of the UCMJ defines rape as "an act of sexual intercourse, by force and without consent." Civilian law generally takes into account that a person of higher status could use that status to coerce a victim into having sex, but the military law has been interpreted to mean that if a victim did not fight off the attacker, then a rape did not occur. Cadets who claim to be victims of sexual assault are being told that if they knew the perpetrator, that could affect their case legally. The UCMJ fails to adequately address acquaintance rape, which makes up the majority of rapes in the country, and probably all of the cadet-on-cadet rapes at the academy since it is such a small school that all of the cadets could feasibly be acquainted with each other.

Beginning in March 2003, in accordance with the Agenda for Change, the confidential sexual assault reporting system at the Air Force Academy was effectively eliminated because confidentiality had the potential to prevent the command staff and law enforcement agencies from learning of serious criminal conduct occurring at the academy. In addition, confidentiality may interfere with the ability of investigators to collect evidence necessary to ensure a successful prosecution of the case.

An investigation of the Air Force Academy Review Panel, headed by former Florida Congresswoman Tillie Fowler (2003), concluded that any problems relating to the confidential reporting system were due to poor implementation of the system and lack of responsible governance and oversight rather than anything inherently wrong with privileged communications. Interestingly, the psychotherapist-patient privilege was not recognized by the military until it was established on November 1, 1999, by Presidential Executive Order 13140 and Military Rules of Evidence 513. Prior to this time, the only communications that were recognized as privileged by the military were those with a lawyer, clergy, or spouse.

Another interesting twist in the administration of the military justice system involves the frequent turnover of command staff. Active-duty officers typically change duty stations every two years, and commanders are no exception. Occasionally they are asked to fill temporary duty positions in other areas, such as during the Gulf wars, in which case an interim commander would step in. Although commanders were aware of the problems and attempted to establish long-term policies regarding the atmosphere conducive to sexual harassment and assault at the academy, frequent turnover interfered with the implementation of these policies.

Base commanders are the ultimate authority and may bestow punishments at their discretion. Commanders have a variety of military justice actions available to them when deciding how to punish a military member for a violation. A commander may use courts-martial, issue nonjudicial punishment under Article 15 of the UCMJ, provide an administrative discharge, or settle on a less severe action, such as a letter of reprimand. If a cadet's case is pending court-martial and there is a change of command, the cadet can request that the new commander withdraw the referral to court-martial and consider an administrative punishment, such as fines, confinement, or dismissal from the academy. No two cases are the same, which can result in different treatment and different punishments of the cases. For this reason, accurately tracking cases and how they are handled is very difficult.

Sexual assault victims are uniquely disadvantaged at the Air Force Academy. If the accused is facing trial at a court-martial, he can request to resign from the academy, denying the victim her right to take her case to court. The academy will pay for cadets to receive drug or alcohol counseling off-campus, but, ignoring the psychology of sexual victimization, requires cadets to pay for rape counseling off-campus. This has a substantially negative impact on the women's meager financial resources (cadets receive a $700 monthly stipend, most of it earmarked for living expenses required by the academy, such as dry cleaning and haircuts). Victims are granted amnesty for honor code violations such as drugs, alcohol, or fraternization when reporting an assault, but that covers only the night of the attack. When a cadet brings charges of rape against another cadet and there is insufficient evidence to convict, the victim is penalized with demerits for having sex in the dorms. Cadets accused of sexually assaulting other cadets were previously removed from the dorms (all cadets are housed in one building, requiring victims to face attackers daily) and separated from other cadets during the investigation. One cadet fought that as being unconstitutional pretrial detention according to *Bell* v. *Wolfish* (1979). Now the victims are removed from the dorms, separating already emotionally distraught people from their support groups, peers, and roommates.

A sexual assault case at the academy is handled very differently from a similar case at other colleges or universities. It is unfortunate that women who are willing to dedicate their lives working for the safety and security of others are subject to such an environment. The Air Force Academy Review Panel made many suggestions that would better balance the needs of the military with the best interests of the victims that, if implemented, would improve the environment at the academy and reduce cases of sexual harassment and assault.

RAPE AND ABORTION

Abortion is a controversial and emotional topic and is also a legal reproductive option for American women. Yet women in the military who are stationed or deployed overseas, including female spouses and children of military members, may have this legal right obstructed. Commanders may decide whether abortion services will be offered in their hospitals or clinics, supervisors may deny subordinates time off for traveling to other locations where abortion services are offered, and the high cost of traveling may be prohibitive to many military members. Military women are working to defend the constitutional rights and freedoms of others. To deny them any one of their constitutional rights is hypocritical and discriminatory.

Estimates of the prevalence of rape indicate that approximately 14.8 percent of adult women in the United States have experienced completed rape in their lifetime, with another 2.8 percent experiencing an attempted rape (Tjaden & Thoennes, 1998). Studies of women veterans reveal much higher rates. As noted earlier, the survey by Skinner et al. (2001) revealed that 23 percent of the women reported being sexually assaulted while in the military. Women in the military are also vulnerable to experiencing rape or attempted rape while on duty (6 percent) (Harned, Ormerod, Palmieri, & Collingsworth, 2002).

There are very few statistics on incidents of incest in the United States or in the military population. A survey of university students revealed that 17 percent of those students reported experiencing some type of physical contact of a sexual nature when they were children, with most of the contacts coming from people related to them by blood or marriage (Justice & Justice, 1979). In the military population, incest resulting in pregnancy could occur with female children of active-duty members and between male sons and female spouses. Not every woman who finds herself pregnant as the result of rape or incest will consider or desire to have an abortion, but being forced to carry a pregnancy to term rather than being able to freely make the choice herself may make a huge difference psychologically. Much more research needs to be done in this area. Nevertheless, these women currently can be prohibited from exercising their fundamental constitutional right to choose simply because of their military service and where they happen to be stationed.

After abortion was legalized with *Roe* v. *Wade*, Congress passed the Hyde Amendment in 1976, which prevents providing abortion services for this population due to the federal funding of the military health care system. In 1985, the Department of Defense (DOD) was prohibited from providing any abortion coverage except when necessary to save the life of a woman. There is no exception in the case where the pregnancy threatens the woman's health but she is not in immediate risk of dying. The Hyde Amendment bans the use of public Medicaid funds for abortions for low-income women, but includes exceptions for victims of rape, incest, and life endangerment (Lutz, 1999). Rape and incest victims stationed at overseas military bases were not protected by this ban. In 1995, Congress passed the DOD appropriations bill, which included a provision prohibiting women from obtaining abortion services at overseas military facilities even with their own funds, except in cases of "promptly" reported rape or incest. Even in these cases, the government will not pay for the abortion; the woman must pay for the abortion on her own. In 1996, this restriction became permanent law.

Emergency contraception, which delays ovulation, blocks fertilization, or prevents implantation of the egg, is generally not considered a form of abortion and is available to women within seventy-two hours of unprotected sexual intercourse. However, some people believe for religious reasons that preventing a pregnancy by any method other than abstinence is a form of abortion. A doctor at a military hospital who holds these beliefs is not required to prescribe emergency contraceptive pills. After seventy-two hours but before five days after the rape, an intrauterine device (IUD) can be inserted to prevent implantation of a fertilized egg in the uterine wall. But again, there must be a health care provider on staff who is willing and able to do that. Many women may not be aware of these options and might not ask for them. After being raped, the thought of a pelvic examination may be too upsetting for many women (World Health Organization, 2002).

This ban, whose only current exceptions are cases of life endangerment, rape, or incest, is especially harmful to women stationed in countries where abortions in the local community are illegal or unsafe. The option of finding an abortion provider in the local area was seriously hindered by the Mexico City Policy, enacted in 1985 by President Reagan, which placed a ban on funding any family planning agencies overseas that provide or promote abortion services. President Clinton repealed this ban in 1992; President G. W. Bush reinstated it in 2001.

The Mexico City policy notwithstanding, a woman stationed overseas who needs an abortion may be forced to seek an abortion in her host country, where abortion may not even be legal. Local facilities are often inadequate or entirely unavailable. Traveling to a safe facility can result in delays that may substantially increase the risks of an abortion procedure. Not all abortion services overseas offer painkillers for the procedure. In Europe especially, there are different cultural expectations regarding nudity, and the modesty of the woman may be violated. Animosity toward the United States often runs high in countries where troops are stationed, potentially jeopardizing the health of anyone who chooses to turn to local medical facilities. If she chooses to return to the United States for the procedure, a military woman must notify her superiors about her need for an abortion, sacrificing her privacy, and hope that their personal opinions about abortion do not influence their decisions to allow taking leave. Then she must wait until there is space available on a military flight back to the United States or purchase a ticket on an international (expensive for the low-income military personnel) flight. It is an outrage that women who have volunteered to serve their country should be subject to such a humiliating policy, even more so since the DOD pays for Viagra for men and federal funding pays for abortions for federal prisoners in the case of rape.

Although abortion services may be available in the local overseas area, there are many restrictions, such as compulsory waiting periods from three days to two weeks, in several of the countries in Europe, sometimes with the result that the woman exceeds the time period for a legal abortion. Some countries include mandatory counseling that must include information about the risks of abortion and alternatives to abortion. The information provided to a woman is often required to be neutral. However, this is not always the case. In Germany, for example, the main provider of this counseling is the Catholic church.

When a woman volunteers for service overseas, she may not realize that her fundamental right to privacy and the freedom to choose to terminate a pregnancy, the very rights she is fighting to preserve, do not exist where she is going. Then this issue becomes not only an employment issue but a health and safety issue of military personnel. At a time when we are expecting so much from military women, it is critical that they have every resource at their disposal to meet their health needs. Now more than ever before, at a time when terrorists are attempting to deny Americans their rights and impose their own moral beliefs on us, it is essential that the fundamental rights of every American be reaffirmed.

The military has inherent problems even with regard to addressing sexual assault cases and providing assistance to victims. Most recently, it has come to light that rape-victim assistance programs in the Air Force have been set up in such a way that if criminal charges are not brought against the accused, the Air Force stops providing assistance to the victim (Burns, 2004).

In the face of the serious issues facing women in the military, the Bush administration has done the following:

• *The Department of Defense (DOD) limited the role of the Defense Advisory Committee on Women in the Services (DACOWITS).* DACOWITS, formed nearly fifty-five years ago to promote the recruitment and retention of women in the armed services, in the past has strongly supported opening more military positions to women and has voiced concerns about and made recommendations to address sexual assault and harassment in the services. Yet Elaine Donnelly, former DACOWITS member and now president of the Center for Military Readiness, a conservative group that advocates limiting positions open to women in the military, has called DACOWITS a "feminist lobby" and her center has urged the administration to dismantle it altogether (Center for Military Readiness, 2002). There are indications that the administration is listening: in March 2002 DOD allowed the DACOWITS charter to expire, terminating the membership of appointees whose terms had not expired. Although DOD then issued a new charter, it allowed President Bush to appoint all new members. Despite being authorized to appoint up to thirty-five members (as had been the case under the old charter), only twelve have been named (DACOWITS, 2004), reducing the committee membership by nearly two-thirds (Scarbough, 2002). One of the new appointees, Catherine L. Aspy, has been outspoken in her opposition to opening ground combat positions to women and has reportedly said that in her view "the Army is a vast day-care center, full of unmarried teenage mothers using it as a welfare home."

The new charter expands DACOWITS's charge to include family issues. Although these issues are important for military men and women, the administration's dramatic reduction in DACOWITS's membership raises the question whether the committee has sufficient resources to handle this expansion in the array of issues within its purview. Moreover, under its new charter DACOWITS is limited to addressing only those issues specified for its attention by the secretary of defense, as opposed to choosing for itself what to focus on from "the full range of issues" under the original charter (Scarbough, 2002). Because the secretary will be choosing from a broader range of issues, it is unclear to what extent DACOWITS will be focusing on women's issues. The full ramifications of the changes to DACOWITS's autonomy and authority remain to be seen.

• *DOD has responded inadequately to allegations of sexual assault.* The military's response to revelations of sexual assault in the services and at the academies has been an ongoing cause for concern. Because of concerns about the thoroughness of internal reviews in the wake of the Air Force Academy sexual assaults, Congress intervened and mandated that an independent commission be created to review the allegations at the academy. The executive director and another member of this commission originally selected by Secretary Rumsfeld were replaced after public outcry: Anita Blair, selected to be executive director, helped found the conservative Independent Women's Forum to "serve as a counterpoint to the National Organization for Women" and later opposed admitting women to the Virginia Military Institute (Soraghan, 2003). Amy McCarthy, named as a commission member, made several public statements questioning the veracity of the women alleging rape at the academy and suggested that the women were engaged in questionable conduct at the time of the incidents (Crist, 2003). (A second controversial selection as a commission member, Sally Satel, a former member of the Independent Women's Forum Advisory Council, was permitted to stay.)

The report issued by the reconstituted commission, chaired by former Republican congresswoman and House Armed Services Committee member Tillie Fowler, sharply criticized a report by the Air Force General Counsel for failing to acknowledge the "chasm in leadership" that "helped create an environment in which sexual assault became a part of life at the Academy" (Report of the Panel to Review Sexual Misconduct, 2003, p. 1) and concluded that "the Air Force General Counsel attempted to shield Air Force Headquarters from public criticism by focusing exclusively on events at the Academy" (p. 4). The report also criticized Agenda for Change, Air Force Secretary James G. Roche's series of policy directives and improvements for the academy, for "effectively eliminat[ing] the Academy's confidential reporting policy for sexual misconduct" (p. 3) by mandating reporting of sexual assaults and failing to recognize the psychotherapist-patient privilege.

Members of Congress recently indicated that they are similarly prepared to intervene if the Department of Defense fails to respond quickly and meaningfully to the recent revelations of allegations of sexual assault against servicewomen in Iraq, Kuwait, and Afghanistan and at other military bases and installations. Although Secretary Rumsfeld has ordered Undersecretary David Chu to conduct a review of the reports and the military response to the allegations, and this issue has been placed on DACOWITS's agenda for the next year, some members of Congress have already expressed concern about the military's willingness to take the allegations seriously. The chairman of the Senate Armed Services Committee has warned that he is prepared to "take over" reform of military practices if the Department of Defense does not fix the ongoing problem of sexual assault in the military (Warner, 2004). Another Republican Committee member expressed concern that nothing had changed for years and wondered why there was "no sense of outrage" among military leaders (Nelson, 2004).

• *DOD has sanctioned restrictive clothing and other discriminatory requirements on female service members overseas.* In 2001 Lieutenant

Colonel Martha McSally, an Air Force fighter pilot, sued the Department of Defense, challenging DOD regulations that required women stationed in Saudi Arabia to wear the traditional Muslim abaya, have a male escort whenever they left the base, and ride in the back seat of all vehicles off the base (*McSally* v. *Rumsfeld*, 2001). No similar restrictions are imposed on male service members. McSally alleges that these regulations discriminate against women and violate her First Amendment right to freedom of religion. In response, the military changed its abaya policy to one that "strongly encourages" women to wear the abaya (Military eases policy, 2002), despite the fact that female State Department employees in Saudi Arabia are not subject to the same requirement and even the Saudi Arabian government does not require non-Muslim women to wear the abaya (*McSally* v. *Rumsfeld*, 2001). In 2002 Congress stepped in and passed a law prohibiting the military from requiring or strongly encouraging female personnel to wear abayas (Bob Stump National Defense Authorization Act, 2002). Other aspects of McSally's suit against the government are still pending.

• *The Bush administration supports restrictions on servicewomen's access to abortion.* Since 1985, Congress has prohibited the use of federal funds to pay for abortions at any military facility, except where the life of the woman is endangered (Title XIV, 1985). Since 1996, Congress has additionally prohibited women from using their own private funds to pay for abortion services at overseas military facilities, unless the pregnancy resulted from rape or incest, or endangered the woman's life (Title VII, 1996). The Bush administration supports this policy, in a reversal of the past DOD position (Enda, 2003). These restrictions force servicewomen facing unwanted pregnancies while stationed overseas, who depend on their base hospitals for medical care, to place their health at risk while they delay the procedure until they can arrange for home leave, or turn to local—and often illegal and unsafe—abortion providers. And even if a servicewoman seeks to terminate a pregnancy caused by a rape, including a rape by another servicemember, although she is permitted to have an abortion on base, she must pay for the procedure with her own money.

CONCLUSION

Opening jobs up for women in the military should be a way to enhance and advance the role of women; it should not be an invitation to sexually harass and assault or erode constitutional rights. Women in the military should not be infantilized and protected by men; rather, they should be protected by the law as equally as civilian women and men in the military are. Access to health care should not depend on a woman's ability to successfully navigate the military legal system or the luck to be stationed with a commander who establishes policies compatible with equal rights for women. It would be unfortunate if a few men were enabled to harass women out of the military given all of the hard work it took to get women where they are now. Women have been essential to military missions throughout history and will continue to be essential, whether they are able to do their jobs while suffering from the actions of their fellow countrymen or not, whether their access to health care is unreasonably restricted or not, and whether they are able to receive military justice for sexual assault or not.

References

Abbey, A. (1991). Acquaintance rape and alcohol consumption on college campuses: How are they linked? *Journal of American College Health, 39,* 165–169.

Barbaree, H. E., Marshall, W. L., Yates, E., & Lightfoot, L. O. (1983). Alcohol intoxication and deviant sexual arousal in male social drinkers. *Behaviour Research and Therapy, 21,* 365–373.

Barstow, A. L. (Ed.). (2000). *War's dirty secret: Rape, prostitution, and other crimes against women.* Cleveland, OH: Pilgrim Press.

Bell v. Wolfish, 441 U.S. 520 (1979).

Bob Stump National Defense Authorization Act for Fiscal Year 2003, Pub. L. No. 107-314, § 563, 116 Stat. 2458 (2002).

Burke, C. (1989). Marching to Vietnam. *Journal of American Folklore, 102,* 424–440.

Burns, R. (2004, March 17) Leader looks at Air Force rape problem. *Seattle Post-Intelligencer.* Retrieved March 21, 2004, from http://seattlepi. nwsource.com/national/apwashington_story.asp?category= 1152&slug=Air percent20Force percent20Rape.

Center for Military Readiness. (2002, January). *Summary and overview: Dismantling the DACOWITS.* Livonia, MI: Author.

Class of '07 selected from pool of over 20,000: Considered the most competitive in Harvard's history. (2003, April 3). *Harvard University Gazette, Harvard Gazette Archives.* Retrieved September 30, 2003, from http://www.news.harvard.edu/gazette/2003/04.03/ 01-admissions.html.

Class of 2007 enters academy. (2003, June 23). Press release no. 028–03. Retrieved September 30, 2003, from http://www.usma.edu/PublicAffairs/PressReleasesbd/NR28–03Class2006EntersAcademy.htm.

Class of 2007 has arrived. (2003, September 12). *Yale Bulletin and Calendar, 32*(2). Retrieved September 30, 2003, from http://www.yale.edu/opa/v32.n2/story1.html.

Class of 2007 profile. (2003a). United States Air Force Academy Undergraduate Admissions Home Page. Retrieved September 30, 2003, from http://academyadmissions.com/home.htm.

Class of 2007 profile. (2003b). United States Naval Academy Admissions home page. Retrieved September 30, 2003 from http://www.usna.edu/Admissions/profile2007.htm.

Crist, G. (2003, June 18). Panelist in AFA inquiry resigns. *Rocky Mountain News.*

Crowell, N. A., & Burgess, A. W. (1996). *Understanding violence against women.* Washington, DC: National Academy Press.

Culbertson, A. L., & Rosenfeld, P. (1994). Assessment of *sexual harassment* in the active-duty navy. *Military Psychology, 6,* 69–93.

DACOWITS. (2004). DACOWITS members. http://www.dtic.mil/dacowits/membrs_SubCom.html.

D'Amico, F., & Weinstein, L. (Ed.). (1999). *Gender camouflage: Women and the U.S. military.* New York: New York University Press.

De Pauw, L. G. (1998). *Battle cries and lullabies: Women in war from prehistory to the present.* Norman: University of Oklahoma Press.

Dead rats left at VMI in apparent rival college stunt. (1997, August 20). CNN.

Enda, J. (2003, July 27). Military women prevented from having abortions overseas. *Women's ENews.* Retrieved from http://www.womensenews.org/article.cfm/dyn/aid/1464/context/archive.

Fitzgerald, L. F., & Shullman, S. L. (1993). Sexual harassment: A research analysis and agenda for the 1990s. *Journal of Vocational Behavior, 42,* 5–27.

Fowler, T. (2003, September 22). *Report of the Panel to Review Sexual Misconduct Allegations at the U.S. Air Force Academy.* Retrieved October 1, 2003, from http://www.defenselink.mil/news/Sep2003/d20030922usafareport.pdf.

Francke, L. B. (1997). *Ground zero: The gender wars in the military.* New York: Simon & Schuster.

Frayne, S. M., Skinner, K. M., Sullivan, L. M., & Freund, K. M. (2003). Sexual assault while in the military: Violence as a predictor of cardiac risk? *Violence and Victims, 18*(2), 219–225.

George, W. H., & Marlatt, G. A. (1986). The effects of alcohol and anger on interest in violence, erotica, and deviance. *Journal of Abnormal Psychology, 95,* 150–158.

Harned, S. H., Ormerod, A. J., Palmieri, P. A., & Collingsworth, L. L. (2002). Sexual assault and other types of sexual harassment by workplace personnel: A comparison of antecedents and consequences. *Journal of Occupational Health Psychology, 7*(2), 1076–8998.

Hillbrand, M., Foster, H., & Hirt, M. (1990). Rapists and child molesters: Psychometric comparisons. *Archives of Sexual Behavior, 19,* 65–71.

Holm, J. (1992). *Women in the military: An unfinished revolution.* Novato, CA: Presidio Press.

Hunter Williams, J., Fitzgerald, L., & Drasgow, F. (1999). The effects of organizational practices on sexual harassment and individual outcomes in the military. *Military Psychology, 11,* 303–328.

Johnson, S. D., Gibson, L., & Linden, R. (1978). Alcohol and rape in Winnipeg, 1966–1975. *Journal of Studies on Alcohol, 39,* 1887–1894.

Jones, D. E. (2000). *Women warriors: A history.* Dulles, VA: Brasseys.

Justice, B., & Justice, R. (1979). *The broken taboo: Sex in the family.* New York: Human Sciences Press.

Kanin, E. J. (1984). Date rape: Unofficial criminals and victims. *Victimology, 9,* 95–108.

Kanin, E. J. (1985). Date rapists: Differential sexual socialization and relative deprivation. *Archives of Sexual Behavior, 14,* 218–232.

Koss, M. P., & Gaines, J. A. (1993). The prediction of sexual aggression by alcohol use, athletic participation, and fraternity affiliation. *Journal of Interpersonal Violence, 8,* 94–108.

Koss, M. P., Gidycz, C. A., & Wisniewski, N. (1987). The scope of rape: Incidence and prevalence of sexual aggression and victimization in a national sample of higher education students. *Journal of Consulting and Clinical Psychology, 55,* 162–170.

Koss, M. P., Koss P. G., & Woodruff W. J. (1991). Deleterious effects of criminal victimization on women's health and medical utilization. *Archives of Internal Medicine, 151,* 342–347.

Leserman J., Drossman D., Zhiming L., Toomey T., & Nachman Glogau, L. (1996). Sexual and physical abuse in a gastroenterology practice: How types of abuse impact health status. *Psychosomatic Medicine, 58,* 4–15.

Lutz, W. J. (1999, May 13). *Double pro-choice victory for military women stationed overseas.* Retrieved October 15, 2003, from http://www.commondreams.org/pressreleases/may99/051399g.htm.

Martin, L., Rosen, L., Durand, D., Knudson, K., & Stretch, R. (Spring 2000). Psychological and physical health effects of sexual assaults and non-sexual traumas among male and female United States Army soldiers. *Behavioral Medicine 26*(1), 23–33.

Martindale, S. (1991). *Sexual harassment* in the military: 1988. Sociological Practice Review, *2*, 200–216.

McIntosh, E. P. (1998). *Sisterhood of spies: The women of the OSS.* Annapolis, MD: Naval Institute Press.

McSally v. Rumsfeld, No. 1:01CV02481 (D.D.C. complaint filed Dec. 13, 2001).

Mercer, I. (2002, July 24). Osama's snickering at our military. *World Net Daily.* www.worldnetdaily.com/news/article.asp?ARTICLE_ID=28381.

Meritor Savings Bank v. Vinson, 477 U.S. 57, 64, 91 L. Ed. 2d 49, 106 S. Ct. 2399 (1986).

Merrill, L. L., Thomsen, C. J., Gold, S. R., & Milner, J. S. (2001). Childhood abuse and premilitary sexual assault in male navy recruits. *Journal of Consulting and Clinical Psychology, 69*(2), 252–261.

Military eases policy, but Muslim-dress flap continues for U.S. women. (2002, Jan. 24). *Newsday,* p. A32.

Mitchell, B. (1998). *Women in the military: Flirting with disaster.* Washington, DC: Regnery.

Muehlenhard, C. L., & Linton, M. A. (1987). Date rape and sexual aggression in dating situations: Incidence and risk factors. *Journal of Counseling Psychology, 34,* 186–196.

Nelson, B. (2004, Feb. 25). Senate Armed Services Committee hearing on prevention of sexual assault: Opening statement.

Quindlen, A. (2003, April 7). Not so safe back home. *Newsweek, 141*(14), p. 72.

Rennison, C. M. (2002). *Rape and sexual assault: Reporting to police and medical attention, 1992–2000.* Washington, DC: U.S. Department of Justice, Office of Justice Statistics. Retrieved March 21, 2004, from http://www.ojp.usdoj.gov/bjs/pub/pdf/rsarp00.pdf.

Report of the Panel to Review Sexual Misconduct Allegations at the U.S. Air Force Academy. (2003, Sept. 22). Available at http://www.usafa.af.mil/d20030922usafareport1.pdf.

Rose, I. M. (2002). Intimate partner violence and sexual harassment in women veterans: Prevalence, provider inquiry, and associated mental health outcomes. *Dissertation Abstracts International, 62*(11-A), 3937.

Rubinstein, M., Yeager, C., Goodstein, C., & Lewis, D. (1993). Sexually assaultive male juveniles: A follow-up. *American Journal of Psychiatry, 150,* 262–265.

Salmonson, J. (1991). *The encyclopedia of Amazons: Women warriors from antiquity to the modern era.* New York: Paragon House.

Scarbough, R. (2002, March 6). Women moved away from combat. *Washington Times.*

The Seville Statement. (1990). *American Psychologist, 45*(10), 1167–1168.

Shilts, R. (1993). *Conduct unbecoming.* New York: St. Martin's Press.

Skinner, K. M., Kressin, N., Frayne, S., Tripp, T. J., Hankin, C. S., Miller, D. R., & Sullivan, L. M. (2000, March). The prevalence of military sexual assault among female Veterans' Administration outpatients. *Journal of Interpersonal Violence, 15*(3), 291–310.

Soraghan, M. (2003, June 2). Some fear AFA inquiry bias: Panel leader fought coed training. *Denver Post.*

Suris, A., Davis, L., Kashner, T., Gillaspy, J., & Petty, F. (1998). A survey of sexual trauma treatment provided by VA medical centers. *Psychiatric Services, 49*(3), 382–384.

Tedeschi, J. T., & Felson, R. B. (1994). *Violence, aggression, and coercive actions.* Washington, DC: American Psychological Association.

Title VII, Subtitle D, § 738(a), (b)(1), 110 Stat. 186, 383 (1996), Pub. L. No. 104-106, Div A.

Title XIV, § 1401(e)(5)(A), 98 Stat. 2492, 2618 (1985), Pub. L. No. 98-525.

Tjaden, P., & Thoennes, N. (1998). Prevalence, incidence and consequences of violence against women: Findings from the National Violence Against Women Survey. *Research in Brief.* Washington, DC: National Institute of Justice, U.S. Department of Justice.

U.S. Air Force Academy. (2003). *Agenda for change—Policy directives and initiatives.* Retrieved October 1, 2003, from http://www.usafa.af.mil/agenda.cfm.

U.S. Congress, House Committee on Armed Services, Subcommittee on Total Force. (2003, April 1). *Hearing on the Air Force Academy Investigation,* 108th Congress, 1st session. http://commdocs.house.gov/committees/security/has091270.000/has091270_0f.htm.

Van Creveld, M. (2001). *Men, women and war: Do women belong in the front line?* London: Cassell.

Warner, J. (2004, Feb. 25). Senate Armed Services Committee hearing on prevention of sexual assault: Opening statement.

Warner, M. (1999). *Joan of Arc: The image of female heroism.* Berkeley: University of California Press.

Webster, G. (1999). *Boudica: The British revolt against Rome, AD 60.* London: Routledge.

World Health Organization. (2002). *Clinical management of rape survivors: A guide to the development of protocols for use in refugee and internally displaced person situations.* Retrieved December 15, 2003, from http://www.who.int/reproductive-health/publications/rhr_02_8/rhr02_8.en.html.

Worth, R. (1999). *Women in combat: The battle for equality.* Springfield, NJ: Enslow Publishers.

CHAPTER FIFTEEN

Discrimination Against Women in the World of Human Rights

The Case of Women in Southern Africa

Teresa Mugadza, J.D.

S outhern African women have suffered sex and gender discrimination over the years (Armstrong, 2000; Ncube, 1997; Ncube & Stewart, 1995; Women and Law in Southern Africa, 1997). This chapter addresses the question of why women are still being discriminated against, particularly in the light of the comprehensive international women's human rights instruments, laws against discrimination, and the strategies being employed by women's activists in the region and elsewhere. This chapter contends that discrimination against women continues because southern African societies have maintained their "culture," which is fraught with customary practices that discriminate against women and is so entrenched in the lives of the people that even though remedies are available, women will not readily make use of them.[1] It describes how the people of southern Africa have several common customary practices (despite coming from different countries and tribes) such as *lobola* (the bride price, or the money, gifts, and cattle paid by the groom to the bride's family), marriage ceremonies, widow mourning rituals, and subsequent inheritance rituals. It highlights how these customary practices have been used to discriminate against women, and in some cases have been incorporated into constitutions and domestic legislation, compounding discrimination against women.

BACKGROUND

Some of the customary practices that pose problems for women today were given prominence by colonialism. When the colonialists came, certain practices were adopted as the way of life of Africans and codified, thus giving them immortality and universality in the colonies.[2] Almost all the countries in southern Africa have a provision in their constitutions that provides for the exercise of culture and customary practices, and in some cases, as in Zimbabwe, the constitutions provide for the preeminence of customary law over general law, thus giving these customary practices the legitimacy and certainty of law.

Colonialism also had an impact on the customary practices of the people of southern Africa. The practices were obviously varied in form and actual implementation, but with colonialism came migration and the intercustomary influences.[3] Once people interact and intermarry, the likelihood of influence is great, and this happened with the people of southern Africa.[4] A very efficient road and rail network was developed to link the colonies. This also made it easy for people to move from as far away as present-day Malawi to work in the mines of present day South Africa, thus increasing the likelihood of intercultural exchange.

Another issue is the existence of two legal regimes in southern African countries. There exists the general law system, initially created to govern the colonial settlers and now applied to all persons because of independence.[5] There is also a customary law system, under which customary practices are recorded and given the force of law. This dual system has complicated the lives of women, who at certain times in their lives are governed by general law and at other times by customary law. Thus, while under general law, a woman has the right to own property in her own right if she has attained the age of majority. But women do not always have a choice of which legal system to marry under, so if she gets married under customary law, she cannot inherit from her husband because at customary law, women do not have property rights.[6]

A WOMAN'S JOURNEY THROUGH MARRIAGE AND WIDOWHOOD

It is against this background that I will examine a southern African woman's life through the process of *lobola*, the marriage ceremony and rituals, and being widowed.

Marriage

There are two types of marriage: civil marriage and customary marriage.[7] The laws that govern civil marriages state that two persons over the age of eighteen can enter into a marriage contract before a judicial officer. The parties must both consent to the marriage and not have another existing marriage. There must also be two witnesses to the marriage. This marriage does not have to be sanctioned or approved by the families of the two parties getting married unless one of the spouses is a minor.

The formal customary marriage process for a woman begins with the introduction of the woman to her in-laws. This is to ensure that the new wife will be acceptable to her new family. In some instances, if a prospective bride is not acceptable to her in-laws, the pending marriage may be called off.[8] After this, the prospective husband's family proposes the date to begin the negotiations for *lobola*, which ordinarily take place between the male members of the families of the bride and groom in those tribes that practice *lobola*. The woman for whom the *lobola* is being negotiated comes to the place where the negotiations are taking place only to acknowledge the groom's delegation. In effect, the process of *lobola* negotiations is the creation of a contract between men about a woman. The woman to be married cannot say anything in the negotiations and has no voice over the *lobola* paid for her.[9] This is the beginning of the disempowerment of a woman as she embarks on her married life.

Women willingly submit to the complexity of a customary marriage for a variety of reasons. First, for the majority of women, *lobola* is more than just a payment. It is about their dignity and esteem. A man who truly respects a woman cannot live with her without paying *lobola* for her. Second, if *lobola* is not paid, then that woman is never considered a real wife in the society or in the family of the man she lives with and her children are considered illegitimate. Women and men submit to these customary practices to appease their extended families and to make themselves fit into their society, regardless of the laws requiring equality of the sexes.

The marriage ceremony begins with preparation of the bride. The bride's aunts (her father's sisters and the wives of her mother's brothers) sit her down for advice on how to conduct herself as a wife. The advice is meant to make her a submissive wife: she must always respect her husband, submit to his sexual advances at all times, and generally persevere in the marriage. Several proverbs designed to make women remain in marriages are also used to make the bride aware that most marriages are not rosy but that she should not give up.[10] What makes this process disempowering for women is that more often than not, women will marry a man who has more economic power than they have, if they even have any economic power. Thus, the woman, who is already vulnerable because of her weak economic condition, is placed at a further disadvantage as she is reminded that she should obey and submit to her already powerful partner.

After the advice session, there is usually a celebration at which the bride is presented to her new family and husband. At these celebrations, there is a lot of food, drink, dance, and song. Even the songs sung at these celebrations are a reminder of the subordinate status of the woman in the marriage. They remind the woman that she has come to stay in this family, although her title is that of an outsider, "the married one."[11] These songs are sung to remind the bride that she is now no longer a part of her family of origin, but at the same time she is reminded that she is not a real part of her new married family. The songs are also designed to remind the bride of her wifely duties, such as welcoming her in-laws and doing household chores.[12] Again, while this is an important aspect of cultural life, the process further disempowers the woman and compounds her unequal position. Thus, although all persons over the age of eighteen at general law can equally contract a marriage, the reality is that at customary law, the marriage partners are made aware at the outset of their unequal status. The man is exhorted to be the head of his household, and the wife is admonished to remain submissive.

Sexual Relations in Marriage

The issue of sexual relations in marriage becomes particularly important in the light of the HIV/AIDS pandemic. A woman is counseled not only to persevere in the marriage but also to submit to her husband in all matters, including sexual relations (Armstrong, 2000). She is told not to deny her husband's advances and is generally cautioned that sexual intercourse is for her husband's pleasure and for procreation. These perceptions persist despite the development that societies in the region have undergone, and it has been cited as one of the major reasons that HIV/AIDS is so prevalent in the region. Thus, the issue of negotiating sexual relations is not considered important or even broached in the counseling of a new wife, because it is assumed that by agreeing to marry a man, she has consented to sex with him at all times.[13] A woman cannot deny her husband even when he has been unfaithful. In some cases, women have continued to have sexual relations with their husbands even when they suspect or know that he has sexually transmitted infections.

There are several reasons that women are more vulnerable under customary law. First, the payment of *lobola* encourages men to feel that they now own their wives' reproductive organs. A man who has paid *lobola* will demand and even force sexual relations with his wife because he feels he has earned that right by virtue of having paid *lobola* (Armstrong, 2000). This is compounded by the fact that some men believe that women will never voluntarily consent to sexual relations, so they never consider their opinions on the matter. Furthermore, because women at customary law did not have any rights, there was no such thing as marital rape, so men could force their wives and face no penalty. In fact, except for South Africa and Zimbabwe, which have some semblance of laws prohibiting marital rape, the general rule in southern Africa is that women are not protected from marital rape.[14]

Second, at customary law, marriage is about procreation. People do not just get married; people get married to have children. The pressure to have children is great, and if a woman fails to conceive after a few months, questions about her fertility and her husband's virility begin to arise. This means that couples will attempt to have children at all costs.[15] Even when they suspect that they have infections that could jeopardize their health, couples will still attempt to have children to avoid the stigma of being childless. Women are expected have children and breast-feed them.[16] Thus, even when women have risked their lives having children, they expose those children to risk by breast-feeding.

Third, the social pressure for women to get married means that women will sometimes expose themselves to situations of infection just to conform. This, combined with other social factors, means that women under customary law are at a great risk of HIV/AIDS infection.

Widowhood

When the man dies, there are several things that must happen. First, the widow is required to sit or lie on a reed mat (which has evolved to carpets and mattresses with modernization) for her to properly mourn. This mat is usually placed in a prominent place in a room where other women sit and comfort her. The widow is covered with a blanket and is expected to wail loudly and generally be so grieved that she is unable to do anything for herself. In some cases, widows have been fed only soft porridge and water because they are too distraught to tolerate their usual food.[17] The widow has to be seen to be mourning; otherwise, she is considered responsible for her husband's death. The widow also must stay in one place, so that the mourners can come to her to offer condolences.

The funeral arrangements will have been taken over by the deceased husband's relatives. The widow will usually concede authority over the funeral arrangements and even the choice of the place of burial to appease the relatives of the deceased husband. Widows are expected to make these concessions as part of the cultural practices relating to death in southern African communities. These practices include adorning the widow in black for a particular period of time, performing various rituals during the preparation of the deceased for burial, conducting the actual burial, and performing subsequent rituals after the burial. In fact, most widows give over all the decision making pertaining to their spouse's burial and the devolution of his estate to allow the necessary rituals to be performed. This is tolerated by the widow despite the enactment of laws that allow women to determine how to dispose of their husband's remains, for fear of being ostracized.

The widow is presented a mourning outfit by her in-laws after the funeral (Ncube & Stewart, 1995). The outfit is generally black and is to show that she is bereaved.[18] This black outfit is to be worn until the cleansing ritual, performed any time from a few months to a year after the burial of the deceased. The widow is required to keep away from public spaces, unless it is unavoidable, because she is in mourning. The widow is also supposed to conduct herself demurely and speak in low tones. In Swaziland, for example, a widow's movement is severely restricted.[19] The mourning period for the widow varies from area to area in the region.[20] It commonly requires that a widow not be seen in the company of males she is not related to, since widows cannot have any sexual relations with any man until after the mourning period.[21] Women often submit to these rituals because they fear antagonizing their in-laws and because failure to engage in them will result in social ostracization.

The cleansing ceremonies vary from area to area, but the principles are the same. The objective of the cleansing ceremony is to separate the widow or widower from the spirit of the deceased spouse and remove the mourning clothes so that the widow may reenter society (Ncube & Stewart, 1995). Most of the cleansing rituals discriminate against women. For example, while in almost all the settings widows and widowers have to bathe in water with herbs, it is the women who undergo tests as to celibacy (Ncube & Stewart, 1995). In some tribes (for example, in Zambia), there has to be sexual cleansing, although this is not widely exercised in the region. It is after the cleansing that the estate of the deceased, in an ideal situation,[22] should be distributed. It is also after the cleansing and as part of distributing the estate that the issue of the wife's inheritance arises, because it is at this ceremony that the widow has to choose a husband from her deceased husband's male relatives.[23] Generally it is after the cleansing ceremony that the estate of the deceased is reviewed with a view to distribution. However, with the changing times, the trend seems to be that families will waive the delay in distributing the estate, with the preliminary procedures for distribution of the estate starting immediately after the burial of the deceased.

Administration of the Deceased's Estate

The subject of inheritance in southern African communities is complex (Ncube & Stewart, 1995; Women and Law in Southern Africa, 1997). Many factors determine a widow's inheritance rights. There is a difference between widows whose husbands had a valid will at the time of their death and those whose husbands did not. Thus, there is a difference between testate (a valid will at death) and intestate (no valid will at death) succession. Furthermore, because of the dual systems of law, widows have different inheritance rights depending on whether their marriage was governed by customary law or the civil law. Under the general law, widows whose marriages were governed by civil law have some right to inherit from their husband's estate.[24] Women who are governed by customary law have to deal with an entirely different system.

In general, under the customary practices of most of the people of southern Africa, women had no right to inherit. The rationale was that women could not be heads of families, and thus could not administer property (Tsanga, 1999), so only males could inherit. This practice still exists in varying degrees in most of the countries in the region. Widows are thus forced to submit to a brother-in-law, who is given the right to administer her late husband's estate; this usually happens when the widow does not have a male child to inherit his father's estate. In some cases, the widow is dispossessed of all authority over her matrimonial property by her deceased husband's male children from previous relationships if she has no male child to inherit. This causes untold problems for women; in some cases, they have to depend on total strangers for their livelihood (where the deceased's out-of-wedlock child inherits). In other instances, widows have to deal with unreasonable in-laws who will either refuse to cooperate with the widow or will just make it difficult for the widow to get access to the inheritance. In some countries this has changed,[25] with new laws that allow women to access their deceased husband's estate, but even those reforms do not protect widows from the ostracism that may come with the widow's inheritance of her husband's property.

CULTURE AND HUMAN RIGHTS

All the countries in southern Africa except Swaziland have signed the major human rights instruments, including the Convention on the Elimination of All Forms of Discrimination Against Women (CEDAW). This should guarantee the rights of women in all areas of their lives, but this has not been the case. The main problem with the implementation of women's rights under the international instrument is the recognition of the exercise of customary law. All the major human rights instruments have clauses promoting the exercise of one's culture in community with others. This right has been endorsed by governments as being important for a number of reasons. The first reason is that men, who have benefited from a patriarchal society, have dominated governments. The patriarchal society has enabled men to maintain control, and there is little incentive to improve the social status of women, let alone their status in their homes, which are considered private spaces. Second, governments, particularly African governments, have used culture and customary practices as a means of preserving cultural identity. These governments fear that changes in the status of women could lead to the erosion of their culture. Furthermore, there is debate as to whether human rights, as they are presented in the international instruments, can work in African societies.

These concerns, of course, come from sources that do not seek to advance the women's rights agenda.

The key to women's emancipation lies in education for these societies as well as a change in the perceptions women have of themselves. Societies need to be educated so that they begin to appreciate women as equal citizens. This goes beyond simplifying and interpreting human rights instruments. Communities need to be educated to internalize equality of women in ways that are real to them. Societies need to understand the disadvantages of marginalizing women, such as underdevelopment and the perpetuation of problems like poverty and HIV/AIDS. If women remain discriminated against, HIV/AIDS will continue to flourish as women will be infected, widowed, and inherited by a man who may or may not be infected, and the cycle will continue. Furthermore, education for women should move beyond helping women know their rights to focus as well on helping women know their own value. As long as women know their rights but do not value themselves, they will succumb to pressures to marry, have children, or forgo their rights. The challenge is to help women appreciate themselves as important and integral members of society and of their communities. Ending discrimination against women requires changing social attitudes, laws, and structures, but this could be the beginning.

Notes

1. Culture here refers to the traditional way of life of the communities. This way of life has evolved with time, but certain practices have been retained in varying degrees of their original forms, for example, the practice of paying bride price, the difference in marital status and rights for spouses, and the difference in inheritance rights between men and women.

2. For example in colonial Zimbabwe, unregistered marriages were not recognized by the colonial power. In order for an African man to be able to live with his wife in an urban area, he had to prove that he was married to her, and the only way to do so was to register the marriage in terms of the African Marriages Act. These marriages were solemnized by the district administrators, and the statute creating these marriages required that before the marriage could be solemnized, the district administrator had to have proof that the man had paid *lobola* for his wife. Thus, *lobola* became a prerequisite for the registration of a customary law marriage, even though payment of *lobola* was not such a high priority in some tribes.

3. There was a lot of intermarriage, and thus transference of customary practices. For example during the time that Malawi, Zambia, and Zimbabwe made up the Federation of Rhodesia and Nyasaland between 1953 and 1963, many men migrated to work in the mines in Zimbabwe. They married local women and created a brand of customary practices that reflected their roots while incorporating the practices of their wives' families.

4. Some of the similarities are so striking that it has become difficult to distinguish between the different tribal groups.

5. The rights and privileges that the colonial settlers granted themselves through the law are now accessible to all persons at majority.

6. See *Magaya* v. *Magaya*, SC-210–98, explaining the principle of women's perpetual minority at customary law. According to Tsanga's critique of this decision (1999), women were excluded from ownership of property because they could not be heads of their families.

7. This is a result of the Roman-Dutch law that still operates in most of southern Africa. For example, the Marriage Act of Zimbabwe and the Botswana Marriage Act of 2000 provide for civil as opposed to customary marriages. Civil marriages were initially intended for non-Africans as they are nonpolygamous; it was assumed that Africans wanted customary marriage, which allows for multiple wives. With independence, Africans can now marry under the civil law, but there still remains a difference between customary and civil marriage with respect to the rights of spouses. Under civil law marriage, women have property rights, while under customary law, these rights are severely limited. See Ncube and Stewart (1995).

8. Among the Zezuru and Karanga of Zimbabwe, this used to be very common. Now the approval is less relevant as people are becoming independent of their extended families.

9. In some cases, women have been subjected to domestic violence by spouses who feel that they bought them and can make unreasonable demands on them and their time (Armstrong, 2000).

10. "*Chakafukidza dzimba matenga*" is a Shona proverb meaning that things are not always what they seem in a marriage and the prospective wife should be prepared to cover the faults and problems in the marriage.

11. For example, "*muroora tauya naye nemagumbeze*" (literally translated: we have brought the bride as well as her blankets) is a popular song at weddings, signifying that the bride has come to stay and hence has come with her bed linen.

12. Another song is "*mai vauya pembererai woye*" (literally translated: a mother has come, let us celebrate). The new bride is being burdened with motherly

responsibility on her first day of marriage, especially in African societies where mothers are known to sacrifice life and limb for their families.

13. The law recognizes this right to sexual intercourse under Roman-Dutch law. It is part of what is called *consortium,* a combination of marital rights, including companionship and sexual intercourse, that accrue to both partners on marriage.

14. The Zimbabwean Sexual Offences Act of 2000 provision came about as a result of the concerns about HIV/AIDS transmission.

15. Among the Shona, if a couple failed to conceive, the husband's brother would secretly be recruited to have sexual relations with the woman in order to have children. In some instances, the woman's family would bring in her younger sister to have children for her.

16. Among some tribes, if a woman did not breast-feed, she was considered a witch or it was assumed the child was rejecting breast milk because the mother had been unfaithful.

17. This is not because the widow will not be hungry; rather, the relatives of the deceased or even her own family will be convinced that she cannot even eat, even though in some cases she can eat. Of course, there are instances where the widow is so grieved that she cannot eat. The widow is also assigned a guard as she is considered to be so grieved as to be potentially suicidal. These societal perceptions may not be necessarily true of all widows.

18. Generally widowers do not have to wear specific attire to show their status. In some tribes, a widower may have to attach a tiny piece of black cloth, no bigger than one square inch, onto a sleeve.

19. A widow cannot even use public transport because she must remain in confinement for the greater period of her mourning. In March 2003, widows were banned from contesting parliamentary elections. See http://www.africaonline.com/site/Articles/1,3,52414.jsp.

20. Among the tribes of Zimbabwe, this period ranges from six months to a year. In Swaziland, the period is longer.

21. Among the Shona of Zimbabwe, one of the cleansing rituals is a check to see if the widow has been celibate. The widow is required to jump over her late husband's staff; if she falls or trips, she is deemed to have been having illicit sexual relations. If she jumps successfully, then she is applauded for having mourned the deceased appropriately.

22. This is because in some instances, the property of the deceased would have been grabbed at his death, or, as is the case these days, the widow and the family of the deceased will have already started these processes to maintain a livelihood for the family.

23. A widow has to choose a husband, but in some instances women choose a symbolic husband, like their deceased husband's sister or their eldest male child. Most women, however, will choose a real man to live with as a husband to avoid antagonizing their in-laws and also to avoid having to deal with difficult in-laws in the distribution of the estate.
24. The portions vary according to whether the inheritance is covered under a will or just by the general law. This system is more generous to widows than the customary law.
25. South Africa and Zimbabwe now have laws that allow women to inherit significant parts of their husbands' estates such as the matrimonial home, but these laws still recognize the symbolic customary inheritance practices, like the inheritance of the deceased's name and title and his staff (*tsvimbo/nduku*) by his son or male relative.

References

Armstrong, A. (2000). *Culture and choice: Lessons from survivors of gender violence in Zimbabwe.* Harare: Legal Resources Foundation.

Ncube, N. (Ed.). (1997). *Law, culture, tradition and children's rights in eastern and southern Africa.* Dartmouth: Ashgate.

Ncube, W., & Stewart, J. (1995). *Women and law in southern Africa research project: Inheritance laws, customs and practises in southern Africa.* Harare: Women and Law in Southern Africa.

Tsanga, A. S. (1999). *Criticism against the Magaya decision: Much ado about something.* http://www.alliancesforafrica.org/Publications/Criticisms%20Against%20the%20Magaya%20Decision.doc.

Women and Law in Southern Africa. (1997). *Uncovering reality: Excavating women's rights in African family law.* Working Paper No. 7.

CHAPTER SIXTEEN

Ugandan Women
Resiliency and Protective Factors in Confronting HIV/AIDS

Valata Jenkins-Monroe, Ph.D.

S ub-Saharan Africa currently bears the heaviest burden of the HIV/AIDS (human immunodeficiency virus/acquired immune deficiency syndrome) pandemic worldwide (World Health Organization/Global Program on AIDS/Surveillance, Forecasting, and Impact Assessment [WHO/GPA/SFI], 1991a, 1991b), while also sharing the plight of ongoing civil wars that have had a tremendous impact on the economy and resources available to fight the deadly disease. Within the first decade of the disease (1980s–1990s), approximately 8 million to 10 million people were infected worldwide, with an estimated 500,000 cases of AIDS among women and children (Chin, 1990; Centers for Disease Control, 1987). Regrettably, since the second decade of the disease battle, more than 3 million additional women have been infected with HIV (Chin, 1990; Ankrah, 1993).

Uganda was one of the first developing countries to encounter HIV/ AIDS. The first two cases were identified as "slim disease" and were reported in 1982 by health workers working on the shores of Lake Victoria in southwestern Uganda (Serwadda et al., 1985). The ideal stage for the rapid spread and quiet course of the disease can be attributed to the country's failing health services (STD/AIDS Control Programme, 2000). According to the Ministry of Health, only 50 percent of the population had access to health care and only 30 percent to safe water (Uganda Demographic and Health Survey, 1995). In addition, drugs and medical supplies were limited, and the availability of blood transfusions was rare.

From those two reported cases in the early 1980s, the Uganda epidemic grew to a cumulative 2 million HIV infections by the end of 2000. HIV/AIDS has had a direct impact on at least one in every ten households in Uganda (Okware, Opio, Musinguzi, & Waibale, 2001). Two of the most vulnerable populations are women and children. In two rural areas of Uganda, the Rakai and Masaka regions, children below fifteen years had lost one or both parents to AIDS. There have been over sixty-seven thousand children infected by the disease and over 1 million children orphaned because of it (Brouwer, Lok, Wolffers, & Serbagalls, 2000). Since newborns are infected with HIV through vertical transmission of the virus from the mother, prevalence rates are up to six times higher in orphans up to four years (Bobat, Coovadia, Coutsoudis, & Moodley, 1996; Brouwer et al., 2000).

Women across the world, and in particular women of color and women in developing countries, are especially vulnerable to the disease. Unlike the transmission patterns in the West, AIDS is a primarily heterosexually transmitted disease in Africa (Green, 1992; Guay et al., 1999). It is no surprise that how women are perceived and how they define their role, their socioeconomic conditions, and their cultural and spiritual practices will influence how sexual behavior is negotiated (Nyanzi, Pool, & Kinsman, 2001; Anyango, Momanyi, & Muriuki, 1995).

What has been promising, however, is Uganda's mounted defense to combat the disease. Beginning in 1996, Uganda was one of the first sub-Saharan countries to report declining trends in HIV infection, and this progress serves as a model that AIDS in Africa is largely preventable. This chapter explores the endeavors and challenges of the women in Uganda to redefine traditional beliefs and practices in their battle to save their families. It relies on discussions with Ugandan women affected by HIV/AIDS who participated in open-ended forums on death and dying issues. These support groups were held during my Fulbright Lecture appointment at Makerere University Medical School from 1995 to 1996.

IMPACT OF HIV/AIDS ON WOMEN

De Bruyn (1992) summarizes the literature addressing the impact of HIV/AIDS on women in developing countries and presents four factors. First, being infected by HIV/AIDS makes women susceptible to stereotypes. It is not uncommon for women to be blamed for the spread of the disease. One relevant stereotype for women in Africa is that AIDS is a "prostitute's" or women's disease. Prostitution is often considered a moral issue, which makes these women especially susceptible to societal judgment. Blaming them by stigmatizing them as sinful and deviant often prevents them from seeking treatment. And although the high incidence of HIV infection among some female sex workers is one source for transmission, the critical issue for prevention is the need to educate them on prevention rather than blame them for having the disease (De Bruyn, 1992).

Second, gender issues related to differences in communication place women at increased risk of exposure to HIV infection (Pitts, Bowman, & McMaster, 1995). Factors that make them more susceptible include lack of access to information, biological and health factors, and some sexual practices (De Bruyn, 1992). Women feel powerless to change their husbands' behavior and thus unable to influence their risk exposure.

The third factor relates to the social demands on, expectations of, and burdens on women. Seropositive women have been shown to have higher risks of pregnancy complications, including spontaneous abortions and premature births (Bulterys et al., 1990). HIV-infected women are confronted with the psychological burden that if the child is healthy, she must worry about its future once she dies; and if the child is unhealthy, she carries the guilt of a possible ill child who may die (De Bruyn, 1992).

Last, and a significant factor for women, is their social position, which makes it difficult for them to take on prevention measures. Women have traditionally been the primary providers of care for all family members. In sub-Saharan Africa, the enormity of the HIV/AIDS epidemic has taxed customary extended care by family members. Women are faced with caring for people with a terminal illness even when they are at risk themselves, and they are not likely to focus on their own needs.

THE COUNTRY OF UGANDA

Uganda is an inland country nestled within the Rift Valley in East Africa. It expands across the equator and is surrounded by Sudan in the north, Kenya in the east, Tanzania and Rwanda in the south, and Zaire in the west. The country is a land of spectacular scenic beauty of mountain ranges, plateaus, hills, freshwater lakes, rivers, waterfalls, and swamps, which contributed to British Prime Minster Winston Churchill's branding Uganda as "the pearl of Africa" when he visited the country in 1908 (Ministry of Information, 1995).

Lake Victoria spans the Kenya-Tanzania border, where it rains throughout the year. In the center of the country is Lake Kyoga, and in the Western Rift Valley are Lakes Albert, George, and Edward. The outstanding river in Uganda is the Nile, the world's second longest river.

In spite of being on the Equator, Uganda has a temperate climate due to the high altitude of the country's plateaus. There is a lot of sunshine, with daylight and night being nearly the same length throughout the year. There are two dry seasons, with the warmest temperature occurring on the flats of Lake Albert and the coldest temperature occurring on the glaciated zone of Mount Rwenzori (Nzita & Niwampa, 1995). A cool night could be below 60 degrees Fahrenheit and on a hot afternoon, the temperature could rise to 85 degrees.

Historical Context

Uganda was forged by the British between 1890 and 1926 (Ministry of Information, 1995). An agreement was made between the Imperial British East Africa Company (IBEA) and King Mwanga of the ancient kingdom of Buganda that had been in existence for nearly five hundred years (Nzita & Niwampa, 1995). The agreement granted IBEA, on behalf of the British government, the right to "maintain order" and intervene in administrative matters of the Kingdom of Buganda.

This was a time when many countries in Europe were competing with each other to carve out empires in Africa. The practice, referred to as "scrambling," was sanctioned by the Berlin Conference (1884–1885), which had formulated the rules of scrambling (Ministry of Information, 1995). In 1890 an agreement between Britain and Germany placed Buganda (now called Uganda) under the British sphere of influence (Ministry of Information, 1995).

At this time, the Kingdom of Buganda was fighting wars with the neighboring Kingdom of Bunyoro, and there were religious conflicts between the Muslims and Christians and between Catholics and Protestants. This was a perfect opportunity for Uganda to be declared a protectorate by the British government and for an expansion of British control to extend to other kingdoms, eventually making them all provinces of Uganda (Ministry of Information, 1995).

By the 1950s, the tide against colonial rule began to rise. Uganda was granted independence from England in 1962, although the queen of England remained the head of state, represented by the governor-general, until that position was abolished a year later. This was followed by a series of leadership changes until a new constitution, the Republic Constitution, which came into power in 1967, made Uganda a unitary state and at the same time abolished the ancient kingdoms of Buganda, Bunyoro, Toro, and Ankole (Ministry of Information, 1995).

In 1971, Major General Idi Amin took power in a bloody coup, declaring himself "life president" and significantly destroying the economy of Uganda. Supported by the Tanzania People's Defense Forces, Idi Amin's regime was toppled after eight years. Following Idi Amin's regime, the fragile government struggled with constant replacements of leaders, until the National Resistance Movement was launched and eventually took over power in 1986. It established a broad-based government, the Resistance Committees, which promoted investing, rehabilitating infrastructures, restoring the economy, and restoring the country's image. Although under this new government many regions began to enjoy peace and security, new armies began to develop to overthrow the government. Some of these armies are today almost nonexistent (including the Force Obote Back and Uganda People's Army), but other relatively active armies are the West Nile Bank Front and the Lord's Resistance Army in northern Uganda (Ministry of Information, 1995).

Setting

Today, Uganda is divided into thirty-nine districts named after major towns. A number of powers and functions have been decentralized to these district service committees. Each district is demarcated into counties and divided into subcounties. Every subcounty is broken down into parishes, and each parish is composed of villages. In a village, all residents over the age of eighteen are members of the village council and elect an executive committee of nine officials. One official committee is the secretary for women's affairs, who controls the one-woman representation to the district council.

The capital of Uganda is Kampala, and its surrounding areas make up the district where most of the women in the discussion groups resided. Makerere University is centrally located in the town of Kampala, and its medical school is housed on the grounds of the public Mulago Hospital. Makerere University was founded before World War II to train the elite of Eastern and Southern Africa. Prior to the civil war, unrest, and some say the "Idi Amin regime," Makerere was thought of as Britain's "Oxford of Africa" (Winter & Shullenberger, 1992–1994). At the time of my Fulbright Lecture appointment, Makerere was struggling to recover from more than a decade of neglect. Furniture and equipment were scarce, and journals and books published since 1970, specifically in the field of psychology, were in short supply. And yet the students were bright, well educated, respectful, and extremely motivated.

The number of women students in the medical school was small—approximately one out of every ten students. However, the women students were unlike what was initially described to me as traditional, in that they would likely stay in the background in relation to the men students. Instead, the women students took on an advocacy role, speaking out about the conditions of women and children patients. During grand rounds supervision, many would highlight the social and emotional needs of the women rather than strictly focus on the behavioral symptoms manifesting their patient's psychological state.

THE WOMEN'S DISCUSSION GROUPS

Residents and upper-level medical students (females and males) rotating through psychiatry were inundated by women either infected with or otherwise affected by HIV/AIDS. Women patients voiced concerns about the future and the plight of their children. Although many mothers were sick with the virus or other conditions, their children often accompanied them to the clinic or remained with them during hospital visits. Along with available family members, children as young as age four cared for their mothers.

The women's discussion groups grew out of the long lines waiting for care and the need expressed by some women to prepare their children for their changing medical conditions. For women who were not now sick, their fears of becoming sick and their existing caretaking responsibilities were the focus of their participation. At any time, a group might have as few as three or as many as eleven women. Often the women were related to each other (for example, sister to sister-in-law, first wife to mother-in-law, mother to daughter, aunt to niece), and multiple generations were not uncommon.

Although the groups were designed to be drop-in and open-ended, many women came weekly until they were unable to travel, due to illness, or until a message was received of their passing. The day of the group was consistent with the clinic day for that week. Since staff patterns and priorities changed from week to week, the discussion group day also changed. The beginning and ending times of group discussions were designed around midday meals. Fruit and a pot dish were provided to participants and their accompanying family members. Transport tokens were also provided for their trip back home.

During my Fulbright year, there were seventeen group discussions with women, and eighty-seven women who participated. Thirty-six of the same women participated in twelve sessions, twenty-one participated in nine sessions, sixteen participated in seven sessions, and eight participated in five sessions. Three women participated in three sessions, two women in two sessions, and one woman in only one session. All participants were mothers and ranged from fifteen to forty-one years old, with the mean age of twenty-four. The average number of children being cared for was six. Many of the mothers and caretakers had assumed the responsibility for children of other family members who had died from AIDS.

Although English is the national language of Uganda, the most widely spoken African language around Kampala is Luganda. While a number of participants had some familiarity with English, two women medical students assumed the role of interpreter during all groups.

Over 40 percent (thirty-four participants) died from complications of HIV/AIDS during the course of the year. In addition, of the fifteen pregnant women infected by the virus, eleven of them lost their infants in early-term deliveries.

THE WOMEN AND CULTURES OF UGANDA

There are several significant cultural communities that make up Uganda. These diverse cultural groups are said to speak over thirty languages and were determined by natural and social environmental demands. There are four classifications of the people of Uganda. The first group, the Pygmoids, are described as the closest relatives to the Stone Age people in Uganda and are said to be the pygmoid Batwa and the Bambuti. Ethnically they are related to the pygmies of the Congo and the Koikoi San and Bushmen and Hottentots of South Africa (Nzita & Niwampa, 1995). Two of the women identified this ethnic group as their family of origin.

The second classification of people is the Bantu. They occupy a large part of Zaire and Southern as well as Eastern Africa. They are credited with introducing ironworking, agriculture, and centralized governments that existed in the Kingdoms of Buganda, Bunyoro-Kitara, Nkore, and Toro. While there are striking similarities in language and customs among the different Bantu groups, each group has its own identifying customs and practices (Nzita & Niwampa, 1995). Eighty-one of the participants in the discussion groups identified this ethnic group as their family of origin.

The third classification of people is known as the Nilotic group and can be divided into the Highland-Nilotes and the Plain-Nilotes. This includes the Nilo-Hamites (the Karimojong, the Iteso, the Kuman, and the Langi). The River-Lake Niolotes are described as the Luo (the Acholi, the Alur, and the Jopadhola). The Luo are related to populations in the Sudan and are credited with introducing the idea of centralized states (districts) (Nzita & Niwampa, 1995). Two of the women identified this group as their family's ethnic origin.

The last group of people in Uganda is known as the Madi-Moru. They originate from southern Sudan, northeastern Zaire, and the Central African Republic. In Uganda, this includes the Lugbara, the Madi, the Metu, the Okebu, and the Lendu. They constitute the largest ethnic group in West Nile, and their language is one of the eastern Sudanic languages of the Madi and the Lugbara. Significant to the Lugbara are two important rituals of tribal identification: face tattooing and the extraction of six frontal teeth from the lower jaw. The ritual is intended as a way of decoration and an initiation into adulthood (Nzita & Niwampa, 1995). Two of the women identified this group as the origin of their family's ethnicity.

THE BAGANDA WOMEN (BANTU CLASSIFICATION)

Given that the Baganda is the largest ethnic group in Uganda and reflects over 90 percent of the women in the discussion groups, this chapter limits its focus to this tribal group. The Baganda are found in the districts of Kampala, Mpigi, Mukono, Masaka, Kalangala, Kiboga, Rakai, and Mubende. These districts also represent the largest concentration of reported HIV/AIDS cases (Uganda AIDS Commission, 1994).

Beliefs in the Supernatural

Belief in superhuman spirits dominated the themes of several group discussions. These spirits were described as representing one of three characteristically different spirits: Mizimu, Misambwa, and Balubaale. The Balubaale were described as men who had lived exceptional lives and had carried this into death. This spirit was often highly respected so the message they delivered was difficult to avoid. The Mizimu were described as the ghosts of dead people who haunted primarily whomever the dead person had a conflict with. There were different experiences in how the Mizimu would be shown. At times, the Mizimu could enter natural objects and would become Misambwa (Nzita & Niwampa, 1995).

Initial discussions around curtailing the spread of HIV/AIDS with condom use were first expressed as symbolic of the Misambwa. The belief that the dead ghost was controlling the deadly virus made many participants skeptical about using condoms consistently. Several researchers have suggested that certain beliefs place women at risk of transmission because preventive measures such as condom use are rejected. A study by Schoepf, wa Nkera, Ntsomo, et al. (1988) found that some women in Zaire feared condoms would injure them and cause sterility.

In addition, some struggled with the desire to have more children, especially since many of their infants died within the first year of life (Schulz, Cates, & O'Mara, 1987).

Nzita and Niwampa (1995) describe the different functions of the Balubaale. The two most significant ones are referred to as the God of the Sky (Katonda, Ggulu) and God of Lightning (Kiwanuka). Balubaale also included the God of Plague (Kawumpuli), God of Smallpox (Ndaula), God of Earthquake (Musisi), God of Lake Wamala (Wamala), and God of Lake Victoria (Mukasa). Some of the women questioned why a powerful past healer had not yet come back as the God of HIV/AIDS.

Discussing Marriage Among Baganda Women

Historically, Baganda were polygamous; a man could have several wives if he could provide for them. Formerly, parents would initiate marriage arrangements for their children, and daughters were not expected to question the wishes of their parents (Heise & Elias, 1995). It was not uncommon for old men to marry young girls in hopes of revitalizing themselves. Similar to the HIV/AIDS epidemic, it was not uncommon for infected men to believe that having sex with virgin or uninfected women might renew their health status. Reports of rape in sub-Saharan Africa have been associated with such beliefs (Reid, 1990). In a study by Bagarukayo (1991), 27 of 184 primary school children in Uganda reported being "forced" to have sexual intercourse.

Today, more young boys and girls participate in selecting their mates, although the economic status of the family greatly influences these decisions. Payment of the appropriate bride wealth is symbolic and expected prior to a formal ceremony, when the bride is officially given to her husband's family. In villages where bride-wealth rates are high, many young men may delay marriage and consequently seek out multiple partners, which increases the risk of contracting HIV and passing it on to their future bride (Willmore, 1990).

Many of the group participants described their families as having few resources. For some of the women, their families handed them over or encouraged them to marry without a bride wealth, or payment of bride wealth was done after the marriage was stabilized. This seemed more related to lessening the burden of caring for them and desiring that they would have a better life. Several of the women discussed having few options in complying with the wishes of their husband or husband's family. For those women who were considered "stubborn," wife battering was not uncommon. And unlike other groups in Uganda, divorce was also very common (Nzita & Niwampa, 1995).

Related to the women's sense of worth or value, in a study examining reactions to repeated STD infections and gender issues, Pitts et al. (1995) found that women feel powerless to negotiate sexual matters. It was not that women lacked the knowledge of the ramifications of sexually transmitted diseases and HIV infection, but rather that their behavior was not consistent with the knowledge (Pitts et al., 1995).

A number of the women (thirty-seven) in the group were widowed and often discussed their husband's sickness and death as related to complications of AIDS, although women would seldom associate their own illness with that of their husband. Regrettably, a woman whose husband dies from AIDS, even if she is seronegative, may be unable to remarry (Toomey, 1989; Rosenbert, Schulz, & Burton, 1986). One theme the women discussed was the change in attention and self-care they were beginning to give themselves following the death of their husbands. At some level, women appeared to be working through the stigma of being ill and were gaining the courage to take care of themselves.

At another level, women faced with economical survival issues after the loss of their husband discussed custom and ritual practices that consisted of their sharing the household of their brother-in-law or father-in-law. The expectations placed on many of them were similar to duties of a second wife. However, most of them accepted this obligation, since prioritizing the care of their children was prominent in their thoughts.

Conversations About Children

Many of the caretakers in the groups discussed finding work for their "orphan" children (as young as nine and ten years old) as a "house girl" or "house boy." In this role, children would live with families and, their mothers hoped, be taken care of. Consistent with research conducted by Brouwer et al. (2000), caretakers discussed the limited resources available to them to care for additional children. There was not enough money to pay school fees, purchase uniforms, buy medicine, or even provide food. There were additional fears that the children would become sick, like the parents who left them. The immediate concerns for providing the orphan children the basic necessities, fear of the children becoming sick, and fear of the children being abandoned to the streets seemed to outweigh concern about the possibility that the children might be victimized as workers (Schussler, 1992; Hunter, 1990; Konde-Lule et al., 1996).

Unfortunately, eleven of the women in the groups had been in house girl roles as young children and reportedly were sexually molested. Seven of these woman discussed repeatedly contracting sexually transmitted diseases (syphilis) and reported symptoms consistent with HIV/AIDS. Interestingly, these young women were more guarded when talking specifically about their bosses, since many of them described supportive relationships with the boss's wife. It was later revealed that in at least four group discussions, participants included the women (the bosses' wives) who had employed the young ladies. Two of the wives reported similar symptoms as their workers and concurred that the mutual supportive relationship was reciprocal.

The discussions with the mothers about their children can be best described as "preparing" or "nestling." Many of the mothers were purposeful in inviting their relatives (caretakers) to the groups with them.

Their fears of abandoning their child and not having anyone to care for their child appeared to be the driving force in sitting through difficult discussions.

A number of infected young mothers struggled with alternatives to breast-feeding. Similar to some of their supernatural beliefs and rituals, they sometimes associated the sick infant with rejecting nursing or being cursed rather than considering the impact of the transmission of the virus. A small number of pregnant women (four of fifteen) identified receiving a "special drink" to help them have healthy babies. These four women were participating in a clinical trail of zidovudine (AZT) to prevent mother-to-child transmission of HIV-1 (Kigotho, 1997). They remained optimistic and attributed the "special drink" to "special powers" of a "special God."

Conversations About Dying and Death

Historically, many Buganda attributed deaths to sorcerers, supernatural spirits, or wizards. It was not uncommon for many women to admit to consulting with a witch doctor. Five participants who identified with the Banyoro tribe within the Bantu group described death as a "real person." They discussed how they would like to be "prepared" (hair combed, clothing and corpse cleaned) and have their body left in the house for family members to pray over. According to Willmore (1990), ritual cleansing, which includes the women having intercourse with a family member, is believed to purify the deceased person and free the dead person's spirit. Unfortunately, this practice may increase the spread of HIV (Willmore, 1990).

According to Nzita and Niwampa (1995), this same tribe traditionally would prepare a millet mixture and place it in the right hand of the deceased. Children were required to take a small quantity of the mixture from the dead man's hand and eat it. Although none of the five Banyoro participants described this practice, they all discussed the desire for their children to have a part of them after death (for example, a lock of hair). The strong fear of death for the Bantu group of women appeared to be centered around how to rid themselves of any bad spirits.

Following the third group meeting, the news of the passing of several previous group members took center stage. Since some group meeting times varied from weekly to biweekly, participants who had passed were already buried. Family members who remained in the group would share the various ceremonial rituals performed on the deceased, and much discussion would follow about ceremonies of other deaths and some of the ritual differences among the tribes and villages.

Participants did not engage in silent meditation; rather, they would cry furiously. In part, the women's sorrow appeared to be related to the long silence of the HIV/AIDS virus. While both the women infected by the virus and the women caregivers in the group openly discussed their losses, these discussions did not include identifying HIV/AIDS as the possible culprit. When symptoms of their various illnesses were discussed, such as persistent diarrhea, oral thrush, respiratory conditions, and fever, participants more readily attributed the symptoms to malaria and other sexually transmitted diseases, such as syphilis, herpes, or gonorrhea.

Although many discussions appeared to avoid linking their symptoms to HIV/AIDS, many women shared cultural remedies with each other for addressing obvious skin rashes typically associated with HIV. Unfortunately, some forms of self-treatment by women may present an increase in risk factors. A study by Dallabetta, Miotti, Chiphangwi, Liomba, & Saah (1990) examining over three thousand pregnant women in Malawi found a significant correlation between HIV infection and the use of topical agents (such as herbs and aluminum hydroxide powder) to treat vaginal discharges. It was hypothesized that because these agents had an irritating and erosive effect on the vaginal mucosa, their use may have facilitated entry of HIV (Dallabetta et al., 1990, 1991).

INFLUENCING FACTORS

Uganda has demonstrated that consistent and early multisectoral control can reduce the prevalence and incidence of HIV infection (Okware, Opio, Musinguzi, & Waibale, 2001). Beginning with the AIDS Control Programme established in 1987 by the Ministry of Health, a countrywide campaign was launched. The primary goal of the program was to fight HIV/AIDS through dissemination of basic information, effective blood transfusion services, and epidemiological surveillance (STD/AIDS Control Programme, 2000). Beginning as a "silent" creeper, HIV/AIDS became the focal issue at every district and community level through legislative, administrative, and political directives (Okware et al., 2001).

The attention to the disease was fueled in part by the rapid increase in infection, morbidity, and death. As HIV/AIDS began to have a direct impact on one in every ten households in Uganda, there were more consistent efforts to develop a multitude of strategies. Through mass media and folk media, the course and causes of HIV/AIDS were reported.

Perhaps one of the most significant influences in understanding the declining incidence of the disease is the availability of drugs to patients free of charge (Okware et al., 2001; Auerbach & Coates, 2000). In addition, the government has strengthened the capacity for comprehensive AIDS case management at all levels of the health care system (Okware et al., 2001).

CONCLUSION

The access, timing, interest, and response to the drop-in and informal discussion groups parallel the country's attention to controlling HIV/AIDS. The psychological impact of the disease was beginning to take precedence for the country and, more important, for families. As women gained access to programs in the clinic, they were also able to experience more women in nontraditional roles.

Not surprisingly, women patients shared concerns and fears related to the social and emotional challenges of being sick, of living, and of dying, to other women in caretaking roles. Equally significant for these women was that they were no longer isolated from each other. These open-ended discussions provided an opportunity for them to grieve, express conflict, acknowledge ambivalence, and talk about the customs and rituals that were challenging their very existence.

References

Ankrah, M. E. (1993). The impact of HIV/AIDS on the family and other significant relationships: the African clan revisited. *AIDS Care, 5*(1), 5–20.

Anyango, O. M., Momanyi, K. J., & Muriuki, J. (1995). *Feelings and experiences of single HIV-positive women about their children.* Paper presented at the Ninth International Conference on AIDS and STDs in Africa, Kampala, Uganda.

Auerbach, J., & Coates, T. (2000). HIV prevention research: Accomplishments and challenges for the third decade of AIDS. *Journal of Public Health, 90*(7), 1029–1032.

Bagarukayo, H. (1991). *KAP study on AIDS among school pupils in Kabale district, Uganda.* Paper presented at the Seventh International Conference on AIDS, Florence, Italy.

Bobat, R., Coovadia, H., Coutsoudis, A., & Moodley, D. (1996). Determinants of mother-to-child transmission of human immunodeficiency virus type I infection in a cohort from Duran, South Africa. *Pediatric Infectious Disease Journal, 15*(7), 604–610.

Brouwer, C.N.M., Lok, C. L., Wolffers, I., & Serbagalls, S. (2000). Psychosocial and economic aspects of HIV/AIDS and counseling of caretakers of HIV-infected children in Uganda. *AIDS Care, 12*(5), 535–540.

Bulterys, M., Chao, A., Saah, A., Dushimamana, A., Habimana, P., Hoover, D., Shea, M., & Duerr, A. (1990). Risk factors for HIV-1 seropositivity among rural and urban pregnant women in Rwanda. *Int. Conf. AIDS, 6*, 269 (abstract no. Th.C.576).

Centers for Disease Control, Center for Infectious Diseases, AIDS Program. (1987). Revision of the CDC surveillance case definition for acquired immunodeficiency syndrome: Council of state and territorial epidemiologists, *MMWR, 36*(1S), 3–13.

Chin, J. (1990). Current and future dimensions of the HIV/AIDS pandemic in women and children. *Lancet, 336*, 221–224.

Crowley, J. L. (1995). Crisis as challenge: Counseling counselors, persons living with HIV/AIDS and survivors. *Journal of Social Development in Africa, 3*(2), 35–52.

Dallabetta, G., Miotti, P., Chiphangwi, J., Liomba, G., & Saah, A. (1990). *Vaginal tightening agents as risk factors for acquisition of HIV.* Paper presented at the Sixth International Conference on AIDS, San Francisco, California.

Dallabetta, G., Odaka, N., Hoover, D., Chiphangwi, J., Liomba, G., Miotti, P., & Saah, A. (1991). High socio-economic status is a risk factor for HIV-1 infection but not for sexually transmitted diseases in Malawian women. Paper presented at the Seventh International Conference on AIDS, Florence, Italy.

De Bruyn, M. (1992). Women and AIDS in developing countries. *Social Science Medicine, 34*(3), 249–262.

Gostin, L. (2002). Aids in Africa among women and infants: A human rights framework. *Hastings Center Report, 32*(5), 9–10.

Green, E. (1992). Sexually transmitted disease, ethno medicine and health policy in Africa. *Social Science Medicine, 35*(2), 121–130.

Guay, L. A., Musoke, P., Fleming, T., Bagenda, D., Allen, M., Nakabiito, C., Sherman, J., Bakaki, P., Ducar, C., Deseyve, M., Emel, L., Mirochnick, M., Fowler, M. G., Mofenson, L., Miotti, P., Dransfield, K., Bray, D., Mmiro, F., & Jackson, J. B. (1999). Intrapartum and neonatal single-dose nevirapine compared with zidovudine for prevention of mother-to-child transmission of HIV-1 in Kampala, Uganda: HIVNET 012 randomised trial. *Lancet, 354*(9181), 795–802.

Heise, L., & Elias, C. (1995). Transforming AIDS prevention to meet women's needs: A focus on developing countries. *Social Science and Medicine, 40,* 931–943.

Hunter, S. S. (1990). Orphans as a window on the AIDS epidemic in sub-Saharan Africa: Initial results and implications of a study in Uganda. *Social Science and Medicine, 31*(6), 681–690.

Kigotho, A. W. (1997). Trial to reduce vertical transmission of HIV-1 on schedule in Uganda. *Lancet, 350,* 1683.

Konde-Lule, J. K., Sewankambo, N., Wawer, M. J., & Sengozi, R. (1996). *The impact of AIDS on families in Rakai District Uganda.* Paper presented at the Eleventh International Conference on AIDS, Vancouver, Canada.

Ministry of Information. (1995). *Uganda: The pearl of Africa.* Kampala, Uganda: Ministry of Information.

Nyanzi, S., Pool, R., & Kinsman, J. (2001). Negotiation of sexual relationships among school pupils in southwestern Uganda. *AIDS Care, 13,* 83–98.

Nzita, R., & Niwampa, M. (1995). *Peoples and cultures of Uganda.* Kampala, Uganda: Fountain Publishers.

Okware, S., Opio, A., Musinguzi, J., & Waibale, P. (2001). Fighting HIV/AIDS: Is success possible? *Bulletin of the World Health Organization, 79*(12), 1113–1120.

Pitts, M., Bowman, M., & McMaster, J. (1995). Reactions to repeated STD infections: Psychosocial aspects and gender issues in Zimbabwe. *Social Science Medicine, 40*(9), 1299–1304.

Reid, E. (1990). Young women and the HIV epidemic. *Development (Journal of the Society of International Development), 1,* 16–19.

Rosenbert, M. J., Schulz, K. F., & Burton, N. (1986). Sexually transmitted diseases in sub-Saharan Africa: A priority list based on Family Health International's Meeting. *Lancet, 2*(8499), 152–153.

Schoepf, B., wa Nkera, R., Ntsomo, P., et al. (1988). AIDS, women and society in Central Africa. In R. Kulstad (Ed.), *AIDS 1988: AAAS symposia papers.* American Association for the Advancement of Science, Compact Library, AIDS. [CD-ROM].

Schulz, K. F., Cates, W., & O'Mara, P. (1987). Pregnancy loss, infant death, and suffering: Legacy of syphilis and gonorrhea in Africa. *Genitourinary Medicine, 63,* 320–325.

Schussler, G. (1992). Coping strategies and individual meanings of illness. *Social Science and Medicine, 34*(4), 427–432.

Serwadda, D., Mugerwa, R. D., Sewankambo, N. K., Lwegaba, A., Carswell, J. W., Kirya, G. B., Bayley, A. C., Downing, R. G., Tedder, R. S., & Clayden, S. A. (1985) Slim disease, a new disease in Uganda and its association with HTLV III infection. *Lancet, 2*(8460), 849–852.

STD/AIDS Control Programme. (2000). *HIV/AIDS surveillance report.* Kampala, Uganda: Ministry of Health.

Toomey, G. (1989) A snake in the house. Living with AIDS in Uganda. *IDRC Reports,* 6–9.

Uganda AIDS Commission. (1994). *HIV/AIDS situation analysis.* Kampala, Uganda: Author.

Uganda Demographic and Health Survey (DHS III). (1995). Kampala, Uganda: Ministry of Health.

Willmore, B. (Ed.). (1990). *Report of the Southern African NGOs Conference on AIDS.* Harare, Zimbabwe.

Winter, E., & Shullenberger, W. (1992–1994). *Uganda: An introduction for Fulbrighters.* Unpublished document.

World Health Organization/Global Program on AIDS/Surveillance, Forecasting, and Impact Assessment (WHO/GPA/SFI). (1991a). *Update: AIDS cases reported to Surveillance, Forecasting and Impact Assessment Unit.* Geneva: Global Program on AIDS.

World Health Organization/Global Program on AIDS/Surveillance, Forecasting, and Impact Assessment (WHO/GPA/SFI). (1991b). *Current and future dimensions of the HIV/AIDS pandemic: A capsule summary.* Geneva: World Health Organization.

CHAPTER SEVENTEEN

Population Control in China

Renee Huebner

T he study of the world's population has been of interest and concern to many international organizations. While natural disasters and epidemic illnesses historically slowed world population growth, diseases that once wiped out an entire culture can now be treated with modern medicine. Through the advancement of modern medicine, people are able to live longer, healthier lives. Consequently, there is an imbalance in the rate of births and deaths per year, and the growing population has become a strain on the world's resources. The U.S. Bureau of Census (1998) reported an estimated 50 million deaths worldwide in 1996 against an estimated 130 million births. Numbers such as these have led developing countries to impose policies that are geared toward controlling such dramatic growth.

China's population control policy has been an issue of debate since its inception. In 1970, China took the initiative to implement a policy designed to keep the country's population growth to a minimum. This policy was also implemented in order to sustain the natural resources and provide a higher quality of life. The policy's original purpose was to limit the number of children per household, thus enhancing socioeconomic development (Yu, 1994).

While there is great concern over the ethical and moral issues involved with the policy, it is important to look at the way the policy is enforced and why this policy was implemented in the first place. Perhaps with a better understanding, those who argue against family planning may find themselves working to reform the policy rather than abolish it. This chapter reviews the policy's history and some of the consequences that Chinese citizens have faced as a result of it.

THE HISTORY OF THE POLICY

The People's Republic of China has the largest population in the world, with an estimated 1.3 billion people (Population World, 2003). In recognition of that, China's government officials need to take into account the growth of population and the decrease of the country's natural resources. In an effort to balance the two, China's government implemented a policy known as the Family Planning Policy or, more commonly, the "population control policy." In order to monitor the growing population, the government created a system to keep track of its current residents. Every resident of China has a household registration, or a *hukou* (Johnson, 1996). This information gives government officials the place of residence and occupation of every person in the country. Family planning officials, or cadres, can then easily assess the rates of pregnancy, births, deaths, and family size. The registration also enables the government to identify couples over the one-child quota. In certain parts of China, families that have more than the allowable number of children can be fined or heavily taxed (Boland, 1997).

China's plan in implementing the one-child policy was to address it through education and persuasion. The government felt that if the people of China had better means of birth control and understood the effects of their chosen birth control method, that alone would constrain the population growth (Isaacs, 1995). The government also felt that giving incentives to those who complied with the new policy would better serve the efforts of control (Boland, 1997). Some incentives included better housing, higher medical and educational benefits, and promotions at work. In contrast, there were penalties for not adhering to the policy: demotions at work, denial of social benefits, and even fines (Boland, 1997).

In 1970, the government decided that placing restrictions on behaviors related to the growing population would better serve the country's growth epidemic (Scotese & Wang, 1995). It was thought that getting married at a later age would help stabilize the country's growth. Those who lived in rural areas would marry no earlier than age twenty-five for men and no earlier than age twenty-three for women. Men and women in urban areas would marry no earlier than age twenty-eight and age twenty-five, respectively (Scotese & Wang, 1995). Couples that married prior to these ages were to space their children five years apart (Boland, 1997). In addition, married couples wishing to have children were encouraged to limit their families to two children for urban areas and three children for rural areas (Scotese & Wang, 1995). In both rural and urban areas, anyone wishing to have a child could not do so until a government-approved application was obtained. This policy was in place for nine years.

In 1979, China's government implemented the one-child policy. The policy stated that married couples living in urban areas were to have no more than one child per household. If the couple lived in a rural part of the country and their firstborn was a girl, they were allowed to have a second child, to attempt to have a boy (Cooney, 1999).

This change in policy has raised a concern related to the abandonment of female babies in the country. When the one-child amendment was added in 1979, the number of missing female babies and abortions increased (Johnson, Banghan, & Liyao, 1998). The number of abortions in 1978 was an estimated 5.3 million, and the estimated number for 1979 was 7.9 million (Johnston, 2004). Unfortunately, there are no records available for the number of missing female babies.

While the government continuously and adamantly denies a sudden increase in abortions and missing girls, research has shown that there is a legitimate reason for concern (Society for the Protection of Unborn Children, 2003). In China, the preference for males has been part of society for centuries. It is thought that this preference is due to the fact that men carry on family names, they carry the financial responsibility, and most important, they carry higher status (Cooney & Li, 1999). In urban parts of the country, where the one-child policy is strictly enforced, women who discover that they are carrying a female fetus may opt for an early abortion (Johnson et al., 1998). Unfortunately, those who find out later in the pregnancy that they are carrying a female sometimes resort to infant abandonment or even infanticide. While the government denies that such practice exists, there are many babies unaccounted for every year (Junhong, 2001).

CHILD ABANDONMENT

One effect of China's policy that is not easily documented is that of infant abandonment. This is an area in which information is extremely difficult to obtain due to the legal consequences of this act. Because of the sensitive nature, most researchers have avoided investigating the problem of the "missing girls" (Johnson et al., 1998). Many in China will argue that the practice of leaving infant girls to be found and cared for by government agencies or others does not exist. When investigating this dilemma, it is important to understand why this sex-selective abandonment began.

As far back as the fourth century, the people of China believed that there was no such thing as "too many sons" (Wolf, 2001). There is no evidence that there was a limiting of male offspring by the government or by the people. It was common in the north to take a fully mature female and marry her off to ensure that she will produce a grandson at the earliest age possible (Wolf, 2001). In the south, female babies were often given away to reduce breast-feeding, as they believed it delayed conception, thus reducing the number of boys the mother could bear (Wolf, 2001). Female infant abandonment increased throughout the 1970s and 1980s so significantly that China's Civil Affairs Office wrote in the *Ministry of Civil Affairs,* a national publication, that "there is a need to strengthen efforts to oppose the practice while taking steps to improve the welfare system's ability to care for the increasing number of abandoned infants" (Johnson, 1996). This statement may have been based on the report of over sixteen thousand abandoned children between 1986 and 1990 (Johnson, 1996). Of these, 92 percent were females, a percentage that makes it difficult to argue that the practice of male preference does not exist. This increase between 1986 and 1990 may be due to the stricter controls by central administration to pressure local authorities to be in better compliance with the policy. Local authorities who failed to meet the birth planning quotas would become ineligible for promotions or bonuses, or their units would be disqualified from being advanced in agricultural production. These advancements often came with many privileges and connections. The result of this pressure was an increase in various types of birth control, such as intrauterine devices (IUDs), sterilization, and abortion, as well as, apparently, abandonment (Wolf, 2001).

ABORTION

One of the major controversies over family planning policy is the way in which the laws are enforced. Is the government of China forcing abortions on women? If so, what can be done to protect the women and children and their human rights? Aird (1972) notes that during 1957, following a directive from the Ministry of Health, induced abortion in the first ten weeks of pregnancy was legalized. However, Tietze and Henshaw (1986) reported that "abortions were not commonly performed until the 1970s, when China instituted the family planning program. The number of reported abortions per 100 known pregnancies increased significantly, from 12 in 1971 to 33 in 1980." By 1983, after the government began promoting the one-child policy, the total number of reported abortions reached more than 14 million. With the amendment of the one-child policy in 1984, the number of reported abortions dropped to 9 million (Hardee-Cleveland & Banister, 1988). However, by the late 1980s, the number of abortions increased again when new requirements were imposed in order to minimize the "unfavorable demographic impact" of the 1984 amendment. The new rules required the woman to be older at the time of a second pregnancy and there was to be a long duration between the first and second birth (Hardee-Cleveland & Banister, 1988). Based on these numbers, it is difficult to argue that abortion was not the main method used to avoid penalties for unplanned births (Ping & Smith, 1995).

With the growing number of abortions, the question of whether the women of China are being forced to abort their babies must be addressed. Some research has suggested that these women are being coerced into aborting pregnancies that fall over the birth quota (Cooney, 1999). Along with various penalties for unplanned pregnancies came other detriments as well. For instance, the children of unplanned, unapproved births would not be listed on the population register (Daen, 2000) and as a result would not receive medical benefits, grain rations, opportunities for school, and chances for employment (Daen, 2000). With various penalties being issued for unplanned births, the consequences of having an abortion or abandoning a child might seem minimal by comparison.

The practice of sex-selective abortion became popular in rural parts of China after the one-child policy took effect (Junhong, 2001). It has been reported that between 1971 and 1985, there were over 100 million "coercive birth control operations" (Society for the Protection of Un-born Children, 2003). These operations include forced abortions and forced sterilization. In 1983, along with the previously reported 14 mil-lion abortions, there were a reported 21 million sterilizations and 18 million IUD insertions (Aird, 1972).

INFANTICIDE

While it is difficult to attribute the number of missing female births to infanticide, it is equally difficult to deny that it occurs. The practice of killing infants is part of China's history. Han Fei Tzu, a Chinese philoso-pher in the third century B.C., wrote, "Moreover, parents' attitude to-ward children is such that when they bear a son, they congratulate each other, but when they bear a daughter they kill her. Both come from the parents' love, but they congratulate each other when it is a boy and kill it if it is a girl because they are considering their later convenience and calculating their long-term interests" (Wu, 2003).

Gender-cide Watch, an organization under the Gender Issues Edu-cation Foundation (GIEF), was developed to educate society about the worldwide phenomenon of infanticide. Even an organization whose sole purpose is to track genocide and gender-selective killings is unable to report an overall number of girls who die annually from infanticide. The organization's difficulty comes from the inability to calculate any actual numbers due to the unreliability and ambiguity of the data. Even so, the estimated numbers of casualties would most likely be in the hundreds of thousands (Jones, 2000). There have been arguments that infanticide in China can be attributed to culture; that is, although the practice of infanticide is illegal and punishable in China for those who are caught, it should be considered acceptable culturally (Isaacs, 1995). It is widely accepted that Eastern cultures do not share the same val-ues as Western cultures, and decisions about family and basic human rights are considered a Western value (Isaacs, 1995). For instance, the women's movement of the Western world occurred over thirty years ago. In China, there have yet to be any major organized movements to improve the social status of women.

We should also consider the alternative to infanticide or abortion for these baby girls. There have been studies showing that orphanages in parts of China are nothing more than torture chambers at best. An article by Hansel (2002) describes one orphanage as a "dying room." It was observed that the children are chained to a chair over a bucket, serving as a toilet, until they are removed, only to be chained to their bed (Hansel, 2002). If the mothers of these babies know that the fate of their child is a long, suffering death, perhaps abortion is the more humane path.

BIRTH RATIOS

One major concern for those who argue against family planning is the difference in sex ratio for men and women. For most of the 1960s and 1970s, the sex ratio at birth in China was close to 106 males per 100 females (Junhong, 2001). The sex ratio has increased to 111 males to every 100 females over the past thirty years, and the answer as to what caused the change is unclear. Researchers speculate that the factors for the differences are underreporting of female births, excess female infant mortality, or sex-selective abortion of female fetuses (Junhong, 2001). The most recent report of gender differences came in 2002, when the ratio was 116 boys to every 100 girls. According to the China Population Information and Resource Center (2003), one of the problems that China will face in the future is this growing difference in number of men and women. It was estimated that by the year 2010, men would outnumber women by 43 million. One of the main consequences of this outcome would be that there would potentially be men who could not find a woman to marry.

GENDER ISSUES

The issue of population control typically raises concerns regarding basic human rights of reproduction. One of the arguments is that humans should have the basic right to procreate and also to decide on family size. However, in China, family size is decided for the people by the government. Often ignored are the effects of this policy on individuals. In 1999, it was reported in the *Psychiatric Times* that there are 300,000 suicides annually in China, ten times the number in the United States (Kaplan, 1999). And the suicide rates for China are two to three times higher than for the United States (Kaplan, 1999). Some would attribute this to higher depression rates since depression has been correlated with suicide. This, however, is not the case in China. While depression is on the rise in China, the occurrence of depression is still lower than that in Western civilization (Kaplan, 1999). Research has found that China is host to 40 percent of the world's suicides, and that

50 percent of the suicides worldwide in women occurred in China (Kleinman & Cohen, 1997). The study noted that China's suicides are more common among women than men and that 90 percent of suicides occur in rural areas.

Lastly, the study found that the suicide rates for women between the ages of sixteen and twenty-six were particularly high (Kleinman & Cohen, 1997). This phenomenon is likely to be related to the one-child policy (Kleinman & Cohen, 1997). Perhaps the cultural pressure to have a son is too overwhelming for these young women, and when they fail to have a son they may feel a loss of self-worth. It is likely that some of these young women turn to suicide rather than live under such extreme and contradictory pressures from their families, who want sons, and the government, which wants to limit births.

A MOVEMENT FOR CHANGE

Journalist Stephen Moore (1999) has written, "To this day no one knows precisely how many babies and women have died at the hands of the population control fanatics in China. What we do know is that this program will go down in history as one of the greatest abuses of human rights in the 20th century. . . . Birth control policy has already claimed an estimated 5–10 million victims. An estimated 80–90 percent of the victims have been girls."

China's one-child policy has been in effect for over two decades and has been the cause of millions of deaths of babies (Hansel, 2002). It is clear that the policy will continue to be in effect and its penalties will continue as well. What the government of China should be working on is to change the policy and how it is enforced. The goals should be complete reform of this policy that clearly evidences inhumane acts of abandonment and murder.

The first consideration in revising a policy is the effect the law is having on the people of China. Who is suffering the most from population control? Research has shown that there are numerous female babies who are abandoned at birth or aborted (Moore, 1999). The women carrying these babies are victims as well. The obvious step to take is to educate these women about birth control. Implementing a major drive throughout China to teach women and men about the different methods of birth control is one strategy. To make a true change in traditional ways of treating women, the change must begin with the women themselves.

In every society, providing women with the same educational opportunities as men has resulted in a decrease in population growth as women find more ways to participate in the activities of their culture.

Once women understand that they are the ones to decide whether they want to have a child, society and traditions will begin to evolve. This evolution in women's thinking has begun in China. As part of the government's new way of dealing with population growth, women are being educated. As a result, the Shanghai Population and Family Planning Committee reported that the number of women choosing not to have more children is increasing. Also, the Women's Federation survey showed that 10 percent of Shanghai's women were deciding against having children at all (China Population Information and Research Center, 2003).

FUNDING

When a country as large as China makes a policy that strips people of the right to reproduce freely, the world takes notice. Because law enforces the population policy, political parties worldwide become involved. One of the main organizations linked to population control is the United Nations Population Fund (UNFPA), which "works in 142 countries to improve women's reproductive health care, including healthy pregnancies and voluntary birth control" (Enda, 2002). The UNFPA was once denied funds by the Reagan administration due to the forms of population control such as forced abortions or sterilizations (Moore, 1999). When the Clinton administration took office, UNFPA restored funding, with an estimated $300 million per year allocated to international population control (Moore, 1999). The Bush administration then cut funding again based on unsupported evidence (Enda, 2002). A report given to the House of Representatives on the United Nations Population Fund (UNFPA) Funding Act of 2003, written by the team appointed by President Bush, found no evidence that UNFPA had supported or participated in any programs that practiced coercion of abortions or involuntary sterilization. The report also recommends that the funds allotted to UNFPA be released. However, the Bush administration eliminated the funding based on its interpretation of federal law allowing them to do so (United Nations Population Fund [UNFPA] Funding Act of 2003). Unfortunately, this move has caused the people of China to lose funding that could have been used to implement progressive medical programs to aid in birth control.

CONCLUSION

It is difficult to defend a practice that seems to be against the very things for which a humanitarian nation fights. The people of the United States value the rights and freedoms that the U.S. Constitution protects. It would be defeating the purpose to support laws that contradict the basis of the Constitution. However, culturally speaking, it is important to remember that China is a country that dictates how many children a family will bear. It fines those who procreate over the allowed number. For the people of China, it may not be a question of what is right and what is wrong, but rather a question of what is right and wrong for society and tradition.

Over the past twenty-five years, China has been strong-arming its citizens into complying with a law that is at odds with culture and tradition. The government has been allowed to punish those who break the law by various means. The country's abortion rates and number of orphans have increased as a direct result of the policy. Suicide rates among women have increased as well. Because of these factors, along with pressure from the United States, China has started to implement changes in the way the government is handling population growth. Educating the women of China can only benefit the country's present and future. By empowering these women, the country could be filled with more informed, intelligent, working women for whom reproduction is only one part of their identity and not the determinant of their cultural value.

Outside China, understanding the population control policy will likely be a struggle for many years to come. Population control is not inhumane; the inhumanity is in how the policy is enforced. Fortunately, movements to change the way China's government enforces the policy are in progress. These, along with educating women (the people who are most directly affected), could possibly be the best solutions to the country's ongoing growth crises since the policy was written.

References

Aird, J. (1972). *Population policy and demographic prospects in the People's Republic of China.* Bethesda, MD: National Institute of Health and Human Development.
Boland, R. (1997). The environment, population and women's human rights [Electronic version]. *Environmental Law, 27.*

China Population Information and Resource Center. (2003). Retrieved November 25, 2003, from http://www.cpirc.org.cn/enews20020617-1. htm.

Cooney, R. S., & Li, J. (1999, March). *Sterilization and financial penalties imposed on registered peasant couples, Hebei Province, China.* Paper presented at the meeting of the Population Association of America, New York.

Daen, C. (2000, June 13). China's population control a sinful solution. *World Tibet Network News.* Retrieved October 2, 2003, from http://www.Tibet.ca/wtnarchive/2000/6/13_7.html.

Enda, J. (2002, September 22). Small advocacy group influences American policy. Knight Ridder News.

Hansel, M. H. (2002). China's one-child policy's effects on women and the paradox of persecution and trafficking. *Southern California Review of Law and Women's Studies, 11,* 369–395.

Hardee-Cleveland, K., & Banister, J. (1988). Fertility policy and implementation in China. *Population and Development Review, 14,* 245–286.

Isaacs, S. L. (1995). Incentives, population policy, and reproductive rights: ethical issues [Electronic version]. *Studies in Family Planning, 26,* 363.

Johnson, K. (1996). The politics of the revival of infant abandonment in China, with special reference to Hunan [Electronic version]. *Population and Development Review, 22,* 77.

Johnson, K., Banghan, H., & Liyao, W. (1998). Infant abandonment and adoption in China [Electronic version]. *Population and Development Review, 24,* 469.

Jones, A. (2000). Gendercide and genocide. *Journal of Genocide Research, 2,* 185–211.

Johnston, W. R. (2004). Historical abortion statistics, People's Republic of China. Retrieved April 1, 2004, from http://www.johnstonsarchive. net/policy/abortion/ab-prchina.html.

Junhong, C. (2001). Prenatal sex determination and sex-selective abortion in rural central China [Electronic version]. *Population and Development Review, 27,* 259.

Kaplan, A. (1999, January 16). China's suicide patterns challenge depression theory [Electronic version]. *Psychiatric Times.*

Kleinman, A., & Cohen, A. (1997). Psychiatry's global challenge [Electronic version]. *Scientific American, 3,* 86–89.

Moore, S. (1999, May 15). Don't fund UNFPA population control. *Washington Times.* Retrieved October 2, 2003, from http://www.cato.org/dailys/05–15–99.html.

Ping, T., & Smith, H. L. (1995). Determinants of induced abortion and their policy implications in four counties in North China [Electronic version]. *Studies in Family Planning, 26.*

Population World (2003). *Population of China.* Retrieved April 1, 2004, from http://www.populationworld.com/China.php.

Scotese, C. A., & Wang, P. (1995, October). Can government enforcement permanently alter fertility? The case of China [Electronic version]. *Economic Inquiry,* 552–569.

Society for the Protection of Unborn Children. (2003). Retrieved October 2, 2003, from http://www.spuc.org.uk/lobbying/popcontrol.htm.

United Nations Population Fund (UNFPA) Funding Act of 2003. (2003). U.S. House, 108th Congress, 1st session, H.R. 1196. Retrieved March 26, 2004, from http://thomas.loc.gov.

Tietze, C., & Henshaw, S. K. (1986) *Induced abortion: A world review.* (6th ed.) New York: Alan Guttmacher Institute.

U.S. Bureau of Census, International Data Base. (1998). Retrieved November 20, 2003, from http://www.census.gov.

Wolf, A. P. (2001). Is there evidence of birth control in late Imperial China? [Electronic version]. *Population and Development Review, 27,* 133–154.

Wu, M. (2003). Culture is no defense for infanticide. *American University Journal of Gender, Social Policy, and the Law, 11,* 975–1022.

Yu, P. (1994). China's experience in population matters: An official statement [Electronic version]. *Population and Development Review, 20*(2), 488–491.

The Editor

Andrea Barnes, J.D., Ph.D., is a clinical psychologist and an attorney. She is currently working in the Learning Disabilities Service of the National Health Service, Lanarkshire, in Bothwell, Scotland. She was previously an associate professor and coordinator of the forensic psychology program at Alliant International University, Los Angeles. She earned her Ph.D. in clinical psychology from the University of Michigan and her J.D. from Boston College Law School. She did postdoctoral training at Children's Hospital/Harvard Medical School, Boston, and at the Eunice Kennedy Shriver Center in Waltham, Massachusetts. She has been studying and writing about women's issues since her undergraduate years at Wellesley College. Her other research interests include parent-child attachment, developmental disabilities, and governmental policy related to mental health and disability.

——ᴗᴗ— The Contributors

Judith C. Appelbaum, J.D., is vice president and legal director at the National Women's Law Center in Washington, D.C.

Nancy Lynn Baker, Ph.D., A.B.P.P., is a member of the core faculty at the Fielding Graduate Institute in San Francisco. She has a long history of interest in the area of women and work in both academic and applied settings. Her dissertation research in the late 1980s dealt with sexual harassment of women in traditionally male occupations. More recently, she has served as chairperson of American Psychological Association's Committee on Women in Psychology and was elected president of the Society for the Psychology of Women for 2004–2005.

Gretchen Borchelt, J.D., earned her law degree from Columbia University. She was a fellow at the Georgetown Women's Law and Public Policy program and has worked with the Center for Reproductive Law and Policy in New York. She is currently a fellow at Physicians for Human Rights in Washington, D.C.

Virginia S. Davis, J.D., is counsel and Women's Law and Public Policy Fellow at the National Women's Law Center in Washington, D.C.

Jay M. Finkelman, Ph.D., C.P.E., is a professor and program director of Alliant International University's California School of Organizational Studies graduate programs in organizational psychology at the Los Angeles campus. He holds a Ph.D. from New York University and an M.B.A. from the City University of New York and a Diplomate from the American Board of Professional Psychology and the American Board of Forensic Psychology. He specializes in employment issues and has extensive experience as an expert witness in legal cases related to employment.

Joyce K. Fletcher, Ph.D., is professor of management at the Simmons School of Management, Affiliated Faculty at the Simmons Center for Gender in Organizations (CGO), and a senior research scholar at the Jean Baker Miller Training Institute at the Wellesley College Centers for Women. In her research, she uses feminist theory to study a wide range of workplace issues. She is a frequent speaker at national and international conferences on the topic of women, power, and leadership and is the coauthor of a widely read *Harvard Business Review* article, "A Modest Manifesto for Shattering the Glass Ceiling." She is the author of *Disappearing Acts: Gender, Power and Relational Practice at Work,* which explores the subtle dynamics that often "disappear" women's leadership behavior at work, and coauthor of *Beyond Work-Family Balance: Advancing Gender Equity and Workplace Performance,* about how to lead organizational change efforts to achieve the dual outcomes of equity and effectiveness.

Phyllis Goldfarb, J.D., is a professor at Boston College Law School. She earned her J.D. at Yale Law School and an LL.M. at Georgetown University. She has directed and administered the Criminal Process clinical program at BC Law School and has taught courses in criminal procedure, gender and legal theory, death penalty, and introduction to lawyering and professional responsibility. Goldfarb's scholarly focus is on the relationship between law practice and legal theory, with attention to the contexts within which legal conflicts arise.

Jennifer R. R. Hightower is a graduate student in forensic psychology at Alliant International University, Los Angeles. After receiving her B.A. from Emory University, she worked in Colorado as a teacher, a counselor for at-risk youth, and a crisis counselor during the Columbine tragedy.

Renee Huebner is a graduate student in forensic psychology at Alliant International University, Los Angeles. She holds a B.A. in psychology from National University. Her research interests include the study of serial killers and serial sex offenders.

Valata Jenkins-Monroe, Ph.D., is an associate professor at Alliant International University-San Francisco Bay Campus. Her research interests include cognitive styles and problem-solving abilities of Third World children, development of children of substance-abusive mothers, child sexual abuse treatment, African American women and substance abuse, intergenerational study of black teen parenting, race and racism, children with special needs, and forensic psychology.

Teresa Mugadza, J.D., is a lawyer by training and a woman's human rights activist who is particularly interested in women's political participation. She earned a bachelor of law honors degree from the University of Zimbabwe, and an LL.M. from Georgetown University Law Center, where she completed a fellowship in Leadership and Advocacy for Women in Africa.

Natalie Porter, Ph.D., was associate vice president for academic affairs at Alliant International University (formerly the California School of Professional Psychology), where she previously served as dean of the clinical psychology programs at the San Francisco Bay campus. She has primarily concentrated on feminist, antiracist, and multicultural frameworks in psychotherapy, ethics, and supervision, particularly with children, adolescents, and women.

Shannon M. Roesler, J.D., earned her J.D. from the University of Kansas School of Law and her LL.M. from Georgetown University Law Center, where she was a Women's Law and Public Policy Fellow and a Georgetown Teaching Fellow. She has taught and supervised law students in the International Women's Human Rights Clinic and has collaborated with lawyers in Africa to design clinical projects focused on reforming discriminatory laws and practices in four African countries.

Patricia D. Rozee, Ph.D., is a professor of psychology and women's studies at California State University, Long Beach. She has worked in the area of rape prevention and education for twenty-five years. Rozee has published numerous articles on violence against women and is coeditor of *Lectures on the Psychology of Women,* now in its third edition.

Catherine Toth is a graduate student in forensic psychology at Alliant International University, Los Angeles. Before attending graduate school, she served in the U.S. Air Force.

Lisa Wilson, J.D., graduated from Harvard Law School, where she was an editor of the *Women's Law Journal.* She completed a fellowship from the Women's Law and Public Policy Fellowship Program, with which she was a staff attorney at the Washington Lawyers' Committee for Civil Rights and Urban Affairs, concentrating on employment discrimination and disability rights litigation. She is currently in private practice.

~ Name Index

‒‒‒ Subject Index